OAKWOOD REMINISCENCES

# Birmingham Footplateman

## *A Job for Life*

*by*
*Dennis Herbert*

THE OAKWOOD PRESS

British Library Cataloguing in Publication Data
A Record for this book is available from the British Library
ISBN 978 0 85361 670 2

Typeset by Oakwood Graphics.
Repro by PKmediaworks, Cranborne, Dorset.
Printed by Cambrian Printers Ltd, Aberystwyth, an ISO14001 and Green Dragon Level 5 certified printer on paper sourced from sustainable forests.

'Grange class 4-6-0 No. 6877 *Llanfair Grange* passes Tyseley with a freight train bound for the North Warwickshire line in 1965. *Michael Mensing*

*Title page:* '28XX' class 2-8-0 No. 3828 receives attention at Acocks Green in 1961. *Michael Mensing*

*Front cover:* Bordesley was the first station out of Birmingham Snow Hill heading south and saw the passage of countless pannier tanks every day on local trip freight workings such as this in charge of No. 4648 heading along the down main line during the early 1960s. This locomotive was a Tyseley engine for many years and was built at Swindon in 1945.
*Rear cover, top:* A view looking south from Tyseley bridge during the mid-1950s showing 'Castle' class 4-6-0 No. 5031 *Totnes Castle* heading 'The Cornishman' off the North Warwickshire line to join the main line to Snow Hill and journey's end at Wolverhampton Low Level, where it will arrive having endured a nine hour marathon from Penzance.
*Rear cover, bottom:* Darkness descends on Bescot yard in the West Midlands as a pair of class '20s' heave a merry-go-round train bound for the Ironbridge power station out of the down yard during 1990. In the background a class '37' ticks over in the shed yard. *(All) Philip D. Hawkins*

To learn more about artist Philip D. Hawkins, his paintings, books and how to go about commissioning work, visit www.philipdhawkins.co.uk
For his Limited and Open Edition fine art prints visit www.quicksilverpublishing.co.uk

Published by The Oakwood Press (Usk), P.O. Box 13, Usk, Mon., NP15 1YS.
E-mail: sales@oakwoodpress.co.uk
Website: www.oakwoodpress.co.uk

# Contents

'Hall' class 4-6-0 No. 5912 *Queen's Hall* arrives at Birmingham Snow Hill with the 9.40 am Bournemouth (West)-Birkenhead (Woodside) train on 4th August, 1962. *Michael Mensing*

# Preface

I have spent many hours of enjoyment reflecting on books written by other railwaymen. Nevertheless, few books seem to bring over to readers a true picture of life on the railways. My aim has been to write more of a social history and I apologise now to those ardent railway enthusiasts whose eyes are dazzled by shining brass work, or just misted over by steam.

The early days were arduous, conditions were dreadful, many times I had thoughts on giving up. I am unable to explain what kept many railwaymen devoted to their work, then again, what keeps a miner going underground for a lifetime?

I devote this book not only to my many lifetime friends, whom it would be difficult to imagine life without, but also to my wife. For her love, for always being there, never grumbling and keeping alive in me the desire always to want to come home.

*Dennis Herbert*

# Acknowledgements

I am most grateful to many people for their help with this book. My wife, for advice on the complexity of the English language and stepdaughter Ann for frequent phone calls on computer technology.

Also, many friends and work colleagues who have readily given their permission to print their photographs. In particular Dick Potts, who at the drop of a hat has found many pictures and jogged my memory.

At a time when I despaired at many hours of work being locked away in a lifeless computer hard drive, Mike Gilmartin of computafixit.com was my saviour.

My sincere thanks.

Driver Bernard Pratt and fireman Dick Potts pose for the photographer with prairie tank No. 5152 at Henley-in-Arden. *Dick Potts Collection*

# Chapter One

## A Job for Life

My reminiscences of early infancy are vague; whilst time ruthlessly edits normality it often leaves memories of just the pinnacles of delight, or perhaps the depths of trauma. Foremost in my mind remains the catastrophic noise, sheer panic and slates cascading from the house roof when our home was struck by a huge thunderbolt. I also remember well, my brother's screams when a deckchair he was kneeling on collapsed, trapping his fingers and tearing off his fingernails. Then again, there was the stark reality of blood when Nellie, our violent neighbour, 'crowned' her husband with a vase. He left the district there and then, empty handed. Amongst a plethora of oaths, I recall him shouting that Wetherfield Road would never see him again. Harry remained a man true to his word and indeed was never seen again.

In contrast to this turmoil, there were seaside holidays in Torquay and New Brighton. I adored New Brighton, as yet, the words 'environment' and 'pollution' seemed tucked away in the dictionary, a terminology used only by academics. Nevertheless, the Mersey Estuary must have been pretty toxic at that time, but this thriving resort had everything a little boy could wish for. Not just the sea, sand and funfair, but my 'dinosaurs' were there too. No fleeting glance either, these monsters seemed to take an age to pass the waterfront. Wisps of dark smoke from one, two, sometimes three tall funnels, I would stand mouth agape at each one's passing. The ocean going liners were all different, flags flying, people waving from crowded decks, many folk possibly having been at sea for weeks. There again, on 'special offer', was the sea trip to Liverpool from the pier-head on the ferryboats *Royal Iris* and *Royal Daffodil*, which departed at frequent intervals. At Liverpool, with the clattering of the electric train on the overhead railway, passing through dockland I could look these enormous smoking wonders right between the eyes. This really was my paradise.

Following the obligatory warning, not to put our feet on the upholstery, my brother and I occasionally went out in our grandparent's car. There were no car owners whatsoever in the road where we lived; therefore this was a very special treat. Our grandfather was a toolmaker; at this point in time he was beginning to reap the benefit of some luxury after many years at work. I was always able to see my reflection in his new Ford Prefect's deep black coachwork. The brilliant chrome work was even better, this became a 'Hall of Mirrors' and I could even make myself look slim. Not that my tubby appearance concerned me, I had already become immune to my older brother's taunts of 'fatty'.

The favoured destination when motoring was Bromyard Common, where my grandparents had become friendly with a number of smallholders. Once in Herefordshire, they would purchase fresh farm produce which was later distributed around the family. From a child's point of view I could never quite see why they always wanted to go to Bromyard, there were never any trains there for me to see!

I had a passion for trains, perhaps I was brainwashed from a very early age, my father being a locomotive fireman for the Great Western Railway (GWR). Occasionally, our mother would take my brother and I to the station to see our dad working on the little 'matchbox' shunting engine that worked in the goods yard adjacent to Tyseley station. This locomotive would shuffle the freight wagons for

Grandad Ravenhall, toolmaker. *Author's Collection*

Seaside holidays in New Brighton. The Mersey Ferry is in the background. *Author's Collection*

My father. *Author's Collection*

*Copy—To be handed to accepted candidate.* (108A)

GREAT WESTERN RAILWAY.

TERMS OF ENGAGEMENT OF WAGES STAFF.

1. An employee must devote himself exclusively to the service of the Company, must reside at or near the place of his employment, attend for duty during such hours as may be required, be loyal and obedient and conform to all Rules and Regulations of the Company.

2. He must abstain from any act that may injuriously affect the interests of the Company, and, except in the proper performance of his duties, must not make public or communicate to any person information concerning the business of the Company.

3. Wages will be calculated as from the day upon which duties are commenced, and will be paid weekly in the course of each following week at such times as may be convenient to the Company, subject to statutory deductions under (for example) the National Health Pensions and Unemployment Insurance Acts, and to deductions of payments due under the Rules of any benefit society established or authorised by the Company. (Particulars of the existing Societies may be obtained on application).

4. Seven days' previous notice in writing of termination of service shall be given on either side, provided that in case of drunkenness, disobedience of orders, negligence, or misconduct or absence from duty without leave, the Company reserve the right to dismiss an employee without notice.

5. No wages will be payable in respect of periods of absence from duty.

6. These terms of engagement will continue to apply throughout the period of employee's service with the Company, subject to any agreed variations.

**To be completed by accepted applicants :—**

I, the undersigned, having made myself acquainted with the above terms and conditions, agree to abide by the same and to conform to all the rules and regulations of the Company.

Signature *Reginald Robert Herbert*
Date *May 5th 1928*

Witness :—

Signature [illegible]
Grade [illegible]

PADDINGTON STATION,
LONDON, W

My father's contract of employment, 1928. *Author's Collection*

My mother. *Author's Collection*

hour upon hour. The engine would make loud puffing noises, billowing clouds of steam and smoke from the tall chimney. When the engine stopped suddenly, the wagons detached by the shunter carrying a long pole would keep running, fanning out on to many different lines in the sidings. I was quite happy to watch this procedure from a distance; near to the engine I wasn't so sure. In close proximity this little locomotive became an ogre, it made all sorts of intimidating hissing and gurgling noises. With the locomotive wheels now towering above my head, it was little wonder that it took some time for my apprehension to pass. Once on the footplate with my dad, however, the heat from the fire, combined with the smell of hot oil, the cab became narcotic. Meanwhile, my mother was left to shiver on the exposed bridge.

We lived on one of the many sprawling council estates which had already consumed much of the countryside around our city. These homes began to materialise during the Chamberlain era, to accommodate Birmingham's exploding population. Many families from the inner city slum clearance areas were also at this period being resettled on these vast new estates. Whilst the majority of residents appreciated their new properties, it only took a small number of bad families soon to have conditions going into decline. Garden gates and paling fences soon became victim to the axe for firewood, in extreme cases, internal doors and cupboards were regarded as consumables in cold weather. These were perhaps drastic measures by some poor souls to combat the severe winters when thick frost covered every window inside the house, often for days on end.

The avenue of saplings planted at every roadside also expired. Any trees that were robust enough to stand up to the natural elements were inclined to suffer at the teeth of every deliveryman's horse. Survival after the bark had been chewed away meant even more torture from the kids aping Tarzan following the frequent showing of Johnny Weissmuller films at the local picture houses. With the demise of the trees, the vandal's attention turned to the gas street lighting, often putting the estate in darkness.

Our home was basic, even by 1930s standards; we had three bedrooms, a living room, kitchen and bathroom. The front door opened directly on to the living room, the focal point of which was a cast iron 'Workwell' range. Maintenance of this fireplace became a chore that my mother always loathed; the weekly cleaning of the flues and polishing the metal work with black lead was smutty work. Yet this she did religiously till the hearth shone.

Our bathroom accommodated just a bath and toilet, which indeed was more than many folk had at that time. A cast-iron cistern at ceiling height, in cold weather dripped icy, toe curling condensation down the back of your neck whilst you were having private moments. A newspaper was always ready for use stuffed conveniently between the cistern down pipe and the bare brick wall. Having the toilet next to the kitchen did have an advantage; with the door ajar my mother could keep a watchful eye on the dinner cooking.

A mangle, with large wooden rollers and oily cogs, perilous to little fingers, folded down to make a kitchen table. The only other furniture in the room was a kitchen cabinet housing the groceries, a gas cooker, wash boiler and a large white porcelain sink, having a solitary cold tap. The coalhouse was under the stairs, the door opening on to the kitchen. If a delivery of coal arrived at meal times there would always be a panic to get the food covered from the clouds of dust as the coalman emptied the hundredweight sacks into the darkness.

We shared our porch entrance with appalling neighbours. Two delinquent teenage sons and constant rowing between them made life very unpleasant for my

Grandma Ravenhall. *Author's Collection*

parents. My mother was always edgy and lived in constant fear; worrying that aggressive Nellie may one day choose to wrangle with her.

The only time I remember my grandfather and grandmother caring for my brother and I whilst our parents went out remains clear. The babble of discontent from next door soon penetrated the wall, Nellie raising her voice and calling,

'Where's the soap?'' A moment later, with no response she again called, 'Where's the soap?' With still no reaction to her 'request', she finally yelled,

'WHERE'S THE SOAP?'

At this point, my grandfather, his irritation at its peak, bellowed back, 'WHY DON'T YOU *LOOK* FOR THE BLEEDING SOAP?'

For some minutes the whole terrace was shrouded in an uncanny silence.

My grandmother found my grandfather's spontaneous response highly amusing. Unfortunately, my mother felt very differently when she became aware of what had taken place. For some days she was in a totally perplexed state, wondering whether there would be repercussions when she came face to face with our unpredictable neighbour.

Whilst the breadwinners next door were out at work, a hoard of teenage truants would let themselves in and out of the house by putting their hands through a missing pane of glass in the front door to release the Yale lock. The youths were a constant menace, the anxiety of what they would get up to next being a perpetual worry. One favourite pastime was putting calcium carbide into screw-top pop bottles half filled with water. This chemical could be purchased readily, as it was still in use for acetylene vehicle lamps. With the bottle stopper on tight, the resulting gas pressure would build inside the bottle until there was a considerable explosion, shattered glass flying everywhere. It was also known for the youths to put bottles filled with water on to a bonfire. The bottle would lie in the embers, perhaps for hours, before exploding without warning with devastating results.

With the exception of Sunday and Monday, shopping was an everyday experience, food had to be purchased fresh. The only means of keeping food cool was a large concrete cold slab in the larder. When shopping, I used to think that the high-speed runs in the pushchair were done for my amusement. The rush, however, was to get home before the bread and milk was delivered. Sometimes my mother's efforts were in vain, grinning faces could be seen in next door's window, munching at our malt loaf!

Following Harry's 'coronation' and subsequent departure, the youths next door had even greater scope for their theft and burglary exploits. My father screwed down any windows that were not essential for ventilation, other windows he fitted with iron bars. These defences did save my struggling parents from the experience of burglary. Other less fortunate neighbours eventually saw fit to raise a petition to get our neighbours evicted. My father readily putting his signature on this petition was an act that worried my mother greatly; again she waited daily for an outburst from Nellie. This petition, however, failed to get the family evicted; they were only to receive a stern warning from the city corporation.

Following this petition, our neighbour set about looking for the person responsible for attempting to get them evicted. When approached, not one of the many residents had the courage to admit to Nellie that they had been involved in raising the petition, all being afraid of her ferocious temper.

The dingy smoke-filled rooms of the old Britannia Inn were a magnet to the community, the deep cool cellar apparently pumped ale that many men would have died for. Here, Nellie caught up with my father as he popped in on his way home from work one evening after a rough turn at work. He was not a big man, but the amount of spirit he had made up for his small stature, he feared no one. Our neighbour had by this time already taken quite a few of her 'usual'. Despite her intimidating looks, plus a real danger from broken glass, my father stood his ground. On approach she came straight to the point, yet the reply she got seemed to take the wind completely out of her sails. My father immediately told her that he had signed the petition, foremost to protect his family from the obscene language and persistent nuisance from her family. Lack of any immediate reaction puzzled my father; Nellie stood at the bar glassy eyed as if counting the gleeds.* She apparently knew nothing of any petition; she had understood that just a single written complaint had been made against her. Realising that every one of her neighbours had denied their action, Nellie remained quite speechless. Eventually, after much pondering, she called the barman over and ordered him to set another pint of Michells and Butler's mild ale in front of my father. She shook her head in disbelief saying, 'Reg, I can only respect your honesty, thank you for being so straightforward with me, at least in future I will know just where I stand with you'.

Following this confrontation there was a vast improvement in our situation at home, although Nellie still had little control of her sons whilst she was out at work. She started to converse with my mother, often confiding in her. Under it all, my mother discovered that Nellie was an extremely sad person, she worked hard, but nothing appeared sacred to her. Her sons apparently constantly pilfered from her too, her inner troubles eventually sending her into a state of total despair. I shall never forget her young daughter's screams the morning that Nellie felt that enough was enough. During one night she latched the door from the stairs, put a pillow in the bottom of the gas stove, turned on the gas and lay down. Ironically, my mother was totally devastated by her tragic death.

Shift work, and lack of rest, made my father not the easiest person to live with. When he was on night shift and in bed during the day, my brother and I were constantly stifled into silence. Our mother ruled us with an attitude of menacing whispers.

Prior to his departure, Harry next door would play the radio at an intolerable volume. He had a passion for military music and would stamp his feet on the bare floorboards in time with the music. Even as a child I could feel my mother's agitation fester at the increasing volume of the radio and her awareness that disturbing my father would go some way to shortening his fuse. We would often sit in silence until a flopping of bare feet was heard on the bedroom oilcloth. Less prominent footsteps on the stair carpet led to the door from the stairs bursting open. My father would appear in just his shirt tails, his trousers and underpants still on the bedroom floor, inside one another, where he had taken them off to get into bed. Bare feet on the cold quarry tiled floor, his direction would be the brass switch on the kitchen wall. With hair dishevelled and puffed eyes he would twiddle with the switch which was faulty. This action brought about arcing inside the switch; this in turn caused the most dreadful grating noise to emit from next-door's radio loudspeaker. My father's 'patience' would be eventually rewarded by Nellie bawling at her husband, 'SWITCH THAT BLEEDING THING ORF WILL YA!'

Silence, and with a smug look of satisfaction, a diminuendo of footsteps would be heard as my father retraced his ground, often not a word being spoken. My father appearing without his trousers points to the fact that he was very confident that my mother would not have had visitors!

Our parents tried to shelter my brother and I from our unsatisfactory surroundings by keeping us in the confines of the garden. It was playing there one

* Gleeds - burning embers.

day that we saw a German airship glide slowly over our house. Nearly 50 years later I became aware that the craft we had seen was probably taking aerial photographs for the Luftwaffe. There were pictures published in a magazine article on World War II, the clarity of the photographs being incredible for those times, our house being clearly visible.

To keep us content in the garden, our father built my brother and I a swing. Unfortunately, at the time of assembly he was unable to get stout enough hooks to attach the ropes. We nagged him to finish the job until he gave way, eventually doing a temporary job of fixing the ropes. He did, however, warn us not to swing too high, until such time as he acquired the appropriate parts. We were quite happy with the arrangement, but it wasn't long before the three older girls from a neighbouring house were peering through the privet hedge with some envy. Our mother was eventually to relent and invite these girls into the garden. Before long the elder of the girls had taken complete charge of the swing. Her incessant blowing of a tin whistle soon made our mother regret her invitation. Despite my brother's advice that she should not swing too high because of the temporary hooks, she began to tempt fate. With her feet stuck straight out in front of her like the nose of 'Concorde', leaning well back on the ropes, the whistle now sounding like a demented ghost, she almost completed the total circle. Contrary to what the record books imply, the first space walk took place in the summer of 1939. Joan Davis's re-entry from orbit, and touchdown, should be recorded as being several yards due east of our swing. Touch down came as she landed on soft ground in the middle of my father's nasturtiums. I am unsure whether it was the sight of her navy blue knickers, or flailing white legs, that doubled us all with laughter. When she got to her feet from this most inelegant flight, she had swallowed the tin whistle! Every time she tried to speak the whistle sounded. To us children this was hysterically funny, but an observant neighbour was quick to realise that the child was in desperate trouble. A frantic few moments with her doubled over and much back slapping by my mother and the neighbour were necessary to free the obstruction. It became a very anxious and serious few moments which came close to tragedy.

My first recollection of Yarnfield Road school was that I was terribly envious of Leslie Dawes, he had a picture of a tram on his coat peg, my picture was only a stupid windmill! In the reception class, my cousin Ernie and I dominated the big wooden toy locomotive, taking turns to push each other around the bare boards of the classroom. Miss Minns, our reception class teacher, was loved by everyone and eventually saw generations of children through the school. I now find it hard to believe that this young woman, with all the distractions of toys around us, could get 40, or so, infants to lie down and rest every afternoon. Although we lay on just a blanket on the hard floor, there was rarely a sound. She either had something very special, or perhaps discipline had already started at home?

With the toys gone, higher classes meant basic learning. Monday morning I went to school with 2½*d.* milk money, and daily with a clean handkerchief and polished shoes, these to be inspected during assembly. Our teacher would stand us round in a circle for us to read aloud. To this day, I have difficulty in reading a passage accurately to others. These reading sessions I would dread. My teacher's patience would soon become exhausted and her shrieking would only serve to make me less fluent. One day, as once again I stumbled over my words, my tutor slapped me very hard around the legs and bottom. What she hoped to gain from this method of teaching still remains a mystery; she did, however, achieve the unexpected. Promptly she had to send a monitor to fetch the caretaker, along with mop, bucket and sawdust! I was sent home in tears and disgrace. I never told my mother of the smacking, but kids are cruel and the incident was a long time being laid to rest.

Miss Wallace, the junior headmistress, was a strong disciplinarian; she would walk about school with her cane tucked under her arm, often having spot checks on clean hands, shoes and handkerchiefs. At the time I started school war had just been declared and a contractor had begun to dig up the playing field to build air raid shelters. The headmistress caught a host of boys playing on the excavations when leaving school one evening. The following morning assembly took nearly all morning whilst she systematically caned almost every boy in the school. There was little point in denial, the 'sugar and spice' would point a finger at the culprits and all was lost, the girls seemingly revelling in the whole event. The headmistress, however, had no further problems with trespass!

My elder brother John was two years my senior and a very hard act to follow. He had a great personality and was extremely clever, every term coming home with prizes for being top of the class. These possessions he would guard with ferocity; if I went closer than three feet he would put his arms around his treasures, inside that boundary he would lash out. My mother consistently sang his praises, which had a tendency to hammer my ego into the ground. Also, there was the practicality, and necessity, for me to have the 'hand me downs'. This I detested, indeed it is a phobia that has always stuck with me until today, I could not now bring myself to wear any hired suit! I also yearned to be clever like John, I wanted more than anything for my mother to be able to say good things about me. This desire eluded me, I was never likely to threaten brilliance and I was always to remain the kind of pupil that teachers had forgotten by the following term.

One morning my teacher gave out our exercise books, to my disbelief I had got a 'gold star', I couldn't wait to get home to tell my mother. All morning I just could not concentrate, I fidgeted about until the bell sounded for lunch. I ran every inch of the way home, out of breath, I slammed the garden gate, ran up the path, my socks around my ankles and the peak of my cap over one ear. Throwing myself against the door I stood on the tips of my toes and lifted the knocker with the ends of my fingers, allowing it to fall heavily on the door. Within a trice the Yale lock was sprung, with my weight still on the door I went skidding across the polished linoleum. A rain of blows fell on the backs of my legs, some around the ears for good measure. Yes, I had been warned, my father was working nights; it had been instilled on me that he would be in bed when I got home. Suddenly the 'gold star' became of little significance and my mother was to remain in ignorance of my achievement, its vital importance to me washed away by a flood of tears.

The first German bombs fell on the city and our parents took us on the 'Outer Circle' bus to see the damage. This was a pretty futile trip, it was only days before a bus ride was unnecessary, the devastation soon being on our doorstep.

I loved to play with the clay from the large hole that my father dug in the garden to accommodate the air raid shelter. The curved corrugated steel sheets bolted together like a giant Meccano. Once the shelter was erected inside the hole, workmen concreted the base and sides. My father then covered the whole structure with the soil taken from the excavation. With a strong metal door fitted, and the inside being equipped with four bunk beds, the shelter was to become well frequented during the nights that followed. These structures must have saved many lives, yet some of our neighbours were saved by not going into their shelter one night. Their 'Anderson' took a direct hit and was blown wholesale out of the ground. Being a cold night they had decided to take their chance in the house!

As children we made good use of the air raid shelter, by day it was our den, climbing on top, it became our castle. Later on it was used for my brother's chemistry laboratory. Along with his Grammar School friend they did experiments, some of which I am pretty sure were not part of the school curriculum! At this period of time my baby sister June had arrived. My brother lost his popularity for a while when the infant ate some copper sulphate crystals from his chemistry set. There were a few anxious moments whilst we waited for the doctor, poisoned she had become very poorly. Thankfully, it was a crisis that was to pass, no lasting harm was done.

With the sound of the sirens our parents would wake us during the night. Often before we had taken shelter the anti-aircraft guns had already opened up at their targets. Sometimes the shelter would take in two or three inches of water during the night if it were raining, the blankets often soaking up the water. Condensation from the cold metal platework dripped uncomfortably, even on dry nights. My father never took shelter; he wore his steel helmet and kept watch for any fires, that is, when he was not at work. Fire fighting equipment was non-existent, therefore the residents of the road started a fund to purchase fire buckets and stirrup-pumps etc. Before any were bought, the man entrusted with the fund absconded with the money!

Nellie's teenage daughter, now being more or less alone and frightened at night, my mother invited her to take cover with us. She was old enough to be company for our mother, our father sometimes being away for long hours at work. Unfortunately, we all soon became infested with head lice. Mother wept uncontrollably as she washed and tooth combed our hair. She combed our hair over a sheet of newspaper and cracked the lice with her thumbnail as they fell, the paper also serving to absorb her flooding tears.

We lived between the industrial area of Tyseley and the large factory complex of Joseph Lucas. Both were prime targets for the German Air Force. The traitor William Joyce, or 'Lord Haw Haw' as he was more broadly known, openly bragged on a broadcast from Germany that the Luftwaffe knew exactly where the Lucas factory was, despite the spider's web camouflage covering the prominent square clock tower. He also mentioned the 31A bus which passed the factory entrance. The factory however, suffered little damage, but our school took a hit along with several houses around. The bomb craters quickly filling with water from fractured mains, gas and electricity supplies were also severed. With the absence of gas it became commonplace for my father to be seen cooking his breakfast on an electric fire laid on its back, plugged into the light socket!

My grandfather gave me a very old flintlock musket; it was pitted with rust, probably having been buried in the ground for decades. Nevertheless, I loved it, lugging it everywhere with me, although it was very weighty and standing on its end it was several inches taller than myself. Along with its ramrod, which screwed in beneath the barrel, the 'weapon' and I became inseparable. Imaginary sorties with the gun took me through El Alamein; on to Berlin and it was well used against the 'Nips' in Okinawa. When the time came in later years for me to be conscripted into the army for National Service, ironically, the last thing I wanted to do was to march and shoot a rifle!

The German air raids became more ferocious, one raid lasting 14 hours. My father often got stranded away from home whilst at work, at such times we usually went underground at my grandparent's home. My grandmother's neighbour was a real comic; her incessant humour always a joy. With the curtain covering the shelter door

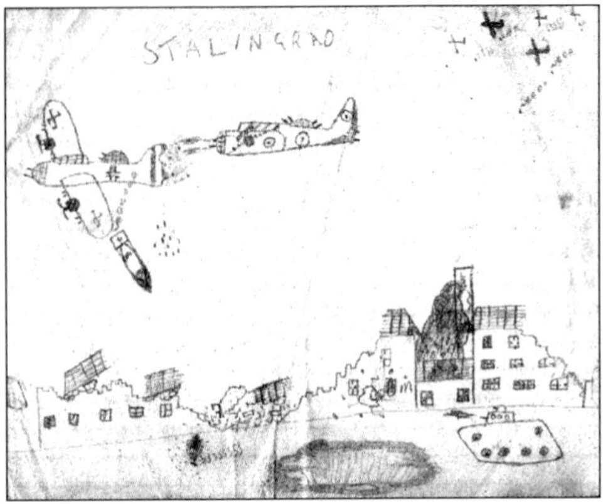


What little boys were drawing in 1942. My 'artwork' found tucked away in a book 60 years later.
*Author*

Aerial photograph taken by the Luftwaffe. The white arrow shows our home, the two small square buildings, above right, was my school and the larger building just above that was the Joseph Lucas factory. *Provenenace Unknown*

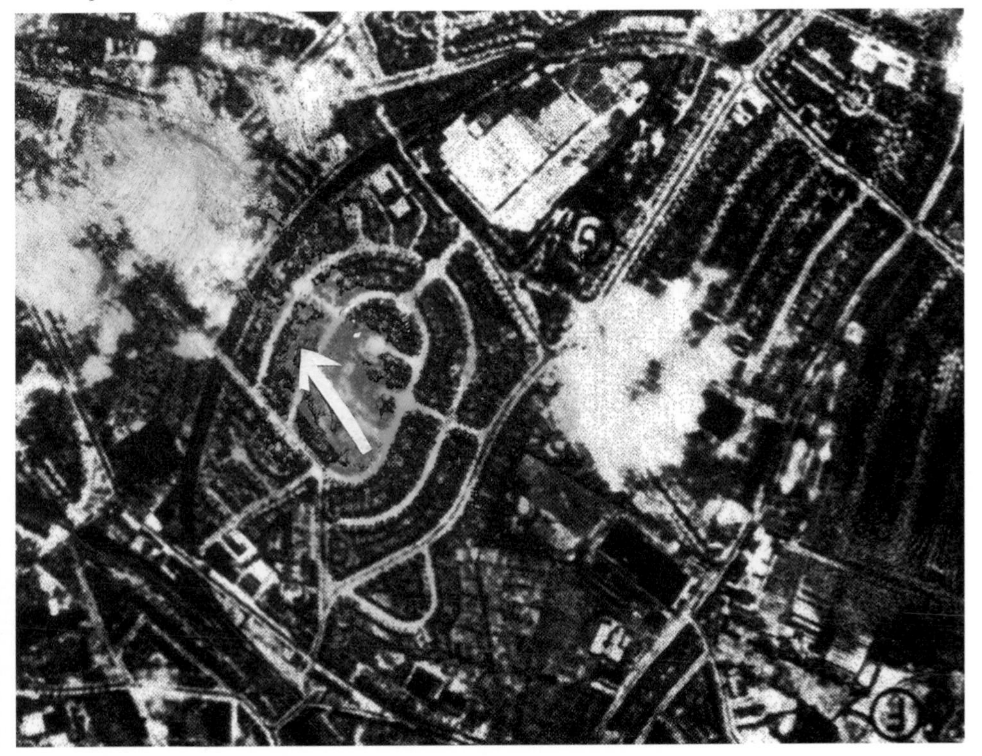

billowing up from the blast of close bombing and the sound of bricks falling, she kept spirits high. With the whistling of a bomb, she would cry out, 'Duck, here comes another Mek-um-shit'. The resulting hilarity usually went some way to dismissing the grim situation. Passing the bucket round was always good for bawdy comments, with the trickling sound of water in the bucket there was little point feeling embarrassed. Grandpa would occasionally pop back from fire watching to ask if all was well. He often got the reply, *'Yes,* empty this!'

Opposites attract; whilst my grandmother kept tight purse strings, I often saw her fishing pennies and halfpennies out of a tin moneybox by inserting a knife into the slot and balancing the coins on the blade. On the other hand, granddad would share his last cigarette with a stranger.

One particularly vicious air raid saw people running in terror. My grandfather called to ask them where they were going.

'To the country', someone replied.

Whilst we were in the air raid shelter, he invited these people into the house and made them toast and sweet tea. Next morning he was to suffer a verbal onslaught from my grandmother, for giving their rations away.

We emerged from the shelter one morning to find an incendiary bomb stuck in the garden lawn. My grandfather picked it up by the fins and carried it to the Air Raid Precaution Post, which was a building on the school premises, the bomb in one hand, me holding the other on my way to school!

It is difficult to imagine now the total darkness experienced with no street lighting and not a trace of light radiating from any house windows, as was experienced during the 'black out'. If anyone opened a house door at night, the room light had to be turned off beforehand, the 'black out' being total, and very necessary.

My uncle did night work for the Birmingham Small Arms factory; thankfully his life was spared on the night the factory was attacked when a great number of people lost their lives, many being buried alive. On the way home in the darkness, he narrowly missed falling through a hole blown in a canal bridge. On arrival home, a huge bomb crater, some 20 feet deep, occupied the ground where his home once stood, the whole terrace of houses being completely destroyed. Fortunately, my aunt had stayed with friends that night. Once daylight came, my relatives went to see what could be salvaged, everything was gone, that is with the exception of their pet canary. The bird had somehow survived miraculously in the battered cage with barely room to move. Tom and Mary found temporary accommodation and replacement cage for the bird. Three days later the canary fell victim to a cat!

With some of the school classrooms demolished learning was disrupted, even with many children being evacuated at one stage there were 53 pupils in my class.

My parents lived from week to week on my father's wages, despite the fact that he was out at work for very long hours. A relative working in an armament factory on an unskilled job actually paid more in income tax than my father bought home in wages. There was much discontent on the railways because of low wages, Winston Churchill begging for the men's loyalty by not taking industrial action at a time of conflict. The rewards would come when the war was over the men were told. A promise that was never to materialise from successive governments, leaving many of the older railwaymen very embittered.

Nevertheless, except for the worst of the war years, helped by my father's railway travel concessions, my parents usually managed to take us to the sea for a holiday. We were always well cared for and my father did his level best to keep a warm house. When desperate, he brought home lumps of coal in his big tin lunch box. If

My grandfather's emblem given for services rendered to his Union which hung in semi-darkness and always attracted me as an infant. *Author*

available, he purchased old railway sleepers, or scrap wood from the wagon repairer's yard. He often worked like the devil sawing through the thick timbers. Burning this creosote-laden fuel made frequent visits from the chimney sweep necessary, my brother and I running to the top of the garden to watch the brush come out from the chimney pot. My father sometimes cleaned his teeth with the soot taken from the chimney, although it beggars belief what it would have tasted like!

On occasions my father used to take me to the Tyseley engine shed to collect his wages. A long path, laid with ash and cinders, led from the Warwick Road up to the locomotive shed door, the path trodden by countless feet and cycle tyres, 24 hours a day, 365 days a year. The roundhouse was a hissing snake pit, heat radiating from hot cylinders and shining piston rods, the wheels on the express locomotives now dwarfing my father. At this point I was allowed to hold on to him, just by his forefinger. The turntable was a huge circular disc which floated under your feet, balanced on a solitary central ball bearing. With the locomotives expertly stopped at the point of balance, turning engines on to the web of berths was achieved purely by manpower. Dodging the puddles, made by dripping hydrants in the hollows of the brick floor, brought us to the narrow passage housing the pay office. Here my father was given a small tin containing his wages and a thin 'ticker-tape' pay slip. After counting and pocketing the money, the tin was placed in a receptacle for use again the following week. If conditions were right I was lifted on to the footplate of one of the big engines and allowed to blow the whistle. I was shown the water bubbling in the boiler water gauge glass; I looked in the big firebox and was shown the silver sand which ran down long pipes on to the rails in front of the driving wheels. This, I was told, was to help the engine get a grip on wet rails.

My father's parent's house backed on to the busy Tyseley South Junction, a home that had sheltered 14 children. It is difficult to imagine how they coped with just three bedrooms. My father used to laugh about it, saying that he used to get up early just to be sure of a dry place on the large roller towel which hung on the back of the kitchen door!

I was fully content once at my grandparents' home, my entertainment being the frequent passing of the trains. The first thing I always wanted to do was look at my grandfather's emblem, presented to him for services rendered to the National Union of Railwaymen. It always sought my gaze hung in the semi-darkness of the terraced house.

Tyseley South Junction was a forest of semaphore signals with a wild undergrowth of rails, wires and point rodding. I would climb high on the strands of the wire fence. Occasionally someone would shout, 'Get off those wires'. I would then scurry back into the house. Minutes later at the first breath of steam, or sound of a whistle, I would be back on the high wire, my neck stretched like a gander.

Grandfather was a carpenter in the railway signal department, a trade union representative and strong socialist. His marriage to my grandmother was also the most unlikely of combinations. In stark contrast to my grandmother, who was a very big woman with a volatile temper, he was a small quiet man who loved to read. He would often get engrossed in his book to the point of letting the coal fire go out. He would then suffer the wrath of my grandmother's tongue.

My ancestors originated from Swindon. Due to the economic situation of the time, my father's parents moved to Birmingham the year the *Titanic* was lost (1912). Grandmother maintained a broad Berkshire accent; this had rubbed off on my father who was only four years of age at the time of the move to Birmingham. Strangely, this accent was never to be eroded by the Birmingham dialect, even after 70 years in the city.

Patience wasn't a virtue that my father held, yet he developed a closeness towards me. On the way home from visits to his parents he would wait on the station bridge with me, I always wanted to see just one more train.

Whilst both grandfathers always got along well, relationships between the remainder of the family were less than harmonious. When my parents married, my grandparents were already related; my mother's brother had already married my father's sister. Invariably, any visits to my father's parent's home were solely with my father. Even at an early age, I realised that he tried to compensate me for the extra attention my brother received, particularly from my mother's mother. Her obvious favouritism often caused rifts between my parents, 'whispering' altercations not entirely kept from my little ears.

With my father working shifts, my grandmother giving both my brother and I a toy drum was at the very least thoughtless. The bother that followed between my mother and father was less than quiet, my father swearing that the 'old mare' had done it on purpose. As once again he was disturbed from his daytime sleep, he had stormed downstairs and stamped the 'instruments' into oblivion under his feet in temper. Nevertheless, in spite of the lack of harmony in their relationship, my father was always the first to help my mother's parents with any physical tasks that needed to be done, his wiry brawn always a very useful commodity. All his efforts at reconciliation, sadly, never went any distance towards improving the relationship with my grandmother. Likewise, my mother often laughed at the unusual way that she could tell whether she was in favour with my father's mother. Her photograph would be removed from the top of the piano in the parlour if grandma had become displeased!

It was probably a sign of the times, but both sets of grandparents did have a common outlook, that was that you never kept a canary and sang yourself! This philosophy rubbed off on both my parents and therefore both my brother and I were put to task early. We never got away with not doing the washing up and there were always errands to be run. Almost daily something had to be taken to my grandmother's house, or an item needed to be fetched. Grandmother, knowing one of us, usually me, would be going, inevitably wanted some shopping done.

'I want a new loaf', she would say. At the local shop I would invariably have to wait in a queue of people purchasing groceries on 'tick'. Several adults would push in before I would get served, children's time being cheap. The shop owner would total everyone's account up on a badly scratched white enamel plate on the counter. If he had only sold a few items, he would lick the ends of his fingers to erase the thick lead pencil from the 'slate'. The next customer may want butter or ham off the bone. The butter patted up from bulk, or the ham sliced on the same grubby enamel plate. Invariably, I would be palmed off with stale bread. This became almost a daily ritual, on returning with the loaf I would be sent back to change it. In later years I found it baffling to understand why my grandmother, who had all day at home alone, would not go to the shop herself, the distance being no more than 30 yards?

After the war, this local shop owner was heard to rail about the authorities not allowing him to sell ice cream. The reason given was that he handled soiled potatoes and other root vegetables. He did have a point went he groused that his rival was allowed to sell ice cream whilst at the same time selling maggots to fishermen by the pint!

The GWR promotion system was that employees had no option but to take the first vacancy that occurred on the promotion ladder. This meant that men moved all over the country within the area covered by the Great Western. For example, perhaps a man, who was an engine cleaner at Chester, could find that the first vacancy occurred for a fireman was at Penzance. Hence he would have to go to Penzance; therefore men often found they were away from home any number of years until a vacancy arrived at their home depot.

Having a spare bedroom, my parents often took in a lodger, always footplate men who had moved depot under this promotion system. The first lodger I remember was a young man from Birkenhead, who had moved to Tyseley depot to become a fireman. Although he stayed with us for only a comparatively short period of time, this was time enough for me to become very attached to him. He became my hero and I was totally devastated when he returned to Birkenhead. Somehow, he always found time for me, any hurried departure into the air raid shelter he would whisk me off to safety. He often sat me on his knee and would read stories from the *Beano* or *Dandy*. 'Desperate Dan' or perhaps 'Boomerang Burke' would become real life characters in my imagination. When he took me anywhere he held my hand firmly, giving me a wonderful feeling of security. His Merseyside humour brought charisma to our home, he made my mother laugh during dire times and I liked that. Comments from my father made me aware that George Siddorn was not only my hero; I understand that under hazardous conditions he bravely released livestock from burning railway wagons during an air raid. Regrettably, the story goes that a senior member of railway staff took the credit for his bravery.

With two working men coming and going at all hours, plus caring for my brother and I, my mother had few spare moments. The cooker worked overtime, washing took a whole day, always Monday. She had a large half beer barrel for a washtub, when we were roused for school this would already be in the kitchen filled with steaming water, the mangle in the upright position ready for action. At mid-day the kitchen would be awash with water, the snow-white sheets blowing on the line in the garden, along with every other woman's washing in the road. The afternoon would be dedicated to scrubbing the oily overalls. Our arrival home after four, the quarry tiles on the floor would be scrubbed and clean newspaper put down to avoid the tread. Invariably, my mother would just be washing down the back yard with the remaining hot suds from the tub.

Many households kept chickens and one evening my father sent me to collect two cock birds that he had purchased from an elderly woman in the neighbourhood. She was a spinster who lived alone, that is, with the exception of a pack of crossbreed terriers. Before I had knocked on the filthy scratched paintwork of the front door, the pack was barking menacingly from inside. Some girls had just passed a comment to me to that a witch lived at that house; I therefore very much hoped that there would be no one in. After a string of obscene curses directed at the dogs, the door opened, to my horror I was asked in. The place was odious, the smell claustrophobic. The old lady went to the back kitchen, treading through chicken droppings on the floor and leaving the pack to guard me. I remember trying to hold my breath, my lungs almost exploding. When she returned with the birds, they were already void of feathers, their necks hanging limp. She hacked off the heads on the living room table and slit up the rear ends with a sharp knife. Stuffing her hand into the birds she drew out the innards and dropped them on the floor under her feet. The dogs went wild, fighting and snapping at each other like a pack of hyenas. They snorted as they gobbled up the still warm entrails until a just a wet patch was left on the brown lino. I felt the need to vomit, by the time she had put the fowl in to a brown paper bag I felt really unwell. In fact, I didn't fancy chicken at all … that is till I smelt it cooking on Sunday morning! I did, however, learn to appreciate the smell of polish when I entered my own home.

Pig bins were put in strategic places in the road, so that residents could throw in stale bread, potato peelings, or indeed any unwanted kitchen waste. In hot weather, before the man in a brown cow gown and leather gaiters could empty them, the smell became pretty obnoxious. When my mother took us out she would detour to avoid the bins, which in warm weather were alive with flies and wasps.

The grapevine had long tendrils during the food shortages of the war years. Every Saturday morning my brother and I were sent to test out the rumour that a certain commodity was on sale at some shop or other. My brother was sent on behalf of our mother; I had to shop for grandmother. More often than not, huge queues would form before the stores opened. Some people seeing a queue had formed waited without knowing exactly what was on offer. Often, on getting to the front of the queue, we were given the third degree by the shopkeeper. Not being satisfied that our mother and grandmother shopped at the establishment regularly, we sometimes left empty handed. In fairness to the trades people, we were often sent to shops that were never part of our mother's usual shopping routine. Most people exploited children this way, so who could blame the shopkeepers for keeping any specialties for good customers. John and I despised Saturdays; it was not as though a few sweets were available at the end of the day.

Neither my mother nor father were religious; nonetheless, my brother and I were sent to Sunday School at St Edmund's Church after Sunday lunch. We were given text cards bearing a quotation from the bible to verify our attendance. For some reason or other, these 'enlightening' afternoons fell through during the war. After which, my brother and I soon found that it was quite easy to get 4½*d.* each from our dad to go for a complete circular ride on the Outer Circle 11 bus. Normally, he did not part with his money readily and this cost was almost that of a pint of beer. The bus route circled the city on the outer ring road and took 2½ hours to complete the 26 mile circuit. We were too young to quite understand why our dad made this sacrifice just to get rid of us for three hours on a Sunday afternoon. We could go in either direction around the route, usually jumping on the first bus with an empty front seat upstairs. Although supervision was never far away, the mostly matronly conductresses stood no nonsense. A longer than usual ticket was issued for the journey, clearly marking the city suburbs in stages, giving us a good grounding of the geography of our city.

It was going for a ride on the Outer Circle that my brother and I got a police record, I was just nine years old. My brother's pal came with us on this occasion and he had with him a tennis ball. Indeed, during the war, the only time we saw a ball any larger was at a football match. Leather footballs were just not available to city boys. On the way up the road we passed the small ball to one another, the road was deserted yet we never noticed a police sergeant riding quietly up behind us on his cycle. Caught in the act, playing football in the street, the sergeant stood us in a line on the kerbstones and propped his bicycle against a privet hedge. He soon made certain that we understood that this was an offence and out came his notebook. He wrote down our names and addresses and made certain we were telling the truth by later asking us to repeat them. We were very quiet on the bus that afternoon, when we did break it to our parents that the policeman had taken our names, our father went into a state of frenzy. We both got a good hiding, and it did hurt.

The following Tuesday morning a small brown envelope came through our letterbox summoning us to attend Acocks Green police station on Friday afternoon. Our father then went into another rage and once again we got cuffed ears. At the police station, the chief constable lectured us at length, he was very intimidating, his flat cap lay on the large polished desk and his uniform was pressed in razor sharp creases, the black serge sporting more chrome work than a 1950s Chevrolet. Not only did this warning frighten us to death, from then on our father watched us like a hawk, ball games of any description being strictly limited to the recreation ground.

There were great celebrations when the war ended; street parties went on for days. Massive bonfires were lit in the middle of the road, ancient oaks in back gardens, those that had survived against all odds, suffered badly to provide fuel. These fires did little for the road surface, large holes evident when the ashes were later cleared. Pianos were dragged out on to the pavement, the keys thrashed throughout the night.

It was some years before commodities got plentiful; therefore my father rented an allotment on the top of the railway embankment. I spent many hours helping him; this was wonderful excuse for me to see the trains go by. Trains crawled passed in both directions on the sharp curve of the North Warwick Line near Tyseley South Junction. Locomotives came by with names like, *Lady of the Lake, Princess Augusta* and *Pershore Plum*. Here I learned the basics of gardening, enjoying the experience. My father loved his garden too, the allotment was not just a necessity, here his normally hasty attitude became relaxed and unhurried. He somehow became a different person.

With his promotion to passenger fireman, my father was allocated his own locomotive, along with a regular driver Frank Hobbs. Frank kindly gave his permission for me to have rides on the footplate. I would be picked up at Spring Road station, *en route* for Stratford-upon-Avon, the train stopping at all stations. The locomotive was one of the numerous prairie class tank engines that worked the suburban services around Birmingham. To passengers, these trains seemed to crawl along over high embankments giving ample opportunity to look down into suburban gardens and to admire the pleasant Warwickshire countryside. In the cab of No. 5156, the brass and copper work glistened and the floorboards were bleached white with the scalding water from the coal-watering pipe. This constant hosing down was necessary to keep down any flying coal dust. To me these unhurried, almost effortless, journeys were absolute bliss and served to add to my addiction to steam locomotives.

On the return journey, the platforms were on the fireman's side, it was therefore necessary for my father to tell his driver when the train was ready to start, that is, after he had seen the green flag given by the guard. My mother was always adamant that my father regularly woke her during the night calling, 'Right away mate!'

At this point in time my parents took in another lodger, a young man from a little village eight miles west of Pwllheli, North Wales. On his arrival in Birmingham, Gwilym, who my father immediately called Bill, was completely alien to city life. Nevertheless, he settled in quickly and soon lost any desire to return to North Wales. He eventually married my cousin Jean, therefore becoming one of the family. Alternately, when he went home to see his parents, Gwilym took either my brother, or me, to his home in the village of Llaniestyn. His home 'Tan-y-ralt' was a little farm in the middle of nowhere. There was no road leading to the house, access was across four fields. The water for use in the house was taken directly from a stream and carried in buckets across three fields. There was no electricity, or gas. The toilet was a plank of wood with a hole in it, having a bin beneath, this was certainly not a place to linger with a book in warm weather! Nevertheless, I adored the place, and it wasn't just because no one took the least notice if I didn't wash my neck! Having said that, Mrs Pritchard did spit on her hankie and wipe out my ears on the way to

Grandad and Grandma Herbert, opposites attract. *Author's Collection*

Gwillym, Mr and Mrs Pritchard and my brother John at Tan-y-ralt. *Author's Collection*

*Above:* My father's regular engine No. 5156 on which I had rides as a boy.

*Colin Jacks Collection*

*Left:* Engineman Frank Hobbs.

*Dick Potts*

chapel on one Sunday afternoon. I shall never forget the welcome I received, Mrs Pritchard hugged me, Gwilym's father lifting me into the air as if I was no weight at all, I immediately felt I had known them all my life. In addition to all this, they owned the most gorgeous black and white Welsh Collie, a most adorable intelligent working dog.

There was no mechanisation on the farm, Mr Pritchard and his three sons scythed whole fields by hand, any heavy hauling tasks being taken on by a solitary pony. This was probably the first time in my life that I had experienced total silence. Incredibly, Mrs Pritchard could hold long conversations with neighbours across two fields; it was barely necessary for her to raise her voice in the still air of the valley. The place was idyllic, yet life can only have been very tough at times for these good people who sang their hearts out at chapel every Sunday.

The house was wholesome, despite the odd inquisitive hen popping in and out of the kitchen. All the cooking was done on an open range in the living room, the fire often brought up to temperature by a pair of large leather bellows. In the subtle yellow glow of the oil lamps at night, it wasn't unknown for the odd cheeky mouse to put in an appearance on the mantelpiece. Food rationing was still in force at home, so the fresh produce on the farm, along with the clean air, made me ravenously hungry. Fresh eggs boiled on the open fire with homemade butter were simple, but had become a forgotten experience. Straight from the cow, the fresh milk had a distinct tang of root vegetables, perhaps swede or mangel. I 'helped' by turning the milk churn, a barrel mounted on a pivot, which rolled over lengthwise when the handle was turned. The milk splashing from one end of the barrel to the other soon had the butter floating on top of the milk. Then there was the grindstone to turn, whilst Mr Pritchard ground the scythe to a razor edge. Another task designated to me was holding the cow's tails while Mrs Pritchard milked on her three-legged stool. The cows tended to swing their tails, flicking her face as she leaned on their bellies to reach the teats. I tried my hand at milking but, as a town boy I was not happy with these beasts, the cows didn't seem to want to co-operate!

Gwilym often carried a shotgun and went in search of rabbits, I never knew him to miss a shot. We climbed Carn Fadryn, which overlooked the farm, feasting on the views over the whole peninsular. I did what I was warned never to do; I drank water straight from the stream. I came to no harm; then again, these people had lived on no other supply of water. All this was a completely new world to me, the almost eternal train ride, the bus skimming hedges on both sides of the narrow lanes, the utility wooden seats, the gearbox screaming on the hills, all this served to make me an extremely happy boy. On arrival home from my first visit to Llaniestyn the bath water was discreetly put on. When Gwilym was out of earshot I was ordered into the bath. The scrubbing, and the humiliating inspection that followed was lesson enough to make it unnecessary in future for my mother ever to see me without all my clothes again.

My brother, having passed the 11 plus examination, was now going to grammar school in his emerald green jacket and cap. Two years later my turn came to sit the same examination, as expected I failed. The rest of my education was therefore furnished at the local secondary modern school. I did have a second opportunity to sit this examination, but I said nothing to my parents. This I was criticised for by my parents, although they had never shown any interest in researching the avenues open to me. I did become indifferent and felt perhaps that they should have made any enquiries necessary to further my education; after all I was yet only 11 years old.

# Chapter Two

## Secondary Modern School

Changing schools meant going from a neat and tidy building to Hartfield Crescent Secondary Modern, which had not only suffered at the hands of boisterous youth, but also much neglect from the wartime years. This, plus a 20 minute walk, four times a day, was an awful shock to my system. The first assembly remains fresh in my mind as I was now standing at the front again, with much larger boys behind towering over me. The first rendering of 'We Plough the Fields and Scatter' sounded hideous, I had to bow down and look at the floor to avoid being seen chuckling. All the angelic female voices were now missing, the girls segregated to a separate part of the school. I had also gone from a school having an all-female staff, to an establishment totally male dominated, it was indeed a traumatic change. Our polished desks reverted to furniture having graffiti and derogatory remarks about middle-aged masters scrawled under the desk lids. Added to this 'artwork', were innumerable dated initials and totems of undying love gouged deeply into the woodwork.

Settling down to lessons, I soon discovered that all the pupils from the same school as myself were well behind with our education. Other scholars were writing free hand, whilst we were still printing letters with the speed of a medieval scribe. Neat and tidiness had always been emphasised to us as a first priority. The first year exams confirmed this, my cousin Ernie and I came 31st and 33rd, out of a class of 35. My cousin later moved schools, but the following year I improved on this place to 16th in the class. My best ever achievement came a further year later, reaching eighth position. The pinnacle of my accomplishment eventually came when I reached top of the class in a Technical Drawing exam. This, unfortunately, gave me little self-satisfaction, I had in reality misunderstood the question, I made alterations to the drawing that were unnecessary. Thankfully, the master felt I had shown initiative and therefore marked me above everyone else. Unfortunately, praise from a teacher did have a down side, other boys labelled you as an 'ear hole'. Thirty-odd kids taking it in turns to have a tug at your ears at breaktime was no picnic and it became easy to see where the term 'cauliflower ear' came from!

A Labour Government had now been elected and many new changes in education were promised. In reality the only modernisation I experienced was that the school was renamed to become a 'Secondary Modern School'. We did have the luxury of a huge playing field, but our gym was the Assembly Hall. Unfortunately for me, much emphasis was put on physical training, a lesson I hated. In the Assembly Hall, a solitary climbing rope hung from the ceiling. I never saw anyone use the rope; perhaps the cracks in the ceiling and the amateurish way it was attached to the roof made everyone rather wary of any ascent. At each lesson we scrambled for lace-less plimsolls, stored in a wire cage having pigeonholes, this attached to the wall in the corner of the hall. The combinations of sizes made it impossible for 35 of us to get footwear that was a correct fit. We therefore often pranced around in plimsolls of odd feet and several sizes too large. During attempts at cartwheels or back flips, it was quite common to have to avoid flying footwear.

A new teacher appeared at the school, a smart upright man much younger that the usual ageing masters. This man's expensive tweeds, arrogance and overly polished shoes set him above the 'down to earth' remainder of the staff. There was a strong prospect that demobilization from a high military rank had reluctantly brought him

Hartfield Crescent Secondary Modern School, at the time of the dedication of the school clock, 1946. The clock was in memory of the old boys killed in the war.

*Provenance Unknown*

back to reality, I feel sure he would have adapted easier to instilling colonialism. Teaching the offspring of the minions was definitely not his forte and he became prone to fits of outrageous fury.

The following term I was to find myself in this man's charge. Being an obedient and middle of the road pupil kept me from his gaze; this was definitely an asset, as I often watched him vent his anger on others less fortunate. On several occasions he did however praise my work. This was not for its academic standard, but for its consistent unaltered tidiness. This he obviously saw as a quality and I was now quite grateful that this teaching had rubbed off on me from my previous school.

Whilst in this class my tutor read a publication to us; to my great surprise the subject was, 'The Locomotive Fireman'. He read in graphic detail the toil of a man obviously on the footplate of one of the 'crack' express trains to the North. After this reading, he set us an essay on the subject, a theme that was unique to me, being the only person the class to have seen, first hand, the working on a locomotive footplate. Once started, my abundant thoughts made the ink flow freely from the sunken inkwell in my desktop as the pen nib scratched over the cheap paper.

The following morning our tutor set us to task and sat high on his pedestal desk, where no one could escape his gaze as he marked our previous day's work. After a time, he rose to his feet and ordered us to pay attention. He started to read from one of the exercise books, my stomach turned when I immediately recognised that he was in fact reading from my hand. In the essay I had made a number of spelling mistakes, these he pronounced exactly as I had written them, emphasising my errors and arousing some amusement from the class. During my work I had also drifted from 'past' to 'present' tense and back again. Here again he stressed these points, serving further to add to my total humiliation. As he read on his anger grew, before completing the text he threw the book aggressively across the room, its pages fluttering in the air like a headless chicken. At this, his face now blood red with anger, he took seven league steps down the aisle between the desks towards me. He then set on me as though I was his most deadly enemy. He slapped me hard around the back of the head and thumped his fist into the middle of my back repeatedly until I felt sick. Under this punishment I desperately wanted to cry, but as 'young men' we were already programmed never to shed tears.

Up until this time, having never as much as experienced any strokes of the cane, the punishment did go some way to raising my 'street credibility' with the rougher boys of the class. Nevertheless, this unjustified attack hurt me terribly. I never told my parents, I was very eager to avoid an inquisition, and perhaps be told that I must have deserved it. I also had to be careful that my brother did not see the bruising when I undressed at night. In later life, my brother and I grew close, but at that age he certainly would never have missed the opportunity to put me down.

After being taught the basic swimming stokes in the Assembly Hall by lying across wooden benches, we were then taken to the local baths. The water looked inviting; I imagined shallow. This first day at the baths I jumped straight in, going immediately to the bottom in deep water. The next 55 minutes of the lesson I spent coughing the chlorinated water from my lungs. I had managed to drag myself out, but this unfortunate experience shattered my confidence and it was 40 years later before I found enough courage to learn to swim!

I enjoyed both woodwork and science lessons, but woodwork frustrated me. I had so many wonderful tools at my disposal, yet the minute I got 'hands on', the master would call yet another halt to work. We all then had to gather round him for yet another demonstration of how to do it. Consequently, it was only after six months that we found ourselves with a completed exercise, two six inch pieces of wood joined together in a 'cross halving' or 'T bridle' joint. It was two years before I paid 3*d*. and took home my first piece of handiwork, a wooden spade scraper! However, although things moved painfully slow, it was a wonderful grounding, they were lessons that I never forgot. The masters were also very strict, no one left after a session until all the benches had been swept and every tool accounted for.

I loved science, we learned about gases, expansion and contraction, heat transfer, and my favourite, electricity and magnetism. At home I made all sorts of gadgetry, an electric bell, a telephone, that only I ever imagined worked, and a gramophone. The gramophone was powered by bits of Meccano and whisked 78 rpm records around somewhat in excess of that speed. The 'sound box' was attached to a large cardboard megaphone, to enhance the volume. My parents must have been much more tolerant than I ever gave them credit for, the ghostly wailing noises emitted from the horn can only have sounded like evening squabbles at a Serengeti watering hole.

Bartering an undersized pair of football boots, I became the owner of a one-valve radio, all its components exposed and screwed to a piece of old floorboard. The valve stood as high as a 150 watt light bulb, the valve itself dwarfed by large coils, which it was necessary to interchange to alter the wavelength. The power source was a double cell cycle lamp battery, the headphones heavy and uncomfortable, feeling rather like having two tins of salmon strapped to your head. Even so, if dad dozed off on the settee and started to snore, the faint reception was totally obliterated.

My five shillings life savings bought me another one valve radio set, this from a man that my father worked with who was an amateur radio enthusiast. The sets he made he took to work, strung an aerial across the locomotive footplate and listened in during quieter moments. I adored my new possession, a brown Bakelite box with large knobs on the front and a push-pull switch to change the wavelength. Two batteries, a 67 volt high tension, and a 2.5 volt low-tension battery powered the radio. With these, the set gave enough volume to loosen the wax in my ears. Even the headset was comfortable enough for me occasionally to doze off whilst it was still switched on.

Eventually, the 67 volt high tension battery became exhausted. I scoured the city on my bicycle for a replacement, all the counter staff frowning and shaking their heads, the battery being obsolete. Some time after, a friend gave me a battery the size of a biscuit tin, giving off 120 volts. If I inadvertently touched the terminals with damp fingers the power was enough to make me jump! I kept the battery for some time before thinking I had little to lose by trying it. With some reluctance, I eventually plugged in. Immediately the headset sprang to life, there also appeared to be no smoke, or tar either, bubbling from any of the components. I was elated; again I was able to listen for any imaginary secret agents, or possible messages of espionage.

With the sheer monotony of hundreds of council houses, the only difference being that one terrace was painted brown, the next green, anyone's status could not be measured by the size of your storm porch, or by the vehicle parked on your block-paved drive. Nevertheless, even under these circumstances people never really became equal, one's standing then being measured by the quality of your radiogram. By this time we had new neighbours; Walter next door bragged he could listen in to radiotelephone conversations and receive messages from Antarctic explorers on his most powerful receiver. I was always so dead green with envy.

Shortly after wiring up my meagre 120 volt, one valve G.T. headphone version, there was an authoritative knock on our front door. Walter, claiming that world searching on my lowly equipment was oscillating, therefore blocking the reception of his 10-valve superhet model. Whether there was any substance in his claim or not, in the interest of good neighbourliness, and the fact that interfering with radio broadcasting was bordering on a hanging offence, my receiver was confiscated. I was shattered and therefore desperately had to search for other interests.

On a rare occasion, when I was 'Home Alone', I resurrected a model steam engine from the garden shed. Some time earlier an older cousin had given my brother and I the moderately-sized engine, which our dad used to run for us fuelled by methylated spirits. When it was running at speed, our dad fed it with enough oil to take the 'Coronation Scot' from Crewe to Carlisle. Unfortunately, the boiler water level gauge glass was now cracked. As the engine was of German manufacture and we had been at war with Germany, inevitably a replacement part was unobtainable. The glass formed a 'U' shape and was pushed through rubber seals into the end of the boiler, the glass then held in place by two screws. My logic was that I could remove the water gauge altogether, block off the holes and therefore run the engine. I deduced that I could always test whether there was any water in the boiler by opening the small tap fitted to one end of the boiler. Walter's son next door lent me his father's soldering iron; so I then set to work removing the boiler from the engine. I made good the repair by soft soldering a brass plate over the holes left by the removal of the broken water gauge glass. Delighted with my handiwork, logic again said that I must test the boiler before I replaced it back into its saddle. The boiler was cylindrical, about three inches in diameter and some nine inches long, the outer barrel being rolled up from brass sheet little thicker than tin plate. I filled the boiler with water and popped it on the gas stove. Satisfaction was achieved, as there were no sign of any leaks. Then, just as a feather of steam began to show from the safety valve, there was a bang and Whoo-oosh!!!. The plate I had newly soldered on blew clean off the end of the boiler, leaving two gaping holes for the steam to escape. The boiler immediately launched itself like an untied balloon in the direction of the first wall of the nine feet by nine feet kitchen. I dived for cover under the large porcelain sink; whilst for the next long seconds the boiler did several orbits of the kitchen, the exactness of my rocket science making Professor Von Braun look like a bungling amateur. With silence restored I emerged from cover. My prototype 'Sam' missile had homed in on saucepans, crockery and condiments, my mother's favourite china teacup now amongst the shards on the red quarry tile floor, it's handle still hanging on the brass hook screwed into the edge of the shelf! The atmosphere was clammy; condensation ran down the painted brick walls and water dripped off the fresh newspaper which lined the shelves. The remaining time until my mother returned I spent on a damage limiting exercise, nevertheless all my efforts failed to avoid the inevitable ear bending.

A job was arranged for me at a grocer's shop which my mother patronised. George Mason's was a household name, having a chain of stores around the Midlands. I was required to work every evening after school, except Wednesday, plus all day Saturday, from 9 am to 6 pm. I was also expected to go in to help out if I was on school holidays, although this never served to swell my pay packet. My main task was to deliver groceries on the purpose-built bicycle having a carrier attach in front of the handlebars. For these hours I was paid 10 shillings per week, which my mother took from me towards my keep. My father, at this time was losing time from work owing to illness and it was then a case of, no work, no money. I was, however, allowed to keep any tips I was given. Rich folk gave me nothing, most people gave three pence, and the most unlikely customers gave me six pence.

The front of the shop was quite elaborate, having the company's name moulded in green and gold glass letters above the windows. Craftsman-built hardwood window frames, nicely varnished, set off the green tiles cladding the brickwork. Arch-shaped bevelled glass was fitted into the grand double front doors, the doors embellished by large brass handles, gleaming and eroded by the interminable use of metal polish. The black and white patterned tiled shop floor was mopped spotlessly by girls in whiter than white overalls, a dressing of clean sawdust sprinkled down after every mopping. Heavy mahogany counters surrounded the rectangular floor, groceries served on the left, meats, butter and cheese on the right. A large bacon-slicing machine dominated the meat counter, usually operated by the shop manager. Cheeses stood on the cool marble topped counter ready to be rationed to customers, these cut through by a single steel wire. Bulk butter waited to be patted into a variety of patterns with wet wooden tools. Towering above all was the polished brass scales, chains hanging taut under the heavy weight of the brass tray. The weights were lined up with military precision, diminishing in size and ready for use.

Opposite the front doors, at the rear of the shop, the cashier's desk stood high overlooking all the counters. For each customer, the girl assistants wrote out a postage stamp sized receipt, the carbon copies in the receipt book being tallied up at the close of each day. Every evening no one left for home until the monies in the cashier's till matched the total of the receipts.

Behind this efficient, cosmetic exterior, the establishment was a shambles. The stock room was overrun with mice; there was no refrigeration and just a single cold tap over a large porcelain sink served all purposes. The toilet was outside; in icy weather therefore, there was little incentive to wash hands under the freezing tap water. Any water for cleaning had to be boiled in a metal bucket, precariously balanced on a solitary gas ring. The only seat in the shop was the cashier's stool, any staff feeling the need to take the weight off their feet sat on the stairs, or any available crate or carton.

I made immeasurable amounts of tea, in jam jars! There was little need for washing up; the girls could distinguish the jar they had used previously by the shade of the lipstick around the rim. Often, I washed the mould off large polony sausage skins, and I even swilled out maggots from lightly infested bacon joints under the cold tap.

The manager and I had regular vendettas against the rodents. I moved the crates and sacks while he splattered the mice as they ran with an inverted broom head. Despite our success rate, with an endless supply of goodies available, the mice were attracted to the shop from as far away as Coventry. In desperation we tried to contact Hamelin, but finally we had to resort to getting a cat.

A customer supplied a young cat, which was eager to stake out its territory. To have any success the animal had to be given a free run of the whole premises. Puss soon began to win the day, but it takes little imagination as to where, and with what, she staked out her boundaries! After a good nights sport, the shop took on the appearance of a disaster area. Tower blocks of 'Rinso', 'Pom' and ' American Dried Egg', had all crashed to the ground, leaving a scene of total devastation. Feline paw marks trekked across the blocks of best lard, greasy footprints leading to the point of triumph, somewhere under collapsed tins of 'Chemico'. The mice finally withdrew, I suspect to the cake shop next door. From this point on, 'Tibs' lived a lazy life of yawning, scratching and licking, often snuggling down on one of the large, fully exposed, slabs of angel cake for some shut eye.

Trade remained brisk, the clientele blissfully unaware of the unhygienic chaos behind the scenes. Everyone wanted groceries delivered, I spent hour upon hour riding the heavy bicycle, the crank wheel being almost the size of the chain sprocket, I peddled furiously, seeming to get nowhere. The tyres on the machine were compatible with those on the nose wheel of a jumbo jet, nevertheless, the bicycle found every pothole. With the carrier bouncing on the front, the eggs in thin brown paper bags buffeted against drums of 'Vim' and tins of 'Mansion Polish'. A safer mode of transport for the eggs would have been an egg and spoon race! Instead, the customers often got a ready-made meringue mix, sometimes on a bed of ginger nut biscuits. I suffered the whims of temperamental housewives and at the teeth of vicious dogs. 'Under the counter' parcels went regularly to one fur-coated customer, delivery to this sizeable detached house became a moment of dread. Within a second of pressing the doorbell, two chows, the size of Bengal tigers, would pin me in the porch, snarling and snapping. There was certainly no escape till the owner called them off. I often wondered if she ever discovered that the bacon hocks had probably earlier been swilled under the tap!

With the increase in custom I began to get behind with the deliveries, having to stay late on Saturday evenings to finish. The girls behind the counter did little to help; they assembled the orders in a box whilst the customer was at the counter. The groceries were then put down behind the counter for me to deliver. When other customers called at the counter, if things got busy and they had run out of items that it was necessary for them to weigh up on the scales, they would then take things out of the orders which were ready for delivery, fully intending to replace the item at a quieter moment. Invariably, the girls forgot and I would arrive on someone's doorstep with groceries missing, making a second journey necessary.

One lady customer refused to accept her sugar ration in four half-pound bags, she insisted in having one two-pound bag. Her argument was that with four half-pound bags she was getting part of her weight in paper. I tried to reason with her, explaining that when the sugar was weighed, a bag of the same size was put on the scales on the side of the weight. Therefore when the scales balanced, the sugar weighed down both the weight and the paper bag, giving her a full half-pound. However, the customer was always right; therefore I still had to retrace my steps with one two-pound bag of sugar.

During my time at secondary school my father was promoted from the local passenger trains on to express work, or No. 1 link in railway terminology.

Regrettably, his new driver was at the other end of the scale from Frank Hobbs, who was his driver on the local trains. In later years, I heard work colleagues comment that my father's latest mate should never have been put in charge of a wheelbarrow, leave alone a locomotive! This driver had spent his working life on the branch line which ran from Bearley Junction up to Alcester, regularly working on an engine nicknamed by the locals as 'The Coffee Pot'. When this branch line closed he was moved to Tyseley depot, his service seniority then putting him in the top link. This was despite the fact that he lacked any experience of main line working.

My father no doubt had the brawn and stamina to cope with this driver's excessive coal consumption, that is, until he met with an accident when turning their locomotive on the turntable at Cardiff. The engine they had worked with on that day was No. 4058, *Princess Augusta*, one of Tyseley's four-cylinder 'Star' class engines. Again, as with many other things, the turntable at Cardiff had suffered lack of maintenance due to the war years. Apparently, it took superhuman strength for men to turn any engine. Consequently, my father sustained a back injury; injuries that tend take a long time to repair without the constant necessity to shovel coal at a frantic rate.

Rare visits to my father's doctor brought him little sympathy; on one visit he was told that it was possible to make a friend of the pain. Another visit brought a comment that perhaps he was being a little bit imaginative! To keep at work my father purchased painkillers, these he took over an extended period. Regrettably, his condition failed to improve until finally he collapsed and was immediately taken to hospital.

Examination showed that he was suffering kidney failure; surgery was then necessary as one kidney was diseased and needed to be removed. His recovery took a very long time and these were very unhappy times. Pain, frustration and lack of income, made my father not the easiest person to live with. After a period of time, the tablets that he had been taking were withdrawn from sale; they were known to cause kidney failure. Any thought of compensation was unheard of.

A man who lived opposite to us returned from the forces and became the first person to park a car in our road, although the car did belong to the company he worked for. Part of our evening entertainment, after 'Dick Barton Special Agent', a radio serial, became watching our neighbours regularly go out for the evening. His wife had long peroxide blond hair; she wore fur coats and the most beautiful tight fitting long dresses, plus outrageously high heels. I was beginning to notice these things! He had any number of smart dress suits; in fact their departure for their evening entertainment became more fitting to Beverley Hills rather than a Birmingham council estate. Conversely, after some time, we had to revert back to 'Albert Sandler and the Palm Court Orchestra,' or 'In Town Tonight' on the 'Home Service', as our neighbour was arrested and wasn't seen again. He was charged with fraud and his family left the district in disgrace whilst he served his time.

I was among the first batch of school leavers who had to stay on an extra year when the school leaving age rose from 14 to 15 years of age. Many employers were at this time desperate for staff, a year without school leavers doing little to help.

During our last year at school we were introduced to industry by visits to various prospective employers. We were taken to a bakery, Derby Locomotive Works, down a coalmine, to a package making company, and Cadbury's chocolate factory. The latter was a favourite with us all, the only visit that came with free samples.

A short while before I left school my form master questioned me as to what I intended to do as a vocation. When I told him I wanted to work on the railway he remained tight lipped. Nevertheless, he hardly hid his disapproval, his grimace was comparable with someone being force-fed with a half ripe lemon!

# Chapter Three

## A Man's World

In 1949 the railway industry suffered acute staff shortages, mediocre pay going most of the way towards causing this shortfall. Having said that, the railways always did hang on to a number of hard-core loyal staff, mostly middle-aged men who remembered the dole queues of the 1920s and 1930s. These workers were prepared to have a small regular income, rather than big money, preferring to hang on to what my father always stressed was a job for life.

The locomotive department of the railway was hit worst by these staff shortages. Arduous filthy work had the added 'attraction' of unsocial hours, 365 days a year. Despite being fully aware of this, I never had any desire to do anything but follow in my father's footsteps on to the footplate.

On leaving school I was a very disappointed young man when my father, who had been negotiating a position of employment for me at Tyseley engine shed, broke the news that it was the locomotive department's policy not to accept employees at less than 15½ years of age. I was five months short of this ludicrous target. Leaving school on that Friday in July 1949 I became completely bewildered as to what I was going to do, knowing the certainty that I would not be allowed to idle my time about the house. Time was money to my father, therefore any hint of a suggestion from me about taking time 'out,' no doubt would have brought forth a stream of colourful expletives to which he could always lay store. I had learned discretion at a very early age!

The weekend passed, nothing was said until Sunday lunchtime when I was told I had to be out of bed on Monday morning early, looking my best. On Monday morning my father and I caught the local train from Tyseley station to Birmingham Snow Hill. The four-coach, non-corridor train, was hauled as usual by one of the countless prairie tank engines that swamped the Birmingham Division. A smoking compartment was chosen, 'off the wheels', the door pulled shut with the sturdy leather window strap and the 'T' handle locked from the outside. With the window closed the train made headway with silence and comfort rarely equalled today. In Snow Hill tunnel the smoke and steam muffled the echo of sound from the rail joints until the 'clapper' at the tunnel exit faithfully counted every axle. Under the cathedral roof, we climbed the stairs with a host of other passengers. At the ticket barrier my thrifty father showed our privilege fare tickets and we made our way to the station offices.

We found our way along a catacomb of passages, thronged with men in tweed jackets having leather-patched elbows. Frumpy women in lovat green cardigans and not the least flattered by round metal-rimmed spectacles busied themselves with much paper. The scene brought back to me the innumerable wartime propaganda films issued by 'The Ministry of Food'.

Arriving at a pre-destined office, the occupant ran a quick eye over me; just to be sure I had two of everything that was necessary for employment. The preliminaries over, I was given a piece of infantile dictation, an eyesight test and asked to sort some beads of different colours into red, yellow and green categories. A discussion followed between the employment officer and my father as to which station I would start work on as lad porter, Tyseley, or Acocks Green. I wasn't consulted at all, Acocks Green was chosen for me because work on Tyseley station involved very heavy parcel traffic. Also, the engine parts from the engine shed bound for Swindon works were loaded at Tyseley. My father obviously didn't want me ruptured early on in my career!

By courtesy of the General Post Office, and a 2½*d*. stamp, two days later I received an appointment for a medical examination. I kept the appointment at a surgery on Coventry Road, Small Heath, where I was given a more stringent vision test. I was then told to strip, again to be sure that I really did have two legs. I was tapped and prodded, took deep breaths and said, 'Arrh'. I then felt myself go fiery red when the doctor put his hands between my legs and I was instructed to 'cough' repeatedly. This was an invasion of privacy that as an adolescent I least expected.

The Post Office operated a wonderful postal service which was cheap even by 1940s standards. On Friday morning I received another letter telling me to report to the station master at Acocks Green station at 9.00 am on the following Monday morning.

All railway stations had a distinctive characteristic smell; my new place of employment no exception. I 'sounded' my arrival at the station master's office door, which was on the main line platforms Nos. 1 & 2, opposite to the bottom of the stairs.

Mr Compton was a fatherly man who put me immediately at ease. He was considerably taller than myself, balding and in the twilight years of his career. His thick-rimmed spectacles gave him dignity; he was in reality a gentleman. He gave me a protective talk, insisting that the railway was a man's world, having dangers that were very real.

The preliminary's over I was taken to platform 3, the station having four platforms in all Nos. 3 and 4 platforms being an island platform between the up and down relief lines. In the porters room I was introduced to Arthur, the leading porter, also Ken, the lad porter, whose place I would eventually be taking. Ken had already been promoted to porter/shunter at Moor Street station. He now had a week to show me the ropes.

Arthur was a middle-aged overweight Scotsman, whom I soon found suffered badly from lethargy. He would loll for hours in the porters room with one leg up on the lockers. He educated himself with two-shilling Hank Jansen paperbacks, completing his relaxation by chain-smoking 'Park Drive'. Along with this lifestyle came the inevitable phlegmy cough, any attempt at conversation would start him 'hacking'. Everyone then within 20 feet would be flecked with spit and fag ash, his face taking on the appearance of an amateur tenor wrestling with the most taxing operatic aria. Before the coughing bout was over both his eyes would be bulging like an antagonised bull.

Ken was about three years my senior and had a youthful physique to be envied. His uniform fitted as though tailor made and he positively bristled with confidence. I felt he had the makings of a born railwayman, he learned exceedingly quickly to make use of the

Mr Compton, station master at Acocks Green, 1949. *Provenance Unknown*

time he had to spare when two people are allocated to do one job. Once he had delegated what was to be done, he was quick to disappear, only to return to check my work and to put me to task on further chores. Surprisingly, when he left Acocks Green, a week later, I never saw him again, probably coupling and uncoupling trains turned out not to be his forte.

My first job was to sweep the platforms; this covered a considerable area, including two overbridges and five flights of stairs. Having worked in the grocery shop for the two years prior to leaving school, I had become pretty adept with a broom. When Ken got the broom out from the storeroom, however, I suffered somewhat of a culture shock, the broom had the wingspan of a 'Lysander'! (A wartime mono-wing aircraft.)

My instructions were that not so much as a match stalk was to be swept over the edge of the platform on to Ted Higgins, the ganger's, prize length of track. This section of track had recently won the district competition for being the best maintained, in fact the Engineering Department had erected two large notices at the end of the station platforms to that effect, saying 'Prize Length'. Ted Higgins and his men were no doubt very proud of their achievement.

I decided to start sweeping on the down main line platform, which had born the brunt of the morning commuters into Birmingham. Ted Higgins stood on the opposite platform taking a break from checking his domain, his keying hammer resting on the floor. He was listening intently to Pat Costello the signal lampman, who came once a week to clean and trim the signal lamps. Pat could talk with the fluency of a cattle market auctioneer on a busy day. Most people only ever got to drawing breath whilst attempting to converse with Pat, but this day it probably gave the ganger an opportunity to keep an eye on what a green new employee was about to do.

Determined to make an impression, I swept with exuberance; pulling out the heavy wooden benches to be certain I did not leave as much as a cigarette end. At the south end of the station I had collected an array of litter, matchboxes, cigarette packets, sweet wrappers and even the remains of some late commuter's breakfast. I was giving some thought to what I was going to do with the litter when there was the sound of a whistle from a train in the distance approaching very fast. I watched with interest as the polished locomotive thundered towards the platform, rolling gently on firm springs. With just a breath of steam from the chimney, the train thrashed through the station, the deafening clatter only dying as the last coach whined away with the tail lamp shaking on the lamp bracket. After the train's passing came 'Hurricane Henry', my collection of sweepings being promptly distributed down the platform again. I flailed about with my feet, attempting to stamp on the litter to avoid it being blown away, this was futile, I needed more feet than a centipede. Pat Costello walked my way carrying eight signal lamps, ready cleaned and trimmed, the lamps spread along two notched wooden batons,

'Have you learnt anything this morning young man?' he offered with a wink. Indeed I had, that was to sweep the down line platforms in the down direction and the up platforms in the up direction!

Between my designated tasks, I helped to see the trains away, soon becoming acquainted with the irritating minority of people who left trains without closing the door. This lack of thought often made it necessary to walk several coaches in length to close a solitary door. These people were probably the first to grumble should their train be a little late. Nevertheless, figures show that 94.3 per cent of the passenger trains that ran in September 1949 arrived within five minutes of their booked time. This was quite remarkable, taking into account that British Railways had inherited a very run-down, neglected railway system.

During the first hours at work I never really felt that I was in a man's world, the only thing I saw of 'Jock', the leading porter, was the soles of his shoes, the rest of him was shrouded in a blue haze of cigarette smoke. When old Harry arrived later, to relieve Arthur, I had no reason to feel any different. Harry was close to 70 years old; BR had kept him on at work due to the staff shortage. Many of the trains that he intended to meet departed before he could shuffle to the appropriate platform. Time had not been kind to Harry; he stooped badly, making his sleeved waistcoat ride high in the middle of his back, exposing his leather bracers. His wizen appearance was not aided by the fact that he wore a permanent scowl; his lower jaw was in permanent protrusion, which tended to give anyone the expression of a man who had just lost his wage packet. Harry intensely disliked the 'present day youth'; he was indeed a man of very few words. When he did choose to speak, it was only in monosyllables, his most prolific utterance, 'Tut'!

To be fair to old Harry, he rarely sat about doing nothing, but tatted about in his own time doing jobs around the station. He would often be seen cleaning windows, polishing the station benches and washing out the toilets. He worked sufficiently to keep the station perhaps a little above average, compared with other stops along the line. Harry was a spotlessly clean man too, his expensive calfskin boots were always highly polished and his starched collar reflected well on the good woman he had left at home.

When Harry sat down for his break, however, nothing but a global catastrophe would move him until he had finished. His meal became a ritual; the time it took him to make a cup of tea was bewildering. It seemed to take an eternity from the time he got the large mug from his locker, till finally he pouted his lips and took the first noisy sip. Harry's dithering drove everyone to distraction, he measured his tea, sugar and milk with the accuracy of an apothecary, dipping the spoon into the caddy and tapping off the excess on the edge of the caddy an interminable amount of times before achieving satisfaction.

My first day was finally brightened when in the afternoon another lad porter signed on duty. Charlie and I immediately developed an affinity, which raised my spirits; I was beginning to wonder how I would cope with the company of my immediate seniors during the next months. When the station master had gone home, Charlie took me to the signal box, which I found interesting and absorbing. He also showed me how to light the station lamps. The gas lamps were all lit individually, with a flame on the end of a long metal pole. Many times over the next few weeks I carried out the task of lighting up the station to some comic's refrain of, 'The Old Lamp Lighter of Long, Long Ago'. Sometimes as I put the flame to the gas, there was a 'pop', and the lamp mantle, as delicate as a butterfly's wings, would disintegrate, leaving just two solitary dull blue flames. The lamp then gave less light than a candle on a first year birthday cake.

The following Monday I took over on the early shift. I was taken by surprise by the volume of people that used the station between 7.00 and 9.00 am. A train left the station every few minutes in one direction or another, every one being seen off promptly. The service really did border on excellent. Even the station master came out of his office, sporting his gold braid hat, to assist with the most patronised trains. Mr Compton insisted that I call out the name of the station, which I felt very awkward about, he stressed that it was for the benefit of passengers with poor vision. I hated doing this, I felt awkward, as though I was drawing attention to myself.

I hadn't been at the station long before two girls invited me to go to their school social evening. They were my age, but continuing their schooling until they were sixteen. They travelled everyday to school by train wearing bright red blazers and straw hats. As the prettiest of them seemed to be showing an interest in me I went through a chemistry change. Despite developing this real soft spot, I could not bring myself to accept the invitation. From the age of 11 at school we had been segregated from the girls. At that point in time I was too timid to handle the invitation, although in fact I desperately wanted to go. Like many teenage young men my hormones were yet in turmoil.

I picked up my first pay packet and took it home unopened. It contained one pound 18 shillings, of which I was given 10 shillings pocket money. The following day I went to Coxhill's, the homemade cake shop; there I bought six jam and cream doughnuts, one for each of the family. Whilst our father always insisted that we shared, the first doughnut was addictive and systematically throughout the day I ate them all. Although no one would have been any the wiser, I never ever forgot my inner feeling of guilt and greed for not sharing with my family as I had planned.

Every few days a large box of fish arrived at the station to be delivered to the fish and chip shop just down the road. I had to deliver the dripping wet box on a sack truck, for which the shop owner very generously gave me two shillings. This perk eked out my pocket money very nicely. Neither Ken, nor Charlie, put me wise to the fact that the station master had a sort of complex towards the rusting fire buckets that hung on the south end of the station buildings. Every morning he would inspect them and ask me to top up the water levels. I am unaware whether the buckets leaked, or perhaps they were just an oasis for all the local wild life. Anyway I struggled, bow-legged, every morning, to lift the heavy buckets back on to their brackets.

Some time later, the ' boss ' gave me a docket instructing me to change the fire buckets from the Swindon stores van. The stores van was attached to the 1.35 pm departure, a train that called at every station to Paddington, via Reading and probably got there sometime the following day! The train was very often hauled by one of the larger classes of engine and was known as the 'Up Cheap'. The 'Up Cheap' was a later description of what in the 'old days' were Parliamentary trains, so called because of a directive from the government of the time that one train during the day must stop at all stations on the line and have cheaper rates. The 'Up Cheap' as we knew it in the Birmingham Area started at Birkenhead, stopping at all stations I can only imagine most passengers avoided this train like the plague. I carried out my instructions and was given new buckets, thickly painted inside with good quality white lead gloss paint. It was unusual, but on the vivid red outside of the buckets was painted the motif 'G.W.R.', this in lovely scroll letters. These buckets, I feel were probably originally destined for the outside of the General Manager's office or somewhere similar. Now the system had become British Railways, all items were now being clearly stamped, 'B.R. (W)'.

After filling the buckets, I hung them on their hooks and watched Mr Compton from the footbridge as he returned from his daily official visit to the signal box, still wearing his gold braid hat. He could not miss the blaze of red that confronted him, it was a wonder that all the trains towards Birmingham had not ground to a halt! With official papers tucked under his arm the station master stood, very upright, nodding approvingly. He was reminiscent of a young second lieutenant taking charge of his first platoon. He lifted himself off his heels, bouncing on the balls of his feet, his body language indicating that he very much approved. He then strode off down the platform with an extra spring in his step, this making the legs of his trousers ride over the tops of his short socks, briefly exposing the white of his calves.

Today, Acocks Green station is staffed by one person and has only two running lines. There are no station buildings whatsoever on the platform, just a bus type shelter. At that time, Mr Compton had under his wing three booking clerks, one ticket collector, two leading porters, two lad porters and three signalmen.

The lady ticket collector left in a hurry to give birth and there was no replacement for her. I was told I would have to stand in for her, although why I was chosen to do the job I will never know. Anyone could have given me a chewing gum wrapper and I may well have accepted it as a ticket! With hundreds of people flooding up the stairs off the evening trains, one 15-year-old had no chance at all of checking all the tickets. Nevertheless, I was paid the rate for the job, five pounds three shillings and six pence. This was just a few shillings less than my father was getting, as he was now newly promoted to engine driver. Nevertheless, I still only got 10 shillings pocket money! Having said that, a short while after I was given a brand new bicycle which I treasured.

It was most probable that a number of people had a free ride during the two weeks that I acted as ticket collector, that is, with the exception of one unfortunate lady who got off a train with a miniature dog. A dog, I might add, that she could almost have concealed in her handbag. The district ticket inspector followed her up the station stairs and chastised me for not asking her for a ticket for the dog. I wasn't even unaware that a dog needed a ticket. Mr Allcock then made me chase after her for 3*d*. excess fare.

A few weeks after I started work on the station the locomotive department decided to reduce the starting age to 15, I suspect on the realisation that they were now losing out on school leavers. As getting on to the engines was my ultimate aim, I immediately applied for a transfer. A short while after my application, I was sent to Swindon Headquarters for a more stringent medical examination. However, time passed and it was the end of November 1949 before a replacement was found for me, therefore I was bound to continue to work on the station.

In the evenings, the leading porter took over the booking office and the lad porter saw the trains away. The train service thinned out at this time and the station became quite lonely. Out of sheer boredom, one night I found a tin of black lead in the storeroom, as I had seen my mother always do, I set to work polishing the fire grate in the porters room. This act had a very unexpected spin off, old Harry started to talk to me … in sentences!

Inevitably, the *entente cordiale* did not last very long. A few days later, Harry, muttering to himself in the gent's toilet heard me sweeping outside and called for my assistance. The urinal outlet pipe was blocked, the fluid topped with 'Craven A' cork tips, match stalks and chewing gum wrappers.

'Put your hand down there will you? Your hand is smaller than mine'.

His intention was for me to get on my knees and remove the obstruction from the pipe by putting my arm down the sewer. I was eager to please … but not that eager! This refusal reversed the relationship again, in Harry's eyes, I yet again became just one of the present day kids and only worthy of 'tuts', nods and monosyllables.

November the fifth was approaching and young men's talk was of fireworks. I happened to comment to Charlie that my brother had discovered that if a thunder flash was allowed to go as far as the fizzing stage, if weighted, the firework would explode underwater, similar to a naval depth charge. I had no reason to doubt my brother's word, although our worlds had become very far apart. He was studying for a Bachelor of Science degree and had girls vying to be noticed by him. Charlie dismissed this as completely impossible and went so far as placing a wager with me for a shilling. I really did not want to lose a shilling and lived in hopes that Charlie would forget the issue.

The following night however, Charlie turned up on the station with a couple of friends, plus the necessary fireworks. Eager to get the experiment under way, he humped one of the heavy fire buckets from the south end of the station, setting it down on No. 3 platform, midway between the stairs and the station buildings. A number of passengers had collected on the down main line platform, they gathered in curiosity as we found an iron hasp which had become detached from one of the porters room lockers to act as a weight. Charlie wedged the thunder flash into the slot of the asp, lit the firework, allowed it to fizz and pitched it into the bucket. Bubbles simmered from the clear water for what seemed an eternity, Charlie had practically got his hand out for the money, when Whoosh!,

BANG! The bucket leapt some two feet into the air, the water then appeared to leave the bucket as if frozen in one piece and shot up towards the apex of the station canopy. Atomising on the complicated girder-work, the water cascaded down, bringing with it at least two decades of grime, soot and pigeon droppings. In a trice the four of us were drenched and looking like the survivors of a mining disaster.

Nevertheless, the following euphoria lasted several minutes, the passengers on No. 2 platform unable to hide their amusement too. Had any of them been going to the pantomime it was the funniest thing they would have seen that evening! After the laughter, my thoughts became pensive, had any of the passengers come into contact with the fall out, we would have been in very deep water. Fortunately the down main line and the up relief line divided the platforms, keeping the public at a safe distance.

With the excitement over, Charlie picked up the bucket and froze in his tracks. The force of the explosion had torn wide open the strongly riveted bucket seam; it was in fact possible to pass an arm through the rent. Immediately realising that we were in dead trouble, we foundered for alibis. Not being clever enough, we would just have to face the music. With the station master's daily inspections it was too much to expect that Mr Compton would not immediately notice the damaged bucket.

I hardly slept that night, the following morning too I was on edge with worry and time came all too quickly for me to go to work. When I went to sign on in the booking office, Winifred was on duty, she was a matronly woman, my mother's age. Before I had chance to close the door by its worn, sloppy brass knob, Winnie developed the nodding dog syndrome. She bit on her bottom lip, exposing false teeth which I think she must have been breaking in for a horse. With her eyes now as prominent as a Madagascan bush baby, she slowly drawled, 'Mr Compton wants to see you'. I got the impression that she had not had so much excitement since the armistice!

Dawdling down the station stairs only fractionally delayed the evil moment. I knocked quietly on the chief's door, he heard me first time. A few steps took me on to the GWR monogrammed 'carpet', taken from a redundant first class coach, which lay in front of his large wooden desk. My superior ignored me, continuing to write while I stood looking at wisps of grey hair sprouting from his polished baldhead.

'Er, you wanted to see me sir?', I offered. Without stopping writing, the station master put his hand left down below the desk and raised the damaged bucket on to the desk, its gaping seam pointing my way like the mouth of a great white shark. He eventually slowly leaned back, tapping his pen in the fork of his hand between his thumb and index finger saying, 'I would appreciate an explanation, Herbert?'

Trotting out my story truthfully angered Mr Compton. He had interviewed Charlie during the morning and our stories happened to tally. He immediately accused me of impudence and colluding with my opposite number, inquiring as to whether I thought he was born yesterday. By this time he was getting pretty angry, he retorted that he knew exactly what we had done and therefore could not understand why we could not be honest. He had often seen boys put tin cans over fireworks and had seen that when they exploded it blew the can into the air. He was wise to what we had done; he insisted that we had placed the inverted bucket over the firework. The more I begged that I had told the truth, the more irritated he became. I seriously thought of suggesting a replay, with another bucket, I could perhaps have a wager with him for half a crown! However, he was definitely not in that frame of mind, so I again used discretion.

Mr Compton didn't carry out his threat to stop the cost of the bucket from our wages, which for me would have brought many awkward questions from home. I was very grateful for this, he was a good man, but the atmosphere was still quite frosty towards both Charlie and myself, when I left to start work at Tyseley engine shed two weeks later.

# Chapter Four

## Cotton Waste and Cleaning Oil

Carrying my new engineman's cap with its small red embroidered roundel indicating GWR, I left home at 7.30 am on 27th November, 1949 to start work at Tyseley. I was wearing a pair of my new overalls given to me when I had attended my medical examination at Swindon. Had I then had the proportions of a sumo wrestler, the stiffened overalls would have been a perfect fit. However, the jacket wrapped right around me, tucking well under my arms, the sleeves being at least three inches too long. My braces were hitched to their limit, already making my trousers uncomfortable to tender parts. Even at these confines, the overall legs still hung like the bellows of a concertina, resting on my tops of my boots and dragging the floor at the heels.

I had made a lot of 'noise' to my mother about tailoring the overalls to fit, but she flatly refused, insisting that after two or three times in the wash they would be alright. She was right of course, having much experience with such matters, yet as usual as a teenager I was too stubborn to admit it. Indeed, when the time came for a second issue of overalls, a year later, I was still growing; the old ones were by then ridiculously short.

Crossing the A41 was easy then, in spite of the 'rush hour 'and this suburb being a heavily industrialised area. There were no traffic lights, no parked cars and no double yellow lines. With nothing to hinder progress, the Co-op milkman delivered milk to most of the terraced houses that stood high above the Warwick Road. As the lovable beast had done for seven days a week, year in year out, the horse drew the cart up the hill facing the oncoming traffic, stopping and starting without command as the milkman progressed with the deliveries. These homes now looking woeful with neglect following the wartime years, paint peeled, guttering hung loose and boundary walls leaned at varying angles towards the road. Some of these walls were already just a heap of rubble on the pavement. This hive of industry housed many famous names, Rover Cars, Girling Brakes, Slumberland Beds, King Dick Spanners, Dawes Cycles, Tucker Switchgear, the list goes on.

The dogs no longer barked from what I had remembered in younger days as the Dog's Home. High on the blue brick wall opposite to the terraced houses, this once stately mansion was now converted to a railwaymen's hostel. The tall tubular fence, erected around the engine sheds and made from old boiler tubes by the thrifty Great Western Railway Company, now corroded badly, offering little protection against intruders. The brook running under the road at the engine shed entrance ran milky white, discoloured by suds oil discharged by industry further upstream. This tended to preserve all and sundry for an eternity, old cycle wheels, bedsteads and countless tin cans. Wild life, long extinct, I suspect even the rats avoided this oily environment.

The gatekeeper's hut door was always open, a cheerful fire burned in the fireplace warming the occupants whilst they studied 'form' from the *Sporting Life*. This morning the gatekeeper was not going to bellow at me to 'bugger off', as he had done many times when I was an inquisitive boy trainspotter.

Along the cinder path an elderly driver nodded as he eyed my garb. His face was smutty, the smell of 'St Bruno' from an old pipe a refreshing change from the yellow sulphur-laden smoke rolling from the chimneys of several locomotives standing adjacent to the path. I dodged the same pools in the sunken loco shed floor as I had

(5719)

THE RAILWAY EXECUTIVE (Western Region).

CHIEF MECHANICAL ENGINEER'S DEPARTMENT,

SWINDON, WILTS.,

Herbert D.C., Tyseley.
Dept 10.55am. ch. Birmingham 11.35am. arr. Swindon 1/56pm. 19
above

Please travel to Swindon for examination by the XXX train on Wed. 10th Aug. and report to the Railway Executive's representative at Park House, Church Place, immediately on arrival.

You should provide yourself with sufficient money to cover out-of-pocket expenses and the payment of the entrance fee (5/-) to the Great Western Railway Enginemen and Fireman's Mutual Assurance, Sick and Superannuation Society, and bring birth certificate if in your possession.

Be prepared to say to what Sick Club, if any you belong, and the amount of sick pay to which you are entitled weekly.

Directions for finding Park House, Church Place, from Swindon Station :—

On leaving station turn sharply to the right and walk straight along Station Road, Sheppard Street, London Street and Bristol Street, turning to the left, near a high tank, at the end of Bristol Street. Keeping the Park on the right proceed for about 200 yards and enter Park House which is on the left at the bottom of this road. Enquire on entering.

2,000-L.C.-1949-(2)

PLEASE BRING YOUR BIRTH CERTIFICATE & SOA

YOU MUST BE PREPARED TO SPEND THE DAY IN SWINDON

The document issued for my medical at Swindon for engine cleaner, 1949.

done years earlier with my father. Crossing the shed, clinker crunched beneath my soles, the hissing 'snake pit' now somewhat tamed by my maturing years.

I was aware of the direction I needed to take to the General Office and found my way along the long passage in semi-darkness. My arrival was acknowledged and I entered the dismal room. The sole occupant was a middle-aged man who eyed me with disdain, making me feel as if I was just another irritation to his day. He wore the 'obligatory' tweed jacket with leather-patched elbows, his dark hair parted with precision down the middle of his head and held firmly in place, I suspect by the hair cream most favoured by the Royal Air Force. I handed to him the small brown envelope that I had received through the post; conversation was for a time impossible, a locomotive blew off steam noisily outside the window. The clerk grimaced at the discharge of steam, he said nothing, I waited. A few moments later another new entrant entered the office receiving the same less than cheerful welcome. At least I was now not alone in this unfriendly environment.

The office filing system appeared to consist of a million drawing pins and paper clips pressed into a wooden partition wall. Memos and pieces of paper hung everywhere, smutty and dog-eared with perpetual thumbing. Three large wooden desks dominated the office, all had brown cork lino tacked to their surface, this medium polished only in the areas in contact with sleeves. Amber low voltage lighting struggled to supplement the daylight from a solitary sash window. The lamps hung on long plaited flex from the high ceiling, hovering just above head height. Plain white disc shades reflected the light on to the desks, in some instances the lamps pulled to a more advantageous position by string nailed at one end to the wall.

During our wait the office door burst noisily open and a youth struggled in with a coalscuttle with the capacity of a wheelbarrow. He humped the heavy scuttle across the office, both hands on the handle, his legs wide apart. He was little older than myself, but he already had the look of a seasoned engineman. His overalls fitted well and he had acquired a black uniform serge jacket, along with a privately purchased greaseproof top for his hat. His face flushed with the crisp air outside, and the effort of carrying the coalscuttle, he raked vigorously at the embers in the grate sending clouds of white dust into the office. The clerk watched the young man's every move as he made entries on the wallpaper size payroll sheets, his rounded shoulders rising and falling as he asthmatically struggled for every breath. Pitching lumps of coal into the grate from some distance, the young man again sent up a further cloud of white dust. Suddenly the clerk leapt to his feet shouting, 'Don't you know the difference between hard and soft coal yet?' The youth replied that he could not find any hard coal. At which the clerk bawled, 'Go back and bloody well look, this place won't get warm till dinner time with that bleeding stuff'. The scuttle was dragged across the brown lino again, the office boy muttering and making two fingered gestures unseen by the clerk. This incident puzzled me, what on earth was the clerk on about, soft coal?

Shortly after the chargeman cleaner entered the office and exchanged words with the clerk, but said nothing to us. I got the immediate impression that they felt that we would not be staying very long. This was certainly the case with my new colleague, he stayed no more than a fortnight! Bill Cox, a jolly man with a 50 inch waist came from behind the wooden partition wall and handed us small brass checks, mine bearing the number 523.

The chargeman cleaner was Frank Chamberlain, anyone could have been forgiven for mistaking him for an elderly engine driver. I estimated his age at 64 years and 11 months, this however was a gross miscalculation, he was more than a decade younger than that. Frank was a short man with snow-white hair and matching white walrus moustache, he also suffered from what seemed to be a stoop. He wore the 'uniform' soft cap, his trouser leg bottoms were noticeably well clear of soft leather polished black boots; a cherry wood pipe peeped from his top jacket pocket.

We followed the chargeman across the engine shed, the design of which was known as a double roundhouse. One side of the shed was designated the 'Passenger Side', the opposite roundhouse was termed the 'Goods Side'. We passed over the 'Goods Side' turntable and followed Frank to the far wall of the depot, his serge jacket pockets bulging with a menagerie of items. It was little wonder he stooped, the bundle of keys he took from his pocket would have been more fitting to a castle dungeon. He unlocked a door and lifted the lever latch, which was more suited to a bank vault. Behind the heavy door the heat met us from a huge fire in the grate; the burning coals piled high in the chimney. These coals only stopped from falling across the room by a sector of steel hacked from a wagon wheel tyre, now acting as a fender. The furniture was a row of cast-iron tables and benches, the wooden tabletops scrubbed white. Traces of white liquid damped the floor, the 'cabin' smelling strongly of carbolescene disinfectant. We disposed of our lunch bags and jackets, whilst the chargeman took a small yellow docket pad and pencil from his pocket. Passing one of the dockets to me he had filled in the date, engine No. 2903 and written, '1 lb. Waste'. Alex and I then retraced our steps behind the man in charge towards the stores, where we exchanged the docket for tight bundles of cotton waste.

Engine No. 2903, named *Lady of Lyons*, was standing near the shed exit doorway in the Passenger Side roundhouse; here we met the only two other engine cleaners at the depot. 2903 was one of only a few 'Saint' class remaining in service and was indeed withdrawn from service later that month. One of the cleaners John Millman needed no introduction; indeed we had gone through senior school together in the same class. I was delighted to meet John, although I was quite surprised that he had chosen to work at an engine shed where most of the locomotives had copper caps around their chimneys. John's father was a freight guard on the ex-London Midland and Scottish Railway (LMS), consequently at school John had always shown a keen interest in locomotives nicknamed 'Crabs', 'Black Fives' and 'Princess Coronations'.

No. 4924 *Eydon Hall* in the shed at Tyseley in 1949, showing the engine pits that we used to crawl beneath the engines, with the author sitting in the cab. *Dick Potts*

No. 6866 *Morfa Grange* after cleaning in Tyseley shed in 1950. *Dick Potts*

My schoolmate had started work two weeks earlier, now I was very pleased that Frank Chamberlain had paired me off with him to learn the ropes. I loosened off the tight bundle of cotton waste, quickly learning that sharp needle like wire from the cotton mill looms was present in the bundle, this could tear quite a nasty gash in the hand if unnoticed. Also, I was quick to realise the futility of our situation; still living in the past, the railway industry had made no extra provision for the appallingly filthy state that the engines were now in, cotton waste being our only cleaning medium. We were instructed to clean only the motion work, names and numbers. The motion work generally meant the parts which it was necessary for a driver to oil before the commencement of a journey, most of which was

The black hand gang on No. 9798. John Millman, *right*; Jim Cullen, Colin Jacks and the author, 1950. *Dick Potts*

underneath the engine. Rubbing at thick gunge with just a patch of cotton waste was useless, we were not given scrapers, nor any form of illumination, yet the chargeman fully expected the job to be done, the situation was simply ludicrous.

John had already learned that paraffin could be acquired from the lamp house, which was under the coaling stage. Unfortunately, to get there the shed yard had to be crossed, right in front of the shed master's and shift foreman's office windows. Getting to the coal stage unnoticed was rather like making an escape from Stalag 13! John had already learned that the chargeman's movements were pretty predictable, so once he was out of sight we set off on a long detour, across the Goods Side shed and up the cover side of a long row of engines, across an engine footplate and under some wagons loaded with ashes. In the lamp house we were just filling the metal can that John had hidden for the purpose when the toolman came in; he was responsible for cleaning and filling the engine headlamps. He wasn't at all pleased, immediately telling us to 'sod off ', he didn't hump paraffin up to the lamp house from the stores for us to pinch it. So we took the same route back with just a drop of the precious oil in the can. This was enough for us to make a presentable job of the coupling rods, which were attached to the 6 ft 8½ in. driving wheels.

I was very apprehensive about going underneath a locomotive for the first time, I thought that the red plate that we had fixed to the front lamp bracket of the engine, announcing 'Not to be Moved,' didn't offer us enough protection. I began to imagine us ending up perhaps in Bristol, riding trapped in the bowels of the engine. However, enginemen were most disciplined with regards to these 'Not to be Moved' targets. No engine was ever moved until the person who had put the red sign on the lamp bracket had personally removed it. I never knew of any incident where this regulation was disregarded.

In the engine shed the engines stood over pits between the rails, the pits only being about three feet deep. It was necessary either to go on hands and knees, which was a bit messy in the wet filthy pit, or by crouching you could edge along doing a subtle kind of 'Cossack' dance with the legs. When going under, however, taking great care that when dripping scalding water penetrated your overalls you didn't shout 'Ouch' and straighten up, hence cracking your head on the anatomy of the locomotive. This day I followed John underneath, scrambling up into the 'works' among the oily rods, it was ridiculously dark. John was already able to name many of the working parts, eccentric rods, quadrant links, weighbar shaft, the list went on, I was impressed. The poor light had one advantage, the chargeman, also not carrying a lamp, was unable to see the extent of our work underneath! So, we rubbed at areas just where we could see, although generally I found the whole situation wasn't going to give me much job satisfaction. When John felt we had done enough we dropped down through the valve gear and slipped through a gap in the brake gear back into the pit. We were still under the allotted two hours when we surfaced; therefore John suggested we had time to go to the canteen for a drink. The smell of frying bacon was irresistible, I felt starving hungry. Having only a sixpence in my pocket, I had four ½*d.* dips in the fat and 2*d.* cup of tea. We were still back in the shed before Frank Chamberlain arrived to allocate another engine for us to clean.

Many boys still wanted to become engine drivers and over the next few weeks there was a steady influx of young men who felt they wanted to fulfil a dream. Any older lads were put on night work, calling up, or 'Knockers Up' as they were known in some parts of the country. Nevertheless, this still left a good body of lads to do the engine cleaning, many of whom had abundant enthusiasm.

Apart from meeting my school pal John Millman, this became a time in my life when I met other men who were to become lifelong friends. Colleagues whom I would now find it difficult to imagine life without their friendship.

Dick Potts was more mature than any of us; he had already served his two years' National Service. Dick's father was a driver at the depot; Sid, was indeed a well-respected engineman. He had however, until that time, refused to allow Dick to follow in his footsteps on to the footplate. He perhaps rightly felt that his son's talents would be of better use elsewhere. Once Dick was 20 years old, the decision was his; he wanted nothing else but to become an engineman. We all looked to Dick's maturity for advice, he educated us on railway matters and he entertained us all with many railway stories, enthralling us with graphic actions. To this day Dick's exceptional power of observation amazes me; this is perhaps why he is such an accomplished railway artist.

Colin Jacks and myself became inseparable friends as single men. We shared holidays and drinking time, often putting the world to right. We shared happy times and moments of emotional turmoil; eventually we became ' Best Man' to each other at our weddings. Colin has always been somewhat more than a railway enthusiast, after retirement putting much time in on the preserved Gloucester and Warwickshire Line, also he has become the author of his railway experiences.

I went through school with Bernard Rainbow; Bernard has also always been more than a railway devotee. He could draw on the intricacies of the railway regulations without reference to the many publications issued to us. He worked conscientiously throughout his lifetime; we started together and retired together from InterCity Cross Country. The demise of steam, however, was a very disconcerting time for Bernard, to compensate he threw great energy into the preservation movement. His tireless work at the concept of Tyseley Railway Museum was legendary. The turnout of the locomotives, on open days, was always fit for royalty; it was such a tragedy that internal politics ruined so much potential. Since then, the Severn Valley Railway Company has no doubt put a greater value on his expertise.

With a host of lads, and abundant enthusiasm, during the weeks that followed the locomotive cleanliness improved greatly. This was no thanks to the immediate management who completely failed to capitalise on the fervour of the young men that they employed. Youngsters so keen, that many of them, I feel sure, would have done the work voluntarily. This has since been proved by today's enthusiasm in the preservation societies. Sadly, because conditions were so awful, it would be no exaggeration to say that 95 per cent of these men left the service over weeks, months, perhaps years. Once on the footplate you were required to turn out to work at all hours around the clock. The money, too, was only enhanced by long working hours and compared unfavourably with outside industry. With all the enthusiasm in the world, this was bound to cause domestic problems. Lifelong footplate men, no doubt, had to have someone very special to go home to.

Starting conditions too were pretty dreadful, much of the engine shed roof was missing and offered little protection from the elements. On a windy day huge panes of wire reinforced glass would fall from the roof. One day I watched as a large shard of glass buried itself into the wooden decking of the turntable; quivering it remained upright like an archer's arrow. Many of the smoke chutes that were designed to take the smoke out of the shed were damaged, or missing altogether. Washing facilities were a wooden trough in the shed, the trough having a pipe along its the length with holes in it through which water came. To heat the water a steam valve had to be opened. We got filthy dirty, although maintenance men got even dirtier, particularly men involved in boiler work. Over time, I saw men stand naked in the shed with each leg in a bucket of hot water having a wash down. Men got so grimed with soot, grease and coal dust that their state was much worse than coalface workers. Miners got pithead baths, these men had nothing.

No. 5907 *Marble Hall* after we had cleaned her, on this diagram she would later work the Swindon Parcels after first working a short local passenger. *Dick Potts*

No. 7001 *Sir James Milne* one of the 'Castle' class engines that worked the Royal Train to Stratford-upon-Avon in 1950. *Dick Potts*

During my lifetime on the railway I was always a moderate, nevertheless, I cannot help feeling that successive governments let down these stalwart employees. Twenty years later, when the shed was demolished to make way for dieselisation, men still washed in buckets, the hot water mostly drawn from the boilers of locomotives. Ironically, the moment there was any industrial dispute the press of the time was inclined to label these good men as 'militant'.

The shed master walked around the shed once a day, wearing a trilby hat, mostly having both hands in his pockets. Many times I politely passed the time of day to him, only on good days receiving a nod in return; I never heard the sound of his voice.

We purchased, or made ourselves, scrapers, even bought emery cloth and metal polish from the local ironmongers, paying for it out of our own pocket. Copper top chimneys and brass safety valve covers began to glisten, along with cab side beading and window frames. We became friendly with footplate men, cadging oil and paraffin, blacking down hot smokeboxes with thick cylinder oil. We took great pride in seeing the engines go off shed, Nos. 5907 *Marble Hall*, 5927 *Guild Hall*, 4924 *Eydon Hall*, there were many. Even the many smaller prairie and 'matchbox' pannier tanks engines got attention, along with the latest wartime 'Austerity' engines, Nos. 77097 and 90685, not forgetting No. 3016, our only Robinson engine.

When we were required to clean the whole of a locomotive, we were issued with half a pint of cleaning oil for a tank engine and a pint of oil for a tender engine. The men in the stores measured the oil as if a weights and measures inspector was breathing down their neck, never a drop extra. One pint of oil was hardly sufficient to clean just a tender, let alone the whole engine.

In 1950 the Royal Train came to Stratford-upon-Avon, we were given the task of cleaning one of our locomotives for the job of hauling the empty train from Stratford-upon-Avon to Tyseley Carriage Sidings for servicing. Engine No. 4980 *Wrottesley Hall* was rostered to do the job, as she was the most recent in having a general mechanical overhaul at Swindon works. Ironically, we were given all the oil and cotton waste that we needed to clean this engine. This, along with electric lead lamps for seeing underneath, and instead of the normal two hours we were given a whole week to get things right! Having said that, the brass safety valve cover and copper chimney top had been painted over, this did mean another trip to the local ironmonger's for emery cloth. At this point in time the shedmaster, Phil Davis, was heard to say, 'They must be bloody barmy'.

When finished No. 4980 looked wonderful to us, yet despite all our work, our lowly 'Hall' class engine was very much overshadowed by the two magnificent 'Castle' class engines that had worked the train from Windsor. Both 'Castle' class engines, Nos. 7001 *Sir James Milne* and 5000 *Launceston Castle*, were a magnificent sight, painted in Brunswick green livery and having glistening brass work, along with burnished steel metal work. In contrast, the Tyseley engine carried the new British Railways standard black livery, this practical colour only brightened with red and grey lining out.

At normal times a collection of youth inevitably bought about some 'horseplay'. We dodged Frank Chamberlain by hiding in empty tender tanks and the fireboxes of engines which were out of service for boiler repairs. Having said that, the throwing of missiles, mainly oily cotton waste, meant dismissal.

If we got to work early, Bill Vaughan, the stationary boilerman, allowed one of us to fill the firebox for him, he was no fool! Officially, we were not allowed on to locomotive footplates, helping on the stationary boiler therefore gave us an insight to the working of injectors, devices for supplying the boiler with water against the steam pressure. We also began to learn of ejectors, which were for creating a vacuum in the train braking system, also the reason for the use of snifting valves and pepperbox valves. There was a wealth of knowledge to be gained along with the relevant terminology.

We worked six days a week, eight hours a day, Sunday work was optional. For a 48 hour week I was paid two pounds eight shillings, less any stoppages.

I was surprised to be called to the chief clerk's office one day; I could not imagine why he wanted to see me. Once in his office Vic Webb spoke affirmatively from behind thick horn rimmed spectacles, urging me to make provision for my future. He was a commission agent for an insurance company and he spoke of figures of money that I had only ever seen as prospective prize money for winning the *News of the World* crossword. In 25 years I would be a rich man, he urged, being able to buy my own house and having money to spare. He talked, or intimidated me, into parting with half my pocket money. When the policy matured, half a lifetime later, the money took my wife and I on our first package holiday abroad, a week in Majorca one Easter and the money was gone.

A locomotive inspector was sent from Wolverhampton to tutor us on the basics of locomotive practice. In the cleaner's cabin, Charlie Weston captivated our interest; he was a good man whom I feel enjoyed our enthusiasm. He was still around in the same capacity 15 years later. He had a pleasant manner and was always very approachable, I never heard anyone say anything critical of him. For someone in management this was pretty unusual at that time, undoubtedly as young men we learned a lot from him. With the amount of interest shown, the mundane subject of engine preparation was soon passed over and we drifted towards locomotive mechanical defects. We touched on unequal exhaust beats, caused by bent valve spindles, shifted sheaves and sprung valve buckles, terminology exclusive to steam engines. Soon most of us could trace the passage of steam through the valve events relative to the position of the 'big ends', or cranks. All drivers had to know this to pass the driver's examination, albeit many years hence for us. The inspector at Swindon Headquarters would place the right hand 'big end', or crank, in a certain position relative to the wheel, then select a reversing lever position, forward, mid, or reverse gear. The driver would then immediately be required to know which steam port opened to allow steam into the cylinders to move the engine. Also the driver had to know which valves were open to exhaust steam. All this was extremely advanced for us, but with concentration we began to get our heads around it. In later weeks we talked of 'Walschaerts' valve gear, as fitted by the GWR locomotive designers to their 'Star' and 'Castle' classes of locomotive, these being the engines which worked the most important express trains.

I continued to clean engines until my 16th birthday, although an incident occurred one day which might have changed my life. I was allocated to clean the underneath of a pannier shunting engine, on this day I was working alone. I put the 'Not to be Moved' target on the front lamp bracket as usual, first checking that the reversing lever was in 'mid gear' and that the cylinder drain cocks were open. Enginemen religiously left stabled engines set in this manner to avoid them inadvertently moving. Opening of the cylinder drains prevented steam pressure building behind the pistons and the 'mid' reverser position put the engine effectively into neutral. Unaware to me, the fireman allocated to take the engine out came to prepare the engine. Parts of the valve gear on locomotives tended to wear to a razors edge, I had my hands in the 'works' when the fireman felt that the reverser, being in the mid position was in his way on the footplate. He knocked the catch out of the lever, which immediately fell into forward gear. This thoughtless act came very close to severing both my hands. A few well-chosen phrases then became necessary, most of which are unprintable!

# Chapter Five

## Doubling my Money

Without the aid of a computer, the roster clerk heralded my 16th birthday by rostering me on my first firing turn, this was a Saturday in June 1950, and as usual he was desperately short of firemen. Because of the night work regulations, firemen were not officially promoted into the grade until they reached the age of seventeen. Engine cleaners under that age could, however, be upgraded to work day turns only. This tended to be somewhat of a farce, as I was to work on upgraded turns until 2.00 am, also often starting work at 4.00 am.

I hadn't slept the night prior to my birthday, I rose at four o'clock before the alarm went off, I was afraid I wouldn't hear it as I signed on duty at 5.05 am for Bordesley Junction shunting engine duty No 9. My driver was Harry Wiggins, who was based at Bordesley, which was an out-station of Tyseley, employing drivers on the shunting duties who had the misfortune of having poor health. These men had to sign on and off duty at Bordesley, therefore I was required to make my own way there and find for myself which one of the seven engines I would be working on. Starting time at Bordesley was 6.00 am, 55 minutes being allowed as walking time from Tyseley. This walking time allowance was via the road, which was quite a detour. I learned that most men walked along the line; so I decided to follow this trend. There were seven running lines between Tyseley and Bordesley, it was daylight, but this was still not the safest of routes for an unseasoned 16 year old to take.

Once I became eligible for upgrading to footplate turns my rate of pay more than doubled, the bottom fireman's basic rate being five pounds, three shillings and six pence. This was good money at my age; unfortunately the rate increased little for the more mature men having homes and families to care for. From this day on, I never did another day as an engine cleaner.

After some wandering around the busy yard at Bordesley I eventually found my engine No. 3646, and relieved the night turn fireman. Engines were never left unattended. My driver soon arrived and I put my cards on the table, telling him that it was my first day as fireman, although, I fear he would have soon guessed. Harry didn't dictate to me, but quietly allowed me to muddle through. My father had already made a point of stressing on me the importance of keeping things tidy on the footplate, which meant regular sweeping up and keeping the coal dust well laid.

No. 9 shunting engine was the heaviest working job at Bordesley, which meant dragging heavy coal trains that had arrived from the Midland Region. We then had to marshal the wagons from these trains to make up fresh formations for the South and West of England. I somehow managed to get all the steam required of me, even if the fire did develop an unorthodox look about it. Starting the heavy trains meant the engine being put into full gear and the throttle, or regulator, opened wide. Smoke shot feet into the air, ash rained down on to the tank tops of the engine and the fire danced on the fire bars, I began to enjoy the exhilarating work. Nevertheless, I can only imagine that it was a one of those periods that the engines were being coaled with hard house coal, in which case my mother would have had no difficulty getting steam. The engine kicked and jerked when passing over bends and points in the yard and I leaned on the rear wheel coil springs protruding up into the cab for some stability. I somehow had to learn to be able to put coal on the fire while the engine was moving. I hit the side of the firehole so many times that the end of the shovel was beginning to turn up. At one point, Harry offered me his pocket knife; at my looking rather puzzled at this gesture, he remarked smiling, 'I thought you needed to make the hole a bit bigger!' In fact I needed a hole three feet in diameter.

It was a hot summer's day and there were soon other disadvantages to be realised. The jam sandwiches in my bag curled up to look like several pairs of kippers well over their 'sell by' date. The milk for my tea refused categorically to leave the bottle. Cling film, polythene and kitchen refrigerators were a blessing yet unheard of.

At the end of the shift, with much of the skin off my knuckles, Harry showed me the engine washing facilities. This was the long rectangular-shaped shovel rammed into the coil springs on the footplate. Falling at just the right angle, the shovel was then filled with hot water from the coal-watering pipe. We used my newly issued soap ration, which looked rather like a piece of sun-dried Double Gloucester ... and seemed to give an equivalent amount of lather. I washed my face, but the caustic affect of this soap on youthful skin tended to make me look as though I was suffering from some rare tropical disease.

Nonetheless, I went home quietly satisfied, my new rate of pay, plus two hours overtime, balancing the scales nicely in my favour. The walk down the line back to Tyseley cut the walking time considerably, I booked relief at two o'clock on my ticket, plus the normal 55 minutes walking time, with an additional 10 minutes for making out the ticket. This made my time to sign off duty at five minutes past three. I then posted my ticket in the office window, but when I was just a few steps away the timeclerk shouted after me, asking had I not learned to tell the time whilst I was at school? He then threw the ticket back out, it was just two thirty; he said five past three was the time I had put on the ticket. Therefore he made me wait up to exactly the minute before letting me go home. I later spoke of the issue to my father, telling him that the clerk had made me wait. My father made me see another point of view, had I met with an accident on my way home when I should have been at work, then the onus fell on the clerk for not doing his job. This was advice that was rekindled a

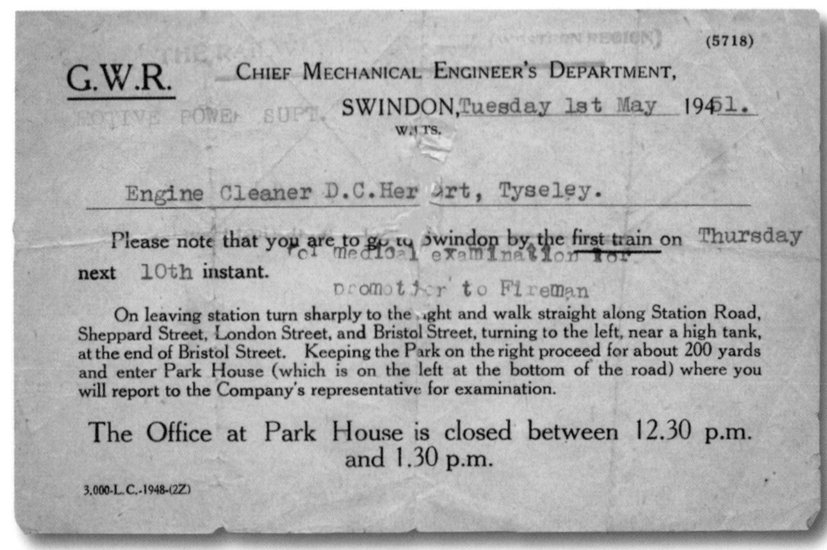
(5718)

G.W.R. CHIEF MECHANICAL ENGINEER'S DEPARTMENT,

SWINDON, Tuesday 1st May 1951.

W.I.TS.

Engine Cleaner D.C.Herbert, Tyseley.

Please note that you are to go to Swindon by the first train on Thursday next 10th instant. for medical examination for promotion to Fireman

On leaving station turn sharply to the right and walk straight along Station Road, Sheppard Street, London Street, and Bristol Street, turning to the left, near a high tank, at the end of Bristol Street. Keeping the Park on the right proceed for about 200 yards and enter Park House (which is on the left at the bottom of the road) where you will report to the Company's representative for examination.

The Office at Park House is closed between 12.30 p.m. and 1.30 p.m.

3,000-L.C.-1948-(2Z)

Document for medical at Swindon for promotion to fireman, 1951

| Gross Wages | Income Tax | Deductions | Date | Ticket No. | Net Wages |
|---|---|---|---|---|---|
| 9.14.3 | 13.0 | 5.1 | JUL 1 | 523 | 8.16.2 |

The author's payslip when doing firing turns, 1951.

number of years later when two Tyseley drivers who lived at Wolverhampton slipped off home early. They caught a late train from Snow Hill station to Wolverhampton Low Level. Arriving at Wolverhampton found them in an empty coach, along with an apparently abandoned large suitcase. This they saw fit to hump across the footbridge and leave in the Lost Property Office. In the early hours, both these men's households were roused by the police, the suitcase having contained a dismembered body! Many questions were asked, most of which were rather awkward.

The following Monday morning I was rostered on duty at 4.15 am, for Hockley shunting engine No. 3, this turn with driver Stan Carter. This was to be my first engine preparation and my first run on the main running lines, albeit 'light' engine, a railway term for running without a train. Forty years on, the eagerness to be out of bed at 3 am had mellowed somewhat, but in the beginning I had profuse enthusiasm.

I signed on and collected the toolbox keys for engine No. 9682 and found her tucked away in the 'Goods' shed. Remembering all I was told by the footplate inspector Charlie Weston, I first checked the boiler water level in the sight glass and the water gauge fittings in general, making sure that he water drained from the glass and returned freely on closing the blow down cock. This proved that the waterways to the gauge were clear and this procedure was to become a religion for our own safety. On my hands and knees I peered up at the fusible plugs in the crown of the firebox to be sure they were not leaking, again checking that all the other things were sound, no leaking fire tubes, firebox stays, or boiler seams. I gave the front and back sanding gear levers a few tugs and then opened the toolboxes checking that we had the vitally important sealed container holding two red flags and 12 detonators. This equipment was used solely in emergencies, for train protection. After screwing on the coal-watering pipe, I put the driver's oil pots to warm in strategic parts of the cab. This was another thing my father had told me, it gave a good impression. Warming the oil made it more fluid.

At this point, it dawned on me that the firehole shield was missing from the firehole. This was a heavy semi-circular casting that sat in the bottom of the firehole to protect the boilerplates from damage by way of fire-irons and shovels. The boilersmiths had obviously removed the shield to access to the firebox for an inspection. It was indeed the boilersmith's job to refit the shield, but after some thought, I felt it didn't really need an expert to drop it back into place. I picked it up, it was considerably heavier than I expected, crouching in front of the firehole I dropped the firehole shield where I thought was about right, but it stuck, half in half out and was quickly getting very hot. Not to be beaten, I got the coal peck and hooked it back on to the footplate. After running cold water on it, I took on the same stance and pitched the ring towards the firehole, only to see it roll down the half burnt coals towards the front of the firebox. I was just beginning to chew at my nails as the cab door eased back and I was greeted with a fresh-faced man with the most infectious smile. At that time in the morning this was quite unique, it wasn't generally a time for smiling faces.

Stan Carter was a happy-go-lucky man who sounded as though he was born within earshot of Bow Bells. He made no bones about it when I confessed that I had dropped the firehole shield into the firebox. He explained that, had the part been refitted, as it should have been, before the fire had been lit, then there would now not be a problem. He told me to alert the boilersmiths, their cabin being next to the engine cleaner's cabin on the far side of the roundhouse.

I quietly opened the boilersmith's cabin door, which was wide enough to wheel a handcart through, the place was in darkness. I switched on the light; a big man lay prone on one of the benches, his head resting on a house brick, interposed with a large patch of cotton waste. He had an array of warts on his face, which made his sooty countenance look quite intimidating. His eyelids were still flickering quicker than a 1920s silent movie when I told him I had dropped the firehole shield into the firebox. His senses still numbed, he asked the engine number as he stretched his stiff limbs. After a quiet pause he then realised what I had said, it dawned on him that the number I had given was that of a pannier having a deep firebox. He then let loose with an absolute stream of curses. I always felt my father was well versed in this field, but this man's vocabulary put my father somewhere in a lower division. I crept out, apologising as I left, yet he was still offering profanities as he tied up his bootlaces.

My driver was now underneath the locomotive with the oil can and flare lamp, a flare lamp being the sort of lamp Aladdin carried, having a lighted wick in a paraffin vessel. I carried on checking around the engine, seeing that the sanding gear was working and tapping out any wet sand from the pipes which may cause a blockage. The sandbox levels also needed to be checked. Opening the smokebox door on the front of the engine, looking inside with my flare lamp, I found nothing leaking and the spark arrester plate was firmly in place, sitting securely on its brackets. The small amount of ashes left in the bottom of the smokebox were found to be evenly distributed, this being a clear indication that the main steam pipe joints were sound. Any leaking joints tended to sweep all the ashes to one side. I then swept further ash from around the smokebox door and slammed it shut and tightened it. After sweeping the remaining ashes from the front of the engine I returned to the cab, checking the other side sand pipes and sandboxes *en route*.

The boilersmith then arrived with a pair of extended handle tongues, asbestos gloves ... and a face like 'four pence'.* He fished about in the hot fire until clean streaks appeared on his face from the sweat running down his sooty cheeks. He eventually negotiated the heavy red-hot cast-iron shield, first on to the footplate, then on to the engine shed floor. After turning the fire hydrant on to cool it, he crouched on the footplate, as I had done, held the casting square with the firehole, got a line with his eye, as though he was going for double top, and pitched the ring towards the firehole, a distance of some two feet. There was a momentary hesitant sound, like a billiard ball not quite making the pocket and the heavy shield dropped snugly around the inside of the firehole. Every man to his trade, I thought. Although I did eventually perfect this technique myself, I did make certain that I didn't drop another one into the fire.

With the footplate to myself again I levelled the fire with the pricker, which was a long 'L' shaped fire-iron. When I opened both of the ashpan dampers to allowed air to flow freely through the fire, this move bought an immediate shout of disapproval by way of a cockney voice from the bowels of the engine. My driver was still underneath the engine and was up behind the crankshaft oiling the 'big ends'. I had just given him a tidy shove up the backside by the opening front damper. Profound apologies were again necessary; this I felt was not going to be my day.

* Face like four pence = looking very glum.

An illustration by Dick Potts which shows how a fireman could find comfort on a pannier tank shunting engine (*see page 62*).

After sweeping up the footplate, I swilled down with the coal watering pipe and trimmed the bunker, breaking up any number of large lumps of coal before they dropped down across the bunker shovelling hole. Shunting engines carried four headlamps, these I fetched from the lamp house, some 200 yards across the shed yard, after which I felt I would have to wear a double truss for the rest of my life. Then again, I still had the experience to come of carrying two scoops of sand for the sandboxes, if you could keep your legs straight whilst carrying these, you almost left footprints in the blue brick floor! This really was a man's world; I was yet desperately short of the required muscle.

We eventually traversed the turntable and went to the water column outside the shed, filling both the boiler and the tanks to capacity, this again being general practice. It was normal for Hockley No. 3 engine to couple to Hockley No. 2 to go light engine to the yard. This we did at the shed departure signal, but outside the Loco Yard signal box the Handsworth shunting engine came up behind us. In this case it was my duty to couple up the rear engine. All three locomotives duly left coupled together and the signalman at Small Heath South signal box turned us out on to the down relief line. All the signals were now showing clear, but when approaching Small Heath station the signals reverted to danger and a red light sprung from the window of Small Heath North signal box. I was the one again who picked up the penalty points; I didn't know that I should have removed the tail lamp from the rear of our engine when I had coupled up. Theoretically, I could have traced complicated mechanical faults on the engine, by listening to the exhaust beats, yet I simply had no idea of the important significance of a tail lamp. This was vital equipment in semaphore signalled areas; each tail lamp indicated to signalmen that a train had passed his signal box complete. It was therefore most important that no intermediate tail lamps were carried. In later years a favourite training class question was, 'When is a red light an all clear signal?' The answer was, 'When it is a tail lamp'.

Hockley was a vast marshalling yard, having four shunting engines in all, Nos. 1 and 4 engines arriving at the sidings some four hours earlier than us. No. 3 engine shunted the 'Round Yard' which was behind Hockley station on the up side, 'up', indicating the direction to Paddington.

Prior to the war, Hockley North signal box had been fully electrified, the power working both points and the semaphore type signals. It was necessary for No. 3 shunting engine continually to cross all six running lines from the down to the up sidings with long rafts of wagons. This meant crossing very complicated pointwork, yet over the many years that I eventually worked in and out of the yard, I never experienced any type of point or signal failure. This can only be attributed to the dedicated men who maintained the system and to the exceptionally rugged design.

The Round Yard shunting spur snaked along the up main line under high retaining walls and tunnels, from this vantage point I was able to watch the many trains go by. Most of the shunting movements were made by way of the shunting horn, or whistle, the man on the ground signalling to the driver by a code on the number of times he pressed the horn, or sounded his whistle, whether to go forward, back, stop or go steady. This made it necessary for the fireman to avoid any noise from blowing off steam from the safety valves so that the shunter's signals could be heard. Even the hissing from the engine blower had to be eased to a minimum for this reason, the blower being a jet of steam directed up the chimney to keep the fire bright when the engine was not working. Shunting 'blind' was quite a primitive operation, yet there were very few accidents, it worked well.

After my earlier problems of the day, things settled down, I was quietly satisfied with my second day's work when later we had relief. Stan Carter had a wonderful sense of humour; he often pulled my leg in an inoffensive way, yet he never forgot seriousness of the job that he performed. I worked with him many times in later years; he was always the same, saw the funny side of everything. He was a respected engineman and a great fellow.

Goods shunting was probably one of the most dangerous jobs on the railway; the men that did this work turned out in all weathers and had a constitution as hard as nails. Shunters worked in pairs, a head shunter and under shunter. The under shunter did the 'fly' shunting; which I had watched from the bridge at Tyseley station as an infant. 'Fly' shunting meant that a long raft of wagons attached to the engine could be sent on to different lines in the yard without the necessity of continually reversing the engine. This speeded up operations and also avoided the necessity for the driver to keep throwing the heavy reversing lever backwards and forwards. On occasions, I saw a number of the more grumpy older drivers get on the floor and remonstrate with the under shunter if he repeatedly failed to 'save the points', meaning that the wagons ran on to points that needed to be turned for the next move.

The head shunter worked furthest away from the engine, turning points as required and making sure that the wagons sent down 'roads' didn't rebound and run back out foul of other lines. 'Fly' shunting did have a drawn back; it did little for consignments of china, or glassware! Shunting was not one of the most glamorous of jobs, yet the shunters at Hockley and Bordesley Junction must have been some of the best in the country. These men on the ground developed an uncanny knack; they never uncoupled, or coupled, anything without the aid of a shunting pole. A shunting pole was made of ash wood, about six feet long and three times as thick as a broom stale. On the end of the pole was a spiral hook, which looped into the wagon couplings. At the end of the day the shunters locked their pole away in a rack, rather like a snooker player locked away his treasured cue. These men could attach and detach wagons on the move, running forward, or back pedalling, it really was an art to behold. I tried on a number of occasions to use a shunting pole, it was very difficult to throw the heavy coupling on to the hooks, I can only imagine that these men had developed muscle in the right places to become so proficient.

The only time shunters got beneath wagons was to couple the vacuum pipes on trains that left the yard with continuous brakes. 'C' headcode trains were braked throughout, 'D' headcode trains left with at least a third of the wagons coupled by the brake pipe. Lower class trains ran with proportionally less fitted. The more wagons that were attached to the engine brake pipe the faster the trains were timed to run. To create a vacuum in what was known as the 'train pipe', the front pipe on the engine had to be placed on a dummy stopper, likewise the pipe at the rear of the train. This leads to a quite amusing story that occurred later at Hockley.

The circus came to town and it was always part of the advertising strategy to parade the animals through the streets to the Big Top. The circus train was accommodated in the redundant cattle pens in the Round Yard. The animals were de-trained, all going well until the grand finale, the elephants. The majestic beasts were eventually lined up in the yard, coupled together, trunk to tail, rather like 'C' headcode fitted freight. The trainer then gave the order to move, but the leading beast wasn't happy, it was obviously intimidated by the slight hissing from our locomotive chimney. Facing the front of a pannier shunting engine, the elephant had every right to imagine it was facing a formidable rival. The keeper whacked the animal with a pole and no amount of prodding at the thick hide would induce the animal to move. Watching this plight the head shunter, who was indeed a real character, approached the keeper and said, 'You'll never get them to move like that mate, the front pipe is off the stopper!' This head shunter, Horace Sparks, was raised in the back streets of Birmingham, these circumstances no doubt helping him to live on his wits. He was not only a total comic, he was completely immune to trauma. On another occasion, there had been a fatality on the line and a young constable was sent to the scene of tragedy. When the policeman approached Horace, it was obvious to him that it was this young man's first encounter with death. Horace, having some compassion, accompanied the reluctant officer to the scene of the accident. Horace picked up the head of the dismembered torso by the hair, looked the corpse in the face, saying, 'It's all right kid, he ain't one of ours!' Meanwhile the young constable could do nothing to avoid the need to vomit.

I muddled through the next few firing turns, gaining much confidence. My first encounter with Welsh steam coal brought me back to earth and I quickly became aware that firing an engine was not just a case of putting the coal on the fire. The following week, I found myself rostered on Bordesley No. 9 shunting engine again. On this occasion I was marked to work with a driver known as 'Big Bill', this tag obviously attributed to his size. I have no idea why he had been demoted to shunting duties, but even as a youngster after a week with him I could have been forgiven for suspecting that it was possibly due to his mental age.

On the first morning, when I relieved the fireman on the night shift, who was an old hand fireman, the pressure gauge was showing rather lower than I had become used to. When I was alone on the footplate I looked at the fire, strangely it had taken on a dull indigo colour. I later became aware of the fact that the night shift had probably built up a huge fire when starting his turn of duty, then sitting down thereafter, he just had to put water in the boiler as necessary, closing down the dampers if the steam pressure became too high. This had made easy work for him, but it did tend to have a disastrous affect on the state of the fire, causing it to clinker badly. Oblivious to this, I opened up the dampers and lifted the firehole flap, turning the blower on a little to brighten the fire. Even so, the boiler pressure increased very little. When 'Big Bill' came to the engine, some 10 minutes later, the engine had still not got to the point anywhere near to blowing off steam. There also looked little change in the state of the fire, except that a brighter glow could be seen round the edges of the fire adjacent to the boilerplates.

It was now more than obvious to me why 'Big Bill' was so called; his cap rubbed on the roof of the '57XX' class engine and his bulk was so great that he had difficulty sitting on the normal seat. He had brought with him from his locker another seat, which hooked over the cab side of the engine cab, on to which he could still only rest a third of his great bulky backside. When in this position he could grab the reversing lever with one hand, the size of a JCB bucket, and throw it backwards and forward with frightening ease.

We backed on to the first train from the Midland Region and dragged it forward. As uninitiated as I was, I knew that there was no point in me adding further coal to the fire, as what was already in the firebox had still not burned through brightly. There was also too thick a fire for me to prod at it effectively with the chisel bar fire-iron, this a straight tool having its end shaped as a normal cold chisel. With my limited experience, I was now totally at a loss to know which road to go down to raise the boiler pressure. I lived in hope that when we started work the blast from the exhaust would brighten the fire. Alas, as we continued to work, the boiler pressure fell even more. The boiler water level began to drop dangerously also. I had no alternative to put more water in to the boiler, an act that reduced the pressure even further. I raked at the fire with the pricker until sweat ran down me in the heat of the summer morning, this in some sort desperation of solving my plight. The second train we backed on to, Bill got the signal from the shunter to move forward and when he put the regulator to full open the engine just stood gasping in a cloud of steam, refusing to move at all. Bill looked over at me wide eyed, as if completely surprised, saying, 'You've got no steam!' He then put his head over the side, saying to the shunters, 'He hasn't got any steam, and if he can't get it we will stay here till he does', further adding, 'They should send firemen who know what they are doing, I'm not doing it'.

Big Bill offered no guidance whatsoever; he sat with a grin on his face, making almost infantile remarks. I was dreadfully upset and embarrassed; I already felt that this was an awful slur on my ability. Big Bill was therefore the first man to shatter the iconic image that I had of men that I had always looked up to, men that had made the grade to engine driver.

Eventually, the boiler pressure rallied a little and we worked on; only to grind to a stop again as things went from bad to worse. This was despite several 'stirs' at the fire with the fire-irons, and the blower being on hard to force extra draught on the fire. Bill just sat ogling at my efforts, obviously gaining some pleasure at the disruption to train working that we were causing. However, I feel that perhaps the yard inspector had sprung into action quite early in the day, just after 9.00 am a fresh engine arrived from Tyseley. With a clean fire I coped admirably without further trouble, that is, with the exception of the damage to my pride and a shattered illusion.

No two men could have been different when a day or so later I was diagrammed to work on another Bordesley shunting engine with driver Bert Brown. Bert was an upright lean man approaching his 60s, yet having a razor sharp personality. He was a smart man too, his overalls were clean and his boots were polished. He sported a starched collar and tie, again reflecting that he was in possession of a little more than just a certificate of marriage. The peak and top of his greaseproof hat was ultra glossy and the brass polished on his brown enamel 'British Railways' cap badge. Although ill health had demoted this man to shunting engines, Bert remained utterly conscientious; he religiously oiled and trimmed the engine as though every run was to be record breaking. He never lost sight that every railwayman had a part to play, he was still, very much so, captain of the ship. I was also quick to learn that when working with Bert, even mature firemen were not allowed to sit and fantasise over 'Jane' in the *Daily Mirror*! Whilst the engine was working, Bert believed that an extra pair of eyes on the 'port' side were imperative. Working in the confines of a busy shunting yard, other engines could inadvertently push wagons out foul of the line on which you were shunting; keeping a sharp look out was vital for safe working.

On the first day Bert looked me up and down and spoke rather abruptly, the exchange going like this,

'Name?'

'Herbert.'

'Number?'

'Five, two, Three.'

'What's your first name?'

'Dennis.'

'How much firing have you done Dennis?'

Rather proudly I said, 'Almost two weeks'.

'Ah!, today you will do it my way.'

Bert opened the firehole doors, taking a look in the firebox. The engine had stood some 30 minutes or so, whilst relief was effected, therefore the fire had cooled. He took the ' L ' shaped pricker fire-iron from its rack on the bunker and hooked it under pieces of clinker that had settled on the fire bars, the clinker looking rather like large pieces of thick Ryvita biscuit. These were lifted and raked to the back end of the firebox where he stood them on their end under the firehole doors. He then rubbed the flat of the pricker along the fire bars, pushing more impurities through the firebars into the ashpan. He closed the firehole doors, lifted the damper and put the blower on a touch. With the air now flowing freely through the thin fire the firebox temperature rose sharply, the pressure gauge needle soon responding in spite of the fact that fire bars were visible in the middle of the firebox. After a while he instructed me to put on four shovelfuls of coal, one in each corner of the firebox. Watching my 'technique', he took the shovel from me and showed me how to get the coal exactly where I wanted it to go. With the fire bed now being at a high temperature there was an instant explosion of activity in the firebox as the coal was added, gases immediately bursting free from the fuel. With the firehole doors left open a little, air passing over the fire aided combustion, burning the gases, therefore avoiding dark smoke from the chimney. This pattern of working was repeated, no more than four shovelfuls at any one time, all around the sides of the firebox.

Bert did not spare the horsepower when working and the thin fire danced freely on the firebars owing to the vigorous blast from the exhaust. He took frequent glances at the fire, to be sure that I didn't fire the engine too frequently, adjusting the firehole doors as necessary to avoid too much smoke from the chimney. Things worked out well and although at times the firebars in the middle of the fire could still be clearly seen I raised all the steam necessary to keep Bert happy.

The following day Bert left me alone, but watched me like a hawk, being sure I followed his method of working. Many firemen resented what they felt was interference from Bert, but his method made sense; it certainly left the fire in good shape for the man on the next shift. The odd wink and broad smile from Bert, after his frequent inspections of the state of the fire, indicated that I was getting the 'drift'. I was at the beginning of a learning curve that 40 years later I was still clinging to, no one person ever knowing all that was to be known of the intricate working of the railway system. I did try to slip a few extra shovelfuls of coal on whilst I felt Bert was otherwise engaged driving. I had not fully accounted for his alertness; he was listening and counting, but not looking. After the fourth shovelful he put one foot over the reversing lever rack on to the shovel, without taking his eye from the man on the ground. I got the message! Those few days' apprenticeship with Bert I never forgot, he taught me of the general pride in the way that men normally left engines for one another.

I was also soon to learn that the firing shovel had other uses, although it is commonly known that enginemen fried their breakfast on it. As I pointed out earlier, jammed into the coil springs of the trailing driving wheels, the shovel filled with hot water became our washing facility. When working with other drivers, apart from hand washing, many times I saw brown snuff laden handkerchiefs 'laundered' in the hot water and hung to dry on the hot pipe work. Snuff taking was an awful habit that I had not encountered until I started work on the footplate; certainly no one in my family followed this pursuit. Many of the older drivers were users and I found the habit very distasteful. Most of the shunting turns that I worked on during these early times were covered by the older enginemen, many of whom had fallen by the wayside through health reasons. A number of these men, over time, lost their self-respect, a continuous wet nose and brown nostrils becoming a pretty obnoxious sight. My young keen sense of smell instantly reacted to the snuffbox being opened; putting my head over the side became the only relief from the awful nauseous smell. One kindly old snuff taker one day offered me one of his pickled onions. He became very insistent that I had an onion with my bread and cheese, stirring them out of the vinegar with his grubby finger just after using his wet snuff laden handkerchief. I didn't feel I wanted to offend him, but without his knowledge the onions were soon on their way to the West of England on the wagon of a passing train.

The back of the shovel, with the blade leaned against the front of the cab in the fireman's corner and the 'T' handle resting on the floor, became a comfortable backrest. Later on, when I got on to quiet night turns, with the weather shield covering half the side of the cab aperture, sitting on the seat with your back resting on the shovel with your feet on the bunker shelf was as snug as anyone was likely to get on any steam locomotive. Eventually, the bottom of your spine would might become numb and in winter your feet felt as though they had encountered the four star facility of a deep freeze, but this was a small price to pay for 'comfort'.

During my first year I worked in all of the shunting yards covered by Tyseley shed. These included Bordesley, Hockley, Handsworth, Moor Street, Tyseley Goods Yard and Hall Green. In addition there were two shunting engines in Tyseley Carriage Sidings, one for coach shunting, the other, known as the Tyseley Pilot, which shunted any freight. There was also a Loco Yard shunting engine, which was quite interesting at times as we sometimes 'ran in' dock shunting engines that had returned from Derby works following a major overhaul. These small locomotives would be hauled to Tyseley in freight trains with their motion removed. The valve gear would later be refitted in Tyseley factory; the engine would then be steamed for the first time and used to work in the loco yard, which could become quite a busy job. Loaded coal wagons for use on the engines needed to be put on the coal stage, any surplus loaded wagons went on towards the coal stack. Loaded ash wagons had to be changed and engines in the factory moved. Some of these little shunting engines still retained their bell for use during dock shunting. Some had open cabs, which was quite a novelty, until it rained.

Handsworth was a very confined yard, having short spurs of track everywhere which held just an odd number of wagons. Hence, this engine seemed to pither about for long periods, seemingly doing nothing really constructive. We pushed wagons into awkward situations with balks of timber interposed between the wagon and the engine. Some we dragged by with bits of rope; it all was a bit Heath-Robinson. This yard was on the down side, behind Handsworth and Smethwick station. However, this engine was also required to cross to the up sidings do any marshalling in Queens Head Yard. In addition, the Handsworth shunting engine took empty wagons to Sandwell Park Colliery, which was behind The Hawthorns Halt north of Handsworth Junction. Sandwell Park Colliery, I understand, had the thickest seam of coal in the country, some 33 feet. However, the mine became uneconomic very early in my working life and therefore became subject to closure.

The Moor Street shunter was very busy on the night turn, likewise on afternoons, but during the day the engine hardly turned a wheel. My heart would sink whenever I was diagrammed to do this day turn. Old Archie Sanders, who worked this turn regularly, rarely spoke to anyone, his facial expression never changing, always looking as though he was in deep mourning. Lads of 16 and men of 60 were never ideal company, but with old Archie you got bored out of your wits, he did nothing but stare into the blue for hours. The only time he spoke, or allowed you to leave the footplate was when he made sure that you cleaned out the toolboxes. It wasn't so bad if the engine stopped where you could watch the trains thrashing across Moor Street viaduct, attacking the gradient in Snow Hill tunnel. However, often our engine was tucked away between two rows of box vans, minutes then became hours, the day seemingly never ending.

For my first year I worked almost entirely on shunting engines, except that occasionally I was rostered on what was known as the 'Target' engine. The purpose of this engine was that when trains arrived from the South destined for Bordesley Junction, the train engine would be detached on the down goods line adjacent to Small Heath South signal box. The 'Target' would then attach to the train and take it to Bordesley. The reason behind this was that there were often long delays getting trains into Bordesley Sidings. Releasing the train engines at Small Heath South meant that the engines could go on shed at Tyseley and after servicing be available for other work.

The 'Target' was usually worked with a 0-6-0 tender engine of the '22XX' class, but in the summer months the shed foremen tried to hang on to any decent engines

A view inside Tyseley shed showing enginemen manually turning the engines. *Gordon Allen*

One of the dock shunters (with an open cab) that we used to work in the Loco Yard after the motion was reassembled in Tyseley factory. *Dick Potts*

belonging to other depots to cover the extra passenger trains that ran on Saturdays. To justify keeping other depot's engines, the foremen had to keep the engine working; putting the engine on the 'Target' was a sure of getting it back on Tyseley shed for the weekend.

Even with Bert Brown's instructions in relation to the technique of how to use the shovel, I now found big engines with long fireboxes a different proposition. Swinging the shovel until my right hand almost touched the cab roof, I would sometimes not quite make the firehole, the shovel crashing heavily on some part of the surrounding metal work. A shattering pain then ran through every muscle in my body as the shovel stopped unexpectedly. This pain was usually followed by some numbness and eventual 'pins and needles'. The coal that should have been projected some 10 feet towards the front of the firebox now remained spread around my feet on the footplate. Nevertheless, I sat on the seat of these big express engines, which sported names and brass beading, trying to look the part. I suspect I fooled nobody.

John Millman was showing an interest in model engineering, and conversations with him must have roused dormant genes in me. I started to buy hand tools, in later years progressing to a turning lathe. At that time I could not quite understand where my desire to do engineering had sprung from, my mother's father, who was a toolmaker, sadly passed away when I was still very young. It was only in later life, via my brother's excursions into genealogy, that I learned that relatives on my father's side had worked in Swindon locomotive works. On my mother's side too, many relatives were toolmakers and engineers, some ancestors in the early days studying under Matthew Boulton and James Watt.

Having said that, I certainly never had my interest in metal work raised by my father, his metal working tools ran to a hammer, cold chisel and a hacksaw ... without a blade! His whole 'workshop' was housed in an apple crate, which during the war co-habited with the chickens in the garden shed. I had good cause to remember this box, the name Francis Nicholls, Birmingham, is etched on my mind as deep as it was branded into the timber sides of the container. As a boy, whenever my father set out to do a job I would cringe. This crate was full of every conceivable item of what my father termed 'useful'. There were bent rusty nails, recycled screws, their heads chewed or bunged up with paint, countless nuts and bolts, cycle parts, in fact every imaginable item of 'tat', down to old collar studs. When dad set about a job, he would first disappear into the semi-darkness of the shed and could be heard raking over the surface of the box. At the same time he would be heard muttering, 'Where's that bloody, thing gone?' A minute or so after would see him, legs wide apart and red in the face, humping the heavy box on to the yard. He would immediately up-end the box, the whole fluid contents spreading over every inch of the yard. A few minutes raking with gusto usually brought satisfaction to his face. When the task on hand was completed, he became utterly predictable. Standing up straight, Woodbine sticking out of the corner of his mouth, he would push his soft cap on to the back of his head. Pulling on his thick silver 'Albert' chain, his pocket watch would emerge from his waist coat pocket, 'Is that the time?, slip these back in the box, there's a good lad!' One hour later I would still be poking washers from the cracks in the yard and fishing ball bearings from the drain.

The seeds of engineering sown by John Millman were eventually germinated by a 9*d*. fortnightly investment in the magazine *Model Engineer*. I also soon fell foul of concentrated advertising, by the purchase of one of the first commercially available power drills. This tool spun drills round at an incredible speed; it would put holes in timber quicker than a .303 rifle bullet. Drilling metal was a different kettle of fish, at such a high speed my carbon steel drills heated up quickly, their ends sometimes glowing red-hot. My whole set of new drills all soon looked like well-sucked sticks of seaside rock!

No one that we knew owned as much as a vacuum cleaner at that time, indeed the houses had no power points for such luxuries. Any electrical equipment was usually plugged into the light socket, once the bulb had been removed. The noise from my new power drill puzzled neighbours to such an extent that they crept round the back entry and peered through the privet hedge to investigate the unusual whine. Also, within an hour of owning the tool, Walter next door complained that the drill was ruining his enjoyment of Shostakovich and Wagner, by again obliterating the reception on his 10 valve superhet radio. This complaint was no doubt justified, the motor armature blotting out the radio reception of probably the whole district!

More pocket money was then necessary to send the new tool back to the manufacturers for the fitting of a radio suppressor. When the drill was returned, it had a piece of equipment hanging on the lead the size of a kilogram bag of sugar. It now needed two hands to hold it, one to support the suppressor!

After a time I bought my first lathe, a 'Portass' plain lathe. Lacking any pre-advice, this machine also proved a poor investment. There were no provisions for milling on the lathe, which severely restricted the machine to plain turning. The lathe also had a flat belt pulley, the belt joined together with anything from fuse wire to bent nails. This gave a constant click, click, click, when the machine was running. I soon learned that when the lathe was running fast, if the click, clicking stopped suddenly, it was wise to take a spirited pace to the right to avoid a slap across the mouth with flying leatherwork!

I was over ambitious, too, with a purchase of casting to make a 3½ inch gauge model of a GWR 'County' class locomotive. The sand embedded in the skin of the castings took the ends off all my turning tools, I might as well have rubbed my thumbnail on the turning metal, it would probably got similar results! I now badly needed a grinder. Because my power drill had proved impractical for metal work and was ruining my drill bits, this tool had for a time been relegated to a shelf in the shed. When the makers of the drill put on the market a drill stand, whereby the drill could be mounted on a bench holding a grinding wheel, I felt that this would be a practical and economic way to fulfil my needs. Unfortunately, the drill chuck was of the keyless variety, anything held in the drill chuck relied on hand pressure to hold it tight. Starting up the drill, the grinding wheel spun at an incredible speed, quite ideal for grinding, but nevertheless the equipment was completely unguarded. Within seconds of the first sparks flying from the grinding wheel, the wheel came loose in the chuck. Before I could make a put for the switch, the gyrating stone wheel almost went into orbit, turning the six by four feet 'workshop' into a miniature squash court. I ducked and dived to avoid the ricocheting object, somewhat more lethal than a rubber ball. With my heart pounding furiously, after I had realised I was indeed unscathed, expeditious steps in the direction of the loo became an urgent necessity. Here, some 30 minutes contemplation was essential to gain my composure. After which, I locked the shed door, only returning some days later to find all my 'work' red with rust.

In the hands of an unseasoned teenager, machine tools can be extremely dangerous. During those early days of attempted engineering I did lose a lot of blood, I was also extremely lucky to reach the age of 18 still having five digits on each hand and the sight in both eyes.

# Chapter Six

## In the Lower Links

One of the good things to come out of the nationalisation of the railways was the abandonment of the GWR promotion system. The later adopted system meant that men were not obliged to leave home for promotion, but could remain at their home depot until a higher grade vacancy was available. Men also had the choice of applying for promotion at other depots if they so wished, the senior applicant always being successful in filling the post. The system was fair, but there was a price to pay, the senior hands at a depot waiting for promotion could see men from other depots filling vacancies at their home depot, because the men filling the vacancy would be more senior.

On my 17th birthday I became eligible for night work and was therefore promoted to fireman at my home depot. Having already completed a year of upgraded firing turns, I went on to second year fireman's rate of pay immediately.

All newly-appointed firemen were normally sent to Bordesley Junction on the shunting engines for a probationary period. As so many men started in the footplate grade, then resigned, I had already become a senior hand to all the firemen who were already at Bordesley. This was a quite unique situation; I was therefore put straight into No. 10 link, the bottom link at the depot. This link did all the mundane jobs, engine preparing, coal stage, turntables and the host of shunting turns not covered by men with ill health, mainly all the night turns.

Everybody had to start at the bottom; my first regular driver was a man from Wolverhampton. Jack Hancock had filled the latest vacancy for a driver at Tyseley.

Men wishing to gain further promotion above the footplate grade, for instance, rising to shed foreman, shed master, locomotive inspector etc., signed on to what was known as the 'Panel'. Once on this list, men could foremost gain experience as foreman's assistant, then go on to act as shed foreman by deputising for the regular foremen during sickness, annual leave etc. There were already any number of Tyseley drivers on this panel list; many by now had become highly capable of doing the running shed foreman's duties, in actual fact, a number of these men were considerably more enthusiastic than the regular foremen.

My new driver was more than ambitious, immediately applying to add to the numbers already on the 'Panel'. Little did I know at the time that in just over a decade I would be sitting in front of him at Swindon, being grilled for my driver's examination, Jack quickly making the grade to chief locomotive inspector. He eventually became chief traction officer, Western Region at Paddington. My new driver was a big man with a most powerful physique; I always felt he must have coped easily with the biggest of engines as a fireman at Wolverhampton. He also had forceful views, his size making it doubtful if anyone would have ever chosen to argue with him.

On his arrival at Tyseley, it was soon obvious to many that someone was giving Jack a 'leg up' the promotional ladder, someone who was more than just a friend of a friend. Once on the 'Panel', he somehow began to take preference over many of the Tyseley men that were old hands at acting as deputy foreman. He began to act as foreman's assistant on more or less a regular basis. Although he had become my regular mate, I doubt, because of the few times that we got to work together, whether he remembered that I was his first fireman when he eventually passed me out to be a driver.

While Jack walked about the shed with a clipboard and wearing a cow-gown, instead of overalls, older hand drivers were now grovelling under engines that he should have been preparing. Drivers were also pushing around turntables and endlessly walking to and from the coal stage to fetch engines into the shed doing this younger hand's job. As more of his mundane work fell to senior men, there was a considerable murmuring of discontent. Not to mention the men already on the 'Panel', who had started to get their nose pushed out to make way for a headquarters man.

Wolverhampton was the headquarters of the Midland Division (Locomotive Dept). The trend for headquarters men to take preference on the promotion ladder started with the onset of nationalisation; indeed it did not take long for this 'Old Pals' act to start. The management at Tyseley was soon completely dominated by men from Wolverhampton, not all of them having the best interests of the depot at heart, they did a job ... just!

Working as a newly-promoted fireman for eight or more hours about the depot was a new experience for me, as was working throughout the night. During the small hours I was constantly in conflict with drowsiness, yet it was absolutely vital that I kept my wits about me. The working environment was extremely hostile, in poor lighting; fireless engines stole about the yard hidden by shrouds of steam, there were many other noises that could muffle their ghostly approach. We never considered the danger when we scrambled up the sides of locomotives to fill tanks, went over cab roofs into coal bunkers, and balanced precariously on coal stage hoists, a precipitous drop to the ash pit below. Miraculously there were few accidents, with no 'Health and Safety at Work Act'; everyone developed a personal sense of self-preservation.

I got unbelievably dirty, ash and Welsh coal dust penetrated my clothing and ground into the pores of my skin, an almost permanent eyeliner visibly imbedded itself into my eyelids. I washed in a bucket with the harsh soap, icy wind sometimes whipping across the cab chapping my skin and cracking my lips.

On reaching home, in the early hours, it was necessary to strip off to wash more thoroughly. The living room fire would be out and the kettles cold on the hob. Heating bath water would have taken two hours or more and would have done nothing for father's strict economy measures; therefore I would have put the larger of the kettles on the gas stove. In the meantime I would rake the grate out and light the coal fire with newspaper and wood sticks. A number of times it was known for me to fall asleep whilst waiting for the kettle to heat. More penalty points were accumulated when mother, or father, came downstairs to find two gallons of water condensed on the cold walls and windows of the small kitchen, the gas on full and no water left in the kettle! I then had to bide my time whilst the whole family shared the solitary sink to get off to work, or school. The whole household stepping around one another, whilst mother cooked the breakfast and at the same time tried to appease my tetchy infant brother. Were these really the good old days I often hear people comment about?

If you passed the medical for the footplate, then it was a sure thing that you wouldn't fail the examination for National Service. All fit young men being conscripted into the forces at the age of 18 aggravated the railway staff shortage, but this did speed promotion for me. In only a few months I moved up to No. 9 link.

This link did the local freight trip work, less taxing and certainly more economical on the soap. We worked trains out of Bordesley Junction to outlying yards at Oldbury and Swan Village. Once at these yards we did the shunting work, having relief around lunchtime. The afternoon shift did the job in reverse, working the traffic from these yards back to Bordesley in the late evening.

My new driver was yet again another 'panel' man, his occasional up grading to foreman's assistant bringing occasional respite from him. Everyone referred to George Taylor as 'Deadeye', he was yet to reach 40, but even at that time I imagined that he looked going on sixty. His short crew cut hair was snow white and he wore an almost permanent perplexed looking frown, as if he was constantly struggling with the penultimate clue of *The Times* crossword. Nevertheless, over all he was a pretty decent mate and quite harmless, despite his traits. He would repeatedly snap orders at me in short sentences,

'Put the injector on'.

'Drop the damper'.

'Water the coal'.

'How's that signal mate?' Yet George's bark was far worse than his bite. George was very hasty too; he handled every spanner as though it was red hot. When doing simple tasks around the engine, like filling the cylinder lubricator, he would mumble swear words under his breath.

'Deadeye' did have a very flexible right elbow too, if at opening time we were not favourably placed in some yard, running loop, or under some water column, I could feel his irritability fester. Once the 'towel' was off, George climbed steep embankments with the stamina of a Himalayan Sherpa; he could scale parapet walls with the agility of an SAS officer and slip through holes in fencing with the stealth of a puma. When moderately satisfied he became half decent to work with, the only problem, by this time he became prime candidate for the presidency of the 'Incontinence Society'. At frequent intervals he would dangle a part of his anatomy over the side, flooding the gangway. The tepid liquid would sometimes splash against the handrails, catching the crosswind. If I had my head down shovelling, I began to catch the unpleasant spray, that is, before I could retire to my corner of the footplate and put my collar up! Frequent use of the coal-watering pipe then became necessary for the sterilization process; even so, I always made sure of leaving the engine via the handrails on my side!

George mellowed in later years; strangely, he hardly looked any different 25 years later when he retired. He did eventually gain a full time management post as diesel multiple unit supervisor in Tyseley Carriage Sidings. This however, was long after the demise of Wolverhampton as headquarters, when we ultimately became under the Midland Region management. In reality, George was not alone, quite a number of Tyseley enginemen eventually gained high positions in management, once that the playing field was level.

Only weeks went by before another 16 places in front of me became vacant and I moved up to the next link. No. 8 link worked the heavy freight trains around the 'Black Country' over some very tricky gradients. These turns were worked with the larger tank engines, '31XX' class prairie tank engines, '66XX' class 0-6-2 tanks, and some of the older '51XX' class prairies that were past their 'sell by' date and therefore taken from passenger train working.

My new link also had the odd local passenger turn, as did all links from here on. This was because No. 2 link, the local passenger link, was unable to cover all the peak hour passenger trains. My new link also worked the trains on Longbridge branch, from Old Hill Junction, via Halesowen. As well as freight, we also worked the passenger turns for the Austin Car Factory workers, small '74XX' pannier tank engines being the only Great Western engines at Tyseley allowed to work on this line.

Up to this point in time I had not really got used to working regularly with one man, both my previous drivers often being substituted for supervisory duties. I now needed badly a mate who would take an interest in my apprenticeship.

My new driver, like the majority of enginemen countrywide, was thoroughly conscientious, he fitted the bill perfectly. He missed nothing, at all hours of the day and night he would grovel beneath engines getting entangled in filthy valve gear and struggling to reach every last cork hole that needed to be oiled. Reg Grafton had served many years as a fireman; I was to learn much from him. He was an excellent engineman too, no one could have driven a steam locomotive any better, he never put a foot wrong. He was methodical, never dictated to me, but made sure I knew exactly how he used to do it, methods that I could not have bettered.

Reg was about 45 years of age, a family man who was buying his own home. Probably through necessity, like many other drivers, once at work he made every effort to stay there as long as he possibly could, the object being to boost his income. I had no commitments, so long hours at work at that time didn't bother me. I could always make use of the money too, now that I was allowed to pay a flat rate housekeeping to my mother.

We almost became nocturnal, much of No. 8 link work being done at night. The train working over the 'Black Country' was exacting, we worked murderously heavy trains with comparatively small locomotives, all trains three-link coupled, having only the engine brake and some brake van assistance. These trains were loaded with anything from pig iron, sand for the glass works, foundry moulding sand, girders, ingots, coal, limestone and oil. We had sparks flying from the chimney one minute, the next, the cast-iron brake blocks would be grinding on the steel wheel rims, generating heat and burning away any surrounding filth from the wheel tyres. This, yet another addition to the many pungent smells around us from every conceivable trade. We would rub the handbrake on when descending long inclines, this would keep the wagons buffered up and 'leaning' on to the engine. Reg would apply the vacuum brake with finesse, cleverly sensing at what point the wheels may lock and start to slide. If the wheels suddenly locked, through grease or damp on the rail, the engine would vibrate viciously and we would then be surrounded by an almost silence as the wheels slid along the rails. Quickly, it was then my job to release the handbrake to allow the wheels to rotate again. Once the wheels were sliding it took very little resistance to keep them sliding, the train speed then increasing very rapidly. On very slippery rails, it was known for drivers to snatch open the regulator momentarily. This just enough to induce the driving wheels to start to turn again, the train speed increasing alarmingly every second the wheels were sliding. Not to mention the 'flats' being ground into the wheel tyres as the wheels were sliding. Once the wheels were turning again, sand was applied to the rail and the brake put hard on again, there was always a sense of touch and go and often a holding of breath!

The many men that worked these trains never got their photograph in *Trains Illustrated*, or indeed found their names in logs mulled over in the *Railway Magazine*. Nonetheless, these men did possess incredible expertise. Little mentioned, but there was a depot full of such men at Stourbridge, conscientious men, who daily worked unglamorous heavy freights over the 'Black Country' gradients.

During the first few weeks of working together, Reg kept a watchful eye on me. Several times I saw him peep into the engine sand boxes to be certain that I had filled them. Who could blame him? I knew that our lives depended on having the sand boxes full and the sanding gear working efficiently. Overflowing the water tanks when filling up at the water column, or over zealous use of the coal-watering pipe, could both cause the sanding gear to clog up and fail. Reg soon developed a trust in me and he was wonderful to work with, his way of working became utterly predictable, making life so much easier. I had already found that some drivers were completely unpredictable in their way of working; you just did not know what they would do next. With my new driver, I knew that in certain places I could carry the boiler water level a bit higher that usual, thus avoiding blowing off steam from the safety valves. I knew also that there would be no snatching at the regulator, which would cause the engine to prime badly. 'Priming' meaning that water was entering the cylinders with the steam and being exhausted out of the chimney. When water entered the cylinders there was a great danger that the cylinder ends could be blown off due to hydraulic pressure.

All these freight trains that we now worked involved loading from Bordesley Junction and heading north. On leaving Tyseley shed it was always policy to take on as much water as possible, filling both the boiler and tanks to capacity. Sometimes, in the short time it took to go light engine to Bordesley and to couple on to your train, if you did happen to depart promptly, the boiler water level could still be quite high. This could be disastrous if leaving the yard with an erratic driver in the direction of Snow Hill tunnel, this gradient being a very taxing start to a journey. These men, who mostly just lacked confidence more than anything, would have water throwing out of the chimney by the gallon with just a few revolutions of the wheels. There was then a good chance of stalling inside the tunnel and having to be dragged out by sometimes two other engines. If a freight train did come to a stand in the tunnel, restarting was impossible unassisted.

When leaving Bordesley with a train, Reg would take it quietly up the short, but quite steep gradient as far as to Bordesley North signal box. He took this rise with a small regulator opening and having the reverser notched up very little. This balance between the regulator opening and 'notching up' on the reverser was the essence of good driving. 'Notching up', shortened the stroke of the valves, which allowed smaller amounts of steam into the cylinders, but gave the steam a chance to expand, therefore making the engine work more efficiently. Once on the long viaduct which precedes Snow Hill tunnel, the line levels out, here he would notch well back and open the regulator almost wide. By the time he needed to work the engine really heavily approaching the tunnel entrance the boiler level would have dropped and there was never any sign of priming. If our train speed had not increased enough to get us through the tunnel gradient, approaching Moor Street signal box Reg would put the reverser, little by little, towards full gear; a sprinkle of sand entering the tunnel always saw us through with the heaviest of trains.

The ascent through Snow Hill tunnel was a challenge to every freight train and the driver's expertise. Inside the tunnel, the gradient rose sharply at 1 in 45 and the line curved to the right. The tunnel was always damp and steamy, causing adhesion problems. During the many years that I was a fireman I never failed to make it through with any Great Western engine. I did however have the 'delight' of sticking three times, once with an 'Iron Lung', our nickname for a wartime Austerity engine; again with a Robinson ex-LNER class 'O4' 2-8-0 World War I engine, and on another occasion with an ex-LMS class '8' freight engine. The latter failure, I might add, being nobody's fault but the driver.

At the time of the latter failure I was already passed for driving and waiting for a driver's vacancy to occur at Tyseley. By this time I had had many years of experience of the tunnel working. I worked on this day with a young Stratford-upon-Avon driver who had been promoted to driver at Tyseley. We departed from Bordesley with an exceedingly heavy train of oil. Vacuum brake-fitted vehicles on freight trains had by this time come into much greater use. On departure, it was soon obvious to me that the brakes on the train were not fully released. It was also soon apparent to me the reason for this problem. Our class '8' was set to create only 21 inches of vacuum in the train pipe; the previous train engine had probably been a Great Western engine which created a higher vacuum, 25 inches. Vacuum brake gauges measured the brake pressure in inches of mercury. My driver, realising that we were not going to make it through the tunnel, stopped the train on the rising gradient towards Bordesley North and went back along the train pulling the release cords on all the wagons to free the brakes. To my total dismay he then decided to continue our journey, although I stressed that we had no chance of making it through the tunnel from where we were standing with a dead start and a load of this nature. To add to this, where we had stopped, other trains could easily have passed us on the main line until an assistant engine could have been attached to the front of us. However, he was an ex-LMS man and had far greater confidence in our class '8' than I had. My warning therefore went unheeded; needless to say we only made it halfway through the tunnel. I then had to walk through the steam-filled tunnel to the signal box conveying the necessary 'Wrong Line Order' form to obtain assistance. It took two other locomotives to drag us out the tunnel and there was an awful lot of choking, coughing and filthy discomfort. Also much delay to other trains. I have to say, this driver was not very popular with the shedmaster when we got back!

Reg Grafton loved a bit of fun and was quite a mimic, although it was a bit unfortunate that his humour was usually at my expense. Adolescents were good entertainment for older people in many industries; I fitted into this category with Reg and he pulled my leg frequently. Although, I wasn't altogether the gullible teenager he thought I was. He could throw his voice quite cleverly; he often had me looking out of the cab mystified for non-existent yard staff that may have been trying to gain our attention. I was keen and alert and he regularly caught me out. When it dawned on me what he was doing, I did not let on, but looked intently as usual, saying, 'There is no one calling on my side Reg, they must be your side'. To keep up the pretence he was then bound to get off his seat to look out on his side. In a very short time he wasn't so keen to pull this one!

Reg's sense of humour did wear a bit thin at times, he developed the habit, when we were at a water column, as soon as the tank had filled he would quickly return to the cab and start moving the engine whilst I was still on top of the tank fastening the lids down. This was an act of utter foolishness, although I did take it in my stride as I did not want our working relationship soured. I admired my driver as an engineman, also his ability to anticipate incidents, or act when the unexpected occurred. I was, however, still basically a boy who was doing a dangerous man's job. I did my work conscientiously; it would have been nice for him to have treated me as an adult.

I found some comfort in little ways of getting my own back, although Reg never suspected. When we were at a stand at a signal that was on my side of the footplate, Reg would watch, or listen, for the signal wires to twitch when the signalman operated the levers, immediately saying, 'How's that signal mate?' This tended to make it look as though I was less than vigilant, although the signal had only cleared at that very second. When I again realised what he was doing, I sometimes got off the footplate and after a short while I would give the wires a good shake. Doing this

I could have Reg's head popping in and out of the cab as regular as a Bavarian cuckoo clock! I slipped in between the engine and the first wagon each time out of sight! Reg never discovered that the joke was on him and the fact that some youths can be quite devious.

One day our engine stopped next to a train of cattle under the cathedral roof of Snow Hill station. The cattle train was waiting for a path through the tunnel after the London express had gone. All the animals were quiet and contented, their breath simmering from the open wagon sides in the cold frosty air. Looking down into one of the wagons, Reg made a loud series of lowing sounds. Within a few minutes the whole trainload of cattle were making the most confounded noise, bellowing, snorting and getting very agitated. I am led to believe that the station master eventually rang Birmingham South signal box, instructing the signalman to get rid of the train immediately, as no one could hear any of the station announcements!

Reg showed me how to fire the '74XX' class pannier tank engines that we worked over the Longbridge branch. Unlike the normal pannier-type shunting engine that had a flat fire grate, the '74XX' class had a sloping grate. By continually dropping coal at the back of the fire, just inside the firehole doors, once the engine started to work there was never any need to throw coal towards the front. The harder these little engines were worked, the better they liked it, the pressure gauge needle would glue itself to the red arrow painted on to the pressure gauge. This red arrow indicated the point that safety valves would blow off steam. I loved working over the Longbridge branch, the gradients were exciting, the slow crawl over Dowery Dell trestle viaduct quite scary. Over this line too, was the first time I was to see kingfishers. Also, it wasn't unknown for us to get some free toffees from the girls working at the 'Blue Bird' toffee factory at Hunnington.

Many of the drivers around Reg's seniority had spent long hours at work during the war years, going without food for long periods. Irregular eating patterns had inevitably taken its toll; Reg suffered badly from stomach ulcers and sometimes came to work looking grey and very poorly. Strangely, this did not always deter him from frying up on the shovel, or indeed make him in any hurry to head for home. I overheard Reg telling another driver one day, in confidence, that he was having problems with itching piles. On side tank engines, where the water tanks extended into the cab, the heat became quite uncomfortable for the driver as he was bound to stand close to the firehole. As young people are, I always got the urge the laugh, or perhaps pull his leg. Indeed, I had previously been on the wrong end of his humour so many times. Nevertheless, I did keep my own counsel; I felt it would have been unwise to embarrass him.

One night we stabled in the north end of Round Oak Yard in the Black Country to have our supper. It was pitch dark and after we had eaten I took the flare lamp on to the cab roof and set about trimming the coalbunker, making ready for the trip towards home. Reg decided to have a look around the engine and put a drop of oil on the valve and piston glands. Suddenly there was with urgent call for help from Reg and I immediately went to his assistance, not knowing quite what to expect. Unfortunately, we had stopped the engine rather inappropriately; Reg had descended from the engine cab where a point handle protruded vertically. As he got down the engine steps, the point handle penetrated his overalls at the seat of his pants, going up the seam of his trousers and straight along the line of his spine between his leather belt. Reg was unhurt, but he was flailing about like a skewered lobster, unable to get free. With my help he was eventually released, the only price he had paid was a gaping hole in the back of his trousers.

On the way home it was impossible for me to keep my composure, Reg drove the engine one-handed, holding the seat of his pants together with the other. He coped well till we had to go into Langley Green Yard to pick up more wagons. Reversing the engine meant that he had to use both hands and put one foot on to the reversing rack to be able to pull the heavy lever backwards. The 'moon' came out every time he had to reverse the engine, at this I just burst into fits of laughter, I was just unable to control myself. Reg didn't like this at all; he just couldn't see the funny side and got pretty furious. Perhaps I was over the top a little, I could not resist it, I remarked to him that there was a plus side to his situation, it was now a lot easier for him to scratch his backside! This was a remark I was very much to regret, yet most of us suffer, at sometime or other, the fact that our tongue gets detached from our brain. I really did get the cold shoulder for quite a long time for my impudence.

Not long after, Reg was promoted to No. 7 link and big Jack Carrigan took his place. Jack, possibly topped the scales at nearly 20 stones, he was also a guy as rough and tough as they came. We got along fine, he was the first man to recognise that I was becoming an adult, and I liked it. He appreciated my help; it was impossible for him to get to all of the oiling points on some classes of engine due to his huge proportions. This was no big deal; I could slip underneath and do what was necessary for him. What I did miss was that Reg and I always cleaned down the cab, blacking the boiler cladding with cylinder oil and rubbing up the pipe work. Jack would have none of this; he regarded it as 'a bleedin' waste of time' and he could not stand the smell of baking oil. I was really unhappy about this, as I enjoyed seeing the cab looking cared for and I felt it would give me a bad reputation with any men who took over the engine from us. Jack also hated having the footplate swilled down; the steam and water, he maintained, had an adverse affect on his rheumatics. He was also a raconteur; I would sit agog at tales of his early sex life, this whilst he simultaneously gained further ecstasy from easing the wax from his ears with the brimstone end of a Swan Vesta match.

Jack and I were together for only a few weeks. Perhaps this was as well because his wife worked in a cake shop, everyday Jack brought a bag full of cakes to work. I imagine the cakes were those that were not sold at the end of each day. Stuffing myself with Eccles cakes and jam doughnuts daily would soon have had the holes in my belt slacking off. Jack did work the engine heavier than my previous driver, although a few extra shovelfuls of coal made little difference on this kind of work. These jobs were busy, but once into a way of working, the work was not over taxing for any fireman.

It was after an overdose of carbohydrate that Jack and I found ourselves walking from Stourbridge Junction to Stourbridge shed to prepare an engine for our return working; it was the middle of the night. The Signal Department was replacing a signal near Stourbridge viaduct and had excavated a considerable hole to take the plinth for the new signal. In the darkness, I walked across the boards covering this hole, Jack following. Suffice to say, boards gave way under Jack's substantial weight and he disappeared down the hole nearly six feet in depth, all I could just see was the top of his cap. Trying to get a 20 stone man out of a 6 ft hole isn't easy, especially when you can't stop laughing! I was in trouble again, Jack saying that I would still have laughed if he had broken both his legs. Once over the shock, however, he bore no resentment, in a few minutes our relationship was as right as rain.

Whilst with Jack, one Saturday afternoon during the summer of 1951, when I signed on duty the shed foreman was waiting for me. A fireman had failed to turn up for work for a turn where the crew travelled to Bristol to work one of the holiday expresses back to Birmingham. Myself, being the only pebble on the proverbial beach, was instructed to travel to Bristol. My driver was Bill Ford, who in later years was to become one of my regular drivers. Bill was a wonderful man; he wore an almost permanent smile across cherry red cheeks. This went in harmony with the most tuneful Somerset/Gloucestershire accent. Bill seemed completely laid back about taking a 17-year-old on what was definitely an experienced fireman's job. I was apprehensive, but this was indeed what I had really come on the footplate to do. I certainly knew there would be little time to lean out of the cab to wave to people as we went by.

We caught a local train from Tyseley station to Moor Street and walked to New Street station to travel to Bristol Temple Meads via the ex-LMS route. This was a new experience for me too, as New Street station had always been out of bounds for me as a young trainspotter.

At Bristol, Bill and I had time for a drink and a sandwich before our train arrived, I was also to learn that these very busy Saturday holiday trains tended to run by the hour, rather than the minute. Perhaps it was also as well that I did not know that it was on these trains that Tyseley firemen could be guaranteed a wet shirt. The engines on these diagrams, I was to discover, invariably arrived at Bristol in a state of weariness, having clinkered fires and any remaining coal would be left at the back in the tender. To have known this earlier would have perhaps intensified my apprehension.

I watched train after train depart, packed to capacity with holidaymakers. An army of engine cleaners were employed at Bristol on Saturdays; as the trains ran on to the avoiding line at St Phillips Marsh the young men invaded the tender with shovels, throwing as much coal forward as time would allow for the tank to fill. Surprisingly, many of these young men were much older than myself.

Our engine received this treatment, conversation with anyone impossible as steam raved from the safely valves, the firebox so full with fire that burning coal dropped out on to the footplate, the cab heat stifling. Dust flew everywhere as the cleaners set to work. In what seemed like only seconds, Bill and I were left alone on the engine and the guard was giving the 'right away'.

We departed in fine shape, the West of England fireman that I had relieved giving me a wonderful start. With No. 5960, *Saint Edmund Hall*, still blowing away steam I swept the footplate, put the injector on, swilled down to lay the dust, I was determined to at least have tidy start. Bill was a good engineman, the steep climb to Filton Junction taken in unhurried fashion. My driver advised me to kept firing straight down the middle of the firebox, keeping the shovel straight. He also suggested that I maintained the huge body of fire that I had inherited.

Our engine was in fine condition and I really did begin to think that I had got the hang of the situation as we approached Westerleigh Junction and took a sharp left turn towards Gloucester. Once past Yate Junction however, our speed started to increase dramatically. The dust really started to fly as the engine rolled on the curves, it was difficult for me to stay upright let alone use the shovel. I had no idea what was going on in the firebox, the white hot temperature was now such as it was like attempting to look into the sun. To maintain the boiler pressure the firehole flap had to be closed between each shovelful of coal. With the roll of the engine, intermittent shovelfuls did not quite make it into fire at all, but crashed against the boilerwork, ending up on the floorboards around our feet. Nevertheless, despite my amateurism, I kept things going. Thankfully, on this occasion I did have the blessing of having a good locomotive and super driver. The line gradients as far as

No. 5960 *Saint Edmund Hall*, the first engine that I worked an express train with. Seen here passing Acocks Green running over Ted Higgins' prize length of track. *Dick Potts*

Cheltenham were not taxing once we had got the train over the summit at Filton Junction. Dragging 10 coaches behind us we still must have easily attained speeds of 75 mph, or more. After departure from Cheltenham Malvern Road, the line climbed quite steeply over the Cotswold Hills as far as Toddington. I lost out a little on boiler water level on this ascent, but Bill knew that the easier running from Broadway to Stratford-upon-Avon would allow me to recover.

I was therefore still in reasonable shape when we eventually stopped at the water column at Stratford-upon-Avon and took on water. At this point I already felt like an Olympic athlete who had just put in every effort to attain gold. I had indeed shovelled coal at a rate that I had not experienced before. Ignorance is bliss and I took the chance of having a breather whilst the tender tank filled. Unfortunately, I was naïve as to what was to come over the next punishing 15 miles up hill. What I should have been doing was frantically shovelling more coal from the back of the tender.

With 10 coaches loaded heavily with holiday makers, there was no easy way up the steep 1 in 75 incline to Wilmcote. It was normal practice for the 'bank engine' to give trains a start out of Stratford, by pushing from behind as far as the East signal box starting signal. This day, the banker had already been sent through to Birmingham to assist a previous train, therefore we were left to fend for ourselves. The fire was now well clinkered and the remaining coal in the tender getting out of reach with the shovel. This meant that I had to rake it forward before I could shovel it into the firebox. With the engine working heavily the fire was disappearing at an alarming rate, the boiler pressure gauge now showing signs of anguish. Bill put the blower on a turn in an attempt to maintain the pressure. I shovelled as fast as possible as we gathered speed again on the short easy gradient on the approach to Bearley Junction, after which the line rises for a further nine miles. Our speed levelled out at about 45 mph as we passed Henley-in-Arden, the regulator now well open and the reverser set with a short cut off. It was a long way to the next distant signal at Danzey for Tanworth; Bill came over my side of the footplate and suggested that I gave the fire a pull through with the long pricker. This brought a pall of dense smoke from the chimney, I could however feel that the fire-iron was rubbing over the hard surface of clinker, the fire was still thin on top of a thick bed of porous ash. Bill took the spare shovel and went to the back of the tender, sending forward some of the better size lumps of coal that remained. Most of the coal that I had been shovelling was slack coal. I shovelled on as more black smoke belched high into the air from the chimney. This was hardly the scientific firing Bert Brown had earlier urged me adopt!

We cleared the summit at Earlswood with an inch of water showing in the bottom of boiler gauge glass and the pressure gauge needle nowhere near the red arrow. Bill eased the regulator and notched the reverser up a little more as our speed increased on the more favourable gradient. The regulator was eventually shut altogether at Shirley and the train allowed to coast as far as Tyseley South Junction, hence I was able to refill the boiler and the boiler pressure began to look more respectable.

I swept up and swilled down, we therefore entered Snow Hill in fine style. When having relief, as the train went forward to Wolverhampton, no one would have been fooled by the tidy condition on the footplate, my face looked like a chimney sweep, even Bill had taken to wearing 'Welsh' mascara!

I staggered down the platform rather dejected; I again felt my reputation was at stake when it had become necessary for Bill to help me out. Nevertheless, I had nothing but encouragement from my driver and he was not a man to indulge in cabin small talk. He assured me that if I intended to stay on the footplate there would be much worse to come, I had seen nothing yet, and I had only worked one way.

Two weeks later I was thrown into the deep end again, almost certainly through necessity. I was diagrammed to work a special day excursion to Windsor. The company that had chartered the train was 'Linread'; their factory at the time being in Livery Street, Birmingham, immediately behind Snow Hill North signal box. The roster clerk must have felt some embarrassment at having to put me on this turn, as he had called my driver into the office during the week and asked him if he would mind taking me. Telling him there was no one else available, I imagine that this was just a matter of courtesy on the clerk's part.

The diagram involved working the excursion to Windsor, and then we had to take the engine 'light' to Old Oak Common shed, London. We were then required to sign off duty until 10.30 pm on Saturday evening. Our duty was then to prepare our engine and work the train back from Paddington to Birmingham. This was in fact a 'Double Home' turn, and accommodation had been reserved for us in Old Oak Common Hostel. I never quite understood how this came about as Tyseley had indeed rejected 'Double Home' working. In this event it was strange to see us diagrammed to do such a turn which gave us much longer off duty in London than the normal meal interval turns. It was little wonder that the roster clerk had found difficulty covering this job; there were not many young firemen eager to stay out at work for so long on a summer Saturday.

I signed on for duty on Saturday morning around 6.30 am and met Arthur Jenkins for the first time. He was a fairly tall, upright man, having snow-white hair and a fresh complexion. In later years I was to work with Arthur any number of times, he appeared to have a inexhaustible supply of clean overalls and starched collars, always coming to work smart enough to be introduced to royalty. This man was a privilege to work with, he never raised his voice, only ever spoke when there was anything constructive to say, and most of all he was an extremely capable engineman.

Catching the local train to Snow Hill, we made our way to No. 7 platform where any number of people had already gathered in party mood. Our train arrived hauled by a 'Grange' class locomotive, No. 6877, *Llanfair Grange*. Inexperience at the time made me unaware that these unglamorous engines were some of the finest engines ever built by the GWR; they were no doubt a credit to their designer. At no time did I ever hear any Great Western engineman say a bad word about these engines. Slightly smaller than a 'Hall' class engine, they had a smaller diameter driving wheel, which made them very strong, whilst still retaining a good turn of speed. In later years I worked one of these engines from Bristol on 'The Cornishman' with 14 coaches packed with holidaymakers behind us, I might add totally unassisted. I also worked a Barry Island excursion with 15 coaches. These engines were also free steaming; it was possible to run for miles without the necessity to close the firehole doors. I remember doing 200 miles, a hundred of which were non-stop, without the necessity to close the firehole doors. There were not many classes of engine that could boast such a performance. It was an awful pity that none of these fine locomotives was to be spared the oxy- acetylene torch at the end of their days.

Luck was with me again as our engine this day had obviously not long had a general overhaul. Her glossy black paintwork was just covered by a thin layer of dust, a good indication that she would be nicely run in. We relieved Stourbridge men, and as one would have expected from the men at this depot, everything was in fine order. The coal was well broken and the dust laid, the cab clean and the footplate swept. I could not have wished for anything better.

We left Snow Hill and the falling gradient down the tunnel quickly aided our speed towards the south. Arthur was also quick to notch the reverser well back, with hardly a sound from the chimney our speed increased further. I fired the best Welsh coal straight down the middle of the fire, the injector was soon running and the pressure gauge needle sat just under the red arrow. There was not the slightest rattle, or knock, from this well-engineered masterpiece. There again, these engines always did appear to hold together well, even after covering a high mileage they never became a rough ride.

At high speed we approached the water troughs at Rowington, Arthur said he would take water for me. This was quite a tricky operation for the unskilled and I suspect he did not want our day spoiled at the onset by me flooding the footplate. If the water scoop was put too deeply into the troughs, it was impossible to get it back out when the train was at speed. In which case the water would overflow from the tender tank lid and cascade over the first coach. Water would also flood from air vents immediately behind the tender toolboxes; this would bring forward coal and silt, which could cover the footplate to a depth of three or four inches. If this happened it made the most dreadful mess and took a long time to clear up. Arthur skimmed the troughs expertly, taking on 2,500 gallons of water in only seconds. Not a drop was spilled.

A fast run down Hatton Bank saw us through Leamington Spa and on to heavier going. The pressure gauge needle now began to linger and I wasn't altogether sure what was wrong. Arthur kept a watchful eye on me and soon realised that I was apprehensive. He also was not going to allow me to get into a mess that it would have been difficult for me to recover from. He came over to my side and screwed up his eyes as he peered into the fire. Courteously he asked, did I mind, as he took hold of the shovel. He then expertly, and effortlessly, swept just two shovelfuls of coal, one into each front corner of the firebox. Grey smoke immediately sprung from the chimney, within less than minute the pressure gauge was showing an increase, on went the injector again, I was back in business. He did not have to touch the shovel again for me, what an almost uncanny expertise these men had.

With all signals cleared we ran through Banbury at speed, at Aynho Junction, Arthur took a gamble with his polished shoes; he let me take water over the troughs. Once again he watched me closely and I suspect ready to put both feet on his seat as he gave me instructions. I wound the scoop down till I felt a slight tug on the handle, watched the tender water gauge float rise, and then quickly returned the scoop to the locked position. None was spilt, and with a further 2,000 gallons of water taken from the troughs this was our licence for a run through Oxford.

The GWR invested heavily in what was known as the Automatic Train Control. This company was the only major railway company to recognise the importance of such equipment to a driver. This system gave an audible warning to the driver in the cab when approaching 'distant' signals. Distant signals were placed approximately ¾ mile from a signal box; if the signalman had cleared all his signals in that direction, then he would clear his distant signal, indicating to a driver that there was now a clear run through his section. If a distant signal was showing clear, the locomotive picked up an electric current from a ramp between the rails; hence a bell rang in the cab. If the signal was, however, at caution, no current was picked up and a siren sounded. It was then necessary for the driver to acknowledge this siren; otherwise the train brakes would be applied. This apparatus was maintained to an extraordinary high standard and this equipment was to become sacred to all Great Western drivers.

There was one minor draw back with the Automatic Train Control (ATC), this was, if the lineside batteries went low at a distant signal ramp, insufficient current was picked up at that clear signal and the siren would sound, thus giving a caution warning, instead of a signal bell indicating clear. This failure was quite rare; even so, it was on the safe side, or what was ultimately known as a 'right side failure'.

Between Fenny Compton and Oxford there were a number of farm crossing on minor roads. These crossings were protected by a distant signal, which the crossing keeper would place at caution when he opened the gates to road traffic. Most of my colleagues never saw one of these road crossing distant signals placed at caution in their lifetime on the footplate. Until the old semaphore signalling system gave way to more modern signalling, some 20 years later, I also never saw any of these crossings used ... that is, with the exception of this day with Arthur Jenkins.

Once clear of Aynho Junction, Arthur felt comfortable enough with our situation to sit down and take the weight off his feet. Things were going so well that even I had time to see some of the lovely Oxfordshire countryside. We approached Fritwell and Somerton and took the wide sweeping curve to the right. Although all the signals were positioned on my side of the track, on this curve looking ahead, Arthur could see all the signals in front clearly. The line then snaked to the left, whereby these signals went out of his view. The distant signal for Somerton road crossing was attached to the same post as the starting signal for Fritwell and Somerton station signal box. A starting signal allowed a train to enter the next section of track towards the next signal box. On this occasion, when the ATC siren wailed at the distant for Somerton Crossing, my driver casually cancelled it and left the regulator open, as he had already seen this crossing distant signal showing clear. Arthur probably felt that on this occasion, the lineside ramp batteries were low and he had received a false indication. Nevertheless, as we passed the 'distant' at considerable speed, he checked this signal by looking at the back of it over our tender. Unfortunately, in the few moments that had lapsed since the signal had gone out of Arthur's sight, the crossing keeper had put his 'distant' to caution to have a farm vehicle across the line.

In extremely rapid succession, with barely enough hands, the regulator was slammed shut, the brake put into the emergency position and the whistle chain hung on. The brakes seemed to take an eternity to operate, the brake blocks eventually grinding hard on the wheels beneath us. When the crossing came into view on the curve, there was a little old lady wearing a red turban and sack cloth apron just clearing the last gate from our path. It was most unlikely that we could have stopped in time, but as we passed over the crossing she gave us a friendly wave. Little did she know that we both almost needed clean underwear! Arthur was a very composed and competent man, but the potential consequences of this incident left him clearly shaken. Thank goodness for the audible warning system and an open cab giving a chance to see the signal from behind. Although my surroundings were unfamiliar in this instance, this proved an all important lesson for me, which was to observe all signals on my side of the footplate.

With mostly favourable gradients in front of us we now ran on to the main line at Didcot, skimmed the water troughs again at Goring and eventually took a right-hand turn at the junction for Windsor at Slough. Passing Eton College we ran into the dead-end station at Windsor. In buoyant mood our passengers filed past the engine. It was a warm summer's morning and I had possibly just burned something like three tons of coal. This point was the nearest I ever came from having a gratuity from any passenger, a joker flicked a beer bottle stopper on to the footplate saying, 'Have a drink on me mate!'

As there was some delay getting another engine on to the back of our train to release us, Arthur suggested, as this would be our engine back this evening, it would be a good idea if I brought some coal forward and filled the 'hole' in the tender well, the space from which I had taken the coal. He rightly said that when the engine went under the coal stage at Old Oak Common shed, large lumps of coal would be dropped behind the tender coal doors which could be difficult to get out once we were on the run home. Filling behind the tender doors again would avoid this problem. This I did, also cleaning and trimming the headlamps and water gauge lamp, before eventually locking them away in the toolboxes in readiness for the evening. Running tender first back up the branch line, we then went round the triangle junction at Slough and ran head first to Old Oak Common. Here we handed the toolbox keys into the stores, washed and signed off duty. Arthur asked me if I felt I would need to rest at the hostel, but I declined and we caught a ride into Paddington on an engine going to work a train out.

At Paddington we met up with our guard, who was one of the more sociable of this elite band of Snow Hill men. We downed a brew of tea, made our way to Hyde Park and watched the world go by as we ate our sandwiches under the reflection of the Serpentine.

In the afternoon we went to Earls Court, where our time was spent browsing around the Radio and Television Exhibition. With the nightlife just coming into bloom, it became time for us to make our way back to Old Oak Common to prepare our engine. There was a train of coaches in No. 5 platform at Paddington, Arthur asked the shunter if it was bound for Old Oak Common Carriage Sidings. We then sat comfortably in the train for a while reading some discarded newspapers and magazines, I now really didn't feel at all like starting work! The platform inspector passed the carriage window and Arthur checked with him the train destination. The train was on the move as we fell back out on the platform, it was indeed going empty - to Exeter!

At the engine shed, we signed on again and went to collect the toolbox keys from the stores. The keys were not there, and the locks from the toolboxes were also missing when we arrived at the engine. There was not a tool of any description in the toolboxes or on the engine. Arthur had been right too; the tender was filled with lumps of Welsh coal the size of meteorites. Much of my earlier preparation work had all been in vain. Ironically, we had gone back to the depot early specially to do our job in a leisurely manner. Before we could start work it was now necessary for me to re-equip the engine with tools, to add to this, it was now changeover time for the shed staff and there was little point in me hanging on until a toolman came on duty at 10 pm. Many of the tools it was necessary for me to carry came from the coal stage engine line, these implements taken from engines that had just arrived on shed.

When at last the engine was fully equipped, I did the preliminary preparation and then spread the fire all over the whole grate area. Engines were always just kept warm on the shed by having a small amount of fire in the back end of the firebox. With the fire spread, I rolled some of the two hundredweight lumps on to the footplate, where I broke them up and made up the fire Reg Grafton style, with pieces of coal the size of a football. We always made the fire up by hand if we had Welsh coal; any attempt to do this job with the shovel was fatal. The fire would take an age to burn through if this type of coal was shovelled into the firebox. Lifting the fire up with the heavy fire irons then became the only option to get the air through to make it burn; Welsh coal would stick together like molten lava. Apart from the resulting steaming problems, lifting the fire with fire-irons could be downright hard work.

I swept the footplate and washed everything down well, but I ran out of time when I should have spent a lot longer trimming the tender. There was only time for me to make many of the huge boulders of coal safe from rolling over the side when we were on the run.

After running light to Paddington we backed on to our train. I did the coupling and we were soon on our way, non-stop to Birmingham, via High Wycombe. We left at 12.30 am and once we had passed the lights from the underground stations at Ruislip I remember little of our trip into the darkness. As usual we had filled the tender and boiler before we left Old Oak Common, therefore there was little room for water when we passed over Ruislip water troughs. Dropping the scoop would certainly have brought a flood on the footplate.

I shovelled on, tired and in robot fashion, with an engine like this it definitely wasn't my skill that got the steam, but I did in fact manage quite well. What I lost on the rise, I recouped on the easier going, with continuous running I had not to worry about blowing steam away from the safety valves. I skimmed the water troughs at Aynho and eventually at Rowington almost expertly. As I shovelled on the coal in the tender got further away from me, the huge lumps of coal that I had not had the time to break up now started to fall in our direction, some of these large enough to break my legs. I cracked the lumps with the coal peck, the wind whipping up the fine dust as we both started to look like the old trade mark for Hartley's marmalade. Arthur's wife would clearly have some difficulty in getting this shirt collar clean!

Running down towards Leamington, Arthur asked me to put some hot water in the bucket for him. With all signals clear, he washed as we passed over the 35 mph speed restriction through the station, although there was still yet time for an awful lot of dust to fly.

It was heavy going on all the Great Western routes into Birmingham, I lost out considerably on the drag up to Knowle and Dorridge; I was getting very tired too. We had run all the way very fast indeed and there were no permanent way speed restrictions at all that would have hindered the spirited run to any degree.

Even with the easier going towards Snow Hill I was still only able to run up No. 5 platform with the boiler water gauge showing just below half full. The time was just 2.30

am; when we had relief I felt a little demoralised at not doing better on the last lap. I did mention this to Arthur; but he remarked that he had 'thumped the engine a bit'. If he had, I had certainly not noticed any sparks from our chimney. I was to later learn that what Arthur termed a 'thumping' was considerable better than many driver's performed on one of their better days! Arthur also paid me an unexpected compliment, saying that he had noticed that I had done the whole trip without touching any of the fire irons whilst we were on the move. He said there were any number of experienced men who could not have done that. I was quite encouraged with what he said, I suddenly became six feet tall, but all in all I had got everything in my favour on this day.

At Snow Hill, after being out at work for some 20 hours, Arthur and I now had to wait on the platform for any kind of lift back to Tyseley that was available, making gestures at passing freight trains, hoping the driver would see us in time and stop. There was no all night bus service. Fortunately, on this occasion our wait was not too long; an engine going to shed picked us up. Back at the depot I washed in a bucket in the engineman's cabin and walked home to a sparse dawn chorus, it was already getting daylight. At home I put the kettles on the stove and washed more thoroughly, lifting my feet into the kitchen sink to wash my legs. My brother and I still shared a bedroom, I dropped the socks he had worn the previous day out of the bedroom window on to the back yard so that I could eventually breathe freely again. I'm pretty certain these were not the good old days!

There was soon another move in the links which took me into No. 7 link. My new link working brought about work on any number of low headcode freight trains to Banbury and Gloucester. There were also a number of what were called 'Zone' turns diagrammed in this link. A 'Zone' turn meant that you went up a grade from being 'Spare', you came under Snow Hill Control, rather than the jurisdiction of the running shed foremen. On 'Zone' turns you were more or less guaranteed train work, whereas if you signed on 'Spare', you tended to be a general dogsbody.

Although it was just coincidence, my new driver was yet again another man who had some desire to become a member of the management team and he was therefore on the 'Panel'. Good fortune was with me again, my new mate and I got along wonderfully. Harold Burton was a man with a 48 inch waist, despite this he was an absolute bundle of energy. No matter what time of day we signed on duty his mood was always jovial; I was to have some great times with this man. He was a railwayman through and through, was very conscientious, and best of all, he had extensive route knowledge. I did hear it said that Harold was a bit 'heavy handed', although I did not find him so, I enjoyed firing to him; it was exhilarating as he worked engines just hard enough to keep a bright fire. More often than not it became easier to get steam to someone like Harold, rather than a driver who worked an engine very economically. I always found this good man very co-operative too, if things were not going well on my side of the footplate, yet he never interfered, or doubted my increasing competence.

Harold was a man who never used bad language; he was a devout Christian who on Sundays would be seen in his bowler hat heading for his place of worship. Many times on the footplate I was inclined to get a rendering of 'All things bright and beautiful', and I got woeful looks if I lapsed into verbal obscenities. Harold also fried up for the England on the shovel; this regular feast carried a large tin lunch box. Many times I saw him put this box on a station barrow sooner than carry it, due to its great weight. His box was full of spanners, corks, trimming wire, water gauge glasses, even a scraper for scraping the dirt away from around the oiling points. A few minutes to spare and he would be along the framing cleaning and trimming the oil cups. I loved working with this man, nothing gave him more pleasure that to see things in good order.

No. 4900 *Saint Martin* on an SLS Special at Gloucester with my old driver Harold Burton proud of his 48 inch waist! *Dick Potts*

With Harold the summer Saturdays of 1952 saw me working express trains to Ruabon, Wrexham and Chester. Hereford also became within our bounds. The drivers in No. 7 link averaged around 50 years of age, although they were comparatively 'young' hands. It was strange therefore how we managed to hold on to such high calibre turns, that is, without older hand drivers in higher links claiming that these were their jobs.

On these express passenger turns, when at our destination, whilst I got the coal forward, Harold would get the clinker shovel and clean the fire, throwing the fire from one side of the firebox to the other as he shovelled the clinker out. Sweat would roll out of him, but he revelled in the work. He never drank anything but water at work.

Like most Tyseley drivers who were on the management panel, Harold stood absolutely no chance of getting a permanent supervisory post. Nevertheless, when he did stand in for the running shed foremen he put abundant enthusiasm into the job. With one or two like him in charge on a regular basis, I feel sure that our working conditions could have improved dramatically. Any important engines going off shed, he would get spare men to make a start in preparing them. This would make sure the engine was fully equipped and generally in good order before the men arrived. Some men resented this, they felt he was a nuisance when they were playing cards in the engineman's cabin. Yet these men only felt Harold was an irritation if they were called to prepare an engine for someone else, it was different if they signed on and found everything in good order themselves. Men often booked on duty to find their engine had been robbed of all its equipment, huge lumps of coal piled on the tender and the pit over which their engine was standing was flooded with water. With just a little interest by some of management our conditions could have been so very different.

One Monday morning whilst Harold was my mate, we signed on at 3.16 am for a freight train to Banbury. It was a damp, warm clammy morning and as I walked to

Pannier tank No. 8700 shunting in the goods yard at Tyseley on 30th August, 1958. Ten years after Nationalization the side tanks still bear the GWR roundel. *Michael Mensing*

work in the dark eerie silence I heard a flip, flopping sound approaching. As I came into the light of a gas lamp a woman approach me, absolutely naked. I suddenly felt pins and needles in my scalp; I really thought I was indeed seeing a ghost. She was quite a shapely woman, yet I was a naïve young man and it was the first time that I had seen a naked woman. The suddenness of the experience was hardly rousing, more frightening than anything. When I told Harold of my confrontation, he showed much interest in my encounter. I understand that for some months he made a detour to work in the early hours on his bicycle, hoping to get a glimpse!

Many of the freight trains that we worked took so long to work one way that we invariably came home on what was termed, 'the cushions', this meaning travelling home on passenger trains. If, however, we did make good time, men were then required to contact the controller for any work that might be going back towards our home depot. With Harold's enthusiasm we often made good time. The more artful drivers on previous freight trains would often get to know that Harold was not far behind them. Consequently they would delay calling the controller, knowing again that immediately Harold arrived he would conscientiously be on the telephone to the control. This did become a bit tough on me as we often found ourselves working trains that others should have been working. Many times I struggled back with rough engines with dirty fires whilst others caught the passenger train home in comfort. To add insult to injury, they were likely to make more money than us, as on night turns there was usually no passenger train home until the first one in the morning. We therefore often signed off duty whilst these men were still waiting for the passenger home. Nevertheless, Harold got much satisfaction from doing a good day's work and in general they were very happy days for me.

# Chapter Seven

## Military Service

After having my medical for National Service I was shown into a room where an officer sat behind an outsized desk. His army uniform had razor sharp creases and his brass buttons gleamed. He wore a leather 'Sam Brown', which had been polished until it had taken on the appearance of a deep lustre varnish; he eyed me critically as I entered. As he took my particulars he snapped questions at me, his attitude as though I was begging for some sort of hand-out. During the interrogation, I was asked if I had any preference as to the branch of the armed forces in which I wished to serve. It was common knowledge that I would have no choice where I was sent, I also didn't really want to be there at all. Nevertheless, I told the officer of my interest in railways, and if possible I would like to go into the railway section of the Royal Engineers. He seemed genuinely taken aback by my quick response, he took on an approving look; I got the impression that he had at last found a 'squaddy' who knew exactly what he wanted. He leaned back in the chair, I felt he was impressed, thoughtfully he tapped his pen between his thumb and forefinger … he then said he would put me down as a trainee lorry driver!

When the dreaded letter finally came for me to go, it informed me that I was to report to No. 6 Training Regiment, Royal Engineers, Norton Barracks, Worcester, on 2nd October, 1952.

My arrival at Worcester station saw a number of other young men obviously heading in the same direction as myself. We were met by military personnel in a lorry with tyres and tread the size of an agricultural tractor. We all scaled the tailboard into the back of the truck and hung on to the metal framework that supported the canvass cover. With the Bedford 'QL' transmission soon screaming beneath our feet, any kind of conversation was now impossible. Nevertheless, the driver seemed intent on cementing an early comradeship; his mode of driving systematically throwing us all alternatively into a heap into every corner of the vehicle. If he intended to deliberately make it uncomfortable for us, then he did do a great job. You could have given me a rough ride on an old 'forty-niner' any day; I was glad the barracks were not too far.

Inside the camp perimeter fence the shouting started, over the next months, had we all been wearing ear protection we would still have heard the incessant bellowing of orders. Standing to attention, looking straight ahead, they got so close to shout their commands at us that we were repeatedly spattered with spit, and could easily have detected what had been on yesterday's menu at the cookhouse.

At the Quartermaster's Stores we were kitted out and we wrapped our civilian clothes in brown paper parcels and addressed them home. This was a precaution against our making our escape. They did stop short of branding us with our military number, but it was instilled so much into our minds that I can instantly repeat it today, 50 years on, Sapper No. 22724525. This number we now had to mark on innumerable items of our kit.

At the 'tailors', we stood in a row whilst he came up behind us and grabbed the back of our battledress tunic and trousers, marking two lines with chalk along the excess of material. Crude as it was, he was better than I gave him credit for; the uniform fitted well when it was returned to me.

They marched us, ran us, physically jerked us, marched us and ran us again; I was starving hungry the whole time. The food was there; they just gave us no time to eat.

I would dash over to the cookhouse in the mornings, only to find, yet again, that un-filleted kippers were on the menu. The mess caterer must have had some scam going with the local fishmonger, I'm sure the amount of times that we had kippers is the reason for today's fish quotas. Trying to eat any kind of fish in a hurry was a hazardous business. Mostly, I would satisfy myself with doorsteps of bread and butter, these pats of butter floated on the top of a large water vat. Once you had 'angled' your butter from the cold water it was like trying to spread a lump of 'Sunlight' soap. When in 'Civvy Street', my work had never left me short of exertion, yet here I lost weight dramatically.

In the evenings, what wasn't wax polished had to be 'Brassoed' or 'Blancoed'. Every night I fell into bed totally exhausted. And did they really need to put bromide in our tea ?

Two weeks initial 'square bashing' saw some of us transferred to Gibraltar Barracks, Aldershot, where the ranting continued in earnest. The polishing and trouser pressing cycle was eternally repeated, in addition we were all issued with rifles. With these weapons, we marched, shot bullets, boiled them out, pulled them through, oiled and polished them and fixed bayonets to them. We almost went to bed with them, thankfully we never had to shoot anyone with them!

Monotonously, everything was done by timing, counting with numbers, one, two, three, one, two, three. Once the driving lessons began, this also was done by numbers, into first gear, two, three, dip the clutch, two, three, look in the mirror, two, three. I hated it. All this training was done on wagons with 'crash' type gearboxes, their shelf life greatly reduced by the interminable grinding of gear teeth beneath the vehicle.

I passed my driving test, as did the majority and the ceremonial passing out parade drew near. All went well on this parade, that is, until the order was given to fix bayonets. This command brought such a complete shambles that the Commanding Officer immediately walked off the parade ground. This was a blunder we all paid dearly for, we were drilled incessantly for the next two weeks! By which time we were bordering on Household Cavalry standard.

My pay for the first six months netted six shillings per week, I now resented very much having to send money home to pay for the insurance policies that I had earlier been talked into by the chief clerk at Tyseley. For this pittance we had to march up to a table where an officer sat, stamp your feet to attention, salute and call out your name, rank and number. The money took little counting; nevertheless, it was one pace backwards, salute again and shout, 'Pay correct, SIR!' This money increased a little after the first six months, but it was always necessary to save religiously if I wanted to get home on any 48 hour passes.

We eventually passed out and in two months I had been stripped of almost 1½ stones in weight, when my mother saw me on my first 48 hour pass, she wept. These tears, plus the regular letters that she always wrote had a profound effect on me; I had previously wrongly felt that she had some indifference towards me. I dearly wanted to give her a huge hug, but emotional contact had never really been part of our family life. It had been my mother's aim to keep all her family looking bonny by way of her cooking. Looking at me on my first leave, she must have felt that much of her life's work had been undone in just two months. Nevertheless, I was fit and healthy and was soon on the move from Aldershot.

Perham Down on Salisbury Plain was my next posting, the camp, 32 Assault Regiment, Royal Engineers, a tank regiment. On arrival I was sent to 26 Assault Squadron. The major in charge eventually interviewed me; during this meeting I was again asked about my interests. I told the officer of my passion for engineering, whereby he concluded that he would put me in the Motor Transport Troop. There, he said, I would have the opportunity for taking a Vehicle Mechanics Course. This was obviously 'pie in the sky', few National Servicemen got on any trade training courses, unless they were prepared to sign on for longer terms. A two-year 'sentence' was ample for most.

My new posting was a disciplined regiment, although more relaxed than the training camps. The almost weekly visits to the regimental barber were also not altogether necessary. Although, with everyone having the same short back and sides at the barbers, we never had to wait long for a hair cut, there was certainly never enough hair left for anyone to have the need for a blow wave! Much of the shrieking orders lessened too, that is, with the exception of our troop sergeant; he had a mouth the size of a parish oven. Sergeant Appleby was an overweight Yorkshire man, who was an authoritarian with a blood red face and a very foul mouth.

On my first day, after morning parade we were marched to the M.T. Hanger. This huge structure was full of vehicles for every military use; the floor was painted green and marked out with white lined bays. The vehicles stood with precision in these bays, they were in immaculate condition, even the wheel nuts were painted alternately in red and white. The whole place was reminiscent of a military museum, rather than a working unit.

We were dismissed to our work, but basically there was nothing left to do. There was only a certain amount that a host of conscripts could eventually do and that limit had obviously been reached much earlier. One of the older soldiers advised me that when the officers were around, you picked up anything close to you and looked busy. I wasn't very good at this and for several days the minutes seemed like hours, the hours like days. I really began to wonder how I would be able to cope with the intense boredom. With 20 months still to go, which was an awful long time, I found this absolute torture. Being alien to my normal environment, this really was going to be equal to a prison sentence.

After a few days I noticed a lance corporal come into the hanger, stand to attention and speak to Sergeant Appleby. At which he looked quickly round the hanger, pointed at me, and bawled, 'Take him, he's useless'. I followed the corporal to the cookhouse, where I was put to work on my hands and knees, scrubbing the quarry tile floor the size of the National Exhibition Centre. To say the least, these kitchens were busy; this was a large regiment with an awful lot of mouths to feed.

Scrubbing this floor was a daunting, almost eternal task, but it was possibly a bit better than washing the countless greasy pans. During this work, I realised that there was some animosity in the camp; the cooks were totally frustrated that the range fires were not up to temperature. The man allocated to do the stoking really had no idea of how to go about it, or he was trying to work his ticket from it. I approached the cooks and then did something that I was warned never to do, I volunteered to help. I raked the ash pans out, opened the dampers and livened the fires with the array of fire irons. I then broke the coal to even size pieces and soon had the pots and pans bubbling merrily and the meat spitting in the ovens. The cooks were delighted; I was indeed their saviour, almost their hero.

So impressed were they that the catering sergeant asked sergeant Appleby to release me to do the stoker's work on a regular basis, although this did mean getting up every morning at 4.30 am. This I didn't mind, at least I would be away from sergeant Appleby, and the time would tend to go a lot quicker with a positive job to do.

Photographs taken during military service of the ship *Narvik* at the time of the East Coast floods in 1953. The rope ladder was a bit precarious to climb with a heavy swell on!

*(Both) Provenance Unknown*

Perhaps two weeks passed before I found myself remonstrating with one of the cooks. He had a large pan of fat on the range and I saw him discreetly spit into it. I wasn't too impressed when he told me that it was normal practice and was a quite hygienic way of telling if the fat was hot enough. Any germs, he insisted would be sterilized by the high temperature of the fat. I really could not get my head round this; I lost more weight as my appetite foundered, wondering what other unsavoury wrinkles some of the cooks got up too. Nonetheless, nature eventually had a way of compensating; I got so hungry that I would finally have eaten a scabby horse!

After only a short period of time I was summoned to the Warrant Officers and Sergeants Mess, the cooks were having similar problems with their stoker. A handful of non-commissioned officers were obviously more important than several hundred other ranks, so I was transferred to do the fires in the kitchen there.

The sergeant's mess kitchen was much smaller and the men I worked with were a great bunch of fellows. We were all conscripted into the same boat, so we mucked in together, covering for each other as necessary. At meal times I got cleaned up, donned a white jacket and waited on the tables. On social evenings I helped with the drink waiter's job, some of these nights became pretty wild. Some compensation for this was that I was moved to a billet out of camp, across the road away from the strict military discipline.

The winter of 1953 saw the East Coast Floods and I had my dream broken when the regiment was called out to repair the breaches in the sea walls. Back under sergeant Appleby we headed for the Crouch Estuary, Essex, where the damaged sea defences had flooded low-lying land. The navy was called out too and our squadron was ferried to a minesweeper which was anchored in the river estuary. During the day we were ferried back to land to fill sand bags by the thousand, in deep mud we braved a biting east wind which blew relentlessly. At night we slept on the steel deck of the ship, cramped and downright uncomfortable. However, a larger vessel was soon sent to accommodate us. On the larger ship, the *Narvik*, we bedded down in the vehicle accommodation hold, but at least we then had folding camp beds.

Fortunately, when we got back to Perham Down I got my old job back in the kitchens of the Warrant Officers Mess. After a while, I was asked to take over the job of looking after the bar. Once in this occupation, I worked one day on and one day off duty. The reason for this being, that whilst there was anyone drinking at the bar it stayed open, all night if necessary. Many wild sessions went on until the early hours and I saw many of my superiors in their true colours. Playing poker dice was a favourite pastime, the first winner named a drink, the second paid for it, and the third drank it. With some daunting cocktails chosen, one by one the players would fall from the bar stools in stupor. In this case, the waiter and I dragged them into the billiard room and laid them on the surrounding couches. Somehow, quite miraculously, they always managed to rally enough to make the morning parade.

Some of these non-commissioned officers were able to forget their rank when in the mess and at quieter times I had heart to heart conversations with many good men.

The upper ranks were allowed to have £5 credit over the bar during each month. Some were always desperately short of money so we would sometimes let them go over this amount, entering the overdraft secretly in the back of the book. They always paid honourably and it was even known for me loan some of the NCOs money from my own pocket.

The regimental sergeant major I found to be a gem of a man, his conservative manner in the mess made him totally unrecognisable from the man we saw in charge of his regiment.

There were three squadron sergeant majors, one was always forced to forget his status when in the mess; he was always short of money, invariably needing our co-operation badly by way of back of the book entries. The other two sergeant majors I have searched the English language for a colourful enough description for each of them. Both military men through and through, rising from boy soldiers, the word 'bastards' I feel would be most apt. Never relaxing; both seemed to keep the proverbial poker up their back even when standing at the bar. One I found was always a joy to watch when one of his subordinates came to the bar, tunic wide open, asking for perhaps a 'Crunchie' bar, chocolate 'Penguin,' or a mineral water. Looking down the length of his nose, his eyes flashed making his thoughts blatantly obvious. Also my squadron sergeant major, I imagine, went to bed in his boots and gaiters, a born soldier, he also never ever let his position of authority waver.

On quiet nights, late when the bar was empty, the lads from the kitchen sometimes came in and with the front doors locked we had social snooker tournaments in the billiard room. Acting as duty Guard Commander one night, my squadron sergeant major came in unexpectedly through the kitchens whilst we were in the middle of a needle match on the billiard table. The sound of his voice would have raised the rafters as he lined us all up and prodded us with his drill stick. When he finally ended his ranting, he ordered us all to report to the regimental sergeant major first thing the following morning, dressed in full battle dress, ready for inspection.

There was absolute panic amongst us, down at the billet, out came the iron, 'Blanco', 'Brasso', and 'Kiwi' boot polish. The following morning we all paraded in line outside the RSM's office. When he saw us standing there, there was a total look of amazement on his face, he had never seen any of us in full uniform before, particularly the cooks. He asked me what on earth was going on, whereby I explained to him that the Orderly Officer had caught us playing on the mess billiard table and we had been ordered to report to him. 'Oh, bugger off will you', he retorted with a contorted face. It was plain that there was some irritation in his need to send us packing. Nothing further was said of the incident.

Brash sergeant Appleby relaxed when amongst the men of his own rank, but never let other subordinates in the mess forget his status. I was far from worldly wise, but with my dislike for this man I soon learned the art of not catching his eye when the bar was busy. The waiters too, made sure he waited longer than anyone else for his meals. He perhaps never realised, but he paid dearly, in time and frustration, for calling me 'useless' and treating the waiters like something the dog had brought home.

It was my responsibility to keep the bar stocked; this could be quite a tricky business as it was not always easy to tell if there was going to be a run on certain items of stock. The efficiency of the British army seemed to depend greatly on me keeping a constant supply of 'Bounty' bars and chocolate 'Penguins' readily available.

Often there were inter-regimental social evenings; the policy was that the losing team paid for a bucket of beer, which the winning team drank, straight from the bucket. This was always our cue to get rid of all the bottles of old stock from the shelves. If our regiment won, some turned up for breakfast next day with deep black rings under their eyes. Fortunately, they never really understood whether it was the quantity, or quality of what they had drunk, which put them off their meal!

One of the sergeants somehow learned that I had an interest in engineering. He had also discovered that army life was not for him as his term was due to expire, he therefore kindly handed me a host of expensive books on this subject. He had set out to get a degree in engineering, but had ultimately found it a bit over his head, I was so grateful to him. I was able to spend the next months with my head buried in these books, also swatting up on my meagre knowledge of engineering mathematics. This attempt at self-education tended to speed the passage of time and narrow the gap dramatically towards demob time.

A warrant officer and a sergeant were periodically elected to run the mess finances; how these were actually chosen I am unaware. Towards the end of my service there was a change of these persons in charge. From this time on money began to go missing from the till, which I found extremely worrying. We checked the stock against the monies taken every night when we closed the bar. The sergeant in charge of this daily audit covered the shortfall from his own pocket on many occasions and any tips we had been given also went the same way. There were four of us with access to the stock and money; at the end of my service we still had not found the culprit. Circumstance no doubt exonerated the other barman, the sergeant in charge and myself, who were indeed on the losing side. Regretfully, the indications were that the highest paid person amongst us was not to be trusted. In this position he now needed fewer entries in the back of the book. I was most relieved when time came for demob.

Without realisation, the discipline of the army training camp rubbed off on me substantially. It wasn't until close to the time of my retirement that it dawned on me that I had never left home for work, whatever time of the morning, without shaving and cleaning my teeth. This had become an unbending ritual. Unfortunately, army discipline didn't affect everyone the same way. A colleague, who had been conscripted to a branch of the Guards, always vowed that he would never polish another pair of boots. His regular appearance showed that he stuck strictly to this resolution!

A 1964 view of large prairie tank No. 4176 at speed on a local passenger service at Tyseley. These engines were used on the Birmingham suburban services until eventual replacement by diesel multiple units. The author's grandparents lived in one of the houses in the terrace that forms the backdrop to this picture. *Michael Mensing*

'28XX' class 2-8-0 No. 3825 ambles through Tyseley station with cattle vans on 30th August, 1958. *Michael Mensing*

# Chapter Eight

## Back on the Shovel

I now longed to get back into my workshop and put into practice many of the things that I had read in the engineering books that I had been given. The desire to invest in a new shed and more versatile machinery also took a hold of me. Unfortunately, during the two years in the army my bank balance had suffered. I had found it necessary to draw on it from time to time to buy clothes and presents for my family at Christmas and birthdays. I also had to send money home to pay for my endowment policies.

I travelled home humping a large kit bag on an early October Thursday in 1954. I went to the locomotive shed office on the following day to report for duty. The roster clerk was still desperate for men, so my appearance was met with a broad beaming smile and the words, 'Can you come in on Sunday?'

Nothing had changed, although it was rumoured that the 'call boys', or 'knockers up', were to be done away with. For some time it had become impracticable for many men to get homes within calling distance of the depot. The wartime bombing had taken its toll on available property and, through necessity, men had moved further afield.

Rumour eventually became reality and this grade of railwayman went into demise, nevertheless, many colourful stories remained of the exploits of these young men. In the 'black out' there had been several occasions when my father was faced with very irate neighbours, the 'call boy' having gone to the wrong house and roused unsuspecting neighbours in the dead of night.

The most popular story was of the fireman who had difficulty getting to work in the morning, despite being called. The call boys were generally inclined to wake the whole neighbourhood in an effort to get this man out of bed. In desperation, on his final warning for being continually late, the fireman suggested that he tied a length of cord around his foot and dangled it from the bedroom window. A few gentle tugs on the cord would surely be sufficient to wake him. Horseplay can be very painful, the temptation was too much for the young men on calling duty; they nearly pulled him through the bedroom window yanking on the cord. So yet again he limped to work late, this time owing to an injured foot! However, the shift foreman had already got 'wind' of what had gone on, he therefore showed some compassion.

Age did little to make this particular man's behaviour become more concentric; he eventually became a chronic hypochondriac. Men got so used to his attention seeking that when he did take a tumble, injuring himself quite badly, it was a long time before anyone responded to his moans of agony. An ambulance was eventually called and the first aid men decided to get him to the yard gate ready to meet the ambulance. The canvas stretcher that had hung since the war years in the shunter's cabin was dusted off and Albert duly loaded. Unfortunately, the stretcher material had deteriorated badly and halfway to the yard gate the stretcher gave way and the poor fellow fell through to the ground. Apparently the much louder wailing that followed did nothing to hide the laughter of the stretcher-bearers on this occasion!

At a later time, Albert turned up at a social evening on crutches. Despite a bad foot, he was not going to miss the darts match. As the evening progressed, others picked up his darts after he had thrown and his ale was fetched from the bar. Albert had a great night and when he got home his wife asked him if his foot was still painful. When he said it was awful, she suggested that he walked back to the club to fetch his crutches, he had indeed walked home without them!

Another driver had a problem getting to work; but not being the nicest of characters, he chose repeatedly to blame the call boys for not rousing him. A driver's word was law; few people could dispute this, least of all the men of the lowest footplate grade. Yet young men can be devious, especially when continually being wrongly chastised. Arriving at work, once again late, the driver again trotted out the excuse that he had not been called. The foreman listened, then said, 'Come along with me a minute Harry'. They made their way along the dark passage towards the call boys' cabin, where the foreman lifted the latch and gently pushed open the door. The driver felt the call boys were in for yet another rousting, until the foreman said, 'Do you recognise anything Harry?'

'That's my bloody front gate!'

'Well you can take it home with you now, and do try to get here right time in the morning.' Justice was done.

I took the roster clerk's bait and started work the following Sunday. Sundays were paid at time and three-quarters, so 14 hours pay was a boost to my first pay packet. Nevertheless, I spent a miserable day on a local passenger turn with an old driver who on a good day was noted for being grumpy. We had his regular engine, prairie No. 4110, I got to work early, as I usually did and gave the cab a special clean down. This did little to enhance any conversation. Verbal exchanges were mostly limited to the words,' Right Away' when we stopped at a station with the platform on my side. That is, until he finally chastised me for not repeating signals to him that he could not immediately see. I did snap back at him, telling him that it was my first day back for two years, things were a bit strange and he would not appreciate any error I might make. This day broke my dream a bit, I was glad to go home and felt a bit apprehensive should I one day find myself with someone like him on a regular basis.

The promotion ladder should now have put me in No. 6 link, but as yet there was no vacancy and I slotted back into No. 7 link, the place from where I left. I need not have worried; my new driver was Jack Payne, who in a short time put a lot of money in both our pockets.

Jack was an excellent engineman, he drove with absolute finesse and he too never put a foot wrong. Although he had a quiet nature and was a man who kept himself to himself, we got along fine. At this point in time Jack was a lithe man, he had a Romany look about him, his swarthy complexion being heavily pock marked. He was completely individual, inasmuch as he always travelled light. Throughout the winter of 1954-55 he never wore any kind of overcoat, or rainwear, he was indeed as hard as nails. Jack wore his overall jacket tucked inside his trousers exposing his bracers; his patent leather shoes would have been more fitting to a ballroom dance floor. His only protection from the weather was his soft cap and the first British Railways issue unlined serge jacket. This jacket he took off, however cold, as soon as we went indoors anywhere. Jack never carried a bag, or brought food of any kind to work, not even a brew of tea. He did have a drink when I made a brew, he then drank from the tea can lid.

One Saturday night Jack and I worked a freight train to Oxford, via Stratford-upon-Avon and Honeybourne. We got stranded, because of engineering work on the line, eventually we were at work for 18 hours. During this time Jack never had a thing to eat, at that time there was nowhere to buy anything early Sunday morning. We travelled home by passenger train and had a short time at Leamington Spa before catching the local train to Tyseley. Jack immediately went to the nearest hostelry and downed several pints of ale. This had no affect on him whatsoever, despite him going without food for a very long time.

When Jack signed on duty he picked up a single driver's daily record sheet, which he folded and slipped into his top jacket pocket. He never carried a watch and if we worked any train where time was a priority we would both peer into darkened signal boxes to catch a glimpse of the signalman's clock. Jack's timekeeping was only just enough to keep any reports from management at bay. His pencil was no more than two inches long; this would be licked so that dark heavy writing would ensue. The only other thing in his pocket would be his roll-up tin. He gave the impression that he had at some time been an old soldier; the roll-ups he produced were little thicker than a straw. These constantly needed to be re-lit and what he saved on tobacco he lost out on matches, at night often tripping across the footplate to light up again from the water gauge lamp. On windy nights the gauge lamp would often blow out, which was a bit irritating, as it was difficult to get a light from the engine fire whilst the regulator was open. Nevertheless, Jack was a pleasant man, we got along wonderfully, he was definitely a culture change from my previous driver Harold Burton. The only time Harold stopped eating was when he had an oilcan in his hand, the box he carried never went empty. He would frequently pat his belly and laugh, saying, 'Kid, you must look after the inner man'.

In the early 1950s the railways had difficulty coping with the volume of traffic and it was commonplace for people to have to stand on crowded express trains for long distances, freight too was heavily congested. Freight yards were overwhelmed and even on short freight journeys we rarely got back home inside our working day of eight hours. Freight trains from the south queued to get into Bordesley Junction and Oxley Yard, the latter yard was just north of Wolverhampton. We were therefore never sure what time we would get home even on the 15 mile trip to Oxley, as trains rowed up on the many goods lines *en route* to this destination. It was quite usual to enter the long goods line between Wednesbury and Bilston and go up behind two other freight trains.

It was mostly on these trips to Oxley Yard that we gained experience of what it was like to ride in a freight train brakevan. Often arriving at the yard after the passenger service had ended, we were sent home in the middle of the night on any of the freight train which stopped at Tyseley for relief. A number of freight guards were injured by incompetent or just thoughtless drivers, therefore this grade of men soon became aware of a driver's reputation. A freight guard boarding his brakevan at Oxley as the train left would say to us, 'You can hold tight tonight chaps', invariably he was right.

If the driver made heavy applications of the vacuum brake without first bringing the train together by gently rubbing on the locomotive hand brake, or tender brake, every wagon could be counted as they buffered up to each other. This momentum increased until inside the brakevan it felt as though you were continually going up against a brick wall. Sometimes, even when you heard it coming and braced yourself, you could be thrown from one end of the van to the other. Thankfully, most drivers were highly skilled; usually all that was felt was the brakevan buffers going up quietly against the wagon in front. Many times, with the most competent of drivers, I did work heavy 'D' headcode fast freight trains to Gloucester without the driver touching the vacuum brake at any time, that is, until the need to stop for water at Gloucester South Junction. As long as we got line clear, the whole journey would be done by using just the tender handbrake. As firemen, we eventually knew exactly where to apply the tender brake and where to slowly release it, this easing of the brake allowing the train to stretch out, thus avoiding any snatching of the loose-coupled wagons behind the brake fitted portion of the train.

Freight trains also queued on the goods line between Tyseley and Bordesley. Many men experienced having relief on the goods line at Tyseley and coming to work the following day to see the same train still in the same position. In bad weather, locomen tended to take refuge in the brakevan of the train in front. When doing this we had to abandon ship in a hurry if the train moved. Despite the brakevan brake being screwed on tight, the train would gather speed quickly to the point where jumping off was dangerous. Enginemen who dozed off in this situation were known to find themselves walking back from Small Heath!

At the time I went with Jack Payne I was yet to have my 21st birthday, although by this time I had had a lot of firing experience. Like all firemen, I had many rough trips, but by this time any steaming problems were not likely to be a problem with my technique, troubles were usually due to poor maintenance, or poor quality coal.

A good grounding with earlier drivers certainly taught me to cope with the abundant Great Western moguls that we took charge of, although these '43XX' class engines did always tend to be the bane of some firemen. These locomotives were very underrated small engines that would do almost any job when in the right hands; they were strong and ran well. The firebox grate sloped steeply and these 2-6-0s only needed to be fired just inside the firehole doors, any coal thrown to the front of the firebox spelt trouble. The motion of the engine and the blast from the exhaust would keep the fire edging its own way towards the front of the firebox. It took some confidence to get the fire right, but steam came freely once this was achieved.

Early in my days with Jack Payne he underestimated my capability and took the shovel from me one day when things were not going well on one of these locomotives. One night we relieved a freight train bound for Banbury at Tyseley station headed by a '43XX' class. This must have been this engine's first trip out following a major overhaul in Wolverhampton factory. The craftsmen in this factory may have equalled that of the men at Swindon, but Wolverhampton factory was not best known for doing a good final paint job. This engine was so fresh from the works that the paint still smelled and where it had been daubed on, it still was not completely dry. Seeing the engine in this condition, I thought the trip was bound to be easier than routine. Fortunately, the engine being newly overhauled, used the steam and water very efficiently and it was only this reason that we limped to Leamington without the necessity to stop to raise steam. This section of line being the easier part of the journey too, I was baffled; there was no way I could get her to make steam. When we took the climb from Leamington, Jack indicated for me to stand on his side, that is, after he set the regulator and reversing lever into the desired notch. Jack looked at the fire over the firehole flap and re-lit his roll-up. He waited a while, until the fire temperature had risen, then expertly flashed two our three shovelfuls of coal on to the fire. Another few puffs at his cigarette and a few more shovelfuls were added. The pressure gauge showed no sign of responding, so off the tender came the long fire-iron, this he threaded over the top of the closed firehole flap and stirred at the front of the fire. The red-hot fire-iron went back on the tender and Jack sat for another few draws at his fag. With the boiler water level now falling, Jack turned on the blower, yet the pressure gauge still failed to respond favourably. The distant signal for Fosse Road signal box was showing clear, but we were already in no state to continue. Jack stopped the train at the home signal and blew the whistle code for the signalman to turn us from the main line on to the loop line. Here, Jack admitted defeat and walked back to the signal box to tell the signalman of our difficulties, leaving me to refill the boiler and attempt to raise the pressure. From here on we limped to each successive signal box in the same manner, stopping to refill the boiler and raise the pressure on every occasion. Jack insisted that the fire was badly clinkered, but even at this stage in my experience, I felt the problem was more likely to have been a mechanical defect. Even if the fire had been very dirty, a newly overhauled engine would have steamed better than this. Jack never took the shovel again!

Jack was not the only driver to make this mistake and take the shovel from me; I had done nearly 10 years as a fireman when another driver felt he could do better than me, this again with the same class of locomotive. My driver on this occasion was a man with an awfully big ego; yet he was undoubtedly a super engineman, who had himself done many years as a fireman. Unfortunately, he always thought that any trouble on the fireman's side was likely to be due to poor firing technique. Even when along with very experienced firemen, he was never prepared to give the benefit of the doubt. On this occasion, we departed from Bordesley Junction with a freight for Swindon; we had indeed prepared this engine ourselves, so as near as I could tell everything was in fine order. The engine didn't respond to normal procedure as it should have done and the steam pressure soon began to fall. Therefore passing Shirley, on the North Warwick Line, I took the long poker from the tender and gave the front of the fire a stir. The fact that I had found the necessity to use the pricker so early in the journey became a reflection on my capability and this driver quickly made his displeasure known. We eventually made the summit at Earlswood, thankfully without the need to stop to raise the steam pressure or apply extra draught by using the blower. The following nine miles were downhill to Bearley Junction, whereby a breath of steam in the cylinders for a short distance took us on to a steep fall again into Stratford-upon-Avon. After filling the tender my driver bade me to stand on his side. He was not going to let me do the driving; I was to watch how it should be done. This was pretty patronising, in view of my already having so much experience.

The first five miles was easy going to Long Marston, but from there on the line climbed steeply over the Cotswolds. With his jacket off, he expertly swept coal into the firebox, but it was soon obvious that this engine would not respond to his talents as well as he thought it would. Several times he asked me to reset the reversing lever cut-off, perhaps thinking a little more draught on the fire would improve things. It beggars belief, the look of disdain that I would have got if I had dared to ask him to alter the valve cut-off! However, with the situation looking sicker with each mile, at Weston-sub-Edge he sheepishly turned on the blower. At Broadway, we were getting quite desperate and off the tender came the long poker! With sweat pouring from his face, he finally said, 'She isn't much good is she?' Whereby I sat on his seat and let him get on with it ... I could have told him that much earlier!

Jack Payne and I turned out for work in appalling winter weather and these slow freight trains exposed us to the elements. Often the preparing engine crew had failed to bother to check that the engine had a storm sheet. Waiting in loop lines, high on embankments, the snow and rain would blow horizontally across the footplate. Many times we took refuge on the framing on the lee side of the boiler when the open cab afforded no protection for us. Crossing the viaduct at Toddington one night, the cross wind actually whipped the coal from the shovel before it reached the fire. Yet Jack never grumbled, he took everything in his stride and his mood always remained affable. He was wonderful to work with and his unhurried approach put a lot of money my way.

One evening, Jack and I were on the platform at Wolverhampton Low Level and we could hardly believe our eyes; a large eight-wheeled van standing on the bay line was rocking quite considerably from one side to the other. Indeed there was nothing anywhere near it to cause this motion. Mystified, we walked over to have a closer look. Inside were two circus elephants, to ease their boredom they had discovered that by shifting their weight from one foot to the other they made their own see-saw!

In general the streets were safe at night, but going to and from work in poor gas street lighting was always a bit eerie. Many pet owners put their dogs out at night and when these animals got bored, they chose night workers like railwaymen for a bit of sport. All too frequently marauding animals snapped at my legs. One night, two German shepherd guard dogs, which had escaped from a nearby scrap yard, pinned me in the opening of an entry, snapping and snarling ferociously at me. I could only keep these beasts at bay by wielding my leather food bag. I was beginning to wonder how this siege would eventually end when suddenly they both simultaneously left. They must have picked up the scent of food, or perhaps an ovulating female. I was very relieved, but my heart still sounded like a forge steam hammer an hour later.

A couple of weeks later, I saw another Alsatian dog in the misty gas light as I walked to work. With the previous encounter still fresh in my mind I tried to stifle my own footsteps as I approached the point where the dog had disappeared into the mist. I first felt that I was safely by, but when I heard the sound of paws on the pavement behind me every hair on the back of my neck felt like an icicle. I strode on 'bravely', till I felt a cold nose on my hand, this animal was as soft as a brush and just wanted company, in fact I had a job to shake her off at the loco shed gate for her own safety.

Two plain-clothes detectives frightened the life out of me on another occasion. In the dead of night they stepped out on me and searched my food bag. Satisfied, they let me go on my way, warning me that I might be stopped again as there was a 'stake out'. It was quite amusing from there on; any felon wishing to avoid arrest would have easily seen the shining chrome tips of the constable's helmets reflecting in the moonlight as they protruded high above the hedges that they were supposed to be hiding behind.

I eventually purchased a new shed for a workshop; the largest the council would allow was eight feet by six feet. The bye-laws gave tenants a choice of what colour to paint any outside building, green, or brown. I chose Brunswick green, although at this point in time I had never worked on any locomotive carrying that colour livery.

I was with Jack Payne for five months until a vacancy occurred in my rightful link; indeed once a place did occur, I was almost the senior hand in No. 6 link also.

My new driver, Charlie Stride, brought another complete change; he wanted only one thing when he got to work ... that was to go home again as quickly as possible. He schemed from the onset to avoid any work likely to involve overtime. Charlie was another man with designs on a management post, he therefore also often deputised as shed foreman, or acted as foreman's assistant. Being one of the older hands on the 'panel' did sometimes give him some sway with his fellow supervisors. He was therefore able to pick his jobs to some degree when we were 'spare', or on 'Zone' turns. Charlie and I got along great; I wasn't bothered if I went home without making overtime. I had just purchased my new Myford Lathe with all its accessories, so I had more than enough to interest me at home in my workshop.

My new mate suffered badly with his stomach, night work obviously proved miserable for him. I imagine that his main interest in doing the management turns was to get some sort of normality to his shift patterns. He never really gave me the impression that he was in any way passionate as to how the railways were run, a management post would just perhaps be convenient for him. However, men make different choices, I myself in later life thrashed many a diesel engine in an effort to get home.

I did get a bit peeved with Charlie one day when as usual he was in a hurry to get finished. He overran a signal at danger, then blamed me for not getting the tender hand brake on quickly enough to bring the wagons against the engine. This was a ludicrous argument, but I said nothing, I was not prepared to quarrel with him.

On the day in question we were working an iron ore train from Banbury to Bilston, West Midland foundry, the train being entirely loose coupled and unbraked. We were on the rising section of line between Lapworth and Dorridge and the Dorridge down relief line distant signal was set at caution. As I said earlier, on level, or falling gradients, the fireman always screwed the hand brake on when a distant signal was at caution; this brought the train gently up against the locomotive before the locomotive vacuum brake was applied. On a rising gradient however, drivers normally tended to ease the regulator and allow the train weight to gradually slow the train down when approaching signals a danger. On this occasion, I repeated to Charlie that the distant signal was against us; also the siren in the cab sounded the appropriate warning. Being in a hurry to get home, he never eased off the regulator so that the train would lose momentum. He leaned well out of the cab on the slight left-hand curve and no doubt could see the outer home signal set at danger for himself. As was commonplace, I called to him that the signal was on. Charlie probably felt that the signalman would clear the signal under what was known as Regulation 5 for Bentley Heath Crossing, but unfortunately the signal remained at danger. In almost one move, the regulator was shut and the brake applied. Charlie had left it too late and the weight of the train pushed us past the danger signal. No damage was done and a few words with the signalman smoothed things over, but I was pretty upset that he chose to blame me.

I might clarify that Signalling Regulation 5 applied when the normal acceptance point for 'line clear' at a station, junction, or road crossing was blocked for any reason. The signal box in rear of the box with the blocked line was also required to keep his signals at caution. This in turn would be an indication to a driver that the line was not clear in advance. The signalman at the box in rear would caution trains by either showing a green flag from the signal box or verbally warning the driver. This method of working was of course a double safety measure. The old railway inspectorate were fully aware that red signals did not always stop trains. If this regulation had still applied today, a number of serious accidents would never have occurred.* Some of the older signalmen that were promoted into the modern power signal boxes still applied this regulation in principle when working the new colour light signalling system, and indeed the railways were no doubt a safer place.

The work in No. 6 link was still mostly freight, but trains of a higher classification. We also had more passenger work to Oxford and some summer Saturday trains to and from Bristol.

In these early days I loved my work and the last thing in the world that concerned me was trade unionism. My grandfather and father had seen the problems of the 1920s and 1930s and had become staunch trade unionists. When I started in the Traffic Department on Acocks Green station, my father was quick to open membership in the National Union of Railwaymen (NUR) for me. Like his father, my father was a member of this trade union. Every three months my father would ask me for my union dues and I paid up without question. He also enrolled me in sick clubs, I' m sure he felt that if I was unfortunate enough to fall sick, my mother's housekeeping would still be there!

Charlie Stride was also one of the minority of locomen who were members of the NUR; most footplate men were members of the Associated Society of Locomotive Engineers and Firemen (ASLEF). I was never approached, or had given any thought to the fact that perhaps I could be in the wrong trade union.

ASLEF had called a strike in the early summer of 1955 and that began to worry me. The reason for the strike was differentials in pay; the locomen's union wanted increased money for footplate workers. The NUR could obviously not support this principle, as the union represented all grades of railway workers. Mostly because of my two years military service, I had just managed to book my first seaside holiday since leaving school; this holiday was due to start two weeks after the strike began.

Because I was worried, I spoke to my father and Charlie as to what we were expected to do should the strike go ahead. The advice given, which I was unhappy

* The Regulation is still retained (although re-numbered) in certain situations in Absolute Block signalling areas.

about, was that we would work as normal, do our own-diagrammed work and not do overtime which would jeopardise the men on strike.

On the weekend before the strike began I was approached for the first time to change unions. Because I had grave doubts about going to work during the strike I could easily have been swayed. Unfortunately, the two young officials of ASLEF who did approach me, didn't ask me to support the strike, they threatened me as to the consequences of going to work. I was already unhappy about the possibility of losing my first holiday, plus the fact that I had just spent two years under military discipline being programmed in what to do. Suffice to say, downright pig-headedness got the better of me, I rebelled at the threat and the conversation became heated.

I then decided to work and do as I had been advised. Sometimes in a life we all make mistakes, going to work was not an act of avarice on my part, but sheer stupidity, and this was a blunder that I shall always regret. With so many good friends around me, under the surface, this was something that I was never really able to come to terms with.

Monday morning we crossed the picket line and Charlie and I worked our own freight train to Gloucester. No relief was available at Gloucester, so we shunted the train into the yard and brought the engine back to Tyseley. On the way home, we were stopped at several sidings and were asked to move wagons into place for unloading, but Charlie refused as this was not our normal work. Possibly, it was more likely that he was in his usual hurry to get home.

Tuesday, we worked another freight, a train of coal for Wednesbury, from Bordesley Junction. Our own train working was cancelled, so doing this would have been normal practice.

Wednesday was a different matter, we were ordered to work a passenger train to Paddington, via Reading. This was certainly not our work; neither did Charlie sign the route to Paddington beyond Oxford. Working this train would mean a long day, therefore I fully expected my mate to turn the job down on principle, and because he was unlikely to get home early. He may have been thinking of his future prospects for a management post, but most surprisingly he agreed to do it. Our pilot driver beyond Oxford was to be another Tyseley driver who was in fact a member of ASLEF and was therefore 'blacklegging' the strike.

Of all the well-maintained Tyseley engines that were available to work this train we were given No. 5983 *Henley Hall,* which was a foreign engine and soon to be found was well overdue for boiler washing. The locomotive itself was in fine order, but when we left Snow Hill with 12 coaches, packed from end to end, she just spewed water out of the chimney for some miles, not that I had overfilled the boiler to any degree before the start of our journey. Each time the regulator was opened a bit more she primed, that is until the boiler water level had dropped to well below the half way mark. Working with a dirty boiler made very hard work of any job, consequently for the rest of the trip the boiler level then had to be kept low at all times. There was then no time at all to relax, normally we worked on the basis of what was lost uphill we gained on easier gradients; with an engine in this condition there was no filling the boiler when going downhill. The uphill sections then had to be started with the boiler level low and hence the injector had to be started quickly to maintain a safe water level. All in all, it was a thorough nuisance.

On arrival at Paddington the train was drawn off us and we took the engine on to Ranelagh Bridge sidings to turn. A labourer then brought the remaining coal on the tender forward for me. During this break, our conductor driver showed some pleasure in working out the large mileage payment that we would receive for doing this job; this bothered me as I could see that the principle of this was wrong. It was at this point that I realised what I had been stupid enough to get sucked into. I also felt that this would surely be the trend of things to come on the consecutive days. I said nothing, but when I got home I never reported for work again until the strike was over. Charlie came to my home to talk to me, but I was having no more.

Tyseley had a mixed breed of men, as all depots did. Nevertheless, there was never any militancy and intelligent ways of settling disputes were always found. These good men, and my many lifelong friends were a privilege to work with; I regretted that I had let them down badly, albeit for very a short time. The strike lasted for perhaps another 10 days, this was time that I used to organize my new workshop. During this period also, I became 21 years of age, any decisions from now were mine and I would have to accept responsibility for my own mistakes.

My annual leave started as the men went back to work; this gave me two weeks breathing space for normality to be restored at the depot. I expected some hostility when I returned, but there was little. I got the cold shoulder from a few, however this was no more than I deserved. The strike was not a great success and men with families had lost their income, they had every right to feel bitter. This was a situation that I never had any desire to let repeat itself, therefore, when the dust had settled I joined ASLEF. Strangely, my father kept his thoughts to himself and said nothing.

About this time I was rostered to work a freight from Bordesley to Moreton Cutting (near Didcot). Charlie had thought better of turning out to work at 12.30 am on Sunday morning and therefore Alf Parsons deputised for him. Alf was a tall thin man with sharp features, he was friendly and talkative and I was to enjoy working with him on several other occasions at later dates. On this morning, I had listened to cabin talk and he appeared to have quite a reputation for being a man who didn't spare the horsepower. To add to this, the engine that was marked on the roster sheet adjacent to our names was No. 3012, a World War I 2-8-0 Robinson-design ex-War Department engine. I am led to believe that engines of this class ran in abundance on the Eastern Region and were reasonably well regarded by their enginemen. The ex-Great Western ones, however, were notorious for their poor steaming qualities, they were certainly not very happy when burning Welsh coal. Over the years, the Swindon draughtsmen had made some alterations to these engines, which it appears were not for their better. The rivets around the base of the smokebox tended to work loose, as the long main frames tended to twist when the locomotives were worked heavily. The smokeboxes then invariably drew in air; this reduced the draught on the fire which spelt death to free steaming. Nevertheless, they were quite strong 2-8-0s and would happily plod along with half the maximum boiler pressure and they rarely stalled. This was quite an asset when the fireman was doing 'rough', a term meaning low on steam pressure.

When I got on No. 3012 this morning, it was obvious she had been stopped for boiler repairs to be done, the grate and tubes were lovely and clean, also a new brick arch had been fitted. The tender was filled with some best quality Welsh coal; all things seemed to be on the plus side for me. I made a huge fire; as usual I made the fire up by hand using moderate sized lumps, as I explained earlier we never used the shovel until the base of fire had burned well through. After preparing the engine we went to Bordesley tender first, here we backed on to a heavy train of coal wagons. I allowed the fire to burn through very slowly; even so it was good fortune that we were soon away from the yard, otherwise the impending noise from the safety valves would, I'm sure, have woken most of the residents of South Birmingham.

I didn't find Alf Parsons a particularly heavy-handed driver, although, he was for sure a man who was not one to hang about. There was an early train home from

Oxford and we were booked to travel home passenger, there was little doubt Alf intended to be on it. The following train was 12.30 pm from Oxford, which would make us a bit late for Sunday lunch!

I remember well dragging the train on to the sharp curve of the North Warwick line, at the back of where I now live and from where in years earlier I had watched the trains from my father's allotment at the quarter mile post. The firelight and glow from the ashpan lit up both sides of the deep cutting as though it was almost daylight. The injector was soon singing away beneath our feet, on this morning I felt that the 14 hours overtime would be easily earned.

I intended to keep the big fire that I had started with and therefore kept firing until we cleared the heavy going as far as Earlswood. This was common practice, but we did let the boiler water level drop as far as we dare. The falling gradient from there on, plus the steep cant on the right-hand curve at The Lakes Halt, made the water in the boiler gauge glass only just visible in the bottom gland nut. During the nine miles down hill to Bearley with the regulator shut, the boiler was then refilled; this prevented steam from being blown away from the safety valves and kept the general scene peaceful. A short pull up to Wilmcote saw us hanging on the brakes again on the steep fall approaching Stratford-upon-Avon.

All slow freight trains normally stopped at Stratford for water, this being Sunday morning, both the East and West signal boxes were switched out, meaning that no signalman was on duty. We were therefore booked on this occasion to run to Moreton-in-Marsh for water. During the steep run down towards Stratford, the tender brake handbrake was left screwed on; this again kept all the wagons leaning against the locomotive until the distant signal for Evesham Road Crossing was spotted. With this signal clear we slowly released the tender brake; this allowed all the link couplings to stretch out again without any snatching. Gradually, Alf opened the regulator and we were fully ready for the heavy going ahead, I still had a big fire and the boiler was as full as I dared.

We took the rise to Honeybourne East Loop and on to the sharp left-hand curve towards Honeybourne South Loop signal box. With this distant signal at caution, I spotted the home signal at clear from some distance and repeated it to my driver. We drew over the junction towards the starting signal and the bank engine was waiting on the main line ready to come behind us. We kept moving and as the signalman switched the points behind our brake van, the banker then came to our rear to push us up as far as Chipping Campden. Honeybourne South Loop starting signal then cleared before we reached it, two crow whistles from the bank engine were echoed from our locomotive and the regulator was put to full open. The exhaust sound on these locomotives always sounded muffled, there were no clear crisp beats from the chimney as on Great Western engines. Nevertheless, the smoke from the chimney shot vertically into the moonlight sky. We forged our way up the incline until we were cocooned in grey clammy steam as we entered the long tunnel. Over the top at Chipping Campden we put our head down on the easier going and we felt a slight tug on the couplings as the banker fell away from the rear of the train. Freight trains were normally given a guaranteed run through Blockley; otherwise they would have difficulty in making the climb into Moreton-in-Marsh. If a banker was required on anything but a rising gradient, then the regulations stated that the bank engine would have to be attached to the rear of the brakevan. The banker leaving us at Chipping Campden therefore avoided attachment to our rear. We stopped at the water column at Moreton-in-Marsh, I put the heavy leather 'bag' into the tank and Alf turned on the water. It was our first stop since leaving Bordesley.

The clear sky of the summer morning brought an early dawn and although most of the work for me was now over, some large lumps of coal had by now become exposed on the tender so, I set about breaking these and laying the dust. The next 20 miles would need just a minimum regulator opening, hence I could take some time to sit and enjoy the countryside.

At this point Alf called to me, asking had I not smelled anything? 'Come and have a look at this', he remarked. The driving wheel axle on my side was actually glowing red-hot in the centre of the wheel. White bearing metal was pouring on to the sleepers from the axlebox like water, indeed the axle was so hot that the metal in the eccentric straps, which were part of the valve gear, had also melted. The liquid metal from the eccentrics had thrown out and had splashed up on to the boiler lagging and had stuck to the filth like plumber's solder. This was quite a sight to behold.

It was probably not a good idea, but after the tank had filled we eased the engine back until the hot axle was in line with the water column. Alf then played cold running water on to the centre of the wheel .We eventually shunted the train back on to the disused Shipston-on-Stour branch and stood there for almost two hours until the axle had cooled further. My driver then did his best to get some oil round the bearings, squeezing himself into the valve gear between the boiler and the main frames. It would have been normal practice for us to leave the train and take the engine slowly to Oxford, but my driver decided that with the favourable gradients it would be perhaps be just as easy to take the train. Once moving, the weight of the wagons would keep up the momentum and it would most likely be less strain on the engine.

We eventually set off at 10 mph towards Oxford, stopping first at the engine shed at Kingham to raid the deserted stores for more oil. It then took us a further two hours to get to Oxford, stopping to examine the engine regularly and pouring more oil on to vital parts. Once at Oxford, we abandoned the train and put the engine on the shed. We were very late for Sunday lunch!

My thoughts were such that it would be the last of that old engine I would see; I felt that the axle journals would be so badly scored that they would surely be beyond repair. Wrong again, 10 days later she passed us by going the other way on another freight, having a set of brand new wheels under her. Full marks were due to the Oxford fitting staff.

Charlie moved up to No. 5 link and my new driver was then Fred Delderfield. During the few months we were together Fred lost his wife of many years, which was extremely sad, and he obviously went through great emotional turmoil. His resulting circumstances then tended to make him throw food into his bag with the intention of frying up on the shovel at work; unfortunately it was not always practical to do this on many of the jobs that we worked. He then went for long periods without food, although the trauma had probably destroyed his appetite.

Fred and I got along extremely well, but he did tend to speak spontaneously, often without thinking, being quite apt at putting his proverbial 'foot in it'. One amusing incident happened when we worked a daytime freight to Gloucester. I made my brew of tea at Bordesley before we departed, this we shared with our guard. We got hung about *en route* and whilst we were shunted into the refuge siding at Long Marston for a faster train to pass, the guard made another can of tea and shared it with us. We got later still and when we had relief at Gloucester South Junction we all decided, as this was a decent day turn, we would make an effort to catch a train home via the Midland Region line, which went from Gloucester Eastgate station to Birmingham New Street station. The mile, or more, walk was taken in some haste and when we arrived on the platform Fred decided to make his brew. The railways had been nationalised for some six years by this time, yet the Midland Region and Western Region were still two completely different entities, the men with the brown cap badges were never known to mix with those with the maroon cap badges. Indeed, the public house near the engine sheds at Gloucester had two bars, Western men to the right and Midland men to the left.

On this day, Fred trespassed on hallowed ground and burst into the Midland men's relief cabin on the station platform, the guard and I reluctantly followed. Fred picked up the heavy cast-iron kettle on the stove and crashed it noisily down on the hob, saying loudly, 'The bloody kettle is cold, I think these buggers in here must see us coming! Put the can on mate', he ordered. I filled the our tea can, lit the stove and we waited for it to boil in complete silence. A number of men sat reading, but I got a definite impression that our intrusion was not appreciated, particularly following Fred's outburst.

'Boil up Fred', I said. At which he went to his bag and found a cardboard Typhoo Tea packet, its inner wrapper twisted tightly round at the top to hold in the mixture of tea and sugar. Fred hastily undid the wrapper, turned the packet upside down, there was a plop, and an egg dropped into the water. Fred had forgotten to bring his tea and sugar! The egg he had brought was for him to cook. The three of us then had to creep sheepishly out of the cabin, without a drink, to some amusement from the Midland men. Fred's size afforded him with broad shoulders, but the guard and I wished for the proverbial big hole in the ground.

One of the turns in No. 6 link was the night Bordesley Junction to Pontypool Road, 'F' headcode freight. One evening Fred and I had the usual '38XX' class 2-8-0 rostered to us. The locomotive had been stopped for boiler washing, a procedure which tended to soot over everything in the cab. When engines were lit up from cold after washing out, smoke and flames from the fire came out into the cab every time the firehole doors were opened because there was no natural draught up the chimney. We normally swilled this soot off with the hot water from the coal-watering pipe, there was always much spitting as the water hit the hot pipe work, the ensuing steam turning the cab into a Turkish bath, but it was better than the dirt blowing about as you got moving on the open road. The water gauge glass and its protector glass on this occasion were also very smutty, so I shut the gauge frame off, cleaned the parts and replaced them. I then became aware of a problem, as the water level in the boiler was now different from when I shut the water gauge frame off. I opened both the test cocks attached to the water gauge and water dripped from them both, so I was quite happy that there was water in the boiler. Before my driver arrived I alerted the foreman fitter; it was obvious to me that the water was not draining from the gauge glass as it should have done when the blow down cock was opened to test the water level.

A fitter eventually arrived, showing some irritation that it had been necessary to call him from the social club to carry out this work. Some of the night staff signed on duty and had the habit of popping to the club to get a couple of pints before the towel went on at 10.30 pm. Besides his obvious bad temper, the fitter brought with him a long stout piece of wire and a spanner; he shut down the water gauge frame, took out the top and bottom waterway plugs and opened the frame again. Scalding water and steam roared ferociously from the plugholes and shot towards the back of the tender. He then stood to one side and poked the rod through the waterways into the boiler whilst the jets of scalding steam and water shot past him. He then shut the frame off again, replaced the plugs and said that it was alright, the waterways were clear, there was absolutely nothing wrong. I then pointed out to him that the gauge glass was not draining as it should, bits of sediment in the glass remained stationary when the blow down cock was opened. His reply to this was that the glass had been changed that very day and he had no intention of pulling it apart again to satisfy a bit of a kid. Fred arrived at this time and unfortunately sided with the fitter. He said that the water gauge had been examined and that I was worrying unduly. I then had to accept what I was told.

After leaving the shed, we stopped the engine clear of the points at Bordesley South signal box ready to reverse into the yard. When the brake was applied to stop here, the boiler water always popped into sight at the top of the gauge glass, this happened however full the boiler was on leaving the shed as the water flowed to the front of the boiler when the engine was braking. The water in the glass did not show on this occasion and I began to get really concerned. When we backed on to our train in the sidings I opened the test cocks again, only to find that the water now only came from the bottom test cock, steam only came from the top cock. I immediately put the injector on, only to be told curtly by Fred not to 'bung' up the boiler for our ascent of Snow Hill tunnel, he did not want the train to stall in the tunnel because the engine was priming.

Fortunately, we left Bordesley with only quite a short train and went into Hockley Yard to make up with further traffic. When we stopped at Hockley I tried the test cocks again, only to find that no water issued from neither of them. We were in fact, very close to the point where the fusible lead plugs fitted to the crown of the firebox would melt. I immediately put both injectors on and whilst Fred was doing the moves to pick up more wagons, I shut off the water gauge again, removed the protector and smashed the gauge glass with a spanner. Fred got downright annoyed with me, he was concerned that whilst I was replacing the gauge glass, if I dropped any parts on the footplate they had a habit of invariably falling through holes in the floor and often could never be found.

In earlier days, Harold Burton had openly encouraged me to replace water gauge glasses if the gland nuts were leaking, or perhaps the glass itself looked thin. White lime scale would bake on to the glass if the nuts were leaking, making the water level difficult to see. Depots should have changed water gauge glasses routinely. Tyseley did this, but at a number of other sheds engines only got a replacement glass when the locomotive went into works for a major overhaul.

A thin gauge glass would be immediately noticeable to enginemen with any length of experience; unfortunately these had a habit of bursting at a most inconvenient time. Over time, the action of the water under pressure eroded the inside of the glass away. I have taken gauge glasses out that had gone wafer thin at the top, how they had stood such great pressure at all was a mystery.

I filled the bucket with cold water and as I dismantled the gauge frame I dropped the parts into the water, these bits were obviously always very hot. When I took out the bottom half of the broken glass the problem came to light. Great Western gauge glasses always had rubber rings as seals; the seals I took out were made of square graphite yarn. The fitter replacing the glass had mistakenly not pushed the glass down on to its seat; the gland nuts had then been over tightened, squeezing the sealing washer under the glass and holding water in the glass, therefore giving a false boiler level reading. As I had done on numerous occasions, I put the new glass in without any trouble, but I did keep the offending parts to show the chargeman fitter when I got back to Tyseley.

The chargeman was pretty angry when I told him of the incident. I feel certain he would have taken the matter up with the man concerned. However, these things usually went no further than that. Higher authority would never have known, although it was quite a serious matter. Had the fusible lead plugs melted, the steam pressure would have been suddenly released into the firebox to smother the heat of the fire; in such circumstances both my driver and I may well have been badly burned. The chargeman fitter did explain that the stores had recently received parts for foreign locomotives that at a later date would perhaps visit the shed. The glass wrongly fitted to our engine was intended for Midland Region engines and was apparently too short for Great Western engines.

Fred and I got into Hockley Yard on the very same job some time after when one of the main steam joints on the boiler started to weep inside the cab. Enginemen always respected joints that fitted directly on to the boiler, as if they did blow out altogether there was no means of shutting them off, and there was a real danger of getting badly scalded. Two of the joints which were prone to blowing out were the main manifold joint, or steam fountain as it was sometimes known, and the ejector box joint. The latter joint was fitted where the driver's brake valve was attached to the boiler and it was this gasket that started to blow on this occasion. Unhappy with our situation, we decided to go back to shed, although it was unlikely that any fitter would attempt to stop this leak whilst the boiler was under pressure.

At Tyseley we dropped into the 'Arcade', a structure built during the war years to shield the light from German bombers when the engine fires were shovelled out. I fetched the examining fitter, who came along with his hammer, this tool he used to tap cotter pins, crankpin washers, etc., to be sure that these fittings were tight. We did always joke that if a fitter came to put a window in, the first thing they threw on the footplate was a hammer! Old Joe Payne climbed the engine steps in his usual unhurried manner, stretched his neck to look at the offending leak, saying, 'Hum, I've seen 'em a lot worse that that'. At which he gave the brake valve the customary tap with the hammer. There was immediately a loud bang and the cab was filled with escaping steam and scalding water. I leapt over the coal on the tender, Fred fell off the steps his side and I never ever saw a fitter move so fast as Joe, he jumped off the other side. Needless to say, we got home very late the following morning! We had to prepare another engine and start again where we had left off.

I soon moved into No. 5 link, undoubtedly the best link at the depot. To add to this my new mate was Bill Ford, with whom I had had my first trip on an express train from Bristol. Bill and I worked together for almost two years and these were probably the happiest days of my working life. He was a great engineman, he was happy go lucky, but never complacent. Whatever the time of day, he was just wonderful to work with, his mood never changed.

Having said that, on two occasions I was present when men who felt Bill was a bit 'half soaked' made remarks that were offensive. Completely out of character, in a flash, he was down the engine steps and ready to spar up with the offenders. On one occasion, the yard inspector in Tyseley Carriage Sidings had loaded us up with so many wagons that our Group 'B' 0-6-0 had no chance of hauling up the gradient out of the sidings. When we set back into the sidings to reduce the train, the inspector remarked that Bill was idle and he hadn't tried. It took three men to hold Bill off this inspector and I was not the only person to be taken completely by surprise by this change of personality.

Anyone could have been forgiven for thinking that Bill was very laid back, yet on the main line he was extremely alert, he misjudged nothing, and in the thickest of fog he knew exactly where he was. Under these conditions, as long as we got line clear and the Automatic Train Control bell kept ringing, we were always on time. At high speeds in inclement weather, I never felt the slightest bit nervous. In my earlier days with him, I would look up from firing, not having the slightest idea where we were, but my life was never in safer hands than those of this extraordinary man.

My new link brought good money and the work was well balanced. The crack job in this link was the Swindon Parcels, a night turn that paid almost double time, taking into account the added mileage payment that we received. On this turn we had the best engines at Tyseley, always one of the newest from Swindon after having a general overhaul. Then again, this train was timed extremely fast. The job involved taking the engine from the depot to Snow Hill, from where we went, via Stratford-upon-Avon, Cheltenham and Stroud, to Swindon, calling at those stations *en route* to load postal traffic. Returning, we stopped nowhere, running to Moor Street, Birmingham, via Didcot, Oxford, Honeybourne and Stratford-upon-Avon. It was extremely rare too, to get stopped by adverse signals at all on this train. On many of the one hundred mile non-stop runs, the speeds achieved would have astonished railway enthusiasts. The super 'Modified Hall' class engines ran like the very devil and their steaming qualities were normally second to none. Bill was really in his element on this turn, I remember roughly timing us from Honeybourne to Stratford East, some eight miles in less than six minutes.

I did, however, have a 'rough trip' on the outward journey one night on this turn. At Swindon we found that the spark arrestor plate in the smokebox had not been refitted properly following boiler washing. The plate was partially fouling the blast pipe exhaust and we both looked like chimney sweeps after refitting it correctly at Swindon, but the good trip home was well worth the effort.

In the summer we worked the Weston-super-Mare trains, again mostly with our own Tyseley engines. We also worked 'The Cornishman' when this train was run in two parts due to heavy loading. Additionally, trains to and from Kingswear, Ilfracombe, and Newquay came into our remit.

The Weston-super-Mare jobs normally went like clockwork; we rarely had any problems, to add to this the coal was usually brought forward on the tender for us by a labourer at Weston, which in itself was a great benefit. The new modified straight-sided tender fitted to our latest modified 'Halls', and some of the other locomotives, was not an asset we would have expected from Swindon. Getting the coal from the back of the tender on these was a difficult job. On the old type tender we aimed to expose the flat plate on the opposite side of the tender to the fire-iron rack. Once this plate was bare of coal, shovelling was easy; it was surprising how much coal could be ladled forward in a short time at a station, or water column. The coal could only be raked forward with the coal peck on the new tenders, that is, until the sloping plate at the very back of the tender could be exposed and this was under quite depth of coal. The new tenders were supposed to be self trimming, but slack Welsh coal would stand almost vertical before it would fall towards the shovelling plate.

The modified tenders did have some benefits, but the new design in general was not well received by enginemen. The extra large tank filler gave surprisingly greater scope when stopping right for water. Running into stations where it was necessary to take water, stopping just right always required a great amount of skill by the driver. Once at a stand, if you had not stopped in the right place, the train could not be moved again as passengers would already be joining, or leaving the train. Waiting for the guard's signal that it was safe to move to take water would then cause delay.

The coal doors on the new type tender opened towards the footplate. This was a great benefit, as on the old tenders the coal doors opened towards the coal. As I said earlier, coal stage coalmen dropped lumps on to tenders weighing several hundredweights, these jammed behind tender doors causing many anxious moments for enginemen. With big engines on express trains, the coal being readily available was vital, any hindrance to supply in the early stages of a journey might well put the fireman in a position that he could not recover. This obviously made unnecessary hard work. On the new tender, firemen tended to stand to one side and

The author working on his 5 inch gauge model locomotive of a Hawksworth '15XX' class 0-6-0PT, 1955. *John Herbert*

The author's nephew, Stephen, and friends have driving turns on my engine in the back garden. *Author*

knock the cross bar holding the doors shut out of its lugs. Expeditious steps to one side were then necessary as huge lumps of coal rolled on to the footplate amongst clouds of dust, but at least they would then be accessible for the use of the coal peck.

The enclosed fire-iron rack on the new tender was also impractical. Only short fire-irons could be stored in it, these capable of only reaching halfway down the length of the firebox. Any longer equipment would need to be threaded through the opened window on the front of the cab on the fireman's side. Once the irons had been used, their temperature made them difficult to handle, restoring them to the rack then became a problem. I might add that not all engines had a fire-iron rack in the fireman's corner at earlier times.

Drivers also complained that the new tender made the cab even more draughty. On the Swindon Parcels turn in winter, I saw drivers come to work clad in so much clothing that they walked as if in a plaster cast. Some resorted to standing in a cardboard box filled with straw to keep their feet warm. When traversing the West Midland Line at night, many times I have seen frost form on the inside of the cab around where my bag and coat were hanging. Whilst the exercise kept the fireman warm, the last thing a driver wanted under these conditions was a swirling draught!

The model steam locomotive that I had started to work on before my military service I now felt was not worth any more effort. Lack of expertise, inadequate machinery and poor workmanship rendered it to gather dust on the shelf. A new set of drawings had now been commercially produced for a Great Western 0-6-0 tank engine in 5 in. gauge. I got the desire to start afresh now that I had more adequate machinery and plenty of reading matter.

A Hawksworth '94XX' class 0-6-0PT No. 9474 crosses from the up main to up relief line near Tyseley on 18th October, 1959. *Michael Mensing*

With these new drawings and the necessary castings purchased I set about doing everything methodically and with great care, reading up on procedures before setting about any tasks that I was uncertain about. Unfortunately, I found that theory and practice were sometimes streets apart. Reaming the wheel centre bores to fit the axles was an instance. I had bought brand new tools and I followed the written method to the letter, yet I was aghast when I looked at the finished holes: instead of being smooth accurate bores, the reamer had chattered and the holes would have been better fitted to a gearbox spline! The books failed to mention that engineering craftsmen preferred to use reamers that were slightly dulled by use; a new reamer would therefore have been slightly burnished to take off the keen edges to prevent the problem that I had encountered. The axles also had to be a press fit into the wheel centres, a thousandth of an inch oversize on the axle and the cast-iron wheels may crack. The same amount too small and the wheels would be loose. To add to this, all the wheels had to be pressed on at exactly 90 degrees to each other, as when the coupling rods were fitted the wheels would not rotate freely. There was absolutely no substitute for experience and I would have given anything for good practical advice. I had earlier joined the Birmingham Society of Model Engineers, but before I got acquainted with anyone the society was forced to move, as their ground was sold for redevelopment. The society then moved out to a site near Earlswood, therefore without transport it became impractical for me to remain a member.

Many parts that I made were scrapped and thrown up the garden in frustration, the use of callipers and micrometers needed a delicate feel, this could only be acquired with hands-on experience. I therefore paid dearly for my experience, in time, blood and very near to tears. It was 10 years before this first locomotive was steamed, another two years was then taken up with modifications, as there were errors on the drawings and the engine would not run efficiently. Determination eventually paid off and it wasn't only the children that got a great deal of pleasure.

My driver Bill Ford fell by the wayside, the doctor at Swindon taking him off main line duties due to high blood pressure. This was not only a great loss of expertise, but for Bill himself to be reduced to shunting duties was a devastating blow. My father and I went to see him in hospital many years later when he was 80 years old. At that time I had never seen anyone so close to death. He miraculously recovered and spent another 10 years of active life, still smiling and always self-dependent. Even at 90 years of age he could still be seen at Cheltenham Races, he was a very remarkable man.

Good fortune was with me again as Harold Burton filled Bill's vacancy and many more enjoyable days at work were to follow. By this time, Harold had got the 'message', that he stood no chance of promotion to a management post. Headquarters men had yet again filled the two vacancies that had occurred for foremen at Tyseley, the old pals' act was as rife as ever. He saw the lie of the land and offered his resignation from the promotion panel. Nevertheless, Harold was still extremely conscientious; he was a Great Western man through and through. He had mellowed and no longer stuck his neck out for other men's work. It seemed that he had now decided to set about feathering his nest for retirement and let those already in management do the managing; this indifference was to put a lot of money our way.

Harold still nurtured every engine; he was often underneath oiling for such long periods that I often got worried and wondered if he was all right. I sometimes walked along the framing to have a look between the boiler and the main frames to check on him. He liked things done properly and one of his little eccentricities was that if we had a good engine and a light train the coal should be burned as it fell.

Firemen, he felt, should save the better lump coal for the more taxing passenger trains at the weekends. I went along with this and night after night on the Swindon Parcels I never shovelled coal forward at Swindon. This could be done, although it did make for extra work raking coal forward with the coal peck whilst running. This method of working did tend to leave a completely empty section at the front of the tender when the engine was put on the shed for coaling. Coalmen, unlike the days when Harold was a fireman, did not bother to break lump coal before they dropped it on the tender. Therefore, the next man that had the engine would find himself digging at boulders of coal several hundredweights in size lying deep in the well of the tender. So this wasn't always a good idea, times had changed.

The principle of taking the coal as it fell backfired badly on me one night. Normally, the trains that we had on the Swindon Parcels return trip averaged 250 tons. The vans contained light produce for Birmingham markets, much of which was flowers, tomatoes and green vegetables from the Channel Islands. When we backed on to the Weymouth portion of the train on this night, this was to be another routine trip home; I could 'eat' this job with the engines that we had allocated to us. The guard eventually gave us the train load and we first felt that he had made an error, 450 tons. This was wishful thinking, we had got a consignment of Jersey Mid new potatoes attached to the rear! I was really caught with my pants down and I paid the price in fluid loss on the way home. The trip, however, was enough for Harold change his views too; I shovelled coal forward at Swindon on future trips!

Harold had an exemplary record and he was always grateful that one day I avoided him from blotting his copybook. We were working a special train for Hereford Races with a mogul and I had previously asked him the details of our diagram. He had told me that we were to stop at all stations to Stourbridge, and then at Kidderminster, Worcester, Great Malvern, Colwall, and Ledbury. We departed from No. 5 & 6 platform at Snow Hill and the signalman at Birmingham North turned us on to the main line. Once over the crossovers, Harold notched up the reverser and opened the regulator more. As we went under Livery Street bridge the Automatic Train Control bell rang for clear signals for Hockley South signal box. Harold had just taken his log book from the cab roof pocket and was making entries when I said to him that I thought that he had told me that we were all stations to Stourbridge? This 'prompt' was sufficient for him to realise that we would be unable to stop at Hockley on the down main line, there was no platform! Suddenly, Harold hadn't got enough hands; he dropped his book and pencil, shut the regulator and applied the brake in a fashion that would have been more fitting in a Laurel and Hardy movie. We stopped at Hockley South home signal, under the Jewellery Quarter tunnels and blew the whistle code to go on to the relief line. Here we were able to make the scheduled stop. He thanked me repeatedly for being alert; yet he rarely slipped up and would no doubt have hated to become the subject of mess room gossip.

There was one driver whose reputation regularly got a going over in the mess room. Firemen normally got to work with most of the drivers at the depot when rostered on 'spare' turns, yet the experience of working with this man in particular had always previously eluded me. I was therefore pretty unhappy when I discovered that my promotion to No. 4 link was to put me alongside him on a regular basis. The promotion ladder had also slowed as I climbed into higher links; therefore it was likely that this man would be my driver for an awfully long time. I hoped for the best, but this man really did drive engines like a fiend; his awful reputation was well justified. The fact that his three previous firemen had thrown in the towel and left the industry wasn't just coincidence.

Promotion to No. 4 link was also something few Tyseley enginemen looked forward to; the link harboured an unprecedented amount of night work. Much of this work was on heavy 'D' headcode freight trains, which ran near to right time, severely cutting any overtime pay. Much of the work also fell just short of the mileage payment margin. In addition to this, the foreign engines that we worked on were the worst that I ever experienced. Night after night we struggled along with heavy, important freight trains, the controllers sent out reports like confetti for lost time, but the root cause of the problem, appalling engines, was never rectified. The situation was absolutely ludicrous.

There must have been any number of locomotives over the Western Region system as a whole which were similar to many Tyseley engines that covered high mileages quickly, on trains having only moderate loads. These engines went in for a general overhaul in far better mechanical condition than of the ones that we were now working with on these heavy 'D' headcode freights. It would only have taken an effective inspectorate to put matters right. Engines thrashed over heavy gradients with maximum loads obviously wore out much more quickly, but because they had not covered the required mileage, they rarely got an overhaul. In the 15 years that I was a fireman, only three times did a locomotive inspector ever ride with me; two of those trains were enthusiast's specials. This in itself was a great tribute to the footplate men who were undoubtedly self-disciplined, but some back up at times from the inspectorate would have been greatly appreciated.

There were never any short apprenticeships for engine drivers; yet in spite of this my latest mate did not apply his trade well. He also had an incessant need to talk, much of which was nonsense, he therefore became more widely known as 'cow mouth'. He was bombastic, every tool that he used he threw back into the toolbox, or just dropped it under his feet. When he took a spanner to any fitting, he was not just content to tighten it, but always put his foot against the tool for extra torque. I was to have many anxious moments when he took spanners to fittings having 200 pounds of steam pressure behind them, brittle brass fittings were well known to sheer off! Fearless, or foolish, he took spanners to parts that artisan staff would have never dared to touch whilst the engine was in steam.

Cliff Rendall began his railway career on the Taff Vale Railway, perhaps it was just loyalty therefore that he seemed intent on keeping at least two South Wales collieries in full production. During World War II he was called to the Railway Section of the Royal Engineers, where he spent the duration around Garloch Head on armoured trains. Although, I feel sure he would have said at some point if he had seen action and the train guns had ever been fired in anger, Cliff's perpetual tales were always such that anyone with the slightest intellect would have readily realised that the stories were untrue. Having said that, his tales were always harmless, never malicious.

Under it all Cliff did have a big heart, he always carried a pocket full of boiled sweets which he distributed to all and sundry, including the many freight guards whose blood sugar level was inclined to drop dramatically when they saw him at the controls.

Cliff always had abounding energy. In the early hours, when many men were nodding by the heat of the fire in relief cabins, he would burst in, slam the door and drop his bag heavily on the table, the tranquillity for everyone was then over. Some of this vigour was to my advantage; he would on a regular basis, scramble on to the tender and shovel coal forward for me. This was never just a token either, he really did put his back in to it, I was very grateful.

The first night we were together we were rostered 'Spare' and we were eventually sent to Banbury to prepare a locomotive and work a train of iron ore from the Ironstone Sidings at Banbury to Steward & Lloyds foundry at Bilston West Midland. We caught the last local train from Tyseley station to Snow Hill, where we boarded the 'Milk' train, which left Birmingham just after midnight. This train ran as a passenger train for the public, having a single brake/third class coach on the rear.

At Banbury shed, luck was with me, we were allocated one of our own engines, a Tyseley 'Grange' class, this engine being in a condition that would have satisfied the most critical. We prepared her and went to the Ironstone Sidings, where we backed on to a heavy train of iron ore. These trains ran totally unbraked, apart from the engine and van brakes, and so ran only at speeds of around 25 mph.

Leaving the yard, Cliff accelerated the train to the point where other drivers would have eased the regulator. Our speed increased further and the rhythmic spitting sound from the vacuum pump quickened. When the ATC bell rang for clear signals at Claydon Crossing we must have reached a speed of 40 mph. I now felt that he must surely shut off steam, as once on the falling gradient towards Fenny Compton we would have no chance of stopping at any adverse signals. The regulator was still open when the bell again sounded for clear signals at Fenny Compton, our speed now far beyond reason for this category of train. In the first few minutes of our journey he had already driven in a way that I had never experienced. I wondered if he really did have some divine preconception of signals that no other driver that I had worked with possessed. All was revealed in the weeks that followed, even the free distribution of sweets failed to smother the look of horror when freight guards saw Cliff at the helm.

The distant signal for Knightcote, and likewise the one for Greaves Cement Sidings could be seen from a long way out. I anxiously looked for these and was relieved to see them showing clear. Southam Road & Harbury signal box was on a slight rise, but I doubt if we could have stopped there should it have become necessary. Cliff had shut off steam after Fenny Compton; nevertheless, the rise towards Harbury was taken purely by the train momentum. Now on the fall again towards Fosse Road, I screwed the tender brake on hard; this made absolutely no effect on the train speed, but it did make the wagons buffer up on to the engine. A clear distant again for Fosse Road and the train speed remained the same to Leamington on the continuing falling gradient. Green signals for Leamington Engine Shed signal box, plus the South and North signal boxes saw the metal wagons clatter over the viaduct; even those in sedated deep slumber would undoubtedly have been roused by our passing.

I eased the tender brake passing through Leamington station and we progressed on to the rising gradient at Avon Bridge, after which the train began to slow. A bank engine for Hatton Bank was not require at Warwick on this day, so with the distant clear Cliff snatched at the regulator. With the long run downhill, I had done as we all usually did; I filled the boiler to the top of the gauge glass to avoid blowing away steam from the safety valves. The whistling sound from the snifting valves, located behind the outside steam pipes on the smokebox, was a sure indicator that the reverser was set towards full forward gear. As one would have expected, this sudden opening of the regulator caused the engine to prime badly, water cascaded from the chimney and spat from every cylinder joint. As the piston glands and cylinder pressure valves oozed water, Cliff just stood there as if this was quite normal. He never even attempted to open the cylinder cocks to drain the excess water away from the cylinders. I was aghast at this complete lack of any finesse;

lumps of fire were propelled from the chimney like an erupting volcano. Drowsy signalmen, otherwise recumbent at this hour, threw open windows and peered out having thoughts of a pending catastrophe. In the deep cutting at Hatton North Junction fire shot feet into the air, I am now quite convinced that what the Neil Armstrong brought home at a later date was not altogether moon dust! In total disbelief, I put my head over the side and burst out laughing. However, this was the last time that I was ever amused by this extraordinary driving technique, this man was to drive me to the point of resignation many times.

Working with a man like this on the type of work that we encountered in No. 4 link bordered on slavery. There was also the continual disadvantage that you never got a head start, as you could not carry the water level in the boiler very high, ham-fisted regulator openings invariable causing the locomotive to prime. Not being able to have a decent start with poorly maintained engines was to become a real problem.

I also soon learned that Cliff had an almost infantile like sense of humour; he would suddenly open the regulator wide, wind the reverser into full gear, open the cylinder drains and simultaneously blow the whistle, sending livestock in fields into a frenzy. Animals stampeded and charged against gates and barbed wire fencing. His success rate was total, yet triumphant frequency never diminished his desire of this obscene pleasure, he would hold his groins and go into tucks of laughter every time.

I became saddled with this man for two years, in which time he never took the tea can to make tea, which he insisted was the fireman's job. When it was made, no matter how busy I was with my work, he would sit with his cup in his hand till I poured it. I tried the 'battle of wits', by letting the tea stew on the dish over the firehole without the milk in it, I always lost, he made sure my need for a drink was always greater than his. His strange diet too is worth a mention: every single day, without any exception, he came to work with a fried egg between two doorsteps of dry bread, this appetisingly wrapped in several sheets of the *Daily Sketch*.

No. 4 link mostly plied the London routes and we worked to and from Reading on a regular basis. In the summer we worked passenger trains to Basinstoke, these being trains for the resorts on the south coast. We also worked in and out of Paddington.

It was on a Basingstoke turn that one day I cleared a modified tender of all its coal; fortunately we had a Tyseley engine which was in first class condition. No. 6904 *Charfield Hall* had recently been in Swindon works for a general overhaul, she had also been fitted with modified draughting. This meant that the chimney blast pipe orifice had been reduced in size and the ' jumper top', fitted by the Great Western to make locomotives more economical, had been removed. This was done to accommodate the poorer quality coal that by this time was becoming common.

We left Birmingham with some good quality quick burning hard coal, much of which was distributed out of the chimney over Warwickshire, Oxfordshire and Berkshire. By the time I detached the engine at Basingstoke to go on the depot to turn, there was already considerably less weight on the tender springs.

Our return working was a day excursion from Portsmouth and Southsea, going forward to Stratford-upon-Avon. Our stops were Oxford, then virtually all stations to Stratford. This meant stopping at any number of stations with short platforms, Kidlington, Bletchington, Heyford, Fritwell & Somerton, Aynho, Kings Sutton, Cropredy, Fenny Compton and Southam Road & Harbury. From Leamington we also stopped at Warwick, Hatton, Claverdon, Bearley and Wilmcote. This took an interminable amount of time, drawing forward to get the rear coaches on the platform each time, sometimes twice at the shortest stations. Each time we started away, sparks shot high in the air. It was dark when we stopped at Leamington and the firelight from the ashpan could still be seen reflecting on the ground. Normally, the amount of coal that had been burned, the fire would have been well clinkered and any glow on the floor long gone. On this occasion, most of the clinker had been thrown out of the chimney or had dropped into the ashpan with Cliff's satanic style of driving.

Our eventual arrival at Stratford-upon-Avon was very late due to the long delays at the small stations. The shunter had therefore gone home, as he had already been on duty many hours. Arrangements were then made for us to take the train to Honeybourne, where we detached, ran round the triangle to turn the engine, and then brought the train back to Tyseley Carriage Sidings. The chimney resembled a Roman Candle going up Stratford Bank and the long rise to Earlswood was taken in similar fashion. Approaching Wood End I put the last shovelful of coal on the fire, I touched Cliff on the arm and pointed to the tender amid the furore. This was the only time I ever saw him ease off and drive anything like reasonably. I then swept up, swilled down, and sat down. The feeling was unique and really most weird. Fortunately there was enough in the firebox to see us dispose of the train in Tyseley Carriage Sidings and leave the engine on the shed.

My thoughts, along with many of my close friends were already on the future driver's examination. This had to be taken at Swindon with an interview with the chief locomotive inspector. I had always been a member of the Mutual Improvement Class, but interest in general by many others had faded, more or less due to the conditions that we encountered. Any study of the subject had to be done on one's own initiative, although the Great Western management had provided an old clerestory-roofed coach body as a classroom, this was positioned outside the front of the goods side engine shed. This classroom was hardly inviting, particularly in winter when the brake van type stove installed in it had to be lit. The coach would barely be warm by the time the lesson was finished. Many older hand drivers gave their time freely in the interest of tutoring others, for which we were always very grateful. If you wanted to become a driver, then it was up to the individual to learn, management provided no tuition. Yet the examination was indeed very comprehensive, the potential driver had to be able to trace the passage of steam into the cylinders and know which steam ports would be open, or closed, in any position that the driving wheel crank was set. When the inspector said the big end was in a certain position, the examinee had to say the valve positions off the top of his head. By knowing this, a driver could accurately test a locomotive for defects. It was unlikely that we could have made any major repairs when out on the line; the tools carried by engines were too basic. Nevertheless, we had to know how to do it. Then again, there were the complex rules and regulations books, which had to be fully understood.

In the first instance, a number of my friends got together and we arranged Sunday afternoons for an improvement class. The venue was anyone's home that had room enough for a collection of eight to ten young men. A number of wives and parents were initially most accommodating, but after a time we all regularly rallied at Dick Potts' parents' home. Dick had the most wonderful parents, who abandoned their sitting room for the kitchen time and time again to accommodate us. Added to this, Mrs Potts baked cakes and made tea by the gallon, eventually we would have indeed been loath to have gone to any other venue. Young drivers, Howard and Dave Jones, Ceri Evans and others kindly gave their time in our interest. Often the subject would stray to other interests, women, or sometimes music. These 'social' occasions introduced me to classical music, Dick having a Hi-fi with speakers as big as a sideboard. The volume rammed home the beauty of Wagner's 'Rhine Journey' and many of the works of Richard Strauss, a composer whose music now haunts me.

Driver Ceri Evans, worked for the benefit of others. He eventually became traction inspector at Derby once the playing field was level. *Author*

A footplate view of driver Bill Timmis and fireman Dick Potts, they worked the final 'Star' class trip together. *Dick Potts Collection*

I turned up regularly for work each day, inwardly hoping that Cliff would either be late, or go sick. He did neither of these and I shovelled coal daily like a lunatic, yet the overtime rewards now came only in minutes, rather than hours.

Ironically, the British Transport Commission had just released educational films aimed at firemen. Scientifically managing the fire and proper use of the dampers would reduce fuel costs we were informed. The films showed a fireman sprinkling coal on the fire and watching the colour of the smoke from the chimney. The aim was to keep a light grey smoke haze emitting from the chimney for total efficiency. Ironically, once a driver was promoted, no one ever questioned his mode of driving, not even locomotive inspectors. Men who drove locomotives in the same manner as Cliff could waste more coal in a single journey than any fireman could save in a lifetime of careful management of the fire. When shown these films, firemen reacted to them rather like a 'Tom and Jerry' cartoon!

One of our turns was the 2.30 am Bordesley Junction to Banbury, a slow 'H' headcode freight. We disposed of the engine on Banbury shed and returned with the Westbury to Oxley Sidings 'D' headcode. Signing on at 1 am was classed as a day turn, the week previous we were on afternoons, going home after midnight, the following week we were on nights. Any social activity was therefore non-existent for three weeks.

On this turn, I usually got to Banbury with drooping eyes, once in the relief cabin Cliff came to life, particularly if there was anything like an audience. His incessant drivel was mind blowing. Our return train arrived regularly at Banbury around 8.30, by which time I usually felt like death warmed up. The train was invariably headed by a mogul, which in itself was getting more tired than myself. Whilst the Westbury engines on this diagram were very well maintained, the fire by now would be heavily clinkered, the coal well back in the tender and the train heavy, in fact just the right scenario for any firemen to have the proverbial 'rough trip'. We regularly followed the 8.30 am express from Banbury; in this path it was normal to have a good run.

When the express had gone and the signals cleared, I would shut the firehole flap and over would go the regulator. If the previous fireman had filled the boiler to any extent, we usually left with the normal cascade of filthy water issuing from the chimney. Cliff never got tuned to any engine priming, even when the sooty water on the window in front of him marred his vision, he still took no evasive action.

My first move would be to thread the long pricker over the firehole flap and feel about at the front of the firebox. The fire was usually thick and sticky with molten clinker. After a few minutes I would repeat this procedure. It may take a third time, when the fire-iron would be almost melting at the end, but I knew that the fire would soon begin to break up under the brick arch by the action of the heavy blast. With the fire lifting off the firebars at the front of the firebox, I then just had to ladle shovelfuls of coal just inside the firehole. Each time I did this, shutting the flap between every shovelful, there was a pall of dark smoke from the chimney. The pressure gauge needle would then come on to the red line and Cliff never beat me. It was indeed far easier doing this than feeding the front end of a long firebox on a big engine.

The following week we signed on at 6.56 pm for what we termed the Reading Biscuits. With Cliff, this turn became nightmare. The job involved travelling to Snow Hill and relieving the 8.08 pm express to Paddington. This train would follow the 8.00 pm express which went via Bicester, our train would go via Reading. We worked this train to Oxford, where we rode 'as passenger' in our own train to Reading. This ride in the train was the only break we had, if the train was full it meant riding in the brake van and sitting on any available suitcase or crate. Sometimes, if the kettle was cold in the relief cabin at Oxford, we never got a drink till we got to Reading shed. At Reading Cliff always insisted on walking through the town to the loco depot. This was a longer way round rather than down the line, therefore by the time we got to the shed, checked that all the tools were on the engine, which was prepared for us, it was time to go off shed.

The 'Biscuits' loaded from Reading West Yard and was a 'D' headcode freight. In the early days the train loaded with Huntley and Palmers biscuits; hence this description always remained with the train. By this time, however, the train carried any kind of traffic and never left the yard with less than the maximum load of 67 wagons in length.

We had big engines on the up express to Oxford, 'Halls', 'Castles', and also 'Counties', Cliff thrashed these unmercifully. Our return engine was generally a Reading 'Hall' class; these engines were as decrepit as any Great Western locomotive ever became. No. 5936 *Oakley Hall* was one, she was terribly steam shy. Another was No. 4961 *Pyrland Hall*; she was just as steam shy and had so much side play in her main axleboxes that she waddled along the track like a pregnant walrus. The whole cab on this engine was actually lop-sided; she was in a dreadful state.

Every night we put off traffic at Banbury Junction for the former Great Central line, making up with further wagons for Birmingham and the North. By the time we arrived there I was soaked to the skin with sweat, medical evidence assures us that getting cold after sweating will not bring on the common cold. However, when we made movements in Banbury Junction sidings, the shunter's signals were on the fireman's side. The wind whipped across open country and I regularly found myself shivering. In winter, I always had to take an overcoat to work on this turn, purely to put on at Banbury Junction. Even with this precaution and the supposed medical evidence, I always caught a dreadful cold, ending the week feeling like death.

Invariably we had to top up the tender water at Banbury Junction yard. The heavy-handed way that Cliff drove any engine meant that when I dropped the water scoop passing over Aynho troughs to fill the tender the boiler level was always getting low. It was only a short distance from there to Banbury Junction, but during this time the injector had to be working all the time. Consequently, by the time we stopped at the water column, and allowed the boiler to fill, a lot of the water we collected over Aynho troughs would already have been consumed. We had to leave

Banbury with as much water as possible as we could not take a chance of reaching the next troughs at Rowington with a low tank. If the tender was low it lifted high on its springs and if you happened to follow immediately behind a train that had taken water from the troughs the water level in the troughs would also be low. These two combinations could make it that you were unable to get water at all. It does seem inconceivable, but with his previous fireman on this turn, Cliff had run out of water before reaching Aynho troughs after leaving Reading shed with a full tank and passing over Goring troughs. With the boiler empty too, the fusible plugs melted in the firebox and they came to a halt standing over the water troughs.

One night we stopped at Banbury Junction next to an Eastern Region man on a 'B1' class locomotive. He was sat comfortably on his bucket seat blowing off his cigarette as he looked out from his homely cab. I took the wet slimy leather column bag out of our tank, dragged it over the coal and let it go. The wet bag inadvertently swung towards the 'B1' and accidentally hit the driver full in the face, knocking his cigarette into a puddle on the floor. I was in no state to apologise, because I couldn't stop laughing! I just had to look the other way as if I had not noticed; I hadn't laughed for months at work, so this minor incident lightened the day.

We arrived at Reading shed one night to find a strange engine allocated to the job, a 'Hall' class looking in half decent condition. We left Reading Yard with the usual sparks flying, yet I began to cope wonderfully. I skimmed the water troughs at Goring and we went round Didcot East Curve with the feather flying from the safety valves. She began to blow off steam passing Culham station which was a blunder on my part. Cliff was not going to let steam go to waste, so he knocked the catch out of the reverser and wound it down even further towards full gear. The pyrotechnics from the chimney were spectacular, as was the continuous thunderous noise. From there on I desperately struggled to maintain things on my side. At Banbury Junction we were in a worse state than ever before, the boiler water barely showing in the bottom of the gauge glass.

From Banbury things got no better, whilst we never had to stop anywhere for a 'blow up', we again arrived at Tyseley Carriage Sidings, where the train terminated, very late and in a total mess. I had struggled to get steam all the way. Feeling that something must have gone wrong mechanically with the engine, I opened the smokebox to try to find an explanation as to what had gone wrong. It seems that Cliff had dislodged the spark arrestor plate when he lengthened the valve travel even more when we passed Culham. The plate was now lying in the bottom of the smokebox, partially covering the blast pipe nozzle. Had this plate fallen in a more drastic position, covering more of the blast pipe, then both Cliff and I may well have been burned to death by the fire being immediately blown back out of the firehole. We were two very lucky people. Ironically, we could have put the matter right at Banbury Junction.

I had some respite from Cliff for one week when we were 'Spare'. I was diagrammed to work the 9.25 am Bordesley to Swindon, 'F' headcode freight with another driver. Backing on to our train at Bordesley our cab stopped opposite the cab of the shunting engine. The interior of the shunting engine was nicely cleaned down, the windows spotless, the floor swept and the dust laid. The young fireman was under the wing of my old mate Bert Brown, a stickler for having things done right. Seeing me, he immediately came over to talk, saying, 'I'm told you are on the 10.10 am Margate on Saturday, Herbert?' Indeed I was, however, could I forget the prospects of yet another wet shirt! With a twinkle in his eyes, he remarked, 'I'm going on my holidays, let's have you right time, no blowing off, or black smoke, I shall be in the train'. His banter brought some amusement, but I knew there would be little chance of any scientific firing, or blowing away steam.

On the following Saturday morning our engine was an unknown quantity to us; she was a 'foreign' 'Hall', dirty but otherwise looked well maintained. The preparation crew had done a fine job for us, the fire was well made up and extra coal had been tipped on to the tender at the coal stage, perhaps whoever did the job realised who the driver was!

We left the depot tender first and took the locomotive to Queens Head Sidings, north of Birmingham. In the sidings we backed on to 10 Southern Region coaches of 'buckeye' stock. These coaches had only just started to infiltrate the area and guards and shunters were being sent for training on the coupling procedure of these vehicles, often using the stock stabled in these sidings for their tuition.

After the shunter had coupled, I screwed the tender brake on and Cliff tried the vacuum for leaks. This being satisfactory the carriage and wagon examiner left us to await the arrival of our guard. I utilised this time to take out the firehole deflector plate, or smoke plate as we called it, and rolled more medium sized lumps of coal into the firebox, only putting the smoke plate back when there was no more room in the firebox. Determined to have a good start, I then heaped well-broken coal high behind the tender toolboxes and gave it a good watering.

Our guard arrived and gave my driver the tonnage, about 330 tons. I watched him climb into the first coach and released the tender brake. As Cliff re-created the vacuum we immediately started to move on the steep falling gradient. After moving just a few yards the vacuum went to zero and we came to an abrupt stand. In seconds, the guard was out of the train and hurrying back towards the engine. The train had in fact come apart in the middle, damaging the vacuum pipes and electrical connections.

I immediately went to alert the carriage and wagon examiner and as I entered his cabin he was just dropping his egg into the bacon fat for his breakfast. He went ballistic, as he had deliberately waited while we checked the vacuum before starting to cook his meal. Obviously, the coaches had been used for the training of shunters and guards on 'buckeye' couplings during the week. Unfortunately, they had not been re-coupled correctly. The carriage and wagon examiner now took on a bloody-minded attitude and it was some time before he emerged with new vacuum pipes. We finally left the sidings 30 minutes late after repairs had been carried out.

Running up No. 7 platform at Birmingham Snow Hill there was a sea of faces, rather like 'Spion Cop' at St Andrews on a Saturday afternoon. However, I spotted Bert Brown with his wife and suitcases. He looked my way, held his nose and made a gesture similar to flushing a toilet chain. I got the message, we were down the proverbial pan.

Leaving Birmingham, Cliff drove like someone possessed, doing irreparable damage to the ozone layer. It was common for folk to stop to watch steam trains go by, this day people froze to the spot, standing agog as we passed. Infants covered sensitive ears, initial delight turning to fright, then tears. The noise from the chimney was again thunderous. Fortunately our charge proved to be a good engine, initially I managed to keep pace with him, but I was soon paying dearly in calories. For all this thrashing of the engine, we barely made a dent on the timetable; a couple of turns on the reversing screw would have seen this fine locomotive go wild with excitement. Cliff never obliged, it was like rather like driving a performance car without using the higher gears.

We stormed up from Aynho Junction into the tunnel at Ardley, lumps of fire ricocheting off the tunnel walls like tracer shells. Out of the tunnel into the deep chalk cutting, through the station, where the American Airbase at Heyford went on to red alert. He was now beginning to beat me, each time I charged the fire I had to go back in the tender to rake more coal forward. Clouds of coal dust now made me look like a miner, Cliff too was catching the slipstream, he too also had the mascara look around his eyes.

The ATC siren screamed at Ashendon Junction distant signal and Cliff slammed the regulator shut with his usual indelicacy. With the injector still on and all the signals in sight from the driver's side, I went into the tender, raking coal forward like fury. This few minutes with the regulator shut was my saviour, drifting towards the home signal I managed to gain on the boiler water level and get some of the bigger lumps of coal from the back of the tender. As we almost came to a stand the signals cleared, over went the regulator again; I had hardly straightened my back.

We eventually took a right-hand turn from the main line at North Acton and came to a stand adjacent to the Underground station. Here fitters were waiting to jack up the ATC shoe to clear electrified lines, we also had relief. I was now wringing wet with sweat and resembled a chimney sweep. With no time to wash, there was no alternative than for me to me join the next tube train full with Saturday shoppers in this wretched embarrassing state.

Alighting at Lancaster Gate, we walked to Paddington, arriving on the station concourse at six minutes to two. Our return working was the 2.10 pm departure to Wolverhampton.

I went to the relief cabin to make a drink, simultaneously downing several cupfuls of hard London water. Cliff made our presence known to the train arranger. Tea can in hand, we walked up our train on No. 4 platform. I began to count the coaches: 14, including the normal 12-wheeled dining and kitchen cars. In addition there were another two 12-wheeled dining and kitchen cars being returned to Wolverhampton empty next to the engine, our total tonnage, 498 tons. I was gutted, what an introduction to my first trip on a 'King'!

No. 6006 *King George I* was simmering well from the safety valves, she was beautifully clean and her brass work shone, we also had the usual audience of enthusiasts. I suppose I should have felt some pride, but I was so anxious at the performance that I knew would follow that this proud moment completely passed me by.

Two 'Kings' at Cannock Road Sidings. No. 6006 *King George I*, my first 'King', seen here next to the 'Inter City', another Tyseley turn; she burned coal at a horrifying rate.

*Dick Potts*

Before I had drunk my second cup of tea, the 'Right Away' indicator lit and I passed the signal to depart on to Cliff. With gritted teeth, he made a grab at the regulator, seemingly determined to make the most spectacular departure since broad gauge days. Ear shattering exhaust beats erupted from the chimney, in little more than one revolution of the driving wheels the four cylinders filled with water. The noise was deafening as filthy water shot feet into the air from the chimney, cascading down on the whole station and obliterating any forward vision from the locomotive windows. The fire turned immediately white with super draught, I dropped the firehole flap in an effort to reduce the turbulence of the water in the boiler. Completely oblivious of the furore of his own making, Cliff casually took his logbook from his pocket; put on his ex-military wire rimmed spectacles and made entries of our departure on time.

With this engineering masterpiece under ultimate torture, I waited with baited breath for sounds that would have indicated that a cylinder cover had blown off, or a connecting rod had bent. With water spitting and oozing from pressure valves and glands, this engine exceeded far more tolerance than any designer could have anticipated. My colleague John Millman and his driver were at the time riding home in our train, he said it sounded as though the train was going through a violent hail storm ... and they were seven coaches back from the engine! We thrashed past Ranelagh Bridge engine sidings, water still issuing from the chimney; here elite enginemen from South Wales and the West of England looked on aghast from elegant 'Castles' and polished 'Britannias'.

Much of the trip home remains blank in my memory. I only put down the shovel to drop the water scoop and operate the injectors. She burned coal at a horrifying rate, mostly from the front end of the firebox. This meant pitching the coal some 11 feet against the natural draught from the exhaust to get it under the firebrick arch. I shovelled coal, uphill and downhill, in an effort to get ahead of this moronic driving, passing points only just registering on my mind; again I barely straightened my back.

It was a warm summer's afternoon and I must have started to dehydrate, as passing Bentley Heath Crossing my legs went weak under me, I also had had nothing to eat since breakfast. I held on to the side of the cab and sat down, I was totally exhausted. At that time I could not have put another shovelful of coal on the fire; fortunately the easier gradient and Cliff eventually shutting off steam for the approach to Birmingham gave me respite. Adverse signals at Bordesley North signal box brought us almost to a stand; I somehow found enough energy to give the fire another charge for the climb into Snow Hill tunnel. Our arrival, exactly on time, yet we were grossly overloaded for the train timing.

Stopped in No. 5 platform, Cliff got down from the engine and strode off to catch an imminent local passenger train back to Tyseley. I made no attempt to keep up with him as he disappeared down the subway. In the subway, hardly able to put one foot in front of the other I took a left-hand turn towards the passenger guard's cabin. This band of elite men were never very accommodating, particularly towards dirty firemen, but there was just a single person inside the room and I asked if I might have a wash as there was nowhere else to go. The guard said it looked as though I needed a drink and he was happy to share his brew with me whilst I had a sandwich. Regaining myself, I later caught a local train to the shed; Cliff had signed me off duty when he had gone home.

I had cycled to work that day, but I had to push the machine home as I was unable get on it. I was off duty on the following Sunday, but I despaired at the thought of the week to come, the Oxley-Bristol, another heavy 'D' headcode freight, returning from Gloucester with the Landore-Moor Street. I knew it would be another agonising week.

The Oxley Sidings-Bristol left Tyseley station just after midnight and this train rarely arrived with less than the maximum 67 wagons in length, again giving Cliff plenty of scope to do the maximum possible amount of environmental damage. On Monday night we signed on, walked to the station and relieved Wolverhampton men.

Wolverhampton depot had a cross section of enginemen who were no different to the men of other depots. Fortunately, the men that we relieved were good and I never had anything to complain about. Regrettably, a number of my colleagues apparently often found things differently, the Wolverhampton men arrived for them with the fire low, the tender untrimmed and the footplate in a filthy state. Apparently, there were odd men at that depot who thought it beyond their dignity to prepare an engine, bring the train 15 miles, picking up wagons at several yards on the way, and then hand the train over to Tyseley men to work to Gloucester. There were some occasions therefore, that Tyseley crews did find it necessary to wait at Tyseley to put things right before departure. It was a severe pull on to the North Warwick Line with a sweeping right-hand curve and it was very heavy going to Earlswood with these trains.

Leaving just after midnight the local passenger service had ended and all the other fast freights would also have left, these included the 'D' headcode Oxley-Westbury and the Oxley-Tavistock Jn 'C' headcode. On the Bristol most drivers therefore made little attempt to reach Earlswood in the diagrammed 17 minutes, knowing that only slow freights were likely to be behind them. On the downhill run to Stratford they were able to recover any amount of time if necessary. The speeds that some wagons of 10 ft wheelbase were inclined to travel over this stretch of line made the 45 mph speed restriction imposed on them in later years look totally farcical.

Cliff had not got around to thinking the way of many other drivers. Every night we left Tyseley with our chimney erupting fire, fertilising all the surrounding suburban gardens and later the fields with potash. At Gloucester, with my usual wet shirt, we walked from the South Junction to the Central station, a walk of perhaps 25 minutes around the road, a route that Cliff again insisted on.

Our return train was another 'D' headcode freight, the Landore to Moor Street. It was common that when we arrived at the Gloucester South Junction the signalman gave the wire for our return train to be turned out from Over Junction into Gloucester Central station. Therefore our return working would just be arriving into the station at the same time as we did on foot. Nevertheless, we did stop to have a quick drink and a sandwich, even if the supervisor's trap door did keep continually opening to see if we were still there, he was always like a cat on hot bricks until we had gone.

Apparently, the commercial department had strived to get a lucrative contract for some of the traffic conveyed on the Landore-Moor Street. This was steel plate for a pressed steel company, Fishers and Ludlow in Birmingham and was supposed to be at Moor Street ready for unloading at a specified time. The controllers were therefore always eager for this train to run on time.

South Wales never suffered the labour shortages of other areas, indeed many men moved from that area to get work in industrial districts elsewhere. It seems strange therefore that the locomotives which worked the Landore-Moor Street were without question the worst-maintained engines that many of us ever worked on. The engines we had on the Reading Biscuits were bad, but they did receive basic maintenance, they were just worn out. However, whenever I saw 87E on a smokebox door, my heart fell. The cabs were unkempt; water gauge glasses were often thin, leaking and covered with lime scale. Joints and glands blew and the engines were just generally uncared for. Many times, after struggling home short of steam, I would kneel on a patch of cotton waste at Moor Street and look up at the boiler tube plate. Invariably the tubes were corked over; some had more 'plaster' on them than the ceiling of the Sistine Chapel. The last few miles up the bank from Stratford became a nightmare; we regularly booked repairs, together with the need for blocked boiler tubes to be cleared. Yet no one could blame Tyseley fitters for sending these engines back to their home depot for what should have been basic maintenance. Consequently, two or three days later we would get on the same engine in the same sorry state. The control kept sending out reports to drivers for time lost, and so the circle went on, it never changed.

At one point I missed the Oxley-Bristol as I was on annual leave. The fireman who happened to deputise for me was taken completely by surprise at Cliff's style of driving on the first night. At Gloucester they relieved the Landore-Moor Street; it was unusual, but at the head of the train was a mogul. Short of steam and boiler water, the first stop was at the foot of the Cotswolds at Bishop's Cleeve. Here, Cliff offered his exasperated fireman a cellophane wrapped consolation from his pocket. Snapping back at Cliff, he told him in no uncertain terms that he could stick his sweets up his arse. With the rest of the week to go, I would have loved to have been the proverbial 'fly on the wall'.

For the whole two years that I was with Cliff he never beat me. I continually struggled and became exhausted time and time again, but we never actually had to stop out of course to raise steam at any time. The irony of this is that with Cliff on holiday, I was rostered with driver Stan Selway, a clean, soft-spoken engineman, who was just another great credit to the Great Western and a total deviation from my regular driver. On Monday evening we worked the express to Oxford; this was a textbook trip that one could read about constantly in books by ex-footplatemen who never appeared to have had any bad times.

At Reading shed, I was surprised to see a Wolverhampton engine rostered to us. No. 6975 *Capesthorne Hall* appeared in fine condition, black paint could still be detected under a light film of dirt on the driving wheels. I could hardly believe my luck. We left the shed bound for the yard, the train now departed from Reading Up Sidings, which meant crossing the four main running lines via the ladder crossing at Scours Lane signal box. Over this extended crossing she rode in almost silence, it was indeed too good to be true.

Leaving the yard with the usual 'full digger' it was soon quite apparent that all was not well with this engine. She wasn't making steam anything like one would have expected for one of these incredible 'Modified Halls'. I took the long pricker and felt about at the front of the firebox; all appear well with the fire. This brought no response and very reluctantly I put the blower on a turn. Even so, things gradually got worse. Approaching Bletchington, Banbury side of Oxford, Stan closed the regulator and allowed the train to drift towards the signal box. I was gutted; it was the first time this had happened to me since my early days with Jack Payne. With the regulator shut the engine made steam rapidly, we stopped at the signalbox with the boiler half full and both injectors running. Six minutes delay and we were away again, with my driver's co-operation we never had to stop again, but we were always in trouble.

At Tyseley, Stan and I examined the engine; there was obviously a problem somewhere. Nothing at all was visible and why she failed to steam remained a mystery.

The following week I got into conversation with driver Bert Watkins, who the previous week had been working out of Paddington. He had worked the 6.08 pm from Paddington; this train ran was a relief to the main train which departed at 6.11 pm. The 6.08 ran first stop Leamington and the main train stopped at Bicester, Banbury and Leamington.

Crossing the concourse at Paddington, Bert had met up with his neighbours, apparently the gentleman had just retired and they had been on the holiday of a lifetime. They had just come across Europe on what was known as the 'Blue Train', which I understand had started from Istanbul and had ran exactly on time to Calais. These people had then crossed the channel and caught the boat train, which had also arrived in Victoria station dead on time. The neighbour's holiday itinerary then told them to catch the 6.11 pm departure, Bert then quite rightly advised them to catch his train, it would be in Birmingham 20 minutes before the later 6.11 pm train.

Bert left Paddington and his fireman soon got into difficulties and they found it necessary to stop at Gerrards Cross for the proverbial 'blow up'. Whilst stopped on the middle line at Gerrards Cross, the signalman reversed the signals and put the 6.11 pm through the platform line in front of the 6.08 train. Eventually arriving in Snow Hill nearly 40 minutes late was hardly a thing Bert was ever likely to live down with his neighbours.

I asked Bert what engine he had had on that evening, '69-er 69-er', he said, then got out his log book, put on his glasses, '6975', he remarked. The same engine as we had a few days earlier on the 'Biscuits', so I did feel some consolation. There was obviously a serious problem with this engine, a difficulty that did from time to time manifest itself with the 'Modified Halls'. When sufficient complaints had been made, the mechanical staff would eventually put this fault right, but I would have been interested to know what this problem was as there was never any visible reason as to why the engines wouldn't steam. Normally this class of engine was an absolute champion of Swindon design and engineering. It was most likely a smokebox problem, perhaps the blast pipe being out of alignment.

At one time No. 1 link men limped about having this steaming problem with No. 7912 *Little Linford Hall* when working the Cardiff service. She was the latest Tyseley engine from Swindon works, but for some days she crawled between stations with only six or eight coaches on continually short of steam. No. 7908 *Henshall Hall* also developed this problem for a time. I also had a dreadful trip with No. 7910 *Hown Hall*, on an Earls Court Motor Show special with Reg Grafton. Had it not been for his fine enginemanship we would have no doubt had to stop *en route* to raise steam. We were diagrammed to leave Snow Hill at 8.55 am non-stop to London, just in front of the 9.00 departure to the same destination. We did manage to keep going, but only arrived just in time to clear for the train behind us that had stopped at Leamington, Banbury and Bicester. We were supposed to work back home with the same engine, but Reg refused to take her back. We were then given another engine that had arrived on a train from the West of England. This engine had a very dirty fire, so we didn't have the best of trips home either. What should have been a lovely day's work with a good mate, turned out quite miserable, but that was footplate work, there were never two days alike.

After two years Cliff was promoted to No. 3 link. He had often worked me to the point of desperation and total exhaustion, but I held my counsel and we never had a miss word. He was basically a nice fellow, he was never malicious and so all in all there was nothing to be gained by us being at loggerheads on the footplate. Cliff drove engines the only way that he knew how, this became obvious. I listened to him telling his tales in mess rooms and he often said that he only ever used what steam was necessary ... but he could have fooled me!

Promotion for firemen was now coming to a standstill as diesel multiple units (dmus) began to arrive to replace the prairie tanks that worked the local passenger services. The early type Inter-City and Cross Country multiple units also began to appear. These

The first dmu on training runs seen at Snow Hill on 17th May, 1957.

trains would replace the Hereford and Cardiff steam services; therefore a number of No. 1 link firemen and all 24 No. 2 link firemen would now not be necessary.

Thinking that the writing was already on the wall, many more good men left the job, some with many years of footplate experience. Quite a number went to the rapidly expanding Bird's Custard Factory where security and better wages were already on offer. From this time on all the work in the links was continually juggled about, basically promotion stood still for firemen as dieselisation took hold.

There had been an earlier attempt to replace the Tyseley GW prairie tanks on the local passenger services, that was when the depot was allocated the first 10 BR Standard '82XXX' class 2-6-2Ts, but these failed miserably to cope, particularly over the Stourbridge Extension Line. They were met unfavourably by Western engineman too, who expected better from Swindon works. Design, rather than poor workmanship made everything tight and stiff to operate on these engines. Elderly drivers now had to yank and tug at things, also they had to open valves by hitting them with a spanner, things that they had previously done easily with one hand on Great Western engines. Probably, the bad language alone bestowed on these Standard machines was enough to give management second thoughts.

I worked on one of the '82XXX' class one day with driver Reg King. He was a small frail man struggling with failing health. Stopping at all stations for eight hours, the poor man yanked, tugged and wound the mangle type reverser until he was totally exhausted. Sick to death of hitting his hands on adjacent pipes and fittings, halfway through the day, he just left the regulator open and stopped at the stations by applying the brake. With the tip to start, he just closed the brake valve and away we went. Hardly the way any mechanical engineer would have expected his engines to be driven, but even at this late stage designers seemed totally detached from what certain locomotives were expected to do.

The Standard engines lasted only nine months at the depot. Some of the replacement engines were the ex-GW '61XX' class, having a higher boiler pressure than the '41XX' class, these were super engines for the work.

This photograph was taken during a Tyseley Drivers' and Firemen's Improvement Class outing to Swindon works in 1951. Little did we know that the first 10 BR Standard class '4' tank engines would come to Tyseley. *Provenance Unknown*

My next driver was Mickey Tolley, I regret that he was only a marginal improvement on Cliff. Mick drove everywhere so fast that he frightened me … and himself! Past experience had brought many, many, fast runs on the Swindon Parcels, but Mick now took speed to new dimensions. We went so fast that the engines would seemingly pass a sound and vibration barrier, they would then appear to float on the rails without actually touching them, it was quite uncanny. On the 8.08 pm Snow Hill to Paddington one night we had No. 7915 *Mere Hall*, a Wolverhampton engine in new condition. We left on time with over 350 tons in weight behind us and stopped in the platform at Leamington at 8.31 pm, 24 miles in 23 minutes. I regret now that I never accurately logged some of these extraordinary runs with Mick, but I never really had time!

Mickey was a small wiry man, my five feet seven inches allowing me easily to look down at the top of his soft cap when we were standing. He was probably of the minimum height allowed for footplate work when he started, and then had lost an inch or so towards old age. Mick had eyes like a possum, making him look as though he was permanently startled, he told whoppers, big whoppers. Then again, like Cliff, these exaggerated fantasies were just ego trips, they did harm to no one. My new mate was excitable: if things didn't go his way, or anything went wrong, he would throw his arms around like an over enthusiastic majorette. He moved with impromptu jerks, rather like a blackbird looking for worms on a wet garden lawn. Sudden moves across the footplate, many times, brought him close to having both his feet severed by the sharp blade of the swinging shovel. Stopping suddenly, the coal I had on the shovel would be spread over the footplate floorboards. I tolerated him … just.

Mick was Grand Primo of the Order of Buffaloes; I was informed at that time that this sect was a poor man's form of Freemasonry. Meetings among this organization were to cost me very dearly in sweat. Instances were all too many, when he burned more coal than I would have saved by economic working of the fire in my lifetime.

One such time was when we relieved a train of 12 empty coaches at North Acton bound for Tyseley Carriage Sidings. We took over from Southern men with a BR Standard '73XXX' class, an engine in lovely condition, not new, but extremely well maintained. The cab also was well cared for and none of the injector steam valves needed the usual spanner to clout them to get them open. After we left North Acton, there was soon fire coming from our chimney that I thought perhaps Mick was having a brainstorm. Having a super engine I had no bother whatsoever maintaining steam, but I hardly stopped shovelling. We ran all the way on green signals, stopping for the first time at the down main line bracket signal at Tyseley South Junction, the signal to turn us from the main line into the sidings. Immediately we stopped, Mick went to get his soap and towel from his attaché case to wash in the bucket of hot water that I had filled earlier to cool. In his food case was the pair of horns that he apparently strapped to his head at meetings, together with other regalia, including his chain of office. He was obviously now very pleased to be getting to his venue on time, but it beggars belief as to how he would have performed had we been delayed anywhere!

Mick and I worked the 10.10 am Birmingham to Margate one day with No. 5912 *Queens Hall*, a Tyseley engine. She was in good order and steaming well when Mick went supersonic down the bank at Hatton. Passing Budbrook signal box there was a bang, followed by an ear rending escape of steam. The cab filled with steam and we both made a put for the tender gangways whilst at speed. After the initial shock, I realised that a newly brazed pipe on the sight feed lubricator condensing pipe had broken off, this was now flapping around under pressure and was banging against other nearby components. I knew that one end of the water gauge spanner fitted the shut-off cock on the steam fountain, but these cocks were inclined to difficult to shut off as they were only ever operated when things went wrong. Even the fitting staff approached these brass cocks with absolute caution, applying only a very limited amount of force when the boiler was in steam. With my jacket over one arm to protect me from the scalding steam I managed to turn the cock enough to bring normality to our surroundings. By this time we were getting towards Leamington, so I did no more until we came to a stand. In this instance we were extremely lucky that the steam shut-off cock operated freely because it had previously been used by the mechanical staff to fit the newly brazed pipe.

By this time Mick's excitable nature was at its height, he was throwing his arms in the air and doing the 'Dance of the Sugar Plum Fairy' around the cab shouting, 'We're a cripple, we're a cripple, go and wire another engine from Banbury'.

Had we have been a failure, he should have not gone from Leamington, as the engine was now getting no lubrication at all to the valves and pistons, running it at speed for the next 15 miles could had done any amount of damage. I tried to suggest to him that the condensing coil was dual-piped, we could indeed use the other pipe quite successfully, the system in fact was made that way. To this he snapped back at me in near fury, shouting, 'Do as you are bloody told, wire for another engine at Banbury'. I went to the signal box and made the necessary arrangements and when I returned Mick had dismantled the lubricator warming cock pipe and hammered it flat with the coal peck. This was now lying on the dish over the firehole, along with an array of spanners and was a completely separate entity to the problem that we were experiencing. Only Mick seemed to know what type of repair he was trying to achieve.

I was loath to give up this good engine, who knows what run down locomotive would be available at Banbury on a summer Saturday morning. Every decent engine would already be out working the innumerable extra holiday trains. After we departed I took the spanner again and turned the cock a little more until the pointer was towards the good pipe. Almost before Mick realised I moved the handle used daily to fill the lubricator to a different position, spots of oil immediately started to rise inside the lubricator the sight glasses. With eyes now like saucers, he reluctantly said, 'We're not a cripple, are we? Keep the fire up, keep the fire up!' If we had given the engine up at Banbury I would obviously have had to run the fire down.

We stopped at Banbury and I looked towards Banbury South signal box; the signalman was looking out from the wide open window. No attempt by me to detach the engine now had him scratching his head. It was quite common for the wires to get crossed, so after a time he cleared his signals. Obviously this could not the train needing a fresh engine, he must have thought. We left Banbury and a very puzzled signalman, as we passed the loco depot there was a very run down mogul standing at the departure signal, a stream of black smoke going vertically into the air as the unsuspecting engine crew made a frantic effort to prepare the engine for us. I was happy with the engine that we had got and Mick showed no remorse for the trouble he had unnecessarily caused.

The rest of the trip went well, but when the cockney driver relieved us at North Acton, he took one look at the bits and pieces lying about, saying, 'Bloody hell! Our fitters will be pleased to see that lot!'

Tyseley did have its fair share of 'genius' when it came to drivers, but about this time one man in particular made an unforgettable impression on me. Mick failed to arrive at work one day, no one else was available with route knowledge and I eventually found myself working out of Paddington with an Old Oak Common driver. This man had obviously served a long apprenticeship on crack trains such as the 'Cornish Riviera' and 'Torbay Express'. At Paddington we took to a rather sad looking 'Castle' and his cockney wit soon had me at ease in his company. However, he must have wondered what on earth I was doing carrying out my usual preliminaries, filling the firebox to capacity as I did to cope with Mick.

When the 'Right Away' indicator lit, the train was eased out of the station, no fuss, no slipping, little noise. We drifted round Old Oak Common Junction, our smoke barely clearing the cab roof. At Greenford I was still waiting for the 'fireworks'. I skimmed the water troughs at Ruislip, swept up, swilled down and only picked up the shovel because I felt I should be doing something. Indeed, I had begun to wonder if this driver was fully aware of how tight the timings were on this particular train. At Tylers Green he cracked the blower and shut the regulator, only lifting his bottom off the seat to apply enough brake to reduce our speed to the regulation 45 mph through the middle road at High Wycombe. I anxiously looked for the station clock, dead on time. With many years experience behind me I found this handling of a locomotive totally unbelievable. I now had an absolute mountain of a fire in the firebox; it was in lovely shape, not as usual torn into holes by excessive blast. The boiler water level was well up the gauge glass, the pressure gauge just behind the red line, the footplate swept and the dust laid.

We made the ascent to Saunderton and negotiated the 60 mph permanent speed restriction down through Princes Risborough. Gathering speed rapidly the engine seemed to enjoy being at the hands of this man. With barely a sound from the chimney, just a quickening spitting from an odd weak cylinder pressure valve, we attained an incredible speed. All so effortless, the engine just trembled with

Driver Jack Payne and fireman John Millman with the Royal Train engine 'Castle' class 4-6-0 No. 7007 *Great Western*. *Bernard Rainbow*

excitement under our feet. We arrived at Bicester two minutes early, the live steam injector just avoiding the point of blowing off. For the first time in weeks I had not taken on the appearance of a miner!

The rest of the journey was taken in a similar vein, in places where my head would normally have been lower than my backside, I was entertained with quips of, the Englishman, Irishman and the Scotsman.

Hatton Bank was taken almost leisurely and we eventually ran up No. 5 platform at Snow Hill with just a whisper from the blower and the rhythmic tick of the vacuum pump, exactly on time. We parted company, I had no idea of his name and I never ever saw him again. Two weeks later, however, his photograph appeared on the front page of the *Birmingham Mail*, having reached the fastest time ever between Paddington and Leamington Spa. His name, George Green; I suspect the train he had worked was a test train prior to the introduction of the Blue Pullman service.

John Millman and Jack Payne worked the Royal Train and when I later saw John I was anxious to hear how he went on. The day apparently went without problems, but John was pretty upset when I spoke to him. He had just travelled to Wolverhampton to the superintendent's office to collect the customary thanks and 10 shillings gratuity given to any firemen who worked the Royal Train. He had specially put on clean overalls for the visit to headquarters, where his presence was eventually made known to the superintendent. John walked into the large office and stood on the proverbial 'carpet' whilst the super thumbed through the papers in front of him. Without actually looking John in the face, the chief said, 'Fireman Millman? … take it', and he pitched the 10 shilling note towards the edge of the desk. In anticipation, John waited a second or two.

'That will be all', the superintendent continued; John then left the office with not so much as eye contact. John was one of the most placid men I have met, but this incident upset him greatly. He swore that he would never work another 'Royal', indeed he kept his word and at a later date caused a dreadful panic at the depot.

# Chapter Nine

## Steam's Declining Years

About 1956 Tyseley's locomotive coal stack was cleared for the building of a new diesel maintenance factory and part of the carriage sidings made way for a refuelling pit. With these projects operative, new diesel multiple unit sets arrived as they were turned out from the factory at Derby.

Men, who had ingrained working habits of 30 or more years, were now subject to vast changes in practice. The promotion system was always fair in respect of drivers and firemen, senior men had the senior work and it was unthinkable that this would ever change. Many of the older men accepted the change to diesel extremely well, but there were a number who never got to grips with the fact that they were now operating electrical switches and not steam valves that may well need the strength of both hands. Some drivers working on the new units operated the controls without quite realising what was going on beneath them. Gearboxes screamed with torture and final drive reversing dogs thumped into engagement whilst the drive shafts were spinning at speed, the consequential damage costs were then very high.

Artisans who had always worked with lead lump hammers, cold chisels and spanners so weighty that they would have made Samson bow-legged, changed to working on relatively delicate electrical switchgear and pneumatic solenoid valves. The transformation was immense, yet these first steps towards modernisation were taken by men in the twilight years of their working lives. Men who had worked years of inhospitable shifts, had been exposed to all weathers and had been at the very forefront during the war years. There is little wonder therefore that many of these good men had aged prematurely. They were wonderful men and deserved far more credit than they ever got.

Drivers were issued with new green serge uniforms, having bright yellow embroidered letters on the lapels. They also now had to carry their own set of driving tools, a brake handle, reversing lever and control circuit key etc. To carry these they were given a leather satchel, making many of them feel like a cross between a bus conductor on the No. 8 Inner Circle and a commissionaire at Selfridges.

For these men, running to time was a way of life; faster running times and quicker turn rounds now caused problems. Drivers sometimes got to the other end of perhaps a six-car unit and found they had forgotten one, or all of the driving tools. The Automatic Train Control isolating flag was also a source of trouble, forgetting to isolate this would not be a problem until the train passed the first distant signal at caution. The train would then come to a stand in the middle of nowhere with the apparatus screaming in the back cab of the unit. Drivers then had to walk back, very embarrassed, along the ballast to cancel the ATC, with the inevitable curious heads looking out of all the windows. I might add that this was not entirely an elderly driver's problem, there were a number of young drivers too, who at sometime or other failed to carry out the necessary procedure in the rear cab of a unit and consequently had to walk back. I was similarly known to fall into this category some years later; it was so very easily done when in a hurry.

Inevitable teething problems, ignorance and some abuse, caused diesel sets to fail, in which case the faithful 2-6-2T prairies were pressed back into their original role. Because of route knowledge, many of the No. 2 link firemen, who were all passed as drivers, found themselves working their own turns as the driver, which was rather ironic. These were very gruelling jobs; quicker turn rounds and the enhanced timings were hard to cope with. Engines worked between Leamington Spa, Wellington, Stratford-upon-Avon, Kidderminster and Bewdley, stopping at all stations. The bunkers on the engines were often exhausted, as were the exasperated enginemen.

The arrival of the diesel units at Tyseley halted my promotion to No. 3 link, which was more commonly known as the 'Spare' link. This link covered the jobs to the North as far as Chester; it also worked the Aberystwyth summer service trains and any extra trains on the Cardiff routes, via Hereford and via Gloucester. In addition, this link covered the Paddington jobs which went via Reading. Although I never made it into this link, most men of my seniority worked all of these routes often when on 'spare' turns.

I worked a day excursion to Barry Island on one Saturday, along with Driver Bert Tucker, our charge being a Tyseley 'Grange' class, No. 6853 *Morehampton Grange*. Due to the extraordinary amount of intending passengers for this train, we finally ended up with 15 coaches behind us. Furthermore, we stopped at all stations to Stourbridge Junction, although by the time we got there, there was no room for any more people to board the 10 coaches with which we had started. It was first arranged for the train to be strengthened by another three coaches from the sidings, making the train up to a full single load for the engine over the gradients of the Malvern Hills. However, our guard objected to this, as this would have contravened the regulations, by putting too many wheels to the rear of his brake van. To avoid further delay, and a number of shunting movements, the whole five-coach set was then coupled to us. This put another brake van at the rear of the train and therefore complied with the Rule Book.

No. 6853 *Morehampton Grange* standing in the shed yard at Tyseley. The author once did over 200 miles on her without the necessity to close the firehole doors. *Dick Potts*

Initially we left Stourbridge unassisted, but a mogul came on to the front of us at Worcester Rainbow Hill Junction, so we went double-headed through to Cardiff. I then had quite an easy trip with a super engine. My mate too was an excellent engineman, but he was indeed a man of very, very few words.

I also booked on for a Cardiff turn one day to find a 'Britannia' class No. 70026 *Polar Star* marked next to our name. On this occasion I had a driver newly promoted to the top link. Charlie Yarwood had been cocooned on the local prairies for some years. Also, at this point in time the 'Britannias' were never frequent visitors to the Birmingham area. I saw my driver screwing his eyes at the roster sheet, obviously puzzled by the unusual number. The engine was prepared for us and he was even more bewildered when he looked at it as it stood in the shed yard. Charlie immediately about turned and went back towards the shift foreman's office. Some minutes later he returned, accompanied by a young Cardiff driver who had just come to Tyseley for promotion. Charlie was in fact a very competent engineman, so after a little 'tuition' from the younger man he was quite happy to cope with this strange craft.

This was only my second time on a 'Britannia', yet this familiarity helped considerably and we had an excellent trip, but things could easily have been very different. As we approached the single bore tunnel between Colwall and Ledbury, I looked and wondered if this large locomotive would indeed fit into the small-looking entrance; the clearance was normally very tight. I did feel some doubt as to the rightful route availability of the machine that we were riding on. The regulator was already closed on the falling gradient and I think Charlie's puzzled looks were an indicator to me that he was having exactly the same thoughts. These few seconds of distraction were almost fatal, as he forgot to put the blower on a touch before the engine threaded itself inside the tunnel with barely inches to spare. The subsequent air pressure as we entered the tunnel immediately brought the fire back out of the open firehole, the flames immediately touching the cab roof and roaring out of the open roof vent. The sudden heat was horrifying and I dropped low on the floor as Charlie threw himself up over the reversing screw into his corner to avoid the searing heat. I did have the habit of putting a drop of cylinder oil on the firehole door runners, as this thick oil did not burn off and it made the doors nice and easy to operate. With my foot, I was therefore able to kick the firehole doors shut; fortunately the handle of the doors was on my side, which saved our lives.

The BR Standard '70XXX' class were undoubtedly the best steaming engines that I ever worked on as a fireman, no doubt due to the generous size of the boiler and the locomotives having only two cylinders. A similar combination duplicated on the Great Western '47XX' class 2-8-0s, these were fine engines too. Even when the large 2-8-0s were worked extremely hard, a fireman would have little problem coping.

Western men tended to maintain very thick fires, mostly through necessity on all Great Western-designed engines. Over-firing a 'Britannia' could lead the engine going beyond control, they would then blow steam away from the safety valves incessantly. Firing a wide firebox was completely alien to us, but I was quick to appreciate the energy it saved. There was no pitching the coal 10 feet or more to the front of a long firebox. On a wide firebox you just had to be sure that the back corners were always well fed. I liked the 'Britannias', but this was not a view shared by many of my colleagues. Most thought they were dirty and noisy engines to work on, giving a harsh ride with the pony truck under the cab. There was obviously some substance to these complaints; the pony truck did thump over anything but the best rail joints. This did make the cab platework rattle and the dust no doubt tended to fly. Nevertheless, they were good engines, but definitely not as sure-footed as any Great Western engine.

BR Standard 'Britannia' Pacific No. 70017 *Arrow* of Cardiff (Canton) shed at Birmingham Snow Hill in 1958. *Michael Mensing*

Churchward '47XX' class 2-8-0 No. 4701 stands at Lapworth station in connection with permanent way work beyond the up end of the station on 8th October, 1961. Single line working is in operation on the down line. *Michael Mensing*

From a fireman's point of view, the '92XXX', or '9Fs', were not in the same street, particularly with Welsh coal. The wide firebox had lost its depth owing to the extra pair of driving wheels, to keep the back corners of the firebox full, firemen invariably discarded the firehole smoke plate, sometimes called a deflector plate. The failure to fit this piece of equipment left the boiler tube plate exposed to cold air being drawn in through the firehole doors. This inevitably had an adverse affect on the efficiency of the boiler, but Western firemen found no other way round the problem when using 'soft' coal. It was probably quite a different story with hard coal, but although I worked on '9Fs' hundreds of times, I never had the luxury of good quality hard coal. The double chimneys fitted to these engines appeared to make no improvement whatsoever to their steaming qualities, in fact, in my opinion the engines with the single chimney were marginally better, although these were rare visitors to the Western Region.

Working over the Aberystwyth route was good experience, although I never worked over this line with a four-wheel-coupled '90XX' class, as many of my colleagues did. I also did not work over the line enough to become totally conversant with it, but I did work these turns with 'Manors', BR Standard class '4s' and moguls. The 'Manors' by this time were super steaming engines and much different from their early days when having the 'jumper' blast pipe top. We had No. 7800 *Torquay Manor* at Tyseley in the early days; her performance was always pretty indifferent until the changes were made to her draughting. Likewise, the '93XX' moguls were subject to improved draughting and renumbered '73XX' onwards. The transformation to all these engines was phenomenal.

I was always full of admiration for the Cambrian men, who seemed to effortlessly pluck the single line tokens from the pick-up points. The high speeds that these men were able to keep and still make the single line token changes was a great advantage to them. All the 26 pick-up points over the route seemed to be in valleys, the quicker the change, the less effort it was climbing the other side. I never ever had a good 'eye' for ball games and I think this is why I found the token changes difficult. There were obviously 26 changes in each direction. On my first trip I threaded my arm through the first pick-up and although we were not going very fast the pain was excruciating as the heavy steel hoop hit my elbow joint. Also, at the first set-down at Westbury, I missed the knob on the arm completely and looked back to see the token bouncing along the ground. I attempted to catch the next with the palm of my hand, but the engine lurched at the last moment and it caught the ends of my fingers, this was very painful too. I never dropped another, but there was a definite pattern, the token hitting either the ends of my fingers or my thumb. Token catching really wasn't my forte in those early days. Changing the token at Dovey Junction on the station platform was amusing, not a bit like changing earlier ones at Rubery, on the Longbridge branch. These were rod type staffs and changing it by hand from a tank engine cab was easy, although there was definitely an art to doing it. The change at Dovey Junction was on the driver's side and I suddenly realised that I needed three hands, at least one to hold on with as there was no cab side to lean on. The ensuing muddle that followed brought visual daggers from Taffy the signalman. There was little doubt as to his thoughts, bloody Brummagem men again. Anyhow, changing the staff at that point, on the move, was only to save him walking to the end of the platform, so it wasn't a big deal.

Eventually, I was able to cope with the tokens, but never in the same expert way as the Cambrian men. The Aberystwyth's were indeed tough jobs, 11 hours on duty, if on time. Often by the time we arrived at Aberystwyth another locomotive would come on the other end of the train and we were more or less straight back. We normally had relief at Snow Hill on our return, as the coaches were stabled out at Solihull. I got back on one turn to find there was no relief and therefore had to take the coaches for stabling, making 13 hours on duty. It was Saturday evening; it wasn't always easy to get younger men to turn out for work.

Until the diesel units came to Tyseley, the links had probably been very similar since the depot had been opened in 1908. From this point on, altered diagrams saw link changes come with regular monotony, hence I lost track of the link renumbering process. My revised links still brought me face to face with the Reading Biscuits and the Landore-Moor Street 'D' head markers, plus regular weekday London passenger work. Extra Paddington work was diagrammed to Tyseley because of the electrification of the West Coast Main Line. The disruption to services on the Euston line saw the Snow Hill- Paddington service very much intensified.

The fact that my latest driver was an utter skinflint made no difference whatsoever to our relationship, he was a superb engineman and wonderful to work with. It made for a very a refreshing change.

Jack Davis went by the name of 'Bicycle Jack', possibly because he came to work every day on a bicycle and tended to walk about the shed for long periods with his trousers held tightly round his legs by cycle clips. His ankle length boots therefore made his feet look rather like something sketched by L.S. Lowry.

Jack loved a game of cards too, which in turn bought him another alias, 'The Coroner'. This was because if he lost a halfpenny, there was always an inquest on everyone's hand and what cards should have been played. My new mate was also a perpetual talker; on the other hand, he was a level-headed man and always good company. He totalled up his predicted wage daily, anticipating that if we made perhaps another 41 minutes overtime by Saturday, this would round his money off to another level pound.

Jack got the best from every engine and it was a joy that our timekeeping on the Londons was monotonously accurate. Old Oak Common depot employed adult engine cleaners and many of the engines in our charge were turned out beautifully, with gleaming brass and polished green paintwork. So well were the engines turned out that it was difficult to judge what condition they were really in, some were not always as good as they looked! I had a habit of looking between the main frames; half an inch of gunge in strategic places was always a good pointer that the engine had been about a bit.

I usually nipped back to the kitchen car when we arrived at Bicester on the 7.10 pm departure to make Jack's brew. He always impressed on me to keep his brew out of sight, just in case the chef was feeling benevolent and put tea in the can for us. He always suggested, too, that I ask if there were any toasted teacakes going begging. I never did, even with Jack's expertise I would hardly have found time to sit and have tea and toasted teacakes!

Apparently, at home, Jack had taken all measures possible to avoid the sharp springs protruding through his bed mattress; these had become painful to him and his wife during their slumber. Finally, he admitted defeat; he would have to get a new bed. Jack had not laid out so much money since the last time he had to buy a puncture repair outfit, consequently he practically broadcast to the entire depot about his latest purchase.

I signed on a couple of weeks later to find Jack had not come to work, the time clerk remarking that he could never remember Jack going sick. I really felt that his illness must be very serious. However, I later learned that he had gone into the garden to do some work; as he bent down he got the most dreadful pain in his back.

He then had to crawl on his hands and knees back into the house and climb the stairs to bed in the same manner. His wife immediately called a doctor, who duly arrived to make his examination.

'Humm, you've got lumbago', he said.

At which the doctor put the flat of his hand on the new mattress, pumping it a few times. 'You'll have to get rid of this bed, it's far too soft', he said. Jack didn't stop spluttering for a week!

Some years later, Jack upgraded his cycle to a moped having a 50 cc engine. My father had been relegated on to the shunting engines at Bordesley Junction for a number of years owing to ill health. He had become friendly with a garage owner, who eventually asked him if he would like a spare time job as petrol pump attendant. My father worked three regular shifts, so doing part time work could be easily accommodated. The men at Bordesley came in for no overtime, so the extra cash was useful towards my father's beer and 'Woodbine' money. Jack used to go into the garage fortnightly to top up his moped with one litre of petrol. My father used to serve him and looked after him by giving him a handful of Green Shield trading stamps; he could do this as many car owners never bothered to collect their stamps. All was well until Jack turned up when my father wasn't at the garage; the boss himself came out to fill up for him. After paying, the boss gave Jack his change and one stamp. Jack looked at this, after checking his change, and said, 'You're a bit skinny with the stamps aren't you mate?, Reg always gives me a lot more than this!' Tact was not one of Jack's finer points. The garage owner then had words with my father for giving the stamps away; after all they did have to be to be paid for.

Jack was not alone when it came to being thrifty. As a youngster I worked to Gloucester with driver Albert Slater. On the way to the station whilst on our way home from Gloucester, I found a pound note. Albert was more than peeved, he continually harped on about the money, stressing that mates always shared and I should split the money between him and our guard. One pound was a day's wage for me, but because of the verbal bombardment that ensued I felt it was far easier to give way and share. Although, I never really found any evidence of 'share and share alike' in later years. All the juggling of the older men's purses and my pockets failed to come up with sufficient change to give Albert his full share; I was just 8*d*. short. I therefore gave Albert the six shillings and told him that I would give him the rest when I saw him again. Unfortunately, I never saw him for perhaps a couple of months; indeed the 'debt' went out of my mind.

I was building the fire up on a big engine in the shed one day when a voice said, 'Have you forgotten anything young man … what about my eight pence?' Albert had perused the roster to see what turn I was on and had come to work a few minutes early specifically to catch me before we went off the shed. I quickly paid up, or my reputation would have suffered!

'Bicycle Jack' did have an obsession about tightening glad nuts and this was to be our downfall when we arrived at Reading shed one Saturday evening for the 'Biscuits'. The engine rostered to us was our very own No. 6866 *Morfa Grange*, in perfect order. I felt like a pools winner, particularly after having a pretty indifferent engine on the up passenger that night. No. 6866 was well prepared for us, but Jack noticed a few drops of cylinder oil had dripped on to the dish above the firehole doors. This was quite common, as the oil came from the 'W' valve gland nut. The 'W' valve was coupled to the regulator handle by linkage and served to atomise the cylinder oil on its way to the valves and pistons from the sight feed lubricator. Any number of footplate men had been known to take a swig of tea from the brew can and had had

The author's father on diesel-shunter No. 15101 at Bordesley Junction. *British Railways*

Driver Albert Slater to whom the author was in debt for 8*d*., seen here on No. 6904 *Charfield Hall* which was the only engine that he totally cleared the tender of coal. *Dick Potts*

their tonsils lubricated with 'black' cylinder oil which had a habit of dripping, unnoticed in the dark, into the tea can. Seeing the spots of oil, Jack immediately needed a one and three-quarter spanner, which I searched Reading shed for. Armed with the tool he put some pressure on the nut, but the cylinder oil had baked hard on to the threads. To get more purchase, he then put one foot on the dish and heaved at the spanner, there was a crack, and the whole valve body moved round instead of the gland nut. This was now obviously a job for the fitters, who took one look at the problem and crippled the engine. Not only did I miss out on a good trip home, but also we now had to set about preparing another engine. The shed foreman went off the deep end and we finally got hold of the most run down '28XX' class 2-8-0, which were super engines, but certainly not cut out for 'D' headcode working as the driving wheels were too small in size. These locomotives were always fine steamers, but this one shook the very life out of us on the way back. Normally, given a locomotive of this calibre to do the job, Jack would have taken his time and made a meal of it, rubbing his hands at any overtime we might make. On this occasion the delay was down to him, so we came home like the wind, the small wheels reaching what must have been maximum revolutions. All round, this was not a good day for us both.

Whilst Jack was sick, I booked on for a ' Zone' turn. This again meant that you always got a train turn, instead of being general dogsbody, preparing engines etc. My driver was 'Cockney' Townsend, although I'm not exactly sure whether he was born within earshot of Bow Bells. He was, however, a man who would give Jack a run for his money when it came to uninterrupted talking. Nevertheless, 'Cockney' was a good engineman and a decent man to work with. He was a sizable man in every direction who always had a rosy red face and tended to look as though he had left his teeth at home on the bathroom shelf. . 'Cockney' also had a placid nature, almost to the point of being 'half soaked', which brought about an amusing incident.

The author stands next to No. 5983 *Henley Hall* at Stratford-upon-Avon *circa* 1962.

We were soon ordered to travel to Honeybourne to relieve Oxford men who were running late on a freight bound for Bordesley Junction. Walking up to Tyseley station we caught the local passenger to Stratford-upon-Avon, this train still being hauled by the usual bunker-first, '51XX' prairie tank engine. At Stratford we joined the ex-Great Western railcar, which stopped at Milcote, Long Marston, Pebworth Halt and Honeybourne, going forward to Worcester, calling at all stations.

At Honeybourne, I followed 'Cockney' round the narrow path in the direction of the Honeybourne East Loop signal box. It was a warm day and 'Cockney' soon began to breathe heavily, but he never economised on chatter as he gasped for air between words. I followed behind him, taking half paces to avoid treading on his heels. His bulk swayed from side to side, allowing his ex-military leather walkie-talkie bag to rub even more of the black serge from a thread bare patch on the back of his jacket. Hair on the jacket made it look rather like it had been the resting place for some albino feline during the previous night.

One of the signalmen that worked in the East Loop signal box was a notorious character, he not only despised locomen, he hated the whole world. Arriving at the signal box, 'Cockney' flopped down on a pile of redundant sleepers, took off his cap and wiped the sweat from around the leather inner band. I fancied a brew, but seeing no movement from the signal box I knew that there was a one in three chance that this fiery signalman could be on duty. For the time being, I opted to wait until we stopped at Stratford-upon-Avon for water. I could quickly nip across to the Relief Cabin whilst the tank was filling, the kettle was usually boiling.

'Cockney', when rested, stood and looked into the distance where an 'Iron Lung' [2-8-0 Austerity ] stood at the head of a freight train simmering from both safety valves after the slow descent of Campden Bank. Puzzled, he went to the bottom of the signalbox stairs, calling in his Bow Bells accent:

'Bi-wll.' No response from up above, he called again a little louder.

'Bi-wll.' Still no reply, 'Cockney' called even louder.

'BI-WLL.' At which the large window at the end of the signal box slid along its runners thumping heavily at its limit, the whole wooden structure of the building reverberating like a huge bass drum. Behold, the man in question leered down at us, his face blood red with anger at his disturbed breakfast.

'Cockney', being as soft natured as the proverbial brush, and completely oblivious of this signalman's fiery reputation called up to him, 'Wos that twain on the Souff Loop Bi-wll?' The signalman looked inquiringly into the distance, then at us, immediately replying, 'How did you know my name was Bill?' 'Cockney', now completely speechless by the signalman's unusual reply, 'Oh ... er ... er, I just guessed', he eventually stammered.

'Well if you are that clever, you will have no trouble at all guessing what that train is will you!' The window slammed shut with percussion that would have done the finale of the 1812 Overture justice. 'Cockney', probably for the first time in his life, was stuck for words and completely bewildered.

Part of one of our summer diagrams was to relieve a train from Hastings at Oxford, then work home to Birmingham. The day that Jack Davis and I worked this turn our train was exceptionally late arriving. It was puzzling therefore, that when we relieved the Southern Region men, someone had shovelled a considerable amount of coal forward on the tender, swept up and the footplate was nicely swilled down. In fact, the condition that the engine arrived in would have been impossible to achieve whilst running. Furthermore, no trains had left Oxford for some time prior to our train's arrival, so it was even more baffling. Our train was therefore

The main part of the northbound 'Cornishman' is banked out of Stratford-upon-Avon by Collett '2251' class 0-6-0 No. 2257 on 23rd May, 1959. *Michael Mensing*

'Modified Hall' class 4-6-0 No. 7918 *Rhose Wood Hall* passes the platform of Stratford Racecourse in 1964. *Michael Mensing*

unlikely to have stood anywhere waiting line clear, which would have given the crew time to get things in such good order.

We eventually left Oxford and it was soon evident that this engine was very poorly; the pressure gauge needle stood where it was and the engine wasn't making enough steam for me to get the injector running. Off the tender came the long pricker for my usual feel round at the front of the firebox. The fire was not unduly thick under the brick arch yet there was already no alternative to turning the blower on. Without Jack's co-operation we would not have gone very far at all, however he drove the engine accordingly; we lost a lot of time, but just kept going, limping into Banbury in a dreadful state. It was now apparent to us now that all the expertise in the world would not have got this train up the bank at Hatton with an engine in this condition, so at Banbury Jack immediately made provisions for an assistant engine from Leamington. Strangely, everything looked fine with our engine, that is, until I got on my knees to check the firebox tube plate for blocked tubes. I was aghast to see several hundredweights of unburned coal piled on top of the brick arch; only the top row of boiler tubes was now visible. I desperately tried to rake some of it away from the tubeplate with the long pricker, I did manage to expose the larger superheater tubes, but the fire-iron soon got too hot to handle and the situation became pretty hopeless. To get coal on top of the brick arch, the engine must have been fired with the firehole smoke plate removed. The young Southern fireman must have thought that he was firing a 'King Arthur' class, when he was indeed throwing the coal against the front tubeplate of the short firebox of a mogul! There was little doubt that the Southern men must have stood somewhere at length prior to arriving at Oxford in an effort to raise steam. Yet when they arrived they said nothing and even indicated to us that all was well.

We made Leamington in our own time, where the Warwick banker was ready in the bay platform and waiting to attach to the front of us. We very much 'leaned' on him to Birmingham, yet still struggled to take our own coaches to Queens Head Sidings and return with the engine light to Tyseley.

I bought my first car, an Austin A40, Somerset; she had the characteristic smell of leather and hard black lustre paint. The car was in my possession for 10 years, in which time Colin Jacks and I explored many of the prettier spots of Great Britain ... and much of its hostelry.

I also became close friends with Paul Cox, whom I first met when I started work on the platform at Acocks Green station. Paul's father was a Signal and Telegraph linesman and if there was trouble on the line I used to have to call him out. I understand that Fred Cox was a very brave man; he was awarded the George Medal during the war years for outstanding bravery.

Paul had a passion for big cars, at one time he owned an outrageously pink Vauxhall Cresta. In turn he also became the owner of several 'big cats', including an E type. Later he was quickly attracted to an Audi, when these cars were rare in this country.

It was a best suit job when I went out with Paul; we went to some very expensive places, entering therein like the Solicitor General and his confidant. We never drank much, but it was an education to see how the other half lived, little did anyone know that we had both probably spent a very long time scouring the coal dust grime from our eyelids before going out! Even so, if the atmosphere became warm during the evening, the grime had a habit of emerging from the pores of your skin and we both probably left at closing time with eyes looking rather like Dusty Springfield.

Paul Cox was not a railway enthusiast, but he was a footplate man through and through. He was not only a wonderful fireman; he was strong and possessed abounding energy. Whenever anyone relieved him, everything was always in excellent condition. Invariably the cab was cleaned down, as he put much emphasis on his own good reputation.

Jack Davis was promoted to a higher link and I lost a champion, Cliff Hinton then became my mate. Cliff was a nice man, but unfortunately he did have trouble running to time on the London work, which was a bit soul destroying. Jack Davis and I had struggled with adverse engines many times, yet it had always given us great job satisfaction to still arrive on time.

On our first job together, we travelled to Paddington to work the 7.10 pm express to Wolverhampton. Whilst travelling in the train, I told Cliff that we never had a 'King' class on this turn; it would always be a 'Castle', or possibly a 'County'. Of course, the inevitable happened; we walked up the train to find a 'King' on the front. This first trip for Cliff must have been a bit daunting, yet things went well initially, indeed we had a fine locomotive. Approaching Ruislip water troughs with the regulator wide open and the reverser notched well back, we were going well and in faultless condition. To my amazement, he shut the regulator and put the engine on the first valve, which meant that the engine was on less than half power with a steep climb immediately in front of us. Almost instinctively, I called to him to keep the regulator wide open; after all I had by now had an awful lot of experience on these turns. Unfortunately my mouth had got the better of my brain; a fireman never told a driver what to do. The look of indignation on Cliff's face was immediately enough to put me in my place. Perhaps my telling him that we never had a 'King' on this job had already put my credibility in a bad light.

Inevitably, only a minute or two later we were on the climb up towards Gerrards Cross and Beaconsfield. The train had now lost momentum and consequently we passed High Wycombe several minutes down.

Initially, I felt that my new mate would learn by this mistake, but regrettably he did the same thing night after night and we were always late passing High Wycombe. From there on he never ran fast enough to recover any time, the work was easy for me, but very unsatisfying. Eventually, even the kitchen car staff got to pulling my leg when I went to make a brew, asking me if we might be right time sometime later in the week. They were men from the North and were always eager to get home.

If Cliff got any reports from management for failing to keep time, which I feel he must have done, then he kept them from me. This actually worried me quite a lot, he could have been blaming poor engines, or in fact shortage of steam, whereby my reputation would have been at stake. However, he kept his cards close to his chest, nothing was ever said, so what actually took place will always remain a mystery.

It was travelling up to London for the 7.10 pm departure that I met a young woman with whom I eventually became totally bewitched. She was a nurse at the Children's Hospital in Birmingham; therefore the shifts that we both worked made courtship very difficult. We saw the most of each other when we were both on night work. I would go home, scrub up and go into town during the morning rush hour traffic; we would then go out for breakfast, often to a tea room in Henley-in-Arden. This relationship lasted for two years, but it wasn't to be, I was devastated when it ended and it wasn't something I was able to shrug off easily. She eventually married and went up north to live, but strangely she always kept in touch with me. Seeing her just occasionally was enough to rekindle what I felt for her and I was never able find the strength to let go.

After a number of other women friends, my wife to be eventually broke this spell, very simply with basic decency and dependable companionship. My wife was a schoolteacher at that time and her honesty, well-organized ways, together with similar interests, became the basis for a relationship that has never faltered. The partnership has always been loving, yet easy going. It is only at a time of sickness, or perhaps just a late arrival home, that inner emotional turmoil brings home just how inseparable we are. I love her dearly.

Cliff Hinton went on annual leave and driver Jack Steventon deputised on a turn which involved working the 6.10 pm departure from Paddington. Jack was an old hand, a quiet, white-haired man, who was an absolute master of his craft, his handling of any engine was nothing short of genius. We took charge of No. 6011 *King James I* and left Paddington on Monday evening with 13 coaches behind us. All Wolverhampton engines now carried Afloc water treatment; therefore I had to keep the boiler water level no more than half full. This water treatment was an addition to many other adversities that we faced, making these big engines prime like the very devil when in the hands of any driver. Nevertheless, with a man of Jack's calibre I was able to 'play' with No. 6011 and barely broke into a sweat. We ran dead on time and I got off her almost as clean as when we started, I have always retained such regard for this extraordinary driver.

On Tuesday evening driver Sid Bagnall was my opposite, another well respected engineman. I was therefore quite happy to see No. 6011 at the head of the train again and we departed with exactly the same coaching stock. Sid Bagnall and I had never previously worked together; I had certainly never heard anyone say he was heavy handed. As experienced as I now was, it was difficult to detect any difference in the way that these two drivers worked the engine. The sound from the chimney was no different to the previous night. Yet the truth of the matter was that I had to shovel like blazes to keep pace. It was difficult for a fireman to see the exact setting of the all important reversing screw, but I suspect Sid was driving with it set at 25 per cent cut off, as most drivers did with two-cylinder engines. The big four-cylinder engines would easily cope with being set at 15 to 18 per cent on the reverser. The difference it made in coal consumption was phenomenal, what a measure of difference I found on two consecutive days with the same engine and train. Many Tyseley drivers had had little experience on the 'Kings' and this comparison of driving was very enlightening for me. There was never a truer word written by O.S. Nock, the eminent railway historian, in later years when he wrote that it appeared with the 'Kings' that the men needed a time of adjustment to them. Unfortunately, there were a number of Tyseley drivers who were never to learn. This, I feel, was purely because they never did any firing on them and did not know what a difference half a turn on the reversing screw would make to the coal consumption. This omission was to make it very hard going indeed for many of Tyseley's firemen.

Nevertheless, this was nothing to compare as on the following Wednesday evening when I left Paddington with Driver Percy Fletcher. The same 13 coaches trailed behind us, but our charge was No. 7008 *Swansea Castle*. The engine was late attaching to the train and our departure right time was a little hurried, so rushed in fact that we left without my driver proving that the train vacuum was not leaking. Indeed there was a leak on the system and we departed with the large four cone vacuum ejector blowing, when he should have had the matter put right prior to leaving the station. We therefore left with the brakes dragging and Percy attempted to combat this with a longer valve travel. The next hour for me was little short of slavery and we eventually arrived into Banbury on a summer evening with the train appearing as it would have done in the depths of winter, with steam rising from the train heating. This was not steam, but smoke from the oil burning off hot coach wheels! The carriage and wagon examiner at Banbury took one look at the train and put a red flag on it, his immediate reaction was that he would terminate the train.

After closer examination, he found a coach brake cylinder release cord had tangled and was holding the release valve open allowing air into the system. A minute or two at Paddington would have put this right and we may well have recovered any time lost following a late departure. As it was, the examiner kept us at Banbury for some 20 minutes before he reluctantly let us continue our journey. More wild fire from the chimney was to follow in a vain attempt to recover time, I was thankful that the diagram changed for us on Thursday for a more relaxing turn.

My friend Paul Cox passed for driving; this was an indication to me that my turn to go to Swindon was now getting close. During the following days, British Railways announced that the Rule Book was to be amended and a completely new General Appendix issued. This was very inappropriate timing for me and my close working friends, who were also due for their driver's examination. There were then urgent sessions at Dick Potts' home so that we could become familiar with this re-issue. This was not easy; we had lived with the old regulations for so long that they were ingrained on all our minds.

About this time, driver Harold Albutt and I travelled to Shrewsbury one Saturday evening to work a return Talyllyn Railway special. We prepared our locomotive on Salop shed and backed our beautifully clean '47XX' class 2-8-0 on to our train, which had arrived from the Aberystwyth line. In the station we were joined by my first regular driver Jack Hancock, he was now locomotive inspector at Swindon and considerably larger than when I knew him 12 years earlier. I don't suppose he now had any idea who I was and remained completely aloof. That day he had already been at work for some 13 hours and still had got to get to Paddington and then back to his home, which I understand was near Bristol. He sat his considerable bulk on my seat, which was somewhat of a hindrance as he kept dozing, almost falling off. Why he chose to ride with us so late at night seems a mystery, this was only the second time that a locomotive inspector had ever accompanied me. The engine was in perfect order, my driver was undoubtedly a fine engineman, most men in Jack's position would have assessed the situation and ridden in the train.

London men relieved us at Snow Hill after a perfect trip and little did I know that only days later I would be in front of Jack at Swindon for my driver's examination.

I had my practical driving test, which entailed working a stopping passenger train from Tyseley station to Wolverhampton. This train was the 7.06 am from Henley-in-Arden, Charlie Weston, the Wolverhampton inspector watched over me and we arrived exactly at 8.40 am at Low Level station, which was right time. Everything went routinely and Charlie took me to the Refreshment Room for a cup of tea and a chat about procedure. He then said he had another pressing matter; he continued that he had no doubts about my capability and left me. I was delighted that this first hurdle was over. He should also have watched me work a freight train, but he deemed this unnecessary, which was flattering, there again, we had all served a very long apprenticeship.

The big day came and I travelled to Swindon with my bowels in turmoil. There was a one in three chance that I would be in front of Jack Hancock. Talk from others suggested that he was the least tolerant amongst his colleagues. I met up with another Wolverhampton fireman with identical reasons for his visit to Swindon and with some comfort to each other we arrived at 'Park House' Headquarters.

The receptionist showed the Wolverhampton man in first and it was not long before a raised voice could be heard from the corridor, there was no doubt it was Jack, I knew the voice well. In a very short time my colleague reappeared, putting both his thumbs down and without saying anything he made his way to the door with some despondency.

My stomach rolled as I was called: There were no introductions, any niceties or an attempt to put me at ease, his first curt words being, 'I hope you know more than that man, he couldn't go round the wheel', which meant that my colleague had found difficulty in tracing the basic valve events.

In reality, this part of the examination could be a real hardship to anyone who was not particularly mechanically minded. Indeed, Alf Smith, who was one of the old Tyseley drivers who gave much of his time to the Improvement Class, spent many hours with my father to get him over this obstacle. Thanks to his interminable patience, my father eventually knew this part of the exam rather like he knew his five times table. Having said that, it is questionable whether knowing this part of the exam by rote allowed him to understand the locomotive any better. I was extremely lucky in this field; I could see the engine in my mind's eye immediately any question was put to me. I therefore knew exactly what should be taking place.

Jack started immediately by saying, 'Both big ends above the axle, lever in mid gear, what is the position of the valves?' The answer came off the top of my head, 'Valve shut at the front, open to exhaust at the back, right hand side'. 'Shut at the back and exhaust at the front, left-hand side'.

He half smiled, 'That has saved yourself half a dozen questions, starting from there usually catches many out', he remarked and I began to feel settled.

There were no catch questions and luckily I had no problem with everything the inspector asked, there again, we had put an awful lot of time into the learning process.

My confidence grew as the examination began to go well; it hardly seemed long at all until he wound the interview up, yet he had covered a great deal when I thought about it, the grilling had taken one and a half hours. I saw doctor in the afternoon and the ordeal was over, the personal relief was astonishing. I made my way home, it had been a long day, I was up at 6 am and would not be home until 8 pm, as it was necessary to change trains at Didcot, Oxford and Leamington on the way home, making for a very tedious journey.

Two weeks later, Cliff and I had prepared our engine in the roundhouse and I was talking to the shed turntable driver when the shed foreman appeared. Old Harry Williams had words with the turntable driver and I had not realised that this individual was in fact at the time deputising for the shedmaster, he always wore a bowler hat anyway. He walked away from us without any acknowledgement to me at all, then stopped in his tracks, about turned and approached me, saying, 'Oh, we have had a directive from the inspector at Swindon about you, we have to congratulate you on your knowledge ... you are only the second man at the depot ever to get that'.

There the conversation ended, he never called me by name, but turned his back on me and walked away. I was speechless, the depot had been open since 1908, I really had every right to feel that it would have been nice had he invited me into his office, shook my hand and said well done. However, this almost insignificant afterthought said everything about our immediate management. It was a good thing that most railwaymen had an in-bred conscientiousness; these people were never likely to get the best from anyone. I was inwardly angry and could only feel some contempt;

whatever my inner thoughts had been, I had always treated these superiors with every respect, they really didn't deserve it.

Another re-organization of the links saw me alongside driver Bernard Pratt. I had been with Bernard several times previously; indeed I always admired his technical understanding of engines and his vast knowledge of the working regulations. I knew him to be a good engineman too; we had worked together from Bristol one day with 'The Cornishman', having 14 coaches behind us with a lowly 'Grange' class engine. We kept time and did the job totally unassisted, which was quite a feat.

Regrettably, working with a driver occasionally was not the same as working with them regularly. Many a good relationship has ended by friends going on holiday and our good working relationship didn't last, our time together became soured, which was a very first for me and it did make me very unhappy. I did later learn from others that he was a difficult man.

I had previously had a number of tough mates to work with, but you could put up with the 'hard hitters' if they were reasonable men. I had never had a miss word with any of them; I had always respected them all for being my senior. Also, I deeply felt that I had a duty to my father not to build a bad reputation for myself.

Bernard had a huge ego and was never happier than when he was the centre of attention. In relief cabins, he would have his audience with their mouths open at events that had been exaggerated to such an extent that I hardly recognised them. Yet I must have been involved in these 'incidents' only a few days earlier. With his infinite knowledge, he had every 'gaffer' licking his boots and begging him to take engines that were not quite perfect. His narratives too, often belittled good men that I had found to be a joy to work with; this unnecessary gossip was therefore a bit hard to swallow. It became embarrassing too, that he always rounded off his exaggerations with the expression, 'Ain't that right mate?', looking at me for support for his fabrications.

He would then pass cakes and pastries my way, but only ever when others were present. His 'tit bits' were the last thing that I needed; I had a wonderful mother who always made sure that I never went hungry.

Bernard became the owner of the first plastic raincoat that I and many others ever saw. What you could buy today in any 'Pound' shop, he paid half a week's wages for. This new concept made him the centre of attention yet again; he revelled in it as the inquisitive questioned him about it. Even at times of drought, he carried it neatly folded over one arm, when he could easily have stowed it in his food bag out of sight. He made a point of putting it down under men's noses in relief cabins, or in trains, so that it would not go unnoticed, therefore inviting conversation.

It was raining hard the day we walked up to Tyseley South relief cabin, or what was known as 'Pneumonia Cabin'. We were to relieve the 5.05 pm Marazion to Oxley Sidings, a 'D' headcode freight. The 'Marazion' arrived regularly with a West of England 'Hall' class engine which was usually in outstandingly clean condition. Nevertheless, the train had come a long way, by which time the engine was usually getting a bit 'tired'.

We relieved Gloucester men and Bernard hung his wet raincoat in my corner to drip dry. On this train it was normal to put off traffic for the Midland Region at Bordesley Junction, this day was no exception. In the yard most of the shunter's signals were on the fireman's side, therefore the fire had to be left alone whilst these movements were made, the fireman relaying the shunter's signals to the driver.

When we were ready to leave, we drew out on to the down goods line behind Bordesley South signal box. This day we happened to be just in time for the signalman to get a margin through Snow Hill tunnel for us. The fire then had to heat up quickly for the assault on the tunnel gradient. The first thing I found necessary was to level over the fire with the long pricker. This tool came out of the fire at a white heat and sparkling at the end as I stowed it up the fire-iron rack in my corner. Passing over the viaduct towards Moor Street there were always any number of unfamiliar smells from small industry under the arches of the viaduct. There was a tannery and an aluminium casting foundry, both of which were inclined to give off obnoxious fumes. Therefore, I paid no attention to the most abnormal stench that hit my nostrils as I stowed away the hot fire-iron.

It was still raining when we put the engine on Oxley shed. When Bernard put his raincoat back on, he never noticed that about 18 inches of it had melted at the back. This was despite me making absolutely sure that the hot fire-iron had never touched, or got too near, his precious attire. Our relationship was still quite amicable at this point, but I was aghast and knew he would be very angry, although I couldn't help seeing the funny side. We caught the trolley bus in Cannock Road and made our way into Wolverhampton town, then back to Tyseley on the local passenger. This journey passed without anyone pointing the damage out to him, or he becoming aware of the yawning hole in the back of his raincoat.

The following day he was absolutely furious when he arrived at work, this undoubtedly being the start of the decline in our relationship. I sincerely apologised, but this was obviously not enough. Most firemen of our era always got to work early to make sure the engine was tooled up before their driver arrived, the oil feeder was always filled and the oil put to warm to make it more fluid. I had done this regularly for Bernard, but from this point on he always found something wrong. His oil feeder wouldn't pour properly, or the flare lamp wick was too short or had water in it. Then again, he found some reason why he always needed a spanner size different from what was available. He had always given the fitters the run around, but now often allowed them to leave the engine before sending me off to fetch them back to do something else minor. It became quite obvious that he was deliberately trying to wind me up.

This was a difficult time, but I said nothing, knowing that it might blow over, or that we probably would not be together for so very long. It was also soon noticeable that he had taken umbrage at the fact that I shied away from backing up his tales of fantasy when we were in mess rooms, or relief cabins. Although, the supply of 'goodies' still came my way whilst others were watching. I suspect that his problem was that he had belittled others to such a degree whilst similarly inflating his own reputation, that he had now become totally paranoid of making any mistakes.

I had learned also that Bernard was not at home on any foreign engine. He tolerated the Robinson 2-8-0s, these were driven from the same side as a Great Western engine. He hated the Riddles Austerities and seemed to go completely to pieces if we were booked a Midland class '8F'. These were normally good engines, but by the time we got hold of them on the Western they were sadly lacking in maintenance. On Great Western engines we had never become used to standing in shrouds of steam, hardly being able to see each other across the footplate. Steam leaks in the cabs of these engines brought condensation dripping from the cab roof in cold weather, making them really miserable to work on. Driving from the other side of the cab, Bernard seemed to suffer a loss of orientation in misty conditions; he would stop yards from signals and get me to walk to see if the signal was 'on' or 'off'. We dropped on to the shed at Tyseley one night in fog with a class '8F' and I walked from the Loco Yard signal box to the last engine on the coal stage line, guiding him in the darkness with a flare lamp. When I got to the last engine, he was nowhere to be seen. When I walked back towards the engine, he inferred that I hadn't left enough steam for him to get enough vacuum to keep the brakes off. He was trembling with temper, or no doubt nerves, although there was still 160 lb. pressure showing on the pressure gauge. I had obviously let the fire down, as we all did when going on shed, but these engines would move with less than 80 lb. showing on the pressure gauge. The prevailing foggy conditions seemed to have driven him almost to the point of breakdown.

We were ordered to work a freight to Oxley Sidings one evening, this train duly arrived at Tyseley with a 'dreaded' Midland class '8F' and a long train. I knew I was in for a miserable time. At Wednesbury North signal box, the signalman turned us towards the long goods loop to Bilston, but first stopped us at the signal box with a red handsignal. He then instructed us that the loop was already blocked with two other trains having no engines on them. As the express was behind us, he wanted us to stop our brakevan clear of the loop points so that when he eventually got line clear for our train, we could back shunt on to the main line again.

It was a filthy night and when the guard signalled to us to stop his van clear of the points we were a long way from the signal box, in fact well ahead of the main line advanced starting signal. As we came to a stand, Bernard decided he wanted a cup of tea. Passing his brew on to me, he told me to walk back to the signal box to make a brew. There was hardly much point in this, as the tea would be stone cold by the time I got back to the engine. Nevertheless, I obediently went a good half mile to the signal box. It was pitch dark and raining hard, yet only minutes after rejoining the engine with the brew, he said I had better walk back to the box and telephone the control to send relief to Wolverhampton Low Level station for us, as it was getting late. This was the last straw and I finally snapped, telling him if that if he wanted relief, then he could walk back to the signal box himself. There was no way I was walking back again in that weather I was already wet through.

The rest of our time together was in acrimony; I tried to break the ice on some days, but he would have none of it. We worked together for probably only weeks afterwards, but it did seem like years.

A Wolverhampton man yet again filled a vacancy for shed foreman at Tyseley. The new foreman was very jolly and seemed to be very friendly with everyone. He was soon well liked by the men in general as he was susceptible to anyone pleading poverty and gave men overtime at the drop of a hat. At this time a number of young Wolverhampton drivers had also come to Tyseley for promotion. As Tyseley men had already come to expect, this foreman again tended to look after his own. I might add that his good turns towards these men were often at the expense of senior Tyseley men.

At quiet times, Bernard Pratt had a habit of sitting in the foreman's office chatting, despite the fact that he told everyone how the management practically licked his boots. Unfortunately, it was not long before the last addition to our management team began to quietly work the oracle on me. There was a general procedure that foremen should have followed when men were 'spare', yet this man began to get me out of the way on dirty, short jobs and then give better work to younger men only minutes after I was away. I first thought that this was co-incidence, but it began to happen all too frequently and I could only conclude that Bernard had laid some poison down. Most of the time we had diagrammed working and therefore we did not come into contact with the shed foremen very often. Although upset by these incidents, I tried to put it behind me. However, although this foreman did still retain an outwardly friendly attitude towards me, later evidence of his actions was to lead to an awful showdown. I was growing older and much wiser. Perhaps Bernard was not a well man, although he never ever implied that he was not well. He died in London shortly after we parted, *en route* for his holidays in the South.

I started to get odd driving turns, which did enhance my pay, but as one would expect they were mundane jobs, mainly shed turns, the coal stage, turntables, or preparing engines. This unfortunately brought me occasionally into contact with the latest addition to our shed foremen, who was again in a position to work things across me. He was still very friendly to my face, but after several encounters it became blatantly obvious that he was indeed holding some grudge.

It is probable that this foreman thought he was working it on me when I booked on one morning 8.00 am 'Spare'. A 'King' class locomotive, No. 6018 *King Henry VI*, had spent some time in Tyseley factory for repairs and he gave me the job of oiling it and taking it up to Snow Hill to go on the 1.00 pm Paddington Pullman. He no doubt thought that I would find it an awful chore, but I had never yet oiled a four-cylinder engine, I also had ample time to do the job, therefore it was quite a good interesting experience. This job, however, had to be done right, all the valve gear, along with the crossheads, connecting and coupling rods, had been re-metalled, the whole lot was bone dry and lacking any corks. I did think at the time that it was questionable as to the wisdom of putting an engine on a hard turn like this without a shorter running-in turn first. No doubt, this was to be a sure test of my capabilities and the outstanding accuracy of the fine work done by the artisans in Tyseley factory.

The fireman who was to work with me preparing this engine was not only a well-known awkward character, but he was downright bloody-minded. As it was some five hours hence until the train left Snow Hill, and I was likely to have to spend a long time underneath the engine in the shed, I therefore asked my fireman if he would mind not making the fire up too early, as we did not want to bring the steam pressure forward too quickly. The last thing we wanted was for this big boiler to be blowing off steam inside the shed.

Needless to say, the engine was ramping steam from the safety valves within 40 minutes and the whole of Warwickshire must have been able to hear it. With my eardrums tingling, I tramped to and from the stores for more oil; it was hard to believe where it all was going. For the next three hours the engine made the most unearthly noise, you could not hear yourself speak. Again, not surprisingly with this young moron, when we finally went to leave the shed for Snow Hill, he then decided that there was something wrong with the coal- watering pipe and disappeared for a long period to find a replacement. Thankfully, there were not many youngsters like Keith!

We had relief at Birmingham and I waited for any later news through the grapevine that the engine had come to grief. After all, the train was timed very sharply and only stopped at Leamington and London. On this particular occasion steam was of course deputising for the 'Blue Pullman' diesel train. However, the days passed, no news was good news, I had obviously done a good job.

I welcomed my next link change; I would have happily gone back to any of my old mates, despite the shortcomings of one or two of them. I hated the atmosphere that Bernard Pratt and I had worked under; yet changing things for the better seemed to be quite out of my hands. The only time I had chosen to speak up for myself, he had found unforgivable, he was adamant and was never going to compromise.

My new mate went by the name of 'The Creep ', although this was by no means a reflection on his character, he was a really nice fellow. Although, to say he was 'laid back' would have been an understatement. There was little anyone could say against his qualities as an engineman, yet he was certainly no 'creep' on express work! With my anxieties over, it was a pleasure to be at to work again. Even so, further altered link arrangements brought me back on jobs like the Reading 'Biscuits' and the Landore to Moor Street again. Harry Howarth was an overtime man; if things were not going well on my side and we were losing time, it was money in his pocket. He had every faith that I could do my job and he would put his nose towards the front window and leave me to it. Although, I did struggle like hell at times and often wondered if he really was awake!

One of the easiest trips I had on the Reading 'Biscuits' was with Harry, albeit with a '9F' on a Saturday night when we were diverted via Honeybourne and Stratford-upon-Avon due to engineering work. Many times I had heard older drivers talking of the super quality Welsh coal that they had used in days gone by. Although we did get some good coal from time to time, there was something special about the coal on this sole occasion. It was in the form of ovoids, which were egg shaped and made of compressed coal dust. Nevertheless, the slack coal quality that went into these particular ovoids was extraordinary, they burned at an incredible temperature and it was certainly unknown to me for a '9F' to steam with the firehole doors open when using soft coal. One shovelful seemed to expand to three times its own volume once on the fire and the temperature in the cab was absolutely scorching. Despite a heavy train, we negotiated the bank at Stratford-upon-Avon and passed Henley-in-Arden with the firehole doors still open. It really was astonishing, I'm sure that if this quality of coal had still been available in quantity, steam locomotives would have been about for much longer. After many years as a fireman this was certainly a very notable experience for me.

There must have been an imbalance in the engine working diagrams on the Reading 'Biscuits' on Saturday nights, as we were rarely saddled with the old Reading 'Halls' that were endowed on us during the week. The following Saturday night when our turn came around, Harry and I found ourselves with a Tyseley engine, No. 75029. Tyseley had quite a stud of these Standard class '4s' and much attention was lavished on them because they regularly worked the Washwood Heath to Southampton fully-fitted freight. This train conveyed very important freight traffic and reports to drivers for any lost time were again distributed like confetti. Despite these engines not being up to the work on this job, the BR Standard '4s' remained on the diagram for a very long time. So poor was the performance of these engines that I never ever heard any locoman say a good word for any of them. Even when the draughting was improved, by the fitting of the double chimney, this made no difference to their steaming qualities whatsoever, they were atrocious engines.

I prepared many on the shed at Tyseley for the Washwood Heath-Southampton and you could not fault the maintenance staff. Looking in the smokebox, you could see firelight through every boiler tube. Even so, the maintenance men still came to put some chemical into the fire, that is, once the fireman had got a hot bed of fire spread over the grate. With this substance in the fire, the blower had to be turned off, so that the varying coloured flames that now ensued could weave some magical process to keep the boiler tubes clear. I think the company that sold this stuff to BR saw them coming, this again made no difference whatsoever to the steaming. These engines made steam freely with the regulator closed, once sustained running was necessary they just would not hold their own. I tried all sorts of methods to try to get the best out of them, like every other fireman, I never found the answer. Even with the firehole flap glowing red-hot the pressure gauge would not hold its own with continuous running. Strangely, by the time you drifted up to a water column for relief, the engine would be blowing away steam wildly from the safety valves. When you eventually came to a stand, having both injectors working, the boiler level would be well up the gauge glass and it would look altogether as if you had had the best trip in the world. A Banbury fireman relieved me one night in this condition and I told him quite frankly that I had struggled to get there. He spoke to me as though I was a novice, so I took it that he was a far better fireman than I was. The following night, the Banbury driver told my driver that they had found it necessary to take the engine on to Didcot shed as he was not prepared to struggle any further, his fireman had been well and truly beaten! And they had negotiated far easier gradients getting to Didcot than we had. Such was the reputation of these machines.

It was therefore with some trepidation that I left Reading with No. 75029 on this Saturday night. I knew exactly what was to come, as yet again we had the usual maximum load. Inevitably, I had the most appalling trip home; I struggled every inch of the way, although I did manage to keep her going. The blower was on all the way and the fire irons never got cool, yet Harry sat in his corner behind the ATC equipment and never said a word.

The following week I was in the enginemen's cabin and I sat listening to a group of men who had got on to the subject of these notorious BR Standard '4s'. With the air getting blue, the old foreman's runner came in, who himself had been a footplate man some years earlier. He listened for a while, then said, 'There can't be much wrong with those engines, Harry Howarth had one on the Reading Biscuits last Saturday night and he never had a scrap of bother!' The foreman's runner could only have got those words from Harry. I began to wonder if we had really been together on the same engine. I had no alternative but to intervene in the conversation and put the record straight.

The Great Western mechanical engineers at Swindon went to great lengths to standardise their locomotives and therefore many of the engine parts were interchangeable. With this in mind, all engines of the same class should have performed equally, depending on their mechanical condition. Strangely, this was not the case; some engines always performed well, even when due for a general overhaul, yet others were mediocre even after major repairs. One case in question was No. 5927 *Guild Hall*, she spent her working life at Tyseley and she was always a pleasure to work on. Prairie tank No. 4170 came to Tyseley brand new; she was always a black sheep. The flagship of the Great Western, No. 6000 *King George V*, was not always the best performer, that is, according to much of the gossip that went on between enginemen. This was certainly the case the only time I worked on her.

One turn in our link was to work the down 'Inter City' from Snow Hill to Wolverhampton, service the engine on Stafford Road shed and work back the up 'Inter City' to Snow Hill. This was a nice job, as it was a decent day turn and you were more or less guaranteed to finish on time. Because of diesel working, we often found ourselves with younger drivers on this turn, this again was a pleasure, with men of a closer age group there was always more in common. It was only 14 miles to Wolverhampton and the younger men would sometimes give the fireman a chance to drive. This was an added interest, as we had little concept of what the future held for us with the inevitable demise of steam. It was on this turn that I worked just once on the only Great Western engine with a bell on the front. The Old Oak Common fireman on this occasion was in a right mess when I relieved him at Snow Hill, the boiler pressure was down and the water low. The trip is memorable because I also fought for enough steam to get us to Wolverhampton. When we stopped at adverse signals outside Low Level tunnel, with the water bobbing in the

A group of young trainspotters record Collett '56XX' class 0-6-2T No. 6667 as it passes through Birmingham Snow Hill with a freight train in 1959. *Michael Mensing*

BR Standard class '4' 4-6-0 No. 75025 hauls the empty stock into Birmingham Snow Hill which will form the 5.45 pm to Stratford-upon-Avon and Worcester on 9th July, 1960. *Michael Mensing*

bottom of the boiler gauge glass, ex-Caledonian Railway 4-2-2 No. 123 steamed by in the opposite direction going for exhibition in Birmingham. She was a magnificent sight in her polished state and powder blue livery.

On Stafford Road shed we always took on coal and made up a fresh fire with large lumps. On this occasion, getting things right to start with helped us have a better trip back to Snow Hill, but I was glad not to be taking *King George V* on to Paddington. Tyseley men relieved us at Snow Hill, so it was always an incentive to get things right for one another, as the relieving turn was in my link also.

On the Wolverhampton part of the 'Inter City' I had a most wonderful week with a young driver who had just come to Tyseley for promotion. He had come from Evesham, a small shed that obviously had not given him a great variety of work. He was really keen and enthusiastic, so it was nice for him to get on a big engine and make the sparks fly, albeit for a short distance. Unfortunately, this particular week there was a 15 mph speed restriction imposed on the compound crossover on the up main line, right outside Handsworth and Smethwick signal box, which indeed we were both fully aware of.

On Monday evening, our enthusiasm got the better of us on the return trip. Determined to be back in Snow Hill on time, one could say the engine was worked in a spirited fashion up the heavy gradient to West Bromwich. Approaching Handsworth Junction my driver eased the regulator and I went over to put on the live steam injector, which was on the right-hand side of the footplate. In doing so, I missed seeing the advanced warning board for the 15 mph speed restriction sited at Handsworth Junction. With downhill running into Snow Hill I took the coal-watering pipe, laid the dust and swept up. It wasn't until we were running into the station that a look of horror came on to my mate's face, 'What about the speed restriction at Handsworth?', he gasped.

We had indeed run over it at approaching 70 mph. Inconceivably, this omission appeared to have gone unnoticed by everyone and nothing was ever said. The following day we looked out when passing in the down direction, the whole crossover under restriction was held up by bits of wood packing as all the ballast had also been removed ready for the relaying project. We thanked our lucky stars, the Gods had been with us that evening! Thirty years later, when we meet at reunions, our greetings are still likely to start with, 'How about that speed restriction at Handsworth?' Light hearted comments, but we both appreciate the seriousness of our error.

Again back with my regular mate, the up 'Inter City' left Snow Hill at 5.00 pm and Harry Howarth and I worked this turn many times, returning with the 8.10 pm Paddington to Wolverhampton. This was an arduous job, as we mostly had 'King' class engines both ways. On these trains Harry tended to work the engines quite hard, but nothing like I had experienced with earlier drivers. Had things still been in their heyday I would no doubt have enjoyed the way he drove.

On the up journey we normally had an Old Oak Common engine and on the return train had a Wolverhampton engine. There was little doubt that by this period the London engines were far better cared for than their counterparts. The Old Oak engines were always beautifully clean and they had the advantage of not having water treatment in their boilers.

Having the water treatment the Wolverhampton engines initially went for long periods without boiler washing, which could be a nightmare to enginemen. After a time, more frequent boiler wash outs were found necessary. More so in the initial period, the boiler water would foam and cause priming, specially if the engine blew off steam, in which case it was likely that much of the boiler water would lift and be thrown out of the safety valves. If you were unlucky enough for this to happen, the water would not stop blowing away until the level was right towards the bottom of the gauge glass, by which time you would be in awful trouble. The foaming could be settled by adding a substance that appeared like milk of magnesia to the boiler. If you were lucky, this fluid was usually contained in a sterilised milk bottle thrown in the bottom of the toolbox with its neck stuffed with newspaper. Such were the niceties of the system. If there was any fluid left in the bottle, it had to be put down a funnel on the tender toolbox once the exhaust injector was working. The chemical action in the boiler was then quite remarkable as the filthy water showing in the gauge glass immediately turned clear with larger lumps of deposits forming. After a time more frequent washouts solved the problem.

Passenger train working was now fast being taken over by diesel traction and the 'Kings' were subject to their last working days. Added to this, Stafford Road shed was down for closure and much of the coal stack, that had probably been on the ground since the depot opened, was now being put on to the engines. With decades of being exposed to all weathers, this coal had broken down to powder. Also, the grab that picked the coal up from the ground had brought with it ballast, tin cans, clinker and any other debris that lay with the coal.

Harry and I worked the up 'Inter City' for the first three evenings of one week and on Monday evening we relieved our men at Snow Hill as usual. The London engine had obviously worked down in the morning and had gone on to Stafford Road shed, were the tender was topped up with this dreadful coal. There was not a lump to be seen and it was rather like shovelling wet sand. Fortunately, the Old Oak Common 'King' was in super condition, therefore despite the fire being dirty and this awful coal we coped, but it was indeed hard work.

We then relieved the 8.10 pm engine as it backed on to our train at Paddington; this engine had worked up in the morning and had been stabled on Ranelagh Bridge engine sidings. The tender had again been filled with this coal from off the ground at Wolverhampton and a labourer at Ranelagh Bridge had shovelled the remaining coal from the back of the tender for us. As the engine had worked the up trip with this powdered poor quality fuel, the fire was already in a dreadful state before we left the station. Also, the engine standing in the sidings for some hours hadn't helped the situation at all; consequently I had the most awful trip home. We always had a big train on the 8. 10. p.m. departure and much of the slack coal seemed to disappear up the boiler tubes without touching the fire. Trying to get this coal towards the front of the firebox was doubly hard, as I was throwing the coal against the natural draught of the exhaust. Harry's forceful driving was not at fault, he was committed to run to time. Nonetheless, I was truly on my last legs when we got back, it had been a laborious day's work.

Tuesday evening was an identical performance, up with No. 6026 and back with No. 6014, with more of this appalling coal. This made for another exceptionally arduous day's work. When I finished my arms and wrists had now become very painful. At home, I ran icy water over my arms for a long period to find some relief; I then took some 'Aspirin' for a painkiller and went to bed.

The situation was no different on Wednesday evening; more 'bug dust' on No. 6026 and I now struggled on the 'easy' bit of the up journey; the constant effort needed was getting the better of me. At Paddington I was in real trouble, my wrists were extremely painful and I again ran the cold tap on them at length to get some respite.

On the return train was No. 6007 looking terribly forlorn, a look in the fire and at the tender again said it all, I was obviously in for another drubbing. To add to my troubles the boilersmiths had repaired the firebrick arch; it seemed possible that the correct type firebricks were now unavailable, as the new arch lay low over the fire and all the boiler tubes were exposed to any cold air entering the firebox via the firehole. In addition the low-lying brick arch prevented me from getting any depth of fire in the middle of the firebox. The engine was also tooled with a set of unsatisfactory tools. That she had been robbed by another engine crew at Ranelagh Bridge seems likely, but the fire-irons were all like a dog's hind leg and the shovel back was split.

When we left Paddington, I did my level best with coal that I could only describe as diseased earth, but passing Gerrards Cross I was already in dire straights. I pointed out to Harry that I felt that there was no way that we were going to get up Hatton Bank with an engine in this condition. Harry agreed and we planned to have assistance from Banbury, indeed there was a pilot engine there which normally stood in the bay line doing nothing, it made sense to utilise him on this occasion.

Again I worked like blazes to keep the engine going, I shovelled uphill and downhill. When we ran into Banbury, Harry felt that I was coping well enough and flatly refused to take the assistant engine. I was gutted, exhausted and at my wit's end. After three days of complete adversity I was totally bewildered at Harry's half-soaked attitude, had he not noticed anything of what was going on my side? With only 40 miles to go my spirit was willing, but I wondered if I had the remaining physical strength to make it to Snow Hill. After Banbury I fought on, firing continuously to keep as much fire in the engine as possible. At Leamington, I had as good a start as we could possibly have hoped for, the water well up in the gauge glass and I had the most enormous fire. Almost legless I was determined that this ogre would not beat me, indeed it was our last night on this job.

I have to deviate from the subject for a while; as we went through a period where new BR coaching stock entering service was fitted with Direct Admission (DA) valves. These valves had already become known by many other expletives from drivers, although they were not a new concept, the Great Western had fitted them to coaching stock for some years. With these modified valves fitted, drivers who had run trains for years now found themselves embarrassingly stopping halfway along platforms, because once a small amount of brake had been applied the vacuum would now not recreate fast enough to get the brakes off again.

The purpose of the Direct Admission valves was to make a faster brake application in emergencies, such as the communication cord being pulled, also dieselisation possibly had some bearing as to why they were fitted in this form. The new DA valves sensed any slight a drop in vacuum, in which case the valve opened an extra port to atmosphere, thus applying the train brakes quicker. These new valves were probably not set correctly and, during braking, drivers reducing the vacuum by only five inches of mercury suddenly found the vacuum gauge went to zero, there was an awful snatch from the train and it was then pot luck if you did not come to a complete stand before the vacuum was recreated. The driver was therefore robbed of any finesse when braking and undue delay was often caused.

On our last night on the 8.10 pm ex-Paddington our train was fitted with the new DA valves, yet Harry had coped well and the obscenities had been kept to a minimum. Leaving Leamington the line dips sharply for about ¾ mile to pass under the Grand Union Canal. This downhill stretch we always used to our advantage to give the train momentum, the burst of speed allowed us to shorten the valve travel for the steep gradient as far as Hatton North.

Great Western engines were fitted with vacuum pumps to maintain the train vacuum whilst running. To avoid the vacuum being re-created by the vacuum pump at the same time as a driver was applying the brake, a device called a retaining valve was fitted to all engines. This retaining valve diverted the action of the pump from the train pipe to the brake 'Reservoir' once the brake was applied (the 'Reservoir' being the vacuum which sucked at the brake pistons and hence applied the brakes). When the pump was operating on the 'Reservoir' it served to counteract any small leaks and therefore make the brake more efficient.

On occasions the retaining valve was known to stick after a brake application had been made, therefore it would allow the pump to keep pumping at the brake 'Reservoir' instead of the train vacuum which kept the brakes off. Drivers always had to watch this carefully and it was sometimes necessary to open the large vacuum ejector and at the same time opening a release valve on the 'Reservoir' to reduce the vacuum therein. With the train vacuum at a higher level than the 'Reservoir', the retaining valve would reseat itself and start to maintain the train pipe again keeping the train brakes off.

Harry slipped up on this occasion and never noticed that the retaining valve had stuck. Because of this, as we had just got the train going nicely, the train pipe vacuum leaked down slightly, the DA valves sensed the drop in vacuum and before Harry realised the vacuum went to zero and we had ground to a complete stand just on the rising gradient at Avon bridge. This indeed was the worst possible place that we could have stopped. Starting from here was bad enough, but Harry then realised that he had 'boobed' and time was lost.

It was unthinkable to imagine that we could recover any time lost with a locomotive in this condition. Passing Budbrook signal box, half way up Hatton Bank, I had not been able to start the injector, in addition the fire was disappearing quicker than I could now get coal into the firebox. Clearing the summit the boiler water was disappearing out of sight in the gauge glass, I went over to Harry and made absolutely sure he was fully aware of the position I was in. He therefore had no alternative to closing the regulator and allowing the train to drift over the slight falling gradient approaching the water troughs at Rowington. With the injector running the boiler water began to show again, but we were now again on a rising gradient and we were forced to come to a stand outside Lapworth signal box as we were in no state to continue. I was not only physically, but morally, beaten, after 12 years as a fireman this had never happened to me on a passenger train. Harry went into the signal box, leaving me to rally the steam pressure. After 10 minutes or so, we left at our own speed; I was practically incapable of doing much more.

At Snow Hill I was in awful pain and couldn't grip anything, I could only get off the engine by wrapping my arms round the handrail and then allow myself to fall on to the platform. This was the last time I set foot on a 'King', and the last time I ever wanted to. In this condition they were just man killers, a galley slave could not have worked harder.

The following morning both my arms had swelled considerably and I could hold nothing, not even to drink, or hold a razor to shave. I obviously could not drive; therefore my father found it necessary to accompany me to the doctor's surgery on public transport. The buses still being rear-entranced, I was unable to hold on to anything.

The doctor I saw told me that he had worked for a long time in a London Teaching Hospital and he had seen my problem a number of times with footplate men, although he stressed he had never seen it so acute. Nevertheless, at that point in time there was nothing he could do until the swelling had gone away.

I went back some days later and he wrapped both my arms completely in a 'Wintergreen' plaster. Several days in this and I was going frantic, I had an allergy to sticking plaster. Back at the surgery I passed out as he took off the wrapping, much of my skin came away with the plaster and I then became a hospital patient.

The doctor at the hospital was aghast, he said it was usual to apply 'Plaster of Paris', but in my condition it was now impossible. When moving my joints they could actually be heard to creak. I was eventually wrapped in yards of crepe bandage and sent home with more painkillers.

I was away from work for six weeks. During this time I was paid Industrial Injury Benefit, but heard nothing from BR management whatsoever as to my welfare.

On return to work I was put on to light duties on the inter-yard trip shunting engines. My mate was another light duty man, driver Fred Scott. Fred had communist tendencies, nevertheless his principles were baffling, he was an ASLEF trade unionist who had for some reason worked during the 1955 strike. Together with his politics, this made him a very unpopular man amongst colleagues. He was a cheerful fellow, but men tended to avoid us both like the plague. It was a long and very lonely three months until the doctor at Swindon passed me fit for my own work.

I changed links again and my new driver was the brother of Charlie Yarwood, who had been my driver to Cardiff with a 'Britannia' and we had both narrowly escaped being badly burned. Bill was the younger of the brothers, who incidentally, both looked like peas in a pod. They were broad Black Country men and although neither of them was very tall, one got the impression that they were rough diamonds in their youth, little doubt they could handle themselves very well. Both brothers rarely smiled and they could certainly be counted on to call a spade, a spade.

I had never worked with Bill previously, so I was pleased to find him a lot more pleasant than he appeared, all round he was a good mate. His absolute 'John Blunt' manner let you know exactly where you stood; I very much admired him for that. He never criticised me, neither did he indulge in mess room small talk, which was gratifying. It was therefore easy to develop a respect for him, although the speed of his driving was to frighten the life out of me on some occasions!

The first diesel-hydraulics were now making an appearance on the Western Region and I came very close one night to being an early fatality of this new concept. I never heard, or saw, an oncoming diesel train, which was terrifying and afterwards turned my legs to total jelly. Link re-organization had put the Swindon Parcels back in my new link and on the night in question it had snowed heavily. We were unusually brought to a stand at the outer home signal for Minety, between Stroud and Swindon. Because we were there for an unusually long time, it was my job to make my way to the signal box in the absence of a telephone at the signal. The snow had drifted high on my side, so I got off the engine on the main line side. Our engine had now begun to blow off steam, which smothered the sound of a parcels train coming in the opposite direction. I was near the cylinders of our engine when the train bore down on me and I had to dodge under the framing of our engine to take refuge as the train thundered by. After this train passed, the signal cleared for us and I rejoined our engine trembling like a leaf. My legs were now barely capable of supporting me and I had to flop down on the seat.

'I bet y'oll be a bit more careful in future?', Bill drawled. How right he was!

The railway was a very dangerous place and I had had a similar experience some years earlier, it was so easy to drop your guard. On the previous occasion, I had again gone to the signal box to carry out my duty as stated in Rule 55. This was at Wilmcote late at night and I saw a freight train coming in the opposite direction and waited. After the train brakevan had passed I went to cross the line, not noticing the

Stratford bank engine that had assisted the train from the rear and by now had eased away from the back of the train. God was with me on that occasion too; the bank engine missed me only by a fraction as I went to step out in front of it to go to the signal box.

Bill was as cool as a cucumber, although his driving was similar to Mickey Tolley, not so heavy handed but rather erratic. He went so fast that we could not always stop; indeed we overran more signals in the few months that we were together than I had experienced in my whole career.

We normally worked the Swindon Parcels on alternate nights, one week, we overran the outer home signal at Kemble on the three nights that we worked this turn. I was on the point of being on first name terms with the signalman on duty! At this period, the traffic carried on the Swindon Parcels had dwindled and we usually left Cheltenham with just three bogie vans. Short trains lacked brake power, so it was always necessary to adjust the train speed accordingly, particularly on falling gradients. Bill went so fast on the uphill gradient from Stroud to Sapperton that each night the distant signal for Kemble was at caution, because a previous train had not cleared. At the speed that we were going we had no chance of stopping at the outer home signal. Thankfully, as usual the signalman was pretty accommodating, as long as no damage was done to any points that may have been set adversely; there was never any backlash from these minor signal overruns.

Shortly after, Bill was trained on the 'Western' diesel-hydraulics; similarly I had training on the 'Spanner Swirliflow' train heating boilers. Eventually, we had this type of diesel on the Swindon Parcels and the Southall Parcels, which we worked from Oxford over the West Midland line to Wolverhampton, via Stratford-upon-Avon and Snow Hill. More often than not, Bill put me in the driving seat on these turns, which was a relief to me. On restricted curves the locomotive would lean over alarmingly and it was some time before I understood that Bill had a problem, and he was not alone.

Until that point in time, drivers were never allowed to wear spectacles on the footplate. Whilst every driver's long distance vision was fine, at their age short distances were a problem, they therefore could not see the speedometer without putting reading glasses on! Without glasses, Bill was taking the 80 mph point on the speedometer to be the 60 mph, there was obviously a good reason why these diesels leaned adversely on the curves! We were quick to realise too, the dangers of it being all too easy to doze off at night. During the early hours, in a warm comfortable cab, it became a nightmare trying to keep awake.

On one of the first trips on Southall Parcels, we cleared Earlswood in good time at 70 mph and Bill closed the power controller. He had got his seat rather too high and being a short man it needed the tips of his toes to keep the deadman's pedal depressed. He began to doze and every dip in the rail that caused the locomotive to bounce, the springs in his seat made him momentarily lose partial contact with the deadman's pedal. There was an intermittent, psss-psss-psss, as air escaped from deadman's operating valve, although this was not quite enough to apply the vacuum brakes. On the driver's console there was an array of blue fault lights, which changed to red as any fault developed. These blue lights reflected back into the cab and looking at the windscreen in the dark was rather like looking at yourself on a black and white television set. These engines carried no headlights, only a headcode number blind, so everything was jet black outside when between signal sections. Wild life was also not yet aware of these silent fast moving objects; at speed there was sometimes the most frightening bang on the front window as the locomotive collided with some large nocturnal bird.

I watched Bill carefully as he dozed and the train speed began to fall. The distant signal for Tyseley South Junction was fixed at caution, due to the severe 15 mph permanent speed restriction over the sharp curve. I knew that when we passed over the Automatic Train Control ramp the warning would sound and Bill would wake. Our speed had dropped to around 45 mph when the ear piercing warning sounded, which was about normal speed; Bill by this time was out of this world. He suddenly leapt up, putting his hands on everything adjacent to him to cancel the warning siren, in doing so he took his foot off the deadman's pedal too. With a slow response from Bill, several of the panel lights changed from blue to red and we came to a stand in the deep cutting in the middle of nowhere. Bill now totally disorientated and seeing the row of red fault lights, immediately said, 'What's gone wrong mate?' 'I think the driver dozed off?', I replied. Bill reluctantly smiled and admitted that he had, it was no big deal, we were in front of time. We just waited until the deadman's device had reset itself and we were away again.

This was not Bill's night; in Snow Hill it was usual to put some of our vans into No. 3 bay platform. We squeezed the vans on to the stop block and thinking that he had left the couplings slack, Bill reversed our engine ready to go forward again. Unfortunately, when the shunter came to detach, the coupling was still tight, therefore the shunter called from between the engine and vans for Bill to 'ease up'. Bill now had to reverse the engine again to slacken the coupling. The diesel-hydraulic final drive gears sometimes needed to turn slightly before they would mesh and allow the engine to reverse. To facilitate this, there was on the panel a 'tooth on tooth' button, which allowed the transmission to move slightly to get the gears to mesh. Regrettably, this button was next to the rear facing horn, now some six inches from the shunter's ears! Because of the noise from the engine, Bill never realised that he was pressing the rear horn, instead of the 'tooth on tooth' button. The shunter was a big man, who walked about as though he had a roll of carpet under each arm; he was also not very amiable at that time of day. Having his eardrums perforated had also done nothing to help his dodgy temperament. The exchange of words that followed is unprintable, Bill eventually got off the engine on to the platform and was ready to spar up to this man who literally towered over him! It was a colourful night, after which Bill was more than happy to let me do the driving. Driving was a good grounding for me as far as route knowledge was concerned; there was now a full view in front of us and all the time in the world to absorb the intricacies of the signalling system.

Bill and I worked well together and again it brought back the joy of being at work; the shifts were bad enough without being on bad terms with your colleague. I shall never understand why Bernard Pratt and I became so alienated. Nevertheless, this was a time when we just had to take the rough with the smooth, as we didn't know until we got to work whether we would be on steam or diesel. This was quite a contrast, as many of the steam locomotives were now well past their best.

One evening turn saw me on a steam engine working a dmu turn to Paddington. The train called at almost every station and I was therefore to have several drivers from varying depots *en route*. I worked the train with the most dilapidated looking 'Castle' and it was quite an experience just seeing the unsuspecting relieving driver's face as the train ran up the platform with a steam locomotive on the front. Most just stood there, thinking that it wasn't their train at all. The Reading driver turned up with immaculately polished shoes, collar and tie and his new green uniform pressed fit for Royal Train duties. The dmu had been established for some time in the London area, so he just stood on the platform agape as if this was not possible. We waited some time on the platform as he refused to get on the footplate and relieve the current driver. After a long exchange he did relent and we eventually worked into Paddington, much coal dust flying as we thumped our way from the numerous stations.

'Western' class diesel-hydraulic No. D1002 *Western Explorer* passes through Knowle & Dorridge with a London-bound passenger train in 1962. *Michael Mensing*

For probably the first time in the history of the railways it was decided that there would be no trains on Christmas Day. I was booked on duty on the following Boxing Day to work the 10 am Snow Hill to Paddington along with driver Ted Davies. When working this turn, we left Snow Hill with the now usual diesel 'Western' class, but between Acocks Green and Olton we ground to a stand with loss of control air pressure. We had only come five miles and our speed had not yet exceeded 60 mph. The diesels were still a new concept to us and despite his training my driver had no idea what the problem was. We were also a long way from any communication with any signalman, Acocks Green signal box being switched out and the signalmen off duty. We then eventually managed to get some power, enough to get the train moving and as we toddled along at 25 mph the Snow Hill pilot engine ran alongside us on the adjacent relief line. The controllers had anticipated that we were in trouble and had already alerted the pilot engine to assist if necessary.

It took us a long time to get to Leamington, where the 'Western' was taken off and we took over the 'Hall' class Snow Hill pilot. Further south we ran into thick fog and we got so late that we changed footplates with our return train at Greenford and never made it to Paddington. Our return train was another steam engine, so we were a bit desperate for a drink by the time we got to Bicester, where thankfully the kitchen car staff obliged us with hot water for our tea.

We discovered later that all that had happened on the diesel was that the locomotive 'overspeed' device had tripped. A new phenomenon had now arisen, with no trains on Christmas Day, the rails had become greasy with atmospheric pollution. The rear bogie of the diesel, unknown to us, had gone into wheel spin and had exceeded the 90 mph maximum locomotive speed, consequently setting off the 'overspeed' device. When trains ran seven days a week, all the year round, we never really had a problem. Unfortunately, this was a locomotive fault that we could easily have rectified had we realised, but we were all on a learning curve and had an awful lot to learn.

On the lighter side, I left the shed for home one night when a driver in a Land Rover stopped and approached me only yards from the depot gate. He said that an animal, the like of which he had never seen before, had just run across the road in front of him. It had now gone into some long grass by an old Victorian house that the local scrapyard was now using for offices. Not quite believing his own eyes, he asked me if I would go with him into the grass to have closer look.

As we approached the area the creature ran back across the road, it was about six feet long and I was pretty sure I recognised it as an anteater. We followed it, as it had now gone into the front garden of one of the local houses and was using its snout as a plough, in doing so was making very short work of the proud owner's half hardy annuals. Another colleague then appeared and he suggested that it must have escaped from the local pet shop, although who would on earth would want this for a pet?

My colleague ran up the Warwick Road to hammer on the door of the pet shop to rouse the owner, only to find that he flatly denied that the escapee was his. Not quite knowing what to do, we then rang the police. The usual beautifully polished, black lustre Farina Austin Cambridge patrol car arrived with its bright chromium plated bell on the front. Two policemen got out, donned their flat hats and approached me, where I explained that I thought the creature at large was an anteater. They looked at me in disbelief.

By this time the animal had gone up a works entrance, so I indicated to the officers the direction that the animal had taken. With flashing torches the constables confidently strode forth. The next few moments were rather like a comic strip in the *Beano*. On sighting the creature they both froze to the spot. Simultaneously, they both turned back towards the patrol car, where they radioed in. The constable said that he was dealing with an unknown species and he was in need of advice, whereby the control suggested to him to put a collar on it. Obviously, he could not do this, as the creature had a tapered head and no neck. The control then asked if he could put it in the back of the car, his answer to that was that he was not having the bloody thing breathing down the back of his neck while he was driving. Eventually, the policemen took a large sack from the boot of the car and confronted the frightened animal. The constables eventually made a rugby tackle on it and finally wrestled the writhing creature into the boot of the car.

The following evening, the story was prominent in the local newspaper. It was indeed a South American anteater and it was in fact in transit from British Guiana to a Belgian zoo, via the pet shop whose owner had denied that it was his. Strangely, this was only one of many exotic species that was eventually to find its way out of these premises; needless to say, all got wide coverage in the *Birmingham Mail*.

First of all Tyseley's steam workshops were demolished in 1963/64, so as to extend the diesel unit factory. We then began to lose more work from the depot, which was very worrying. Many fine young men were sadly forced to leave the industry.

Then the Regional boundaries were altered and Tyseley became part of the Midland Region. The depot was immediately upgraded and the shed code changed from being 84E and under Wolverhampton, to become 2A. This 'A' status brought much speculation that our futures were assured, particularly when the 'Goods Side' roundhouse was demolished to make way for a new locomotive repair factory. A wheel turning lathe was also to be installed, this lathe would unbelievably, re-profile worn wheels without them being removed from any type of traction unit, it was an amazing step forward.

From this time on, a number of Tyseley men also began to get promotion to management. For the first time promotion was made on capability, rather than who anyone was likely to know. Older colleagues therefore started to go up the promotional ladder, which was refreshing; particularly knowing that many of these good men had always been conscientious and had our industry at heart.

The effects of the Beeching Report in 1963 soon began to show on freight traffic, small consignments of goods were deemed unprofitable. This in turn saw many small yards close and an ever-diminishing number of shunting engines at Bordesley Junction and Hockley. This in turn meant less work for drivers having poor health.

The author's father back on main line duties, seen here driver training on English Electric type '4's. Left to right are, father, the train guard, Stan Rosamond, Tyseley roster clerk, driver Stan Carter and tutor driver Harry Mason. *Provenance Unknown*

My father was sent for a medical examination and, much to his delight, was passed fit for his own jobs on the main line. At the time I felt there was something a bit cynical about this, as he had now spent 20 years on the shunting engines; perhaps it was a sinister way of avoiding the payment of a redundancy package? Yet I can only admire my father for what he took on, as he now found himself in No. 1 link. Indeed he had not set foot on any of the 'Standard' engines, or any of the 'foreign' steam engines which were now in abundance. He also had to be trained on the 'Western' hydraulics, the Brush 2,750 hp locomotives, English Electric type '4s' and the diesel multiple units. All these forms of traction were now becoming part of our lives. Along with this, he had to learn hundreds of miles of routes, which were as yet predominantly semaphore signalled. This was quite a task for a man nearing 60 years of age and I shall always be very proud that he took it all in his stride and enjoyed the challenge. For the first time in his life, too, he was able to make some money towards his retirement.

My seniority now brought more driving turns, many of which were conducting the engineering department tamping machines. These new machines had taken over the role of packing the ballast under the track sleepers and it was originally intended that they would be worked with just the driver operator. This plan never bore fruit as the machine drivers refused to sign a route card and therefore take on responsibility for themselves, until they were paid the same rate of pay as train driver. Long negotiations eventually reached stalemate and for many years a pilot driver was always supplied when these machines worked on any running lines.

The original tamping machines were four-wheeled vehicles, which ran at a top speed of 15 mph, reducing to 5 mph over any crossovers. All drivers hated these jobs, particularly if the machine was moving some distance, perhaps to do work in another district. The machines were unsprung and the pilot driver had to stand, legs apart on the steel chassis as there was no floor, or sides, just a roof on four outer struts.

I had to go with a machine on one occasion from Solihull Yard to Banbury, in a blizzard. I had the most dreadful day, the signalmen would not entertain letting us run because of our slow speed and the snow was already blocking back other trains. To add to this, these machines could not be relied upon to operate any track circuits; this meant that you were never sure that the signalman knew exactly where you were. Therefore, I had to keep walking in the snow to the signal box to sign the train register to make sure that the machine was protected by the necessary signalling instruments. It was a bitterly cold day, there was no heat on the machine whatsoever, the warmth from the engine was blown out of the side on to the track by the radiator fan, consequently this fan drew cold air across the engine just where you were standing. The machine operator, who was some 20 years my senior, never moved from his seat and said practically nothing for the eight hours that it took us to get to Banbury. What a way to earn a living, I thought? At Banbury we finally stabled the machine and as I walked away to catch a train home, the operator said, 'Kid, I'm glad that's over'. He was human after all!

The speculation that our jobs were assured was very short lived, more work went from the depot and we saw Wolverhampton and Saltley men start to work jobs that had traditionally been at Tyseley for decades. This was galling, as we knew that the diagrams given to both these depots could not be achieved within the eight-hour working day of these men. Things got so bad that on some occasions we were ordered not to report for work at all, this was to save the new 40 minutes booking-on allowance that had been negotiated for enginemen during the last pay talks. Consequently, we were all completely demoralised, we had reached rock bottom, as we knew that the depot would eventually close as a running shed. The opinion of management was that Tyseley was not well placed strategically for any future plans. There was a future for Tyseley, but it was only for maintenance purposes. We therefore waited daily for news of our demise.

One week, I signed on 6.00 am 'Spare' and never had a job for the whole week. The place was as quiet as a church crypt and I was bored out of my brains. It seemed that Tyseley men were only to be utilised to cover the diagrammed jobs at the depot, we were not given any extra work whatsoever. This was most likely a preliminary trial to see if in fact the depot could be closed. A strategy that was confirmed to us later by Bill Stanley, who started as an engine cleaner with us, but ill health had diverted his career to the control office.

On Saturday of that week, I had planned to go to St Andrews to watch the 'City' play, as I was always a keen 'Blues' supporter. By this time we had moved into a new amenity block attached to the new diesel factory and the telephone office was only separated from the engineman's cabin by a glass screen. Unfortunately, my 'favourite' foreman had been on duty all the week and at 1.00 pm on Saturday I had thoughts on asking him if I could go home early to get changed before going to the match. Surprisingly, at this time I heard the foreman say to the telephone operator, 'I'll give him that job, he's sure to give me a shilling'. In the next breath he was round to the cabin ordering me to go to relieve a Wolverhampton fireman on a freight train now standing on the down goods line at Tyseley. This foreman was obviously looking after his own mates again at my expense. Ironically, the train that he wanted me to relieve happened to be one of the jobs that we had always worked; the train was now standing on the goods line behind another train, which had no engine on it. The train was now unable to get into Bordesley Junction to detach traffic, because the 'Target' engine was already on a train at Small Heath and also waiting to get into Bordesley.

'Manor' class 4-6-0 No. 7805 *Broome Manor* and '9F' class 2-10-0 No. 92237 in the shed yard at Tyseley in 1964. *Michael Mensing*

'Austerity' 2-8-0 No. 90268 trundles through Acocks Green wth a freight train in 1961. *Michael Mensing*

Years of experience told me that, at this time of day, no freight trains would move until the afternoon shift at Bordesley started work after 2.00 pm, when indeed my eight hour day would be up. After they signed on duty, the shunters at Bordesley would then have to clear at least two trains before the train I was asked to relieve could detach traffic.

It was therefore blatantly obvious to me that the earliest that I was likely to finish work would be something like 5.00 pm, and only then if we had a clear run to Oxley, which in itself was extremely unlikely.

It was unfair for this foreman to ask me to take on a job of this nature under these circumstances; he was being unreasonable. I pointed this out to him and he then accused me of refusing duty. I knew I could not win with this man, so I chose not to argue with him. I signed off duty and lost the remaining one-hour pay. I went to the football match rather annoyed, but I dismissed the issue and thought that would be the last I heard of it ... I was wrong again.

Although dispirited by the loss of work from the depot and an uncertain future, I finally made it to No. 1 link. Fortunately, my new mate was a great man, he raised my state of mind at work during troubled times and we became good friends. During his time as a fireman, Fred Gay had also fired to a number of drivers who could hardly have been called enginemen. Fred therefore never knocked any engine about; he was another thoroughbred Great Western man. In his early 50s he was the youngest regular driver I had worked with for a decade and he willingly changed sides with me to let me do the driving. He did, however, make one proviso, he was having none of those 'Stanier' engines, Austerities, or '9Fs', I was happy with that.

One night, Fred said that he intended to do the firing; as we walked up to relieve the Washwood Heath to Southampton fully fitted freight. Working freight trains at night had not gone down well with the men in the top link, but unfortunately the timekeeping on this particular train had long been abysmal and as I said earlier, it did convey very important traffic. In desperation the management entrusted the working of the train to the most experienced men at the depot, in a desperate attempt to improve matters. At long last, regular use of the wretched Standard '4s' had also been abandoned on this service.

My mate was quite happy when he saw a 'Grange' at head of the train. This class of engine was a firm favourite with all Great Western men; indeed I had never ever experienced any of this class of engine to be steam shy... that is until that night!

Fred hung his coat in the fireman's corner, wiped the shovel handle with a wad of cotton waste, along with all the other implements that he would touch. On the gentle rise from Tyseley it soon became apparent that all was not well in the firebox. The pressure gauge needle stood still just on the 200 psi mark and the boiler water level began to drop with each mile as we were yet to get the injector going. Off the tender came the long fire-iron and into the fire it went. The beads of sweat appeared on Fred's face as he gave the fire a good root up. This made little difference and soon the blower was turned on. At this point I felt enough was enough, I begged him to return to his own side of the footplate. But he was having none of it, he had agreed to do the firing and nothing would change his mind. He toiled on sweaty and dirty, until we reached our destination, such were his principles. Fred's skill with the shovel equalled that of his driving, but this locomotive was just another engine sadly lacking in general maintenance.

The return job after working the Washwood Heath to Southampton was a Hoo to Handsworth bulk cement train; another fully fitted train, which was always headed by a BR Standard '9F'. The onus of firing on our return was therefore always mine. Fair play to the '9Fs', they coped well with this murderously heavy train, but we

Ex-GWR Churchward '28XX' class 2-8-0 No. 2875 (*left*) and ex-LMS Stanier 'Black Five' 4-6-0 No. 44663 with freight trains near Knowle & Dorridge on 7th March, 1962. *Michael Mensing*

Ex-GWR mogul No. 6364 approaches Acocks Green with a short freight train on 25th February, 1964. *Michael Mensing*

always had to keep the firebox full to capacity. Ironically, the first time that we were to work this job with a Brush type '4' diesel, we broke down at Leamington as the engine went short of radiator water.

The Snow Hill pilot engine was always a top link turn, the engine could be called away at any time so the men with the widest route knowledge took charge of the turn. In general, we just shunted coaching stock and parcel vans around the station. In the early days, the pilot always employed one of Tyseley's best engines, unfortunately at this time most of the engines were now neglected. Tyseley had taken in some unusual motive power too, 'Castles', 'Black Fives', and a '47XX' class 2-8-0. Some of these engines were absolutely decrepit, we had No. 5014 *Goodrich Castle* on the pilot one day and we were in dread of being called to work anything. The strengthening stay across the top of the cab was cracked, each time we went over uneven rail joints the cab roof buckled and the sides of the cab went outwards. This along with excessive side play in the rear axle boxes made her hardly fit for the shunting let alone express work.

One winter's morning we were called to go on the 10 am departure to Paddington as the diesel's steam heating boiler had failed. Basically we were required just to heat the train. Our charge this day was No. 5900 *Hinderton Hall*, she had been a Tyseley engine for some time; nevertheless she also was terribly run down. The 'Western' hydraulic locomotive detached, we backed on to the train and the diesel came on to the front of us and we left some 15 minutes late.

I think from the onset, that the Wolverhampton driver on the diesel intended to give us the ride of a lifetime ... to Leamington he succeeded!

It was doubtful if, even in its heyday, our engine had ever been so fast as on this occasion. In her present condition however, she bucked, rocked and vibrated like crazy. At such speed the asbestos lagging began to shake from under the boiler cladding. Despite my flooding of the footplate with water from the coal-watering pipe, both Fred and I soon took on the appearance of a pair of millers. With the flour like substance stuck to our eyebrows, we watched aghast as the boiler moved between the main frames. Both of the rear boiler keys had worked themselves out.

We had not quite come to a stand at Leamington when Fred was off the footplate and heading towards the front engine. I could see his finger shaking at the man in the driving seat, he was indeed livid. There was little doubt, much of what had taken place was deliberate; unfortunately this had backfired, as our locomotive had now thrown all the corks from out of the side rods and big ends. Fred and I did have some replacement corks, but our supply was insufficient, I therefore had to go scrounging corks from drivers on other engines around the station. Fred refilled the rods with oil, but standing in the station platform this was not easy. Considerable delay accrued by the time we were in a fit state to continue.

We ran at a speed within reason for a while but as we made the climb to Ardley tunnel, the second man on the diesel came to the rear cab making gestures towards us. We eventually gathered that one of the twin diesel engines had shut down and they now needed some extra help. We ran well from there on with us doing our best, but passing Denham the diesel's second engine also shut down. So our outmoded, dirty, rundown steam engine ignominiously pushed the shining maroon diesel silently into Paddington!

Bernard Rainbow had a similar experience with his regular driver Fred Matthews. A 'Hymek' type diesel hydraulic locomotive was put on the front of their engine at Swindon when working a train from Weymouth. The train was being hauled by a mogul, but the diesel was going light engine to Oxford anyway, so it was felt expedient to attach it to the train. Bernard and his mate were then also subjected to a ride to remember. Fred Matthews was not going to give the Oxford men the satisfaction of knowing what a rough ride they had experienced. When a smug looking fireman came to detach at Oxford, Fred took out his watch and quietly said, 'We are timed a little bit faster than that, but we should recover the time by Banbury!'

Old rough engines often shook the asbestos from under the boiler lagging, yet we were totally ignorant of the dangers of this substance and we just dusted ourselves down as necessary. Breathing in this dust becomes a 30-year time bomb and a number of my colleagues have since suffered the dreadful consequences. Forty years have passed since being exposed to the dangers of asbestos, perhaps I am lucky?

The 'King' class locomotives were all withdrawn from service in 1962. It fell to Dick Potts to be the fireman on the last special train in April 1963 from Birmingham to Swindon with No. 6018 *King Henry VI,* this along with his regular driver Albert Slater. Colin Jacks and his mate Joe Hackett hold the laurels for taking this engine on its final journey to Swindon works for dismantling. Whilst this was a sad occasion for railway enthusiasts and some enginemen, the majority of men that had worked on them in their final run-down condition were only too glad to see the back of them. So great was the desire for some enginemen at other depots to fight shy of working on steam engines, particularly after a taste of the 'Westerns', that they went to great lengths to avoid failures often only caused by the lack of steam heating for the train. Men were known to carry cloths pegs which they used to hold vital safety devices from operating just to keep the train heating boiler working. The pegs were sometimes put on low water relays and there was obviously some good fortune that a catastrophic boiler explosion did not occur. The BR management were probably quite unaware of the utter stupidity of some men and issued photographs of the damage sustained to the inside of the 'Spanner' boilers. The photographs showed bulging platework caused by the shortage of water supply to the boiler and the publication urged men to be conscientious in carrying out the correct 'blowing down' procedure to avoid this failure.

With some 14 years experience now behind me, on 20th September, 1964 it became the duty of Fred Gay and myself to work the Stephenson Locomotive Society special train, 'Farewell to the Counties'. In spite of my great enthusiasm for steam locomotives, and an awful lot of hard work on my part, this trip was to produce very little personal satisfaction for either of us. The tour must have been a great disappointment to the many railway enthusiasts who rode in the train; at no time in over 200 miles did our speed exceed much in excess of 60 mph. I have to admit this was a dismal performance by any standards, but it was completely out of our hands.

Designed by the chief mechanical engineer of the time F.W. Hawksworth, 30 of these 4-6-0 'County' class locomotives were built at Swindon after World War II. These locomotives were the last express engines to be designed by the GWR and had deviated to some degree from usual Swindon practice. This class of engine, however, was not generally well received by enginemen. With the many years of design work available to the engineers at Swindon at that time, Great Western enginemen were entitled to expect much more from their centre of engineering excellence.

The 'Counties' were never part of the regular diagrams worked by Tyseley. Therefore Tyseley enginemen only took charge of these engines occasionally, sometimes on the 8.08 pm Snow Hill to Paddington, or the 7.10 pm Paddington to Wolverhampton, otherwise these engines were limited to Saturday holiday trains or specials.

Working on any of this class had eluded me altogether whilst they were in their original condition, that is when they had a very high boiler pressure of 280 psi and had the original single chimney. Nevertheless, my keen interest made me seek the opinions of many of my colleagues that did encounter them as they were originally built. Stock answers always seemed to be that although the locomotives had a high boiler pressure, firemen were generally unable to keep the pressure gauge needle anywhere near the point of blowing off with sustained running. Apparently, the more co-operative drivers, seeking to get the best from these new engines, found it made life easier for their fireman if they used only a small regulator opening and kept a longer valve travel. This obviously went right against the general principles of efficient working of any locomotive.

All 30 engines were eventually modified by fitting a redesigned double chimney. The boiler pressure was also dropped to 250 psi. Originally, the first engine to be built, No. 1000, did have an experimental double chimney, but the remainder all had single blast pipes. The later modification transformed the steaming rate of the whole class, but unfortunately another problem developed which took a long time to identify. This became another set back to the popularity of this class of locomotive as far as enginemen were concerned. This further irritation was caused by cylinder oil carbonising in the blast pipe casting, which in turn interrupted the exhaust flow. This fault was not immediately apparent, hence for a long time many other things got blamed for the return to indifferent steaming. These included poor quality coal, choked boiler tubes, even poor firing technique. Meanwhile the list of expletives grew as men found themselves rostered to work on a class of locomotive that seemed to be dogged with problems.

During the war Swindon had taken to building the Stanier class '8Fs' for War Department use. Swindon apparently used the boiler plate formers for these engines for the new 'County' class, which I suspect was an economy measure at austere times. Therefore, a further irritation for firemen was that the 'Counties' were the only Great Western engines not fitted with the standard firehole shield and smokeplate. Even the old Robinson ROD's were converted and had this equipment. The '1000' class were fitted with the type fitted to Riddles Austerities and Stanier locomotives, probably because they had used the LMS-designed boiler formers.

All was well with the firehole furniture when the engines came new from the works, but heat distortion and interchanging of smokeplates from other engines eventually made getting anything that was a good fit almost impossible. If the smokeplate did not fit snugly into the firehole, it would sag and lie down at the front. This would impede shovelling and make it difficult to keep an even fire bed at the front end of the firebox. Firemen then had to resort to jamming all sorts of paraphernalia between the top of the firehole and the smokeplate to get the deflection right, this so that the cold air entering the firebox through the firehole was directed just below the brick arch, whilst at the same time allowing ample clearance for the shovel to bring about even firing. Spanners of every description were used for this purpose, but the favourite device for packing was the square headed screw bolt which was used to screw rail chairs to the sleepers. Even so, vibration when running often shook the packing out, usually at a critical time. The firehole doors would jam with hot spanners, or bolts, wedged in the door runners. More streams of curses then evident as everything would now be very hot. With overalls scorching, the smokeplate would then probably end up thrown in the corner of the cab, or in extreme cases out through the gangway to end up as cowling for the chimneys of every lineside cabin. Men got so fed up with ill-fitting smokeplates that the engines

BR.7945/2

**BRITISH RAILWAYS BOARD**
**222 MARYLEBONE ROAD**
**LONDON, N.W.1.**

**(Conciliation Staff)** Date....29 SEP 1964....196

# CONTRACTS OF EMPLOYMENT ACT 1963

To :—

Name...HERBERT D. C..... Grade:....FIREMAN....

1. In this statement under Section 4 of the Contracts of Employment Act, 1963, the British Railways Board give you those particulars required by the Act of the terms and conditions of your employment at the date above. Your employment with the Board or their predeeessors began ~~*[on.........................................]~~ *[at least 5 years ago]. Such terms and conditions are either set out below or may be found in the documents mentioned in this statement.

*Delete whichever is inapplicable

2. **Rates of Pay, Hours of Work, Holidays and Holiday Pay.**

The terms and conditions of your employment relating to the method of calculating your remuneration, your hours of work and your holidays and holiday pay are contained in a series of agreements made with the Trade Unions who are party to the Machinery of Negotiation for Railway Staff. Summaries of such parts of these agreements as relate to your employment at the present day will be made available to you for reference upon application to your local officer. Any changes in these terms will be entered up in these summaries.

3. **Payment Period.**

Wages are paid weekly in respect of each week ending with Saturday and are paid to you not later than 7 days after the end of the week for which payment is due.

4. **Sickness or Injury.**

Your terms and conditions relating to incapacity for work due to sickness or injury and sick pay are set out in a Booklet No. BR.6909/1 which will be made available to you for reference upon application to your local officer. No sick pay is payable to male employees until they have attained the age of 18 years and completed 12 months' service and no sick pay is payable to female employees until they have attained the age of 25 years and completed 5 years' service.

*Delete whichever paragraph is inapplicable

*5 ~~**Pensions and Pension Schemes (Female Employees).**~~

You are not subject to any pension scheme and you will not be entitled to a pension.

*5. **Pensions and Pension Schemes (Male Employees).**

If you have no rights under sub-paragraphs (A) and (B) below, you are not subject to any pension scheme and you will not be entitled to a pension.

**(A) Pension Schemes.**

If you are already a member of a pension scheme (including the British Transport Commission (Male Wages Grades) Pension Scheme) you will have received a copy of the Rules which set out your rights under the scheme.

Otherwise, if you were under 45 years of age at the date of your entry into the service of the British Transport Commission or the British Railways Board, you will become subject to the British Transport Commission (Male Wages Grades) Pension Scheme when you have completed 12 months' service and have attained the age of 21 years.

**Note:** If you entered into the service of the British Transport Commission or their predecessors on or before the 1st October, 1954, and have not already become a member of the British Transport Commission (Male Wages Grades) Pension Scheme, you cannot join that Scheme now.

**(B) Customary Practice.**

If you entered into the service of the British Transport Commission, or their predecessors, on or before the 1st October, 1954, you may become entitled to a pension as a result of customary practices of those bodies by virtue of the provisions of Section 99(2) of the Transport Act, 1947, or the British Transport Commission (Ex-Gratia Pensions) (No. 2) Scheme 1962 made by the British Transport Commission under the British Transport Reorganisation (Pensions of Employees) (No. 2) Order 1962. Details relating to entitlement under these practices are contained in a memorandum which will be made available to you for reference upon application to your local officer.

**6. National Insurance Acts.**

Paragraphs 4 and 5 above set out the terms of your employment relating to sick and injury pay, pensions and pension schemes, but you may be entitled to benefits under the National Insurance Acts.

**7. Notice.**

Your terms and conditions relating to the length of notice which you are entitled to receive to terminate your contract of employment are contained in the agreements mentioned in paragraph 2 above. Changes in these terms will similarly be entered up. If you have no rights under these agreements you will be entitled to receive one week's notice.

You may terminate your contract of employment by giving one week's notice.

Your contract may be terminated without notice if you have been engaged before the Board have received references or medical reports and such references or medical reports prove unsatisfactory, or in the event of your being guilty of misconduct.

**8. Uniform Clothing.**

The issue of uniform clothing is as set out in a Booklet No. BR.6519, a copy of which will be made available to you for reference upon application to your local officer.

---

Driver Fred Gay and the author at Swindon with *County of Chester* during the last 'County' run.
*Bernard Rainbow*

No. 1011 *County of Chester* taking water at Stourbridge Junction on the farewell tour.
*Bernard Rainbow*

often left depots without this equipment at all, as most depots carried no spares for this class of locomotive. This obviously led to inefficient combustion and the likelihood of boiler problems. Without the smokeplate being fitted cold air entering the firehole was thus directed straight on to the tube plate. The whole class of engines ran around for all their working lifetime without this simple problem ever being solved. Any liaison between locomotive inspectors and the mechanical engineers seemed totally non-existent. A directive was eventually issued to enginemen, banning the putting of packing between the smokeplate and firehole. Foreign objects were the cause of damage to the boilerplates in the vicinity of the firehole seam; strangely nothing was ever done to rectify the root cause of the problem.

The firehole on these engines was also set at a higher level from the footplate. This followed the trend of locomotive designers of other companies and again came about by the use of 'foreign' boiler formers. Other companies' mechanical engineers did provide a higher shovelling plate on the tender, or bunker, which made shovelling easier at equal heights. Mr Hawksworth, however, still made his firemen get the coal from out of the cellar!

The only surviving 'County', No. 1011 *County of Chester* arrived at Tyseley a week prior to the Stephenson Locomotive Society farewell tour. She blended well with the sorry looking stud of locomotives that remained at the depot. The colour of her livery was unrecognisable, one of her nameplates had disappeared, and she stood, filthy dirty, in a shroud of steam.

We often grumbled about our fitting staff, but the standard of maintenance on Tyseley engines was well above that of many of the surrounding depots. During the following week many repairs were carried out on No. 1011, along with a boiler wash out and tube clean.

On the eve of the tour, some of the members of the Stephenson Locomotive Society set about cleaning the engine. Another member had made a very creditable job of producing a replica nameplate. Made from wood, this reproduction was barely recognisable from the real thing.

On the morning of the tour, *County of Chester* looked in very fine condition. Our charge was prepared for us; the preparation crew had done a super job. A huge fire had been made up, the tender topped up with coal, the footplate nicely swept and the cab cleaned down. We could not have wished for a better start.

Our footplate inspector, Reg Morgan, met us after backing on to our 10 coaches in Tyseley Carriage Sidings, the train weight being 325 tons. His first comments to me were, 'I hope that you can cope with this engine Dennis, because if you can't, I can't, I have never fired one of these in my life'. I can't imagine why he said that; at this point in time my pride would never have allowed him to take over.

After Fred had conferred with our guard, the signal cleared for our departure towards Snow Hill. Unfortunately, it did not take many revolutions of the wheels for us to realise we were in for a very rough ride. A characteristic of the 'Counties' when they had covered some miles was a heavy steam hammer effect under the footplate; this was already evident, even at low speed. Reg Morgan wasn't so very long before he took the advantage of a more comfortable seat in the train!

When the Snow Hill platform signal cleared, our journey was to take us to Stourbridge, Worcester, Cheltenham, Gloucester and Swindon. Returning we came, via Didcot, Oxford, Banbury and Leamington.

With a green flag from the guard we headed north into the tunnels under Birmingham's jewellery quarter, snaking out over reverse curves past the vast

Hockley Freight Yard. A solitary diesel shunter now stood silent where four pannier tank engines had once shuffled the pack for seven days a week. With our acceleration on to the rise towards Handsworth Junction the truth of the discomfort we were about to experience became evident. The thrashing under the footplate as bad as we had both ever encountered. Fred and I looked at one another, the exchange was non-verbal, the expressions on our faces spoke volumes, 200 miles still to go!

Passing Queens Head signal box, I attempted to start the exhaust injector. This important component failed to work at all once the regulator was open. After a great deal of water had spilled on to the track ballast, I gave up and put on the live steam injector.

We took the left-hand bracket signal at Handsworth Junction on to the Stourbridge Extension Line, this line devoid of any straight sections. As the engine lurched on the junction points, so the live steam injector kicked off, more water going on to the ballast. This was the first of innumerable times this injector was going to splutter, in fact every time we encountered a rough bit of track. I attuned my hearing to listen to the sound of it working, that is, over and above all the other clatter. Nevertheless, I still had to rely on any guest on the footplate, whoever was standing behind the driver had to watch that the injector was still working. It soon became evident that the injector was slow supplying the boiler; therefore it was imperative that I kept it working for long periods.

We headed towards the Black Country, on this line, had we been blind, we still could have said exactly where we were, surrounding sounds and smells said it all. The putrid smell of the iron foundry at The Hawthorns Halt, then the stomach-rending odour of rotting animal flesh at the fertiliser factory at Langley Green. Scorching heat blown from extractor fans at the bottle making plant. Breathing would become wheezy at only a brief passing of the chemical works at Oldbury. Then the perpetual sound of the heavy drop forge at Rowley Regis followed by the anvils of the chain makers at Cradley Heath, all pointers to a train's progress.

A signal check at Oldbury and engineering work at Rowley Regis, added further to our seven minutes late departure from Birmingham.

Our engine eventually put her head down the 1 in 51 gradient through Old Hill tunnel, out over the Longbridge branch and Bumble Hole junctions. Flash memories came of earlier days on 'A' group pannier tank engines, working passenger trains to the Austin works. Many recollections also of the grinding freight trains to Round Oak Steel Works. Regrettably, the rails into the distance on these lines were now red rusty.

At Stourbridge Junction we topped up the tender tank, this was only a precaution as on a Sunday we could have been delayed by further engineering work. The injector problem was also a contributing factor that we should not ignore this chance to take water. After a short rise out of Stourbridge, things took a turn for the better on the easier gradients towards Worcester. With less curvature on the line the riding improved, Fred had the engine well notched up on the reverser, keeping on just a breath of steam to the cylinders, which had a tendency to cushion some of the wear and tear. We attained 62 mph approaching Cutnall Green, but further delay was caused by signals and engineering work at Droitwich, this requiring reversal on to the opposite line as single line working was in operation.

A short stop at Worcester saw us on to the short rise to Norton Junction and over Abbotswood Junction. Straight, easy running, allowed us to reach 60 mph again, but signals at Defford and single line working between Eckington and Ashchurch hindered progress further. Once past Cheltenham, we ran on to the four-line section of track to Gloucester Engine Shed Junction, the scene of many a race between a 'Forty-niner' and a 'Black Five'.

We took water at Gloucester South Junction, where the stock market price of Kodak must have improved dramatically. Easy running from Cheltenham and a 10-minute stop at the water column allowed my fire to burn hollow and cool somewhat. The start from Gloucester South also took me by surprise; in all my years as a fireman I had never made a start from that point. We only ever stopped there with freight trains and usually had relief. Our start ripped the fire into holes; ideally, I should have got out the long fire-iron and levelled the fire. Having guests on the footplate made this manoeuvre difficult, that is without someone getting branded! I used my skill with the shovel in an attempt to get an even fire bed again, but the boiler water level was already dropping. I knew I could sacrifice the boiler level to some degree for the easy run from Sapperton to Swindon. Nevertheless, I was quickly reaching the point where the injector would have to go on, and stay on, if a dangerous situation was to be avoided when the engine put her head downhill at Sapperton. The pressure gauge needle sat at about 230 lb., but at Stroud she still was not making steam freely enough to hold the pressure with the injector working. My driver also needed a full head of steam to get us over the top. I had no alternative but to get hold of the long pricker fire-iron to root up the fire. My action did little for the environment over the Golden Valley, but it saved the day for me, we went over the summit with the water just in sight in the gauge glass. We crept over the top at just 16 mph, then averaged just over 60 mph to Swindon, our fastest speed for the day at Minety, 62.6 mph.

Our arrival at Swindon was 29 minutes late according to the handout sheet issued to SLS members. However, my driver had been issued with a Special Train Notice when signing on duty; this was due to the extra engineering work involved that day. This notice recorded us to be just 2 minutes late, which was probably down to me, having struggled for steam on the last leg of the journey. Fred, seeing me in trouble, obviously did not work the engine has hard as he should have done. Then again, that was teamwork.

After unloading the passengers, we reversed into Swindon Factory Sidings, stabled the train and then filled the tank and boiler to capacity. With the boiler pressure reduced and the dampers closed we took a break, whilst a host of volunteers invaded the tender and brought the coal forward for me. I was most grateful.

Returning to the engine the fire looked lifeless; the only flames were short and blue in colour. It was obvious to me that a thin layer of clinker had set on the firebars. Some Welsh coal formed a treacle-like substance when hot; any attempt to get air through the fire with a chisel bar fire-iron whilst the fire was in this state would be futile. The substance would settle straight back and stick to the firebars, maintaining steam would then become difficult. However, with a period without draught on the fire, the clinker would cool and set hard, therefore it would become brittle and could quite easily be broken with a chisel bar. Once the clinker was broken and air could pass through the fire any impurities would remain porous.

After the use of the fire-iron, I made up the fire again for our return journey. I built up a very large fire, keeping the dampers closed to allow the fire to burn through slowly, there was still some time to go before departure, the last thing we wanted was noise of steam blowing away from the safety valves. A few minutes before departure I raised the dampers, closed the firehole doors and turned on the blower a little. At the time of departure everything was just right; I had a mountainous fire which was well burned through.

Swindon to Didcot was the best section of track that we would encounter for the whole trip, having few curves and mostly being a gentle fall. If we were going to get any speed at all it was now. We did attain 57.6 mph at Uffington, but were then to suffer repeated signal checks, as we were behind another train. Nevertheless, according to the log we passed Didcot North Junction on time and were also on time reaching Oxford.

Between Oxford and Kidlington we got tied up with more engineering work, this again involving crossing over on to the up line. Once clear, we ran over sweeping curves through the beautiful Oxfordshire countryside, the line chasing the River Cherwell for some miles. Stately homes overlooked the line, mostly a safe distance from smoke and whistle noise.

A clear distant signal for Aynho Junction was our licence to get water from the troughs, therefore avoiding the necessity to stop at the water column at Banbury. Just a few seconds saw the tank full over the troughs and clear signals gave us a run through Banbury station.

Once clear of the rise as far as Wormleighton Crossing, Fred asked me how I felt about livening up the performance a little. I was having no problems and still had energy to spare, I therefore I had no objections. Unfortunately the line from Fenny Compton to Harbury had always been a problem to the Engineering Department. As we attempted to gain speed and provide some fireworks, No. 1011 went into several alarming rolls; once again I had to juggle with the injector to get it started again. As seasoned enginemen, we realised that the locomotive was just too unstable to be pushed at greater speed. On the run down from Harbury to Leamington, we both took refuge on the tender to escape the pitching and dreadful vibration under our feet.

When the signalman at Leamington North gave the 'train entering section' for 1X83, according to our notice we were on time. With the hardest part of the journey now to face, it would have been naïve to expect that the climb to Hatton would not to have taken its toll on our reserves. Surprisingly, we cleared the deep cutting at Hatton North at 31 mph, the pressure gauge needle still just behind the red line. The boiler water level had dropped, despite the injector working continuously, but at this stage it was no problem.

After topping the tank again on Rowington water troughs we were soon on the four-line section past Lapworth. Here it was necessary for me to level over the fire to avoid too much fire being in the firebox when we went on shed. Our guest was ousted from my corner again, whilst I drew the long pricker from the rack. The fire-iron came out of the fire with its end white-hot and sparkling, everyone on the footplate then finding it necessary to do the 'Boston Two Step' to avoid its lethal end. The wad of cotton waste used to hold the pricker was smouldering and filling the cab with an acrid smell.

Again, according to our late notice, we were on time running up No 1 Platform at Snow Hill. At that point in time, neither Fred Gay, or myself would have had any sentiment about seeing No. 1011 going straight to the scrap yard. Many finer engines had already been sacrificed. We really had done our level best, we were not looking for any laurels, the star of the show had not performed well. Then again, few stars do at the twilight of their career. As I put the tail lamp on the tender to run-round the train, I did get one 'Brummie' comment from a young man, 'Yer dain't break many records down Fosse Road'. Quite honestly, I could quietly have stuffed this youth where I had just put several tons of coal. Then again, it was a sad time for steam enthusiasts, their majesties, the 'Kings', having already gone some two years earlier.

On reflection, I now feel it was sad that none of these 'County' class survived the acetylene torch. I never remember any of them getting 'Blue Ribands', but the engines were no doubt an important part of Great Western history.

Fred Gay was a good man who was devoted to his home and family. It was not only his good enginemanship that I respected; he was also a keen first aid man. I had avoided gore and tragedy until this time, but one night we were first on the scene when an unfortunate man had both of his legs severed by a train. Fred could do little without medical supplies, but he did what he could, remaining calm and reassuring. My admiration for him remains strong; he was just another unsung hero, whilst I fought against the need to vomit.

The top link now lost much of its stature, although the Swindon Parcels had now found its way into the link, this turn was one of the few remaining decent jobs at the depot as the work dwindled further. Fred and I were now often separated whilst he worked single-manned diesel multiple unit turns.

I was soon trained on the 350 hp diesel shunting engines; otherwise this may have meant that if there happened to be a driver short, it could have become necessary for me to work a main line turn while an older hand driver was left to drive a shunting diesel. Training all passed firemen on the diesel shunting engines therefore kept strictly to the principle of senior men doing the senior work.

Regrettably, my now often being 'spare' whilst Fred worked the passenger turns was to put me in contact with the shed foreman again who was set on maintaining a grudge.

One Saturday afternoon I worked a trip job with a driver that worked turns in what was known as the 'Cripple Link'. Men having poor health were relegated to this link; the jobs therein were usually short and at reasonable times. There was very little freight traffic about locally by now; much of Hockley Sidings had closed, along with many of the other local yards. On this day we were sent to shed early, if there was no other work available the shed foreman would then sign the driver's daily record sheet and we would go home. We would of course still be paid our guaranteed day of eight hours.

The elderly driver took his record to be signed on this day and when he came out of the office he asked me what had gone on between this particular foreman and myself. The foreman had said to him that he did not mind signing the ticket for the driver, but was very reluctant to sign it for me; I had let him down two years earlier when I signed myself off duty to go to the football match. Whilst I always knew this man was holding something against me, these words were indeed clear proof. It was now five years since I had worked with Bernard Pratt and the time when I first noticed that this foreman was holding something against me.

I obviously became very angry and really felt that the time had at last come for a show down. I got along fine with everyone else in management; I really needed to know why there was this long-standing problem with this man. My driver felt some embarrassment when I became heated and begged me not to approach the foreman right then as he would know that he had been talking. Against my better judgement I very reluctantly went home, only to chew the situation over in my mind for the whole weekend.

I signed on around lunchtime on the following Monday, I was 'Spare' again, so I waited again with other men in the mess room for work. I had only been in the cabin a few minutes when the foreman involved entered. Putting his arms around me like a long lost son he put a florin in my hand saying, 'Dennis, how would you like to fetch me some fish and chips?'

This I did, but when I put his meal on his desk I quietly asked him about the problem between us, I told him that I was fully aware that he had borne some resentment against me for a very long time. Unfortunately, face to face with me he was first taken by surprise, he then flatly denied that there was any problem at all. I have never been very proud of the conversation that followed. This Monday lunchtime was to become perhaps the lowest point in my life, one word led to another and I called him a sneaky, creepy, crawly, two faced, bastard. I was so angry that I would happily have fought with this man. As I ranted these words I looked the shedmaster, Tom Field, straight in the face, he having entered the office at a most inopportune moment. Tom Field was the first man to be promoted to shedmaster at Tyseley who was not from the footplate grade; he had risen from the artisan grades. I understand that he was a good man, but he was yet another shedmaster with whom I had never spoken. Inexplicably, on this occasion he turned and walked out of the office and remained totally uninvolved, whilst the telephonist stood agape, his eyes as wide as frightened rabbit. I slammed the office door in temper and returned to the mess room, every minute waiting for further repercussions. No doubt I had given this man very good grounds for my dismissal. Strangely, this foreman was always well liked by everybody and it now seems even stranger as to how we got to this point. Whether Bernard Pratt did blacken my character early on, or whether this was just a clash of personality still remains very much a mystery.

Each subsequent day that passed brought relief; I heard no more about it and no action was taken against me. Our relationship if anything improved, however, with the demise of the Wolverhampton Low Level to Snow Hill local train service, which made travelling to Tyseley from Wolverhampton difficult for him, he took early retirement. This unfortunate episode was finally over and I was very relieved that the atmosphere had cleared.

Until this time, men worked all their life on the railway and walked away on retirement with no more than a handshake from colleagues who happened to be there when the men signed off duty for the last time. This was extremely sad, but management finally made amends and men were eventually given a gold watch, but at this time only after 50 years' service. Only a handful of men were to qualify for this award and after a time the period was reduced to 45 years service, nevertheless this was a step in the right direction.

Unfortunately, one national newspaper of the time found this 'generosity' too much to bear and printed a small item which read: 'The British Transport Commission has just spent £40,000 on gold watches for long serving employees'. In very bold type they then printed a footnote expressing the total losses of British Railways the previous year, which unfortunately ran into millions of pounds. Nevertheless, I have never bought that newspaper since.

I noticed one day that my friend John Millman was again rostered on Royal Train working; it would now be interesting to see how he would react following his snub by the superintendent at Wolverhampton. John had once vowed never to work another 'Royal'. The motive power on the Royal Train was now a 'Western' hydraulic and only a handful of us had been trained to work the steam heating boilers. John, true to his word, never turned up for work, his excuse being that he had overslept. John's failure to arrive brought total panic to the depot; the only other fireman available was a man who had signed on at 10 pm the previous evening and he had spent the night marshalling in the diesel factory. This was the filthiest of jobs, which meant us scrambling between units to couple or detach. Also, we often found ourselves splitting diesel trains which were locked together with grime; some had never been separated since they came out of the factory brand new. This was usually necessary to get them on to the wheel turning lathe. Therefore, the only man available to work the Royal Train was very dirty and unshaven. He was quickly asked to clean up, whilst the shed foreman broke into the clothing stores to find him some new overalls. So John quietly had his pound of flesh, after all everyone was likely to oversleep at some time!

'Modified Hall' class 4-6-0 No. 6999 *Capel Dewi Hall* at Stratford-upon-Avon on the author's last day as fireman with driver Jack Higgins. *Provenance Unknown*

Shortly after, John applied for promotion at Water Orton, an out station of Saltley; Saltley being another Birmingham depot only about three miles away.

In late July 1965 I also received notice of my promotion to driver. My last day on the shovel came on 7th August that year. On a very hot Saturday afternoon driver Jack Higgins and I travelled to Bristol Barrow Road shed, here we prepared No. 6999 *Capel Dewi Hall* for the trip home. This fine locomotive was now filthy dirty and was devoid of any of the brass number plates and names. Nevertheless, she was a game performer, as was my driver. We recovered a considerable amount of lost time getting to Stratford-upon-Avon and unavoidably polluted the atmosphere with a well-heaped tender full of 'Midland' hard coal. We stopped at the water column at Stratford with a fair chance of arriving in Snow Hill right time, but the water column there was situated half a coach length off the end of the platform; regrettably a motorcycle whose owner alighted at Stratford had earlier been loaded into the front brake van. This was unusual and it meant that we now had to get permission to set back onto the platform to unload this machine, obviously costing us some time.

On my last day as a fireman our engine gave a sparkling performance, which was rare on any of the return West of England trains. I suspect that our train had been hauled from Newquay to Bristol by diesel traction as it had never previously been normal practice to change engines at Bristol. Having a fresh engine I was quite happy for Jack to thrash the engine a bit. We cleared Earlswood summit in effortless fashion, albeit with a very sorry looking Swindon masterpiece, thus ended a long chapter in my life.

Colin Jacks. He is seen here on a 'Midland' engine, but the Great Western badge on his cap shows where his true loyalties lie. *Dick Potts Collection*

# Chapter Ten

## Promotion to Driver ... and Redundancy

Promotion put me back at the bottom of the pile and becoming a driver was nothing like the day that every young boy of earlier times would have dreamed of. There was one consolation, the number of driving turns that I had worked as a passed fireman immediately put me on to top driver's pay. All the work was now unglamorous, engine preparation, shed work and shunting. Added to this, the engines were now filthy dirty, uncared for machines, name and numberless, their identities scrawled in infantile white painted numbers on their cab sides. Also, the uncertainty of depot closure still hung over us; it was a soul destroying depressing time. Tyseley was in the death throes for a very long time, it is possible that the management found that depot closure was more difficult than they first thought. Waves of extra work would come to the depot and shortly after there would be redundancies, therefore everyone was just kept in limbo.

A number of my close friends had already moved away from Tyseley for promotion, my friends John Millman and Colin Jacks amongst them; they had moved to the ex-LMS depots at Water Orton and Saltley. Soon disillusioned, both of these colleagues were amongst many of the fine footplate men who left the industry. Countless hours of dedicated, irreplaceable apprenticeship were lost, it was indeed sinful. There were always vacancies for drivers on the Southern Region electric trains, but most steam men never saw this as their forte. John Millman and his family took advantage of the £5 passages that were on offer to Australia. The Beeching Report was drastically to change so many railwaymen's lives.

Senior drivers were mostly utilised on the diesel trains, so I eventually I got out on to some train work with steam engines. I had a thrill one night when I worked a train of carflats to Oxford with an un-named 'Britannia' No. 70053. This engine was still in fine mechanical condition, most rare for this time. My young fireman did a wonderful job and effortlessly swept coal into the firebox with great skill. He was one of a number of young men who were to impress me over the next months. Regretfully, he too was to become just one of a number to be later forced off the footplate and into outside industry.

I had driven express trains as a fireman, that is, when I had worked with a young driver who was still willing to take to the shovel. Nevertheless, I did get to drive an express in my own right when I was rostered to work the early Leamington to Birkenhead one Sunday morning. Unfortunately, being let out on the loose on the expresses was only short lived, as we only worked this train from Leamington to Snow Hill.

Our engine was No. 6848 *Toddington Grange* and my fireman was John Butler, a pert young man who nonetheless was a good fireman. After preparing the engine we took the stock from Tyseley Carriage Sidings to Leamington. We turned the engine on Leamington shed and left the station at 9.02 am. No. 6848 looked in pretty sad condition, but she was better than her looks and my logbook says that we arrived in Snow Hill at 9.41 am. I didn't enter the intermediate stops, which suggest we were on time. At least, we stopped at Knowle and Dorridge and Solihull, so we must have run quite well at times.

Late one afternoon I was ordered to work a train of iron ore from Tyseley South to Bilston West. As well as good firemen, there were bad, and also the inexperienced.

Empty stock movements at Tyseley in 1964. A 'Modified Hall' can be seen in the background on a mineral train. *Michael Mensing*

BR Standard class '9F' 2-10-0 No. 92215 passes through Snow Hill station in 1961. A Cross-Country dmu set stands in the platform road. *Michael Mensing*

This day, it was my young fireman's first day on the main line; indeed he had been on nothing bigger than a pannier shunter. We relieved Banbury men at Tyseley with No. 92212 and 40, sixteen-ton tippler wagons behind us. It was no fault of the young man, but he was totally bewildered and unfortunately showed little initiative.

There was a torturous few miles in front of us to start with, beginning with the ascent of Snow Hill Tunnel, which in itself was always a drain on the boiler. Whilst filling the tender at Bordesley I made sure the fire was right, adding a good charge of coal myself. I then did both the driving and the firing, which wasn't as difficult as it sounds. Once through the tunnel, we were then only moving quite slowly over the reverse curves through Hockley and taking the rise to Handsworth Junction. The line dropped sharply from West Bromwich station and halfway down the bank was Swan Village road crossing. With just the engine brake and a murderous weight behind the engine, I had to be sure I was able to keep the train in check. With the steam brake hard on, smoke poured from the 10 driving wheels as they heated up with the friction of the brake blocks. The road crossing distant signal was against us, it was rush hour and the signalman wanted to keep the road traffic moving. I was just beginning to wonder whether I would really be able to stop if the signals remained against us when the engine vibrated madly and she started to slide. This was pretty unusual with one of these heavy '9F' locomotives on a dry rail. With the train speed now quickly rising, I released the brake to get the wheels turning again and rammed it back on hard. The next seconds were tense, as the signalman slowly manually wound the crossing gates from out of our path and cleared his signals. Thankfully, my early record as a driver remained unblemished.

With the heavy work done I allowed my young mate to muddle on, after all it was the best way for him to learn. Having said that, I didn't get the impression that he was at all enthusiastic. I did feel that he would soon become just another name and

The author as a young driver doing engine preparation work. The manual turntable at Tyseley had by this time been mechanised. *Dick Potts*

face to be forgotten. However, he somehow survived the mass redundancies that occurred over the next months and eventually became a train crew leader at Saltley depot. Some 25 years later, he was seen hiding behind a building spying on me, and others, as we left the depot. He was making sure we that were all wearing our high visibility clothing and changing cabs when we made reverse movements. A number of accidents had occurred whilst drivers were propelling locomotives from the rear cab, therefore changing cabs became law. After many years on the footplate, being spied on was an irritation that I could easily have done without. I felt that over-concentrated supervision only served to erode self-discipline that was naturally instilled into most railwaymen from their early days.

One evening I was sent to Stratford-upon-Avon to work the Honeybourne Goods to Bordesley. At Stratford shed I was joined by my fireman Dave Rogers, who was a Stratford fireman and was in fact older than myself. We prepared our engine No. 43115, an Ivatt mogul; little did I know then that this was going to turn out to be 'just one of those days'. We moved from the coal stage line to fill the tank, whereby the glass weather shield smashed into a million pieces as it caught the very limited clearance on the coal tip. The weather shield was a strip of glass which was outside the cab, this was an aid to vision and was a very useful accessory.

After fetching our train from Long Marston we got as far as Bearley Junction where the signalman had us routed via Hatton North Junction, instead of the booked route over the North Warwick Line. After challenging the change of route, we eventually went forward as routed and on arrival at Acocks Green we were turned on to the goods loop. As we approached the exit signal from the loop it was showing clear. This mode of signalling entitled me to believe that the advanced starting signal should now also be clear. The advanced starting signal was badly sited behind the road bridge; consequently I didn't see it until the last moment and found it to be at danger. I then had to brake hard quite suddenly, which was certainly against the principles of working loose-coupled freight trains and it was quite worrying for me for a time as I felt that I may have given the guard a bump. Strangely, this was the only time in my working life that I ever saw any train stop at this signal. It was common practice for signalmen at Acocks Green to either hold trains at the starting signal, which was at the end of the station platform, or hold the train in the goods loop until they got 'line clear' from Tyseley South Junction.

After disposing of the train at Bordesley and apologising to our guard for the sudden stop, we turned the engine on Tyseley shed and then took it back to Stratford. *En route* we were next stopped at Shirley with a red hand signal exhibited from the signal box, as our tail lamp had gone out. On arrival at Stratford, I stopped at the east end of the station platform where a ground signal was to turn us towards the shed. I heard the ground signal clear with a thump, although it was on my fireman's side, he rightly repeated the clear signal to me. On reversing there was a succession of bumps and bangs and we then had rather a rough ride as the engine ran along the sleepers! When we got on the ground to investigate, every wheel was derailed, except the leading pair of tender wheels, which had oddly gone back towards the main line from were we had come. This made things look pretty bad for me, as it looked as though I had reversed before the signal had cleared. Fortunately, when I alerted the signalman by telephone that we were derailed, he immediately admitted that he had turned the points again while we were moving over them.

It had been a hot day and during such weather the signal wires tended to expand, hence the afternoon signalman had found it necessary to tighten the wire to get the ground signal to show clear. With the cool of night, when the night signalman pulled the lever, the wire had shortened and it would not latch back into the signal frame. He then thought that the point detection hadn't lined up and tried the points again, just as we were passing over them. I was very grateful for his honesty as we did block the main line for four hours. Clearing the line in such a short period of time was remarkably good going for the Tyseley breakdown gang. They first had to be alerted, an engine and crew provided, and it was some 40 minutes run from Tyseley.

Single line working was soon initiated to keep trains moving in both directions whilst the fitters re-railed the engine. This work was done only with baulks of timber and heavy traversing jacks.

A complete change then came about when I was eventually trained to drive the diesel multiple units. Probably 80 per cent of the work at Tyseley was now with this form of traction and many of the older hand drivers didn't now mind the younger men taking more of the demoralizing turns that some of these trains involved.

Snow Hill tunnel eventually closed, along with most of this landmark station; there were now more pigeons than passengers. Just the north end low numbered bay lines remained in operation. From these platforms we worked to and from Langley Green with a single one-coach unit, soon to be aptly called 'Bubble Cars'. These units could be quite unpredictable to drive; they were prone to sliding and very indifferent brake adjustment. These single units were also involved in a number of mishaps, as it took one and a half minutes for the brake to be fully operative after the unit had stood for some time. Men tended to get into the cab at the last minute, created the vacuum and depart almost immediately. If signals were against them soon after leaving, they found they had virtually no brake, as all the air had not yet been exhausted from the reservoir side of the brake pistons.

On these single unit turns, a two-hour break at Langley Green could be pretty monotonous too on a winter's evening; the cab lights were too dim for you to read for any length of time and if you sat in the train compartment with the lights on, the batteries would soon go flat.

At this time there was so much uncertainty in the railway industry as a whole that vast numbers of men began to leave other grades also. The railways were then forced to employ a great deal of immigrant labour, particularly as guards. Many of these new entrants were soon acting as guards on these insignificant passenger turns and at the very least, conversation would prove difficult. It was little wonder therefore, that the takings at the local boozer at Langley Green took a turn for the better!

In due course, the relief lines from Tyseley South Junction to Lapworth were closed and the rails recovered. Station canopies and footbridge roofs were removed; many station buildings were also demolished to save money on local rates and further maintenance. Weeds now grew on station platforms, and also on the permanent way, as further economy measures were made by the engineering department. Many of the manual signal boxes failed to escape these drastic cut backs; they too were razed to the ground and therefore made the signal sections longer. This in turn left trainmen without communication for long distances, should there have been any difficulties encountered.

It soon became almost a pleasure for me to just get a turn where I worked to Stratford-upon-Avon, although this route too had not escaped management vandalism. Small stations were lit only by paraffin 'Tilley' lamps, drinking water to signal boxes was still delivered in cans. In a very short time, the whole railway infrastructure seemed to have collapsed and it was difficult to imagine that a short time earlier I had been storming up these inclines from Stratford with a polished 'Castle' on 'The Cornishman'.

Diesel units at Birmingham (Moor Street) with Gloucester Railway Carriage & Wagon Co. driving trailer second No. W56295 in the foreground. *Michael Mensing*

A three-car suburbam multiple unit arrives at The Lakes Halt with the 6.10 pm Birmingham (Moor Street) to Henley-in-Arden on 26th May, 1964. *Michael Mensing*

The maintenance staff got to grips with the units and all in all they were quite robust machines, in fact, it was quite rare to become a total failure. We often limped along with two of the four engines shut down and no heat in the train or cab, but most drivers conscientiously did their very best to keep the service going. Instead of water columns, knowledge of where taps and watering cans were situated became a priority. This supply of water to top up engine radiators and these taps became just as important as the positioning of any emergency telephones along the route.

One problem with these early units was that they were prone to the fire alarm ringing in the cab for no reason. This happened so frequently in the summer that men eventually began to ignore the alarm. At first drivers would stop immediately to investigate only to find no sign of fire, although the fire bell would usually stop ringing after a time.

I fell into this category on a summer Saturday lunchtime when apathy got the better of me. I was standing in the bay line at Henley-in-Arden waiting to leave calling at all stations to Moor Street. The 30 minutes that I had there was a convenient time for me to have a sandwich and a cup of tea. The fire bell started to ring, but as many others had done, I ignored it for a while. As this unearthly ringing noise persisted, I eventually stepped out on to the platform and was aghast to see flames leaping up the sides of the rear coach! I dropped my sandwich, pressed the engine stop button, grabbed the fire extinguisher and then alerted the guard whilst running to the rear of the train. With one extinguisher exhausted, I took a second from the rear driving cab, whilst the newly-trained immigrant guard kept tapping me on the shoulder and asking if he should protect the opposite running line. As the immediate situation was a bit desperate, and we were standing in the bay line some yards from any other passing train, my reply was a bit curt and undignified, thus warranting a later apology.

With the fire out, my thoughts turned to keeping the service going, so I set about the procedure of isolating the damaged vehicle. This meant isolating it electrically and centralising the final drive reversing dogs. Obviously, the offending coach also had to be locked out of service. With passengers now arriving for their afternoon shopping in Birmingham, filthy dirty I went to the signal box and explained to the control what had taken place. I advised the controller that I would now be leaving Henley-in Arden with only half power, which would mean I would be late arriving in Moor Street. Also I knew that this unit then went back out of Moor Street on a service to Leamington, I told the control that another unit would be needed for this service.

On departure, I began to have some regrets about leaving Henley-in-Arden in this state; perhaps I should after all have advised the control to the cancel the train. As it was a Saturday the next open signal box was at Shirley, some 10 miles away. The unit crawled up the incline and it seemed to take forever between stations. Under these circumstances, should there have been a problem I have no idea how I would have contacted anyone, except for a very long walk!

My shift was over at Moor Street and I eventually arrived 20 minutes late, but I did have the satisfaction that I got the passengers into town, which I felt was important. Despite my advice to the control, on arrival two fitters met me to repair the unit. Obviously, immediately they saw the blackened coachwork they had other ideas; they put the unit out of service. Already any initiatives taken by drivers had begun to be disregarded; the control chose to send the fitting staff to Moor Street, instead of turning off another unit from the sidings to work the Leamington service. The Leamington service was then cancelled.

After training on dmus I often fell for what were known as ferrying turns. This meant marshalling the units at Tyseley Carriage Siding after they had been refuelled and serviced. It also involved taking trains into the maintenance factory for the more complicated jobs. These turns were not very economical on the footwear, we spent hour upon hour walking about the sidings, and climbing in and out of cabs, so they were very tiring turns. Fuel and lubricating oil dripped badly from the units, the ballast got sodden and the work became equally as dirty as working on steam engines. Fitting staff, who had just come from the pit beneath the unit after doing repairs, then sat in driving seats to test their adjustments. They trod oil into the cab; covered controls with filth from their hands and their impregnated overalls transferred dirt to the seats. We went home reeking from pungent diesel oil.

Battery maintenance with the diesel units proved an awful problem, the batteries were only charged when the train was running in excess of 17 mph. If train guards left the lights on during the day, the batteries never had a chance to recover. After the engines had been stopped and started a few times on the fuelling pit, in addition the carriage cleaners had to leave the lights on whilst doing their work, in which case the following morning the engines would not start. Some of the units could be attached to battery chargers, but in most cases it was found necessary to keep the engines running all night; otherwise the engines would not have started. Initially, not all drivers were issued with torches, in the darkness therefore it was not unknown for units to leave the siding towing several battery chargers! This tended to create yards of copper wire and a very spectacular electrical storm. Because the engines had to be left running all night, each unit departed in an absolute smog of white fumes, on still days a blanket of choking obnoxious vapour covered the whole area. Residents living near the line had an awful lot to contend with.

My romance ended and my circumstances at home were also changing, indications were that I should give some thought to buying my own home. Council houses had been put up for sale for the first time and my parents were offered the chance to buy their house for £1,200. My elder brother already had a well-paid job as a laboratory technician and he immediately saw this sale as a good investment. He quickly convinced my parents and hence stood guarantor for the purchase. Unfortunately, he then often referred to the family home as his house, which tended to make me feel rather uncomfortable about my future.

Unfortunately, my young sister had also earlier married and her situation was now pretty desperate. Initially, the newly weds had purchased a house in Coventry and now had an infant son. My sister was also towards the end of her second pregnancy when problems had arisen. It had been a normal weekend for them; her husband had spent time decorating the bathroom and had left for work as usual on Monday morning. A short while after his departure, the bailiffs arrived, put all their furniture on the front garden and secured the doors. It made no difference that my sister had an18-month-old son and was heavily pregnant. Apparently, her husband had not paid any of the bills and my sister was totally unaware of any difficulties that he may have had.

My mother and father took them into our already overcrowded house and my parents were reduced to sleeping on the living room floor. This was a pretty awkward situation with both my father and I working shifts, as the front door opened directly into the living room. My father then took out loans on some endowment policies and cleared outstanding payments on other items for them.

During their stay with us, my sister gave birth to a daughter and my father contacted her husband's place of work to advise him of the happy event. Unfortunately, my father was told that he hadn't been to work for some days. At his normal time, my sister's husband arrived home from work, paper under his arm and carrying his brief case as usual. When questioned by my father, he insisted that he had been at work. Perhaps it was a good thing that he was far more nimble than my father, my father's temper had risen to such heights that he may well have killed him. Quite rightly, my father doted on his only daughter; it was therefore difficult to imagine what pain he was inwardly feeling. My sister's husband left there and then and was never seen or heard of again.

My sister eventually found lodgings, but her situation still proved very unsatisfactory. My parents were beside themselves with worry, my mother developed bouts of nervous asthma, during which we could hear her fighting for breath, which indeed was pretty frightening.

A house went up for sale locally; I not only fell for the location, but also its large side garage. Unfortunately, I looked for the good points and was somewhat blind to its poor general condition. Yet money was tight; building societies would only lend money to anyone who was an investor. Fortunately, I had a long-standing account with the Co-operative Building Society and this put me in a good position to be granted a mortgage.

At an interview with my solicitor, I asked him if I should employ a surveyor. The advice that I was furnished with was that if the house wasn't worth the money, the building society wouldn't release their money. I was pretty gullible and felt this was fair comment. At a later interview with the building society manager, he hinted that I go back and renegotiate the price; the look on his face told me that the price was too high. This I did and £200 was eventually reduced off the asking price of £3,800.

At a further visit to my solicitor, his telephone rang whilst I was with him; it was the house agent dealing with my sale. It then became obvious that they were more than well acquainted, they were on first name terms! Hence, at the time I still paid more than I should have done, but there was soon some equity in it.

My own judgement had already been that the house would at least need re-wiring, but when I got the keys, a look round soon revealed that the up stairs floorboards were infested with woodworm. They were so bad that the boards gave way under my feet. The owner of the house had previously visited me at home to ask if I wished to purchase the floor covering up stairs. She said she would accept £3 for the lino and I had gladly paid her, as I had absolutely nothing. This I found also to be full of holes and had to be thrown away, perhaps she thought I wouldn't notice the woodworm with the lino down!

However, the problem now became mine, I had to put it down to experience. The whole of the upstairs floor in three bedrooms had to be renewed. Fortunately, the joists were quite sound, so as I lifted the floorboards I vacuumed the whole lot out. I then treated the joists and the new floorboards to avoid any recurrence. It was three months before I could consider moving in, the fumes from the wood treatment must have killed every living creature and seemed to last for ever.

I had anticipated the cost of the re-wiring and the decorating, but the cost of this extra work was crippling. I had already sold my latest asset, my pride and joy, a Wolesley 16/60 with its red leather seats and walnut veneer dashboard.

Eventually it was all worth while, although at one time I did feel that I was about to become the first person ever to lose money buying a house. With all the mess and turmoil around me, I sat one day on a wooden crate near to despair and tears. The doorbell rang, it was Dick Potts and his wife Joy, they had come to see if I needed help! Had they just sat and talked I would have been grateful, but they soon set to work with scrapers and brooms, I was so glad to see them. My friend Paul Cox also

My friend Paul Cox and fireman Peter Gilbin seen on the footplate of ex-LMS Stanier '8F' class 2-8-0 No. 48669 at Tyseley in 1966.

mucked in with a blow lamp and scraper, all in all, this was to teach me much about the value of good friends. I have never forgotten their help at a difficult time.

My sister and the children moved in with me, they now had a big garden to play in in safety and we were close to my old primary school when this became necessary. Unfortunately, I got another financial set back: the moment my sister came under the roof of a relative all her social benefits were stopped, something neither of us had anticipated. However, the benefits of house purchase still outweighed the difficulties. Miraculously my mother never gasped for breath again; it was almost as if someone had waved a magic wand. She eventually lived until she was 92 years of age.

Even so, it was 1968 before I could afford to have a night out; things at work also went from bad to worse. Increase in car ownership brought about a further decline of the local train services and the Sunday service around the Midlands was therefore abandoned. This loss of Sunday work meant that the majority of Tyseley drivers now went home regularly with just basic pay.

A welcome diversion came when I was sent to the training school at Derby for a week to learn diesel-electric traction. No doubt an uncertain future did tend to make it hard for me to put my heart into this studying. Nevertheless, I did find the course interesting. This again was a new concept and it wasn't surprising that some men found the terminology baffling; talk of 'field diversion' and 'back electric motive force' initially was a bit over all of our heads.

The running side of Tyseley was now supervised almost entirely by ex-Tyseley drivers; men were promoted to shift foremen and diesel supervisors. In general, they ran a tight ship; they knew all the diagrams like the back of their hand and also the calibre of their men. Their relationship with the workforce was also good, however, little missed their attention. If you slipped away early and passed your daily record sheet on to someone else to put in the time office for you, it was often mentioned next day. This never became an issue, but they let you know that it had been noticed. The timekeepers, too, were now surrounded with glass and it wasn't easy to put in someone else's ticket unnoticed. The most sensible amongst us accepted this; perhaps this efficiency would save our jobs.

I was eventually trained to drive the new 'D15XX' class, Sulzer locomotives; these 2,750 hp engines were later to become the class '47s'. A number of English Electric 2,000 hp type '4s' had also become common in our area, as the new Sulzer's had taken over their work in other districts. Amongst these locomotives was the infamous No. D326, which was involved in the Great Train Robbery. These early locomotives were rugged and reliable, they had to be, some drivers operated the controller as though it was a stiff regulator on a Riddles Austerity! The resulting 'lightning' from high amperage electrical current in the control boxes in the engine room could be quite spectacular. Unfortunately, these locomotives did have a major problem - when stabled in sidings they had a habit of running away! The parking brakes were useless, with both handbrakes in each cab screwed on tight, they were still known to move unexpectedly when the air pressure had leaked away. Each locomotive therefore had to carry four wheel chocks. These chocks became a problem in their own right, in the pitch darkness encountered in some siding they were apt to get forgotten. Drivers were known to drive over them and end up on the proverbial dirt! It does remain a mystery how these locomotives could have been accepted for service in the first instance; this was obviously a dangerous design fault.

My time eventually came to do my training on the English Electric type '4s' and my tutor was driver Joe Hackett. Joe was a great guy; he was nearing retirement and

A Stanier '8F' class 2-8-0 hauls a train of new vehicles, including Minis and Land-Rovers, near Lapworth in 1966. *Michael Mensing*

English Electric type '4' (later class '40') No. D226 and a Brush type '4' (later class '47') attract the attention of young trainspotters at Birmingham Snow Hill in 1966. *Michael Mensing*

always full of fun. He made no bones about the fact that he only became a diesel tutor because he hated shift work. Each tutor took on two pupils and my colleague in this instance was a man who had come from Stourbridge to Tyseley for promotion to driver. This man had already been involved in a number of incidents and wasn't particularly able. We were given one week of training, which included the handling of the locomotive. Daily, we worked a train of empty coaches to Toddington, ran round the train and worked back. *En route*, we made stops at some stations to improve our skills.

Joe came on Monday morning and foremost in his mind was that he could do with some help putting a new window frame into his back bedroom at home. Normally, the inspector came on Friday to pass us out, so Joe said that if we got down to the training we could go to his house on Thursday to help fit the new window. In general, with so much uncertainty we all found it a bit difficult to be very conscientious about the training, the depot could close at anytime and we could be out of work.

I absorbed the training quite well, but it was a different story with my colleague; here Joe was hitting his head against a brick wall. Nevertheless, on Thursday Joe parked his car up towards Tyseley station and after signing on we walked out through the carriage sidings. At the house we put in the new window, fitted the glass and even had time to help him repair the garden fence. At booking off time we left his car in the same place and returned to the shed.

Walter Hill the shift foreman saw us coming and was soon out of his office. He immediately asked Joe where he had been; the inspector had come a day early to pass us out, as he needed to attend a more pressing engagement on the Friday. I first thought that this had caught Joe on one leg, but he was cute and quickly reacted by saying that the fitters were working on the engine that was allocated to us when we signed on duty, he had therefore taken us to Bescot to do some static training on a locomotive there. This was a plausible excuse; but it was fortunate no one checked up with the maintenance staff!

The inspector turned up again the following day in an awful mood, he threw his briefcase on to the cab floor and kicked it heavily to one side as he made his entrance. Eddy Allcock, the inspector, I understand was an ex-Crewe driver, he certainly seemed to have an intolerant attitude toward anyone who wasn't weaned on the West Coast Main Line, particularly Tyseley men. He had an abrasive manner; this was something we had never encountered with any of the local footplate inspectors on the Western. Although there had always been an undercurrent that Wolverhampton men were always promoted to these jobs, it would have been difficult to criticize most of them. They were all good men, certainly competent and all generally had a quiet and sensible approach. Inspectors like Bill Parcell and Charlie Weston were no doubt gentlemen. Arthur Rogers and Reg Morgan, men that were later promoted after the decline of headquarters, were also their equal.

On the day of our passing out, our inspector was met with a further irritation; the locomotive allocated to us had a problem by way of a generator fault. The technicians had wired the engine room with electronic equipment so that they could monitor the power output under working conditions; this meant that the maintenance staff would also be accompanying us. This not only delayed our departure, but the extra men on the engine were obviously a hindrance when he took us through the engine room to see if we knew what he was talking about.

My colleague was first in the driving seat on the way to Toddington; things went well until the signals were against us at Milcote level crossing. There was an error of judgement and my colleague overran the home signal which protected the crossing. Fortunately the crossing gates were clear of the railway, otherwise they would have become matchwood! This obviously did little for our superior's state of mind.

After running the engine around the train at Toddington, we adjourned to a compartment in the train where he could give us our oral examination without the encumbrance of technicians. Eddy Allcock first started to grill my colleague, who now began to agonise over the way that he interpreted his questions. He later started to snap questions at me; fortunately I was able to furnish most of the answers that he was seeking, that is, until he enquired as to the causes of high engine water temperature. I first told him that I would check to be sure that the radiator shutters were open and that the fans were working. If the problem persisted I would have to operate the water bypass valve to isolate the engine thermostat. 'What else?' he snapped. I pondered and glanced at Joe for inspiration, Joe looked blank; this was obviously a new one on him. I then had to say that I was sorry, but the answer eluded me.

'What about low water level?', he retorted.

'I didn't think that one was in our driver's manual', I replied.

'If you have less water in a kettle, it boils quicker doesn't it?', he bellowed. By this time the English Electric type '4s' had covered considerable service on the West Coast Main Line; because the inspector must have had great experience with these locomotives, I said nothing. In actual fact, he wasn't right; I later learned by experience that the radiator header tank float always shut the engine down as soon as the radiator water began to get low. In normal circumstances, this was always well before a high water temperature warning light would appear.

The inspector then watched me do the driving on the return journey and signed both our certificates of competence *en route*. At Tyseley station, we dropped him off on the barrow crossing so that he could catch a train home to Crewe. As he got off the engine he turned on Joe, saying, 'These pair are of little credit to you', and he stormed off down the platform.

Although this remark was water off Joe's back, it did make its mark on me. Perhaps I hadn't been as conscientious as I should have been, but I felt competent about my training and that I could cover normal eventualities. We were all dispirited by the thoughts of the depot closure and it was very difficult to give one's best. Nonetheless, no one had ever openly criticised me in such a way before and I was certainly very unhappy about that.

It was some weeks before I drove one of the English Electric type '4s' in my own right, but part of one of our diagrams was to act as secondman to another driver who worked a freight from the sidings at Tyseley North. One evening, after completing the first part of my dmu working, I walked back to the depot where the driver was preparing the type '4' on what was known as the 'Middle Pit'. The locomotive was standing on an incline and as I approached the engine it started to move towards me. My immediate reaction was that the driver had seen me coming and was going to pick me up. As it approached me it gathered speed and I could see that there was no one in the driver's seat! I then dropped my bag and had to run to get on board. On the verge of a coronary I clambered into the cab and I put the brake on. This was just as the driver calmly emerged from the nose end, which he had been checking during his preparation duties. With the noise from the compressors therein he had no idea that the engine had moved at all, when it was well on its way to blocking the Warwick Road! Like myself, he was also newly trained; he had in fact started the diesel engine, taken the chocks away after seeing that there was air pressure holding the brakes on, then continued with his preparation work. Unfortunately, when the brake main air pressure reservoir reached 80 psi, the vacuum exhausters automatically started to create vacuum in the train pipe. This in turn released the air from the bogie brakes; hence the locomotive ran away because the parking brakes were useless. A week of training was one thing, but being fully conversant with this new type of traction was only eventually to come about by many hours of hands-on experience.

Then again, it took only my first trip to realise that all these diesels were not the warm, clean, comfortable things that we compared with steam engines. My first experience with a type '4' was with a freight to Banbury and the only time the cab got warm was when I thrashed the engine up the bank from Leamington to Harbury, minutes after easing the controller the cab was freezing again.

After the engine was detached from the train at Banbury, I went down what was called the escape road towards the station. When I telephoned the signalman, he said that the diesel hydraulic standing in the station on the express had a partial loss of power and the control wanted me to go on the front of the train to assist. This was my first experience of express driving over this section with a diesel and it was only minutes before backed on to the front of the disabled D800 'Warship' class. With the power of my engine and the remaining power on the 'Warship', we soon had the 12 coaches up to 90 mph.

On the run down into Leamington, it went through my mind that all my drivers on steam used to apply the brake somewhere by Leamington Carriage Sidings. What I didn't realise was, that on steam trains we were probably never doing 90 mph at that point! I was soon alarmed that I was going far too fast and the vacuum brake was full on and the gauge showing zero. With fire coming from the brake blocks we entered the platform far faster than we should have done and I really thought I was going to miss the station altogether. Fortunately the brakes then bit, and I finally ground to a stand with both of the locomotives standing off the platform and all 12 coaches standing just right in the station. I bet the cockney driver on the rear locomotive thought that I was pretty confident, when in fact I had frightened the life out of myself. I then had a thought, had the driver on the second engine switched off his vacuum exhausters? This he should have done automatically when coupling to another diesel. I should also have checked with him that he had carried out this procedure. He had indeed failed to switch off his exhausters; therefore both locomotives were recreating the vacuum brake as I was applying it, this therefore made the train brakes much less effective. Again there was an awful lot for us to remember and there was no substitute for experience.

The axe eventually fell again and on 12th August, 1968 I received my redundancy notice. Having just bought the house, I really didn't feel I wanted to move from Tyseley to remain a driver. Sixteen drivers were given the opportunity to stay at Tyseley to act as secondmen on the remaining work with diesel locomotives. Dick Potts, Bernard Rainbow and myself just crept into this last 16; we retained our driver's rate of pay, but were re-graded under the category of 'Put Back Driver'. Management made some effort to get us to transfer to the engineering department to drive tamping machines, but we all would probably have left the railway rather than accept this. This move was probably only an attempt at breaking the stalemate with the machine operators, who were members of the National Union of Railwaymen.

There was some irony in receiving my redundancy notice and being downgraded. Although I didn't realise it at the time, it was to be the turning point to much happier times.

Tyseley still retained some Paddington work and now worked the Bournemouth trains as far as Reading. These top link diesel turns now needed a secondman for the train heating boiler and all these turns paid mileage. These trains to the South were now routed out of Birmingham New Street via Grand Jn and the Camp Hill line to Bordesley Jn. The old ex-LMS goods line from Bordesley Junction connecting with the ex-GW lines at Bordesley South Jn was upgraded for passenger trains.

Tyseley also now had a night car transporter train to Dover, which loaded from either the remaining part of Bordesley, or Knowle and Dorridge. This train we worked to Old Oak Common, or Acton Yard, this too was a mileage turn; being paid night rate on this turn and mileage it became a nice little earner.

The building of Saltley power signal box and consequent alterations to the track layout also meant more Sunday work on engineering trains. With just 16 secondmen left at Tyseley, the management were now crying out for us to work every available Sunday to cover 'ballast' working. Also, any special passenger trains needed to have a secondman to operate the train-heating boiler. Overnight, my income almost doubled, another bonus was that I now got the chance of working with my father. He shared the driving with me, as most of the other drivers did as we were qualified. Father and son working together was never allowed on steam engines on the 'Western'.

As a young driver I had never been able to spread my wings much, these jobs now gave me a vast amount of experience and the opportunity to remain fully conversant with the many miles of routes.

I did work to Paddington with driver Bert Watkins one day. Bert was a super engineman and was one of those people who were always completely unruffled, yet was wholly competent. On the up trip to London we noticed that the engineers were removing the crossovers operated by the redundant Tyseley North signal box. We therefore knew that there would be a speed restriction on when we came back. This restriction of 20 mph was published in our 'Speed Notice'.

On the return journey, we approached Acocks Green at 90 mph and watched closely for the advance warning board for this new speed restriction. When the warning board had not come into view when approaching Tyseley South Junction Bert applied the brakes. Approaching the former Tyseley North signal box, there was the 20 mph commencement of the speed restriction. The engineering department had omitted to put out the advanced warning board! Fortunately we were the first train to approach this speed restriction and we were able to stop and report the oversight, otherwise someone else may have passed over this rather rickety bit of relayed track at speed.

On diesels we greatly missed having a constant supply of hot water and a bucket to wash in, which had always been on hand with steam engines. The handrails of diesel locomotives were always smothered in grime and on the ' Western ' hydraulics the dust that blew up from under the floorboards was always a problem. At speed, if you opened the door to the engine room, or opened one of the cab side windows, all the floor inspection hatches lifted and started to hover. This in turn brought an unimaginable cloud of fag ash and dust into the cab.

The extra money I now earned was my saviour; my sister and I had spent most of the first year living from hand to mouth. Having said that, our existence was a happy one and there were never any regrets. I was king of my own castle and my sister and the children had settled into a good environment.

On one Sunday excursion with a diesel unit we worked through to Ramsgate, although I would now question the safety issue of diagramming footplatemen on duty for so long. We left Tyseley Carriage Sidings early and went empty to Wolverhampton. From here we worked through to Ramsgate, via North Pole Junction, near Old Oak Common, where we picked up Southern Region conductor driver. After having seven hours at Ramsgate we worked back to Wolverhampton and then came empty back to Tyseley. Unfortunately on the way home from Ramsgate, three of the eight engines of the unit shut down. Owing to this problem we had to be diverted via Southall, where the artisans put the problem right. This was the most I ever earned for one day at work, when I picked up my wages on the Thursday after I was paid 86½ hours pay. I never made any overtime during the week that followed this excursion, it therefore worked out that I had earned 46½ hours for one day, as we were on a 40 hour week. This Sunday turn was obviously very much enhanced by a large mileage payment and the Sunday rate of time and three-quarters.

The 'good fortune' of the 16 'Put Back Drivers' didn't go unnoticed, our situation soon met with some envy from drivers who were on bare earnings whilst working on the local passenger turns. With no local service on Sundays, there was also very little other overtime, except for a few odd shed turns. The additional engineering turns that we were now getting added little to drivers' earnings, as these few turns were distributed between more than 100 men.

There were a few rabble rousers who therefore began to raise their voices at the earnings of the few 'Put Back Drivers'. It was felt that drivers too could sit on a diesel locomotive and act as secondmen. These men were quite prepared to do the secondman's job, with the exception of one thing, and that was to attach and detach locomotives. Once a man was promoted to driver he was never expected to do the coupling again, although it was always a driver's responsibility to supervise these operations.

The discontent grew, until the union representatives were forced to call a meeting. This meeting was held in the Staff Social Club at Tyseley and I was one of only about half a dozen of the 16 'Put Back Drivers' who were able to attend. Some 50 or 60 drivers attended, so if it came to a show of hands the minority had little chance of winning. One driver addressed the meeting and said that the 'greedy should share with the needy'; and there were a number of other passionate orations of a similar vein. Then another driver voiced an opinion and said that in accepting the duties of a secondman, they would no doubt be expected to attach and detach locomotives. Someone else intervened, suggesting that on engineering turns when a driver acted as secondman the coupling duty could be passed onto the train guard. There was an argument against this, as it could put locomen's jobs at risk, as single manning was the ultimate aim of BR management. Some of the more portly drivers then became adamant that they were not prepared to do any coupling up; indeed there were a number of men who were now physically incapable of doing such a task.

With the issue put to the vote, the drivers themselves overwhelmingly rejected the motion that drivers would opt to do secondman's duties. So once again militancy never got the upper hand at Tyseley. As I said it was always a middle of the road depot where issues were aired sensibly, collectively these men were wonderful to work with.

At the end of the summer service in 1969 a number of vacancies for drivers were created at Saltley. With the future of Tyseley still not settled I felt it would be wise to apply, that is, if I wanted to remain a footplate man. It was hard decision to give up the great position I was now in, good money and not being wholly responsible. Nevertheless, I had to look to the future.

My application was successful and I transferred to Saltley as a driver again on the 13th October. Some of my colleagues who were 'Put Back Drivers' also saw fit to apply, so I was in very good company, including Paul Cox and Dick Potts.

# Chapter Eleven

## Saltley

Enginemen were fiercely loyal to the locomotives they were accustomed to and the companies, or eventual Regions, that they worked on. As a fireman, a Midland Region driver from Saltley depot rode with us one day to learn the road. My driver was somewhat curt with him, so during our journey on a freight to Banbury he spent most of the time talking to me. I was enthusiastic and was able to put him right on a number of points. He was a nice fellow and our sociable chat was quite enjoyable. When he left us at Banbury, my driver immediately went off the deep end at me. He criticised me for talking to him, these Midland men were poaching our work and taking the bread and butter from our mouths, he claimed. His temper rose until he was red in the face and he finally shouted at me, 'Tell them nothing in future!'

This incident made its mark on me and I wondered what kind of reception I could expect from the old LMS drivers, now that the boot was on the other foot. Some 10 ex-Western Region men going as drivers to Saltley all at once must surely have some impact. I therefore felt some apprehension when Dick Potts and I met up on that Monday morning to start on a new venture. I was extremely glad of Dick's company and his extensive geographical knowledge of railways outside the Western Region. My younger days of train-spotting were limited to the Great Western, and even after nearly 20 years on the railway I still tended to think that there was no railway of any significance north of a diagonal line from Paddington to Birkenhead. What a shock I was in for!

In the General Office at Saltley we were given our new pay check numbers, Dick was 475, mine 474. The office was as big as a school hall and I had never seen so many clerical people concentrated in one area of railway premises before. The enginemen's cabin was twice this size, one half of which was closed on alternate days for cleaning. This was such a contrast to the 4 x 4 metre cubby-hole that the new premises at Tyseley had provided for us. In the mess room there were literally dozens of enginemen and guards waiting for trains, or standing 'spare'. I wondered how the management could keep a track of such numbers ... in reality they couldn't!

We signed on and off duty on a card left in the lobby, no one seemed to submit a driver's daily record sheet unless they were on a mileage turn, and this only because the clerk needed to tally up the miles worked so that they could be correctly paid. To us this was unbelievable slackness, yet we were quick to learn that we could sign off duty for the previous day when we came to work the following morning, as the cards were not taken into the office for checking until after 8 am. This perk was to become very useful, as Saltley was a bit out of the way for us to get home to Tyseley. Therefore, when we had had enough of road learning, or the weather was lousy, we were able to just go home and sign off the following morning. This system was open to abuse, no one bothered if you were inclined to book overtime for the previous day when signing on the day after. Indeed, some men were eventually taken to task at one period for booking a Sunday turn when they signed on duty on Monday morning. I might add, a dim view of this was taken! Nevertheless, even this fraud failed to tighten any slackness; this was a completely different world for us. It was difficult to understand that three miles away at Tyseley, there was this programme of continual cut backs and efficiency, yet here at Saltley there was this almost ludicrous situation of freedom and waste of manpower. Initially, the old hand Saltley men laughed at our honesty, but eventually we were only too happy to fall in line with general policy.

Dick and I were rostered together whilst road learning and foremost we spent some two weeks looking around the local area and yards. Whilst we had already worked in and out of Washwood Heath Yard and as far as Water Orton there were still a vast amount of sidings to become familiar with. There were four signal boxes in Washwood Heath Yard alone, and another two in Lawley Street Sidings. Much of the signalling system terminology was alien to us. The Western Region never had distant signals on permissive block goods lines which was commonplace all over the ex-LMS lines. Then again, what was a 'Jacko' or a 'Dodger'? Learning just the local layout was a daunting task, you had to be sure that you knew exactly where you were, should you have to work in the densest of fog. Our seniority too, put us well up the links at Saltley; it would therefore be necessary for us eventually to learn hundreds of miles of routes, much of which carried no audible warning system as a guide in foul weather.

Any fears of resentment that I felt might come from the Midland men were totally unfounded. Like all enginemen countrywide, many drivers with whom we rode were conscientious men who were only too willing to offer their guidance. Little doubt, the driving antics of a few were surprising, but the majority were enthusiastic men who had not suffered the years of uncertainty that we had been subjected to. When riding with some drivers, their eagerness made me feel a little embarrassed at how my own attitude towards the job had developed. A position of permanent security had obviously been a great encouragement to men at depots having a future.

Our closeness in seniority kept Dick Potts and I together during much our traction training too, we had an incredible amount to learn in this field also. Foremost, we were trained on the Sulzer Crompton Parkinson 2,500 hp locomotives, along with their sister engines the Sulzer Brush type '4' 2,500 hp. These locomotives were eventually to become the class '45s' and '46s' and were widely used from Plymouth to Newcastle, including Leeds, and also Derby to St Pancras.

Our training then stretched to the Sulzer type '2s', which were to become the class '24' and '25s', locomotives that were extensively used on local freight trip work. Also, we came under instruction on the eventual class '31s', which worked the New Street to Norwich passenger trains. Then again there was the sister engines to the English Electric class '40' 2,000 hp locomotives, the smaller class '37' English Electric then called type '3s'. These had better parking brakes - but only just! Further more, the English Electric type '1s' had to come under our belts, these locomotives were the favourite of very few drivers - if any!

During these training sessions I was to meet some extraordinarily fine railwaymen whose knowledge of diesel locomotives was to astound me. These tutor drivers included Cliff Fletcher, Len Stokes, Wally Rowe and Arthur Thomas, then there was Harry Willetts, who was a fellow model engineer - our mutual interest was to eventually make us good friends. These dedicated men could drum enough knowledge into the thickest of us so that we could pass the inspector at the end of a week's training. I felt very humbled by the expertise of such men.

Harry Willetts would never have stood out amongst other locomen, yet he had an almost saintly disposition to be envied. He criticised no one, would do anything for anyone, and was never seen to vent any anger. Some men unfortunately used Harry as their first and last answer to all their mechanical problems. In later years I saw him under someone's car in the car park, he was lying in snow doing a repair. At a later date, I asked him if he ever felt that some people might be taking advantage of him, he shrugged his shoulders and quietly said, 'We are all mates, aren't we?' It was more than sad that Harry had a very short retirement; men literally came from the length and breadth of the country to pay their last respects. Personally, I was very proud to have just known this 'Midland' man.

BR Sulzer Bo-Bo diesel-electric No. D7579 passes through Acocks Green with an up freight on 4th August, 1964. *Michael Mensing*

Our latest traction inspector had just been promoted to Saltley and also originated from the Great Western at Oswestry. He was a 'new broom', who took on an unimaginably difficult roll. Saltley had the largest concentration of locomen in the country and trade unionism was strong. It needed much diplomacy and great tact to keep the wheels turning at such a significant depot. Regretfully, although he was a tireless inspector, Les Durnell had an unfortunate manner which tended to make life difficult for himself. He lacked any kind of discretion and on approach he tended immediately to put men's backs up. From the start he was fully intent on wielding the proverbial ' big stick' to tame this 'unruly' depot, but this was far from the best technique to gain the men's co-operation in general. On one occasion, he slipped unnoticed into the rear cab of a locomotive leaving New Street on the Newcastle service. This act to check that the driver observed the permanent 10 mph permanent speed restriction out of the station. Whilst passing through the tunnel, he then went via the engineroom and burst into the cab at the other end of the locomotive to the great surprise of the driver. This act infuriated the man in charge, who immediately put the brakes on and stopped. There was an altercation, whereby an ultimatum was given that one of them was going to get off! The inspector had no alternative but to leave the engine, otherwise much delay would have occurred. Ignominiously, he then had to walk back through the tunnel to the station; no doubt what the inspector had done had been very unwise.

Part of our training extended to the British Railways Automatic Warning System (AWS), by which time the system had already been installed over some routes of other Regions. The new power signal boxes at New Street and Saltley now brought the new AWS system on to our doorstep.

This latest cab warning system was an update of the Great Western Automatic Train Control. With trains now running at 100 mph, the engineers did not want a shoe making direct contact with a ramp on the permanent way at such speeds, therefore the new equipment worked entirely on electro-magnetism. The new apparatus also provided a visual indicator in the cab. This looked rather like a dartboard, which showed yellow segments when a signal was set at caution or danger, whilst at clear signals the indicator showed all black. This was an added extra, which was useful to a driver as he could always check on the last indication that he had received. The old ATC was sacred to all Western men, therefore the management, quite rightly, were eager that the latest warning system was treated with the same respect. Any wrong indication given in the cab needed to be reported in a specific way to keep the system in tip-top order. Installing the warning system countrywide was a vast improvement to safety on the railways. With line magnets placed at every distant signal in Absolute Block Working areas, and a magnet in rear of every colour light signal in Multiple Aspect Signalling areas, the system was to give innumerable correct indications to drivers daily.

I never knew of any incident where the old Great Western ATC gave a serious 'wrong side' indication to any driver, that is, telling him that the signals were clear when they were not. One incident did occur, but at the subsequent inquiry the signalman admitted to reversing his signals after the train had passed a clear distant signal.

The modern AWS system was obviously more complicated than its predecessor and was unfortunately known to give 'wrong side' indications. However, these were extremely rare, once reported the equipment was removed from the locomotive, or unit, and sent to Derby Research Centre for a thorough examination. The driver then always got a report from the technicians explaining why the fault occurred, which served to maintain complete confidence in the equipment. More often than not, any problems were simply caused by moisture getting into the apparatus.

'Wrong side' failures were coded 5 and 7, these had to be reported immediately by stopping at the first signal telephone, or signal box. These included receiving the bell, indicating clear signals, when the signal was at caution or danger. The second was when no indication at all was received when passing over a magnet when a signal was set at danger or caution. This 'nothing received' indication only became a 'wrong side' failure in the absence of the normal automatic application of the brakes if the driver had failed to respond. All other secondary faults had to be reported at the first convenient place.

The early Sulzer (later class '47') 2,750 hp locomotives allocated to the Western Region had dual Great Western ATC and British Railways AWS fitted. This did prove somewhat unreliable, as the shoe fitted to the locomotive body tended to strike things other than the ramp between the rails. Greater flexibility of the springing was the cause of this when passing over poor rail joints near to road crossings or junctions. The shoe would then often be inadvertently be pushed up causing the warning horn to sound. The ATC equipment was finally removed from the Western Region diesels when the shoe on a locomotive caught the barrow crossing at Tyseley station on 22nd May, 1967. The bolts holding the shoe sheared off and the cradle fell beneath the train derailing it at speed. Several coaches of the Poole to New Street service then overturned (*see photographs*).

Following my initial training on the AWS, for the next 20 years the apparatus was well maintained and undoubtedly was a wonderful asset. We were to utterly rely on it in dense fog. Regretfully, on the run up to the privatisation of the railways, the system did get downgraded. A change of thinking by management, and cutbacks to save on maintenance costs, eventually saw locomotives being returned into service with serious faults on the apparatus. If a 'wrong side' failure had previously occurred, it was deemed sufficient to test the equipment whilst the locomotive was being refuelled. If the fault did not recur during this brief test, the engine was kept in service. Strong complaints by drivers, myself included, now brought the response from management that the AWS was only a guide to drivers, it should never be relied upon

Two views of the accident at Tyseley due to the failure of the ATC shoe bolts.

*(Both) Dick Potts*

totally. Having equipment that was inclined to give a clear indication at signals set at danger was indeed a problem. By this time the Thatcher government had curbed the trade unions; there was also a 'dog eats dog' situation in lower management, particularly in the inspectorate. These inspectors now felt it unwise to rock the management boat for fear of their own jobs. Inevitably, drivers who saw serious safety issues looming had nowhere to register their concerns. The appalling accident at Southall in the early days of privatisation was the result of such thinking by the management. The AWS apparatus in this instance was isolated, as it was out of order.

Our road learning continued, first to Leicester, where many of the Leicester drivers that we rode with were quite willing to allow us to drive, telling us it was the quickest way to learn. This would have been good experience, but the offer of driving was only taken up once we had a good idea of where we were.

We then learned Derby, and Gloucester via Spetchley and via Worcester. Steam engines were now history, but the incline working at Bromsgrove was the same with diesel locomotives as bankers. The 'Lickey Bank' commanded the respect of every driver, whether ascending, or descending.

My first day of revenue earning came when I signed on 'spare' one Monday morning. I first went into the mess room among great numbers of other enginemen and waited for work. After 1½ hours, I was given a job to relieve a freight train at Landor Street Junction, take it into Washwood Heath Yard and bring the locomotive back to Saltley. My train was waiting after the five-minute walk to Landor Street relieving point and we were soon on our way towards the sidings. Entering Washwood Heath Up Sidings we went up behind another freight train. When the shunt signal cleared, it was normal practice to 'hump shunt' the train in front, by pushing it as slowly as possible over the hump. The shunter then detached the wagons as necessary and they ran on to the appropriate roads for their northern destinations. To avoid the wagons colliding heavily against one another, brakesmen were employed to chase the wagons and apply the hand brakes. This was probably the most dangerous job on the railway, as the brakesmen had to run alongside the wagons and pin the brake down with a stout ash wood brake stick.

We eventually hump shunted the train in front and the shunter detached us from our train and we went back to Saltley. I had only been on duty just over three hours, so I went back to the foreman's assistant and told him I was back. This of course is what we would have normally done at Tyseley. The man in charge then gave me a rather odd inquiring look, saying, 'Would you rather sit here then, or at home?' He then turned his back on me; I got the message and went home. I was obviously unaware this was the usual way of working, once you were given a job the foremen didn't expect to see you again. However, it soon became apparent that this was how the shift foremen were able to gain the men's full co-operation. If you had already been on duty three hours and you were given a diagram which was for a full eight hour turn, then you were expected to finish that diagram without crying out for relief. With the full co-operation of the men, Saltley was able to cover a vast amount of work and the diagramming office at Crewe, wise to the fact that any work would always be covered, kept numerous special diagrams flowing to the depot on a daily basis.

The depot management of the time seemed to settle for the 'anything for a quiet life' approach; the result was that things did run extremely smoothly. The depot therefore was able to cover a vast amount of work over a large part of the country. Unfortunately, this countrywide coverage did bring unflattering remarks aimed at Saltley drivers from men of other depots. The depot drivers then became known as 'Seagulls', notably because Saltley men went everywhere on the system.

My friend Paul Cox was sent for his medical as he had reached his 40th birthday. It was inconceivable that he would fail; he was healthy, strong and had never lost a day from work through sickness. Although Paul had gone through the same rigorous vision tests as all Tyseley men did at Swindon, regrettably he was now deemed colour blind. He was now mentally in tatters, as he was doomed to shed work only.

Two sets of shed men booked on every four hours, this was a dirty filthy job, as large numbers of locomotives came on and off the depot for re-fuelling and servicing. There was some consolation in working the shed turns, as each set of men signed on duty, the earlier sets of men went home. Whilst these men did only work four hours a day, they all mucked in, there was no demarcation of jobs, men did everything necessary. Drivers would couple on if necessary and secondmen moved engines, there was never any delay, the men co-operated to the full to see that things ran smoothly. I couldn't help but compare this way of working with Tyseley; I felt certain that some cutbacks would soon come to this depot too. Men going home after only half their working day couldn't possibly last. How wrong can anybody be, the system was still the same on the day that I retired!

Perhaps two years went by and I watched my friend Paul working on the shed, he made the best of it, yet I couldn't help noticing that he knew every engine that went on and off the depot. This knowledge extended to the diagrams that the locomotives worked. Every time I saw him I hinted to him that he shouldn't consider doing the shed work until he retired. I urged him to apply for supervisory posts. This he eventually did, becoming an engine arranger at first, then rose to train crew supervisor at Saltley. He seemed to enjoy this very much and he became popular with everyone. Although I would never have compromised him, he knew what I wanted as I grew older; I never wanted to hang around doing long hours. We later had to sign on and off on a daily record ticket, as we had done at Tyseley. Later years saw some tightening of the system, but Paul would often take my ticket and slip it into his top pocket at quiet times so that I could go home. I was very grateful for his friendship.

Long before retirement Paul sadly died, despite him never losing a single day from work through sickness. His death was a devastating experience for me; an absolute multitude of colleagues paid their last respects at his funeral, which said everything about this man.

I eventually began to drive trains over the new routes with strange forms of traction; this was where the learning really began. When working within the vicinity of a manual signal box, if the signalman wanted you to make a certain move he could come to the window and shout, or wave his duster at you. Under 'power box' signalling, in the absence of a nearby telephone, in many ways you needed to 'read' what the signalman might intend you to do. Knowing the signals was one thing, knowing the countless moves was another.

When walking to Tyseley to sign on duty it had taken me just 10 minutes. At night, with the absence of public transport, walking to Saltley took 1¼ hours through a very unsavoury area. I now needed another car. I eventually paid £230 for a 1964 Vauxhall Viva. There was no walnut dash or leather seats in this motor, it was six years old, tinny and if the sun shone on it, the plastic seats scorched your bottom. Nonetheless, for 13 years I used it every day for work. I went courting and on holidays in it, no one else ever put a spanner on it, what a bargain that was.

Saltley had a large complement of young men who were now in the grade of 'secondman'. I have to admit that I was often very grateful to some of these younger men for explaining the usual procedures on some of the diagrams. Most of these youngsters were extremely keen and competent and I never had any doubts about sharing the driving with many of them. Having said that, there were some whom I only let drive once, their over confidence was to leave me pressing my feet on the floor boards with my toes curled up! I wasn't about to have an early coronary!

Despite the fact that overtime was easily come by and Sunday work was regular, greed again reared its ugly head. As had previously happened at Tyseley, Saltley drivers now wanted to share the secondmen's turns on Sundays. I felt strongly against this, as did a number of my colleagues from Tyseley who had been 'Put Back' to act as secondmen. Regrettably, this time we were on the losing side when it came to a show of hands. On principle, following this vote, some of us did put a letter into management to say that we were not prepared to work secondmen's turns on Sundays. Yet I was disappointed to see one ex-Tyseley man vote for the motion. He had originally moved from Banbury to Tyseley to become a driver and had ended up being 'Put Back' with the rest of us. After the vote, I approached him and suggested that he had a very short memory. He looked puzzled, so I reminded him that 12 months earlier he had in fact voted the other way when the boot was on the other foot, his principles were obviously only as deep as his pocket.

My first trip to Leicester came on a Sunday afternoon; I was diagrammed to do one trip with a multiple unit and a second with a locomotive and coaches on the Norwich service. When I signed on, I was surprised to find a young Saltley driver there to conduct me. He was busting with confidence and was quick to make me realise that what he did not know about the railway wasn't really worth knowing. Apparently, engineering work was scheduled in Arley tunnel; my train was therefore diverted via Coventry and Three Spires Junction. I had not yet learned this section of track, so a conductor needed to be provided.

Changing ends and a reverse movement at Coventry, together with a slow run over a line which was normally used only for freight trains, obviously made us late arriving at Nuneaton. Here another change of cabs and another reverse movement was now necessary. My conductor had been doing the driving up until that point and I took over from him from there on. Here, he pointed out to me that he was diagrammed to conduct me on the return journey also; therefore he suggested that he might as well come with me to Leicester. My thoughts were, as it was my first trip, that two heads were better than one, I may well be glad of his company.

After leaving Nuneaton I made the usual stop at Hinkley. The line rises out of Hinkley and at the brow of the rise our speed had risen to 45 mph. As we went through an overbridge on to the falling gradient, children had piled rubbish on the line in our path. This behaviour was commonplace to train drivers and I felt that the type of material on the line would be easily pushed aside by the train. My thinking was right, but I had not seen a large loop of wire which happened to wrap itself around the control air pipe on the front of the unit, regretfully the wire was stout enough to break the isolating cock clean off. The control air pressure immediately went to zero, the engines returned to idling and there was now no control over the gearboxes. In this condition we were reduced to coasting on the slightly falling gradient.

In a trice my colleague had got a mass of paperwork over the cab console and was anxiously thumbing through it. My comments to him were that he could put the manuals away, what had happened here was unlikely to be in there. I then had to ask his advice on how far he felt we might run in this condition. He thought that we might coast as far as Croft Sidings signal box. I then asked him if it was normal for this signal box to be 'switched in' on a Sunday afternoon. He was not sure, but we had just passed an engineering train going in the other direction and our speed was now down to 20 mph. As we approached the signal box, however, the starting signal for the opposite line was still showing clear, so I quickly deduced that had the signalman been on duty this signal would have been set to danger to protect the train that we had just passed. There was no point in stopping here, so I left the brake alone. This action allowed us to coast at just 10 mph up to crossing gates at Narborough signal box.

The moment we came to a stand, Tony was out of the cab and in the signal box telling the signalman of our plight. Brought about by many hours plodding around the dmu sidings at Tyseley, my knowledge of the units now became of great use. I walked back down the train, shut off the control airline between the front power car and the intermediate coach, or trailer car as we termed it. I then went to the rear power car, where I revved one of the engines with the manual throttle. This built up the air pressure quickly in the rear power car, whereby I returned to the front cab knowing that I would now have electrical control of the rear two engines. I then put my hand up to the signalman to indicate that I was ready to go; he then opened the crossing gates and cleared his signals. When I picked my conductor driver up at the signal box, his hat was now on the back of his head and he couldn't get his breath on how quickly I had got out of trouble. I now only had half power, but at least we were moving again and all the gradients from there on were level to falling.

At Leicester we were just 12 minutes late on the retimed schedule, I was happy with that, a driver from out of the' sticks' had proved his worth, I thought?

At the time, I also felt that there was sure to be a replacement unit around the station somewhere at Leicester that could be used for our return trip. I was wrong, neither were there any fitters on duty who might furnish a repair. The station inspector eventually informed us that a Sulzer type '2' locomotive was being turned off the depot for us to tow the train back to Birmingham. My expertise from Tyseley now came in use again; it was now my duty to fully isolate both power cars on the unit. Centralising the final drives could also only be achieved with air pressure in the damaged coach. With the help of the carriage and wagon examiner, a wooded peg was shaped and we hammered this plug into the broken pipe. This allowed me to gain enough air pressure to centralise the four final drives. Failing to carry out this procedure could have resulted in the engines being turned in the wrong direction whilst we were towing, the ensuing damage could have been catastrophic. I was now dressed in my new blue uniform and would have been very glad of a pair of overalls. I got filthy dirty as I had to lie on the station platform to isolate the final drives.

With the job done I was now grateful of the company of my pilot driver, as on the return journey we had to detach the locomotive and run round the unit to attach to the other end at Nuneaton. This performance had to be repeated again at Coventry. All these movements took time and we finally arrived back in New Street station very late. Because the drive shafts were isolated, the alternators were not working to charge the batteries. In turn the unit batteries went flat because the train lights had to be left on for the passengers. This again caused the train heating to fail.

We got the passengers to Birmingham, but they were undoubtedly pretty unhappy, most of their journey had been in total darkness and in an uninviting temperature. I was also too late to work the Norwich; again I was happy with that, I went home to clean up.

My conductor driver was a budding tutor driver and he was often seen rubbing shoulders with our new inspector. During the following week Les Durnell was waiting for me when I arrived at work. He started by saying that he understood there had been an incident during my turn of duty on the previous Sunday. There was indeed little doubt in my mind from whom he had obtained that information! I initially felt that he might offer me some encouragement for the way I dealt with the situation. This was a gross misapprehension, he criticised me for working the train forward without a warning horn. With no air pressure in the leading vehicle when I left Narborough, the horns obviously did not work. I could feel myself beginning to fester inwardly and I put it to him as to what he thought I should have done, other than stand at Narborough to wait for an assistant engine to come from Leicester. His reply to this was that I should have driven the train from the rear cab of the unit were the horn was working. He added that the pilot driver should have sat in the leading cab and indicate on the unit buzzer each time it was necessary to sound the horn. I then put it to him as to how I would have gone on if I had been alone, as under normal conditions I would have been. His answer to this was that the train guard should have then ridden in the leading cab whilst I drove from the rear cab.

Without degrading the many well trained and conscientious guards that I worked with, there were some of the recent arrivals in the grade who were unable to name the stations that we called at, let alone be responsible for observing the signals while I drove the train from the rear end. I pointed out to him that the incident had occurred late on a Sunday afternoon, the only people on the line were likely to be trespassers. I walked away from him in disgust, what he had proposed was totally impracticable and I could not help losing some respect for him.

On the same day I was on a local freight trip job and our locomotive was the usual Sulzer type '2', or eventual class '25'. These small engines, being light in weight and only having four-wheeled bogies, didn't hold their 'feet' too well on a heavy freight train.

The last part of our trip working on this turn was to load out of Cadbury's Sidings at Bournville. This was prized traffic to the railways; this train was possibly the only freight train that was allowed through New Street station just prior to the evening commuter trains. On this afternoon, the weight of the chocolate products took me by surprise. Having left Cadbury's Sidings, we ran on to the down gradient entering the tunnels towards New Street. Having never worked a freight over this section of track, I was already rather cautious, better safe than sorry. Nevertheless, the train soon began to push the locomotive and the locomotive brake was immediately put on to its extent. As was usual, we only had the engine brake; none of the wagons were vacuum piped to the locomotive. The fire from the locomotive brake blocks was soon illuminating the tunnel sides, the wheels smelling of burning oil. At this point, I was anxious not allow the locomotive to start to slide on the damp rail of the tunnel, so I had to keep the sanding gear working. We were down to only 15 mph, but the train kept pushing and it certainly did not look as if I was going to stop at that all-important signal protecting the station. My secondman was well aware of this and prepared to 'abandon ship'; he was soon standing on the bottom step ready to jump off. Who could blame him; the consequences of overrunning this signal were likely to be pretty devastating, as passenger trains were departing from the station every few minutes at this hour. With my heart thumping like a drop forge, only feet from the signal it cleared in our favour, what relief I felt, but this experience did absolutely nothing for my blood pressure! The train was eventually left in Washwood Heath Yard for the journey north and I was certainly a much wiser man.

The following day we were on the same turn, my guard was a young blonde curly-headed lad, as yet with little experience. On the way to work his 'Reliant Robin' had caught fire, he told me how frustrated he had been as his vehicle was gutted. He had been near to a telephone box when his car caught fire, but he hadn't got any loose change to ring 999 for the fire brigade! Not surprisingly, I immediately realised that it was not only my own back I was watching.

When we left Cadbury's Sidings on this second evening, our train tonnage was similar to the previous day, I was therefore extremely anxious not to have a similar experience approaching New Street station. Alas, the shunter in charge of the siding at Cadbury's had more than an aggressive streak; in fact he seemed to hate everyone and went around with the expression of a rabid dog. Nonetheless, I approached him quietly and explained to him that I had experienced problems controlling the train on the previous evening. I informed him that I felt it was unwise to approach the station with such a load with only the locomotive brake to rely on. I then asked him if he could put a couple of vacuum brake fitted vehicles next to the locomotive to assist me in stopping. This would have taken only five minutes, but his eyes flashed and he pushed his shunting pole towards me saying, 'Mate, if you want any fitted, here's the pole'.

Angered at his attitude, I told the shunter that I wouldn't be leaving the sidings until I had got some braked vehicles attached to the engine. Once I had made my decision I had to stick to it and eventually we missed our margin for a path through the busy station. Whether it was getting towards his home time, or he eventually realised that I meant what I said, the shunter then furiously began to re-marshal the train. Now totally bloody-minded, he shunted every fitted wagon out of the train and connected them all to the locomotive, I now had some 15-braked vehicles of which I had control. To do this he had to occupy the up main running line for some time, this in turn causing delay to other passing passenger trains.

When we were finally ready to leave, the signalman at New Street refused to accept the train, as the commuter service was now in full flow. The control then ordered us to take the train forward to Selly Oak Sidings, where we were to run round the train and take it to Washwood Heath Yard via Lifford Curve and Camp Hill. If my memory serves me right, the longest train we could run round at Selly Oak was 44 standard wagons length. On arrival at Selly Oak, when we came to run-round the train, our train was half a wagon length too long! My young guard then got into an awful mess, and further delay occurred to passenger trains needing to go south out of New Street. We eventually arrived at Washwood Heath about 8.30 pm, some three hours late for this lucrative freight traffic, so it was little wonder that the telephone wires had by now got red hot.

I signed on again next day and for the second time in a week our traction inspector was waiting for me. Ted Brown, the shift foreman, looked at me over his half spectacles as if to say that I was already getting a reputation.

When I had explained the events of the previous days, I have to give Les Durnell full credit; he backed my actions to the hilt. In fact, he was quite angry at what had taken place. He left me saying, 'You leave this to me, but I want it all on paper'. I heard no more of the incident, however I suspect the shunter had the blue touch paper lit near to his rear end!

Les Durnell wanted everything in writing, yet at this period of time all reports appeared to sink into a morass of correspondence in the general office. Indeed, if we reported anything, even if it was a safety issue, we never got any response from management, not as much as an acknowledgement. It was little wonder therefore that some drivers eventually became quite apathetic to situations that arose. However, some weeks after my incident with Cadbury's traffic, a comprehensive train loading procedure was implemented. This calculated trainloads by, 'standard wagon length units'. Every vehicle now had its brake force calculated and stencilled on the vehicle chassis, along with other dimensions, including its route availability.

Our new loading books contained innumerable pages of tables for every gradient and route that the depot worked over. All routes had a designated brake force, calculated to incorporate the speed of all classes of freight trains. Initially it was the guard's job to total up the train tonnage and be sure that enough vacuum fitted vehicles had been attached to the locomotive to give at least the minimum required brake force. However, the onus was on the driver to be sure the calculations had been worked out correctly. Although we almost needed 'A' level maths to be sure of the figures, these tables were indeed a step in the right direction.

Every day I learned something afresh as I felt my way in this very different environment. The very much outnumbered 'Western' men were inclined to get a lot of good-humoured banter from the 'Midland' men, although many of my colleagues were always able to give as much as they got. The engine arranger, who was the outside foreman at Saltley, tried to wind me up one day by making comments about the Great Western. I let it wash over me and as I left his office he said, 'You don't bite do you?' I then remarked that I had learned quickly. To which he replied, 'Geoff Morris has been here three years and he still bites!' This said it all; I was right to keep my own counsel, once you got wound up you became a constant target for a bit of fun.

On one occasion a secondman did annoy me with his persistent carping, there were obviously a few young men who undoubtedly thought that all 'Western' men had straw sticking out of their ears. I did have to 'count ten' on a number of times with this fellow, happily I did manage to hold my composure. However, I was pleasantly surprised to be able to get my own back much sooner than I expected.

We were diagrammed to work an excursion train from Derby to Stratford-upon-Avon and we had to travel to Derby to get our locomotive from off the depot there. This thick set young man towered over me and walked about as though he was held in a straightjacket. He snapped at me in monosyllables when he spoke, I had not been spoken to in that manner since I had left senior school. At Derby, we were allocated a Crompton Parkinson type '4'. These 2,500 hp locomotives were probably the best all round engines that I ever worked on, in reality, I never heard a single word of complaint from any driver about these locomotives. They were rugged, strong and reliable, with eight-wheeled bogies they were extremely stable at speed and their cabs were comfortable and warm. Their sister engines, the Brush type '4s' were a good comparison, but the Crompton's had the edge for power.

After preparing our locomotive we left the depot; this was the first occasion that I had made movements around Derby station. There were several ways that the signalman could have routed me to get into the station; again it was a case to some degree that I had to read the signalman's mind. I had quickly assessed that I would not be able to count on the moron that was sitting in the other seat.

Our train duly arrived into the station from Skegness and I made moves to attach to the back end to draw the train out of Derby towards Birmingham. These moves were made with some caution, as I was eager not to make any mistakes. Needless to say, this caution did not go without comment from the other side of the cab, he seemed only too keen for me to give him the opportunity to gloat.

I finally got the 'right away' and we left on time. Before I had got the last of the 12 coaches clear of the 15 mph permanent speed restriction leaving the station, a voice from my right was telling me to, 'Open her up, we haven't got all day'.

As yet, the maximum line speed from Derby to Birmingham was 75 mph and I passed Burton-on-Trent on time. At Landor Street Junction, adjacent to Saltley Depot, we were still on time as we took the left-hand curve to pass behind St Andrews Football Ground. A further sweep to the left at Bordesley Junction took us on to the 20 mph wide curve leading to the ex-Great Western lines. Here I couldn't resist saying to my colleague, 'You are on a good bit of railway now David, you are on the old Great Western, it's 90 mph over here, not 75 mph'. This was met with his usual expressionless look and the comment, 'Huh! There's woodworm in the sleepers over here'.

Clear of the restriction of speed, the locomotive was put on full power and we passed Solihull at 80 mph. With easier going the speed increased further. I happened to glance over at my mate; he now had his nose up against the window and was looking straight ahead. He was gripping the frame of his seat with both hands; his hold was so tight that his knuckles were white and I realised that he had never been this fast before ... I was beginning to enjoy this! Our speed at Knowle and Dorridge was now just over 90 mph and I left the controller full open. At 95 mph David could contain himself no longer; he leapt from his seat and shouted, 'You're mad you are'. Perhaps ... but I cured him, the rest of our time together was in total silence and he has always given me a wide berth since.

The Cromptons, or class '45s', did have one peculiarity, this we were warned about when we did our traction training. I was to drive these engines for thousands of miles, yet this anomaly only ever happened to me once. All diesel locomotives of that time had 'load regulators'. On most locomotives, when power was shut off quickly there was a delay before power could be regained. This delay was caused by the 'load regulator' running back to normal or what we termed 'stud forty'. With Sulzer type '4' 2,750 hp locomotives it could be the best part of a minute before the 'load regulator' ran back to normal after shutting off power quickly. When you did regain power, if you were still in the higher speed range, it could still take a further minute and a half to get back on to full power whilst the load regulator went through its sequence. Therefore, if signalmen kept their signals at caution, yet still cleared them before you had to apply the brake, time could still be lost due to the slow operation of the 'load regulator'. There again, if the 'load regulator' failed to run back to normal on most locomotives, you would be unable to regain power at all and the locomotive would become a failure, that is, if you could not get it to run back after the engine had been shut down for a few minutes as we were instructed to do in our driver's manual.

When the 'load regulator' stuck on a Crompton Parkinson, power could always be gained instantly. Unfortunately the 'load regulator' would then deal you the amount of power at the point at which it had stuck. This was alright at speed, but it was quite alarming to put the controller in the 'on' position and then have the locomotive surge forward on full power when you were making a standing start! I might add that a driver would be quite unaware of this prematurely. This could be really dangerous if you were making moves in a siding. You could only cope with this situation by holding the air brake full on, apply power, then slowly release the brake in an effort to counteract the surge of power. On a freight train, however, if you were unaware, this could easily tear out the wagon draw hooks, or break the couplings. I was glad this fault only happened to me once!

The axe fell on Tyseley and it was finally closed as a running depot in 1970, although it remained for maintenance purposes as we expected. The older men took a redundancy package, my father included; he was just 61 years of age. A new 'Booking on Point' had been created at New Street station; some Tyseley drivers moved there, this along with men from Aston, Monument Lane and Wolverhampton depots, which were originally the ex-London & North Western Railway sheds. The majority of Tyseley men did have the chance to move to Saltley, or go even further afield. My old 'Top Link' driver Fred Gay was a little younger than my father; he walked to the Rover factory, which was only a short distance from his home in Solihull. At the factory he asked for work, after telling the personnel officer that he had spent his life as a train driver. The lady in charge frowned sympathetically when she offered him the only position available because of the low salary that went with it. Fred had difficulty keeping his composure when he was told that the wages were indeed half as much again as he had been getting as a top paid train driver! He therefore spent the rest of his working life in a white coat, checking the electrical equipment of the cars as they came off the production line.

I had already made friends with many of the men at Saltley, but it was now good to see a lot more familiar faces at my new depot. I had some fine friends at Tyseley and it was nice to have Bernard Rainbow, Howard Jones and his brother Dave amongst us again, to name just a few. Both Howard and Dave helped most of my friends through their driver's examination. Howard Jones and Ray Hopkins were also our Committeemen for GWR Engineman's and Fireman's Mutual Assurance Sick and Superannuation Society, which was our all important pension fund. Both these men freely dedicated much of their time in the interest of Tyseley men by visiting the sick and bereaved. As the pension fund members diminished, this was a position later taken up by Don Magson, who also set aside many hours of his time in our interest.

Our pension fund, the MAS as we knew it, was a fund set up by the foresight of the Directors of the old GWR and was years ahead of its time. All GWR enginemen had to pay five shillings to join; there was no option, other than to leave the service or grade. The fund was virtually free, I paid 33p per week up until the time I retired, this payment made me a first class member. At the time of nationalisation there were few other pension funds on the railway system, most locomotive men had none at all. I suspect that this railway pension fund must have eventually been protected by government agreements at that time of nationalisation; the GWR pension fund was no doubt the envy of many enginemen of other companies.

The British Railways pension fund was eventually set up and ex-Western men were pressured to leave the MAS and join the new scheme. The figures that I was furnished with at that time indicated that I would pay £5 per week into the new scheme to get slightly less pension. I would also lose 15 years of service by joining the BR new scheme. The only benefit on offer with the BR scheme was that if I died in service my widow would get the equivalent of initially two years' wages as life assurance. In later years this did rise to three years' wages.

The new scheme did not appear to be a viable option, nevertheless, I was urged by our union representatives to become a member of the BR pension fund; the union felt all locomotive men should be under one roof. No doubt, pension funds are an extremely complex issue; the committeemen who represented us were not sure themselves over the issue that confronted us. There again, trade union men, who were totally unqualified to offer any opinion, tried to twist our arms to join the new BR scheme. The logic of this has always confounded me and I therefore remained in the Great Western pension fund.

The amalgamation into the Saltley diagrams of some of the remaining work from Tyseley meant that I would again be working regularly over my old hunting ground, roads that I knew like the back of my hand and I have to admit felt more comfortable driving over.

Once at Saltley one job had often come into my remit, and that was the up passenger/postal which left New Street in the early hours at around 4 am. On one Monday morning, engineering work had taken place at Kingsbury and a temporary

Driver Jack Higgins and the author on the footplate of 'Castle' class 4-6-0 No. 7029 *Clun Castle* at the time when Bernard Rainbow and others turned the engines out of Tyseley Museum fit for royalty. *Les Dearson/Colin Jacks Collection*

Howard Jones at the controls of a class '45' diesel locomotive. He was our pension fund representative and spent many hours tutoring us for our driver's examination. He spent many hours in the interest of others, visiting the sick and bereaved, yet still found time for union activities and his work as a JP. *Provenance Unknown*

speed restriction was in force according to my weekly notice. At this period, much track work was being done on the former Midland main lines to bring them up to 90 mph running. This work became so frequent that the engineering department had trouble getting enough men to work every Saturday night and Sunday. The large projects that they took on therefore became a problem to complete. It seemed that as long as the two ends of the track were tied back together for trains to run, the work was left, sometimes in an awful state. There were occasions when the normal temporary speed restriction of 20 mph was far too fast for the precarious way in which the track was left. Trains snaked over rails that were like a dog's hind leg and the locomotive pitched and rolled on the uneven ballast. Drivers, therefore, had to use much discretion when passing over such works.

I left New Street on this morning and my secondman went into the engine room to turn the train steam heating back on. The steam had to be shut off whilst we were in the station to avoid the shunter getting scalded as the post office vans to the rear of the train were often re-marshalled. My mate had trouble getting the boiler going again and didn't emerge from the engine room until we were well past Water Orton Junction. We had run into heavy mist and as he entered the cab the engine room lights, together with light from the Stones vaporising boiler, made it briefly difficult to see out. I was also momentarily distracted by him telling me of a problem with the boiler. The split second normality was restored, I just caught a glimpse out of the corner of my eye of a very poorly lit advanced warning board for the 20 mph speed restriction. I immediately applied the brakes hard, yet before I had reduced the speed sufficiently we passed the restriction commencement indicator at something like 35 mph. The locomotive pitched and rolled alarmingly on the uneven track and it was difficult to imagine how it stayed on the rails, had we had anything other than a stable Crompton Parkinson type '4', it may well have been another story. We were the first train over the new track and it had been left in a dreadful state. I stopped at the next signal telephone and informed the signalman of the incident, I also advised him that the advanced warning board was very poorly lit and wasn't the prescribed ¾ mile from the speed restriction. The signalman would then have to stop and warn following trains until the situation was put right.

The siting of temporary speed restriction advanced warning boards was also becoming a problem, now that the permanent way gangs had gone mobile with road vehicles. Not surprisingly, warning boards now tended to be put at a point of the nearest access that the platelayers had got from the road to the trackside. Often they were sited either much too far out or too close to the commencement to give adequate braking distance.

Realising how close I had come to disaster, on returning to the depot I made a report out, emphasizing on the poor standard of warning board lighting and the importance of correct siting. This communication went completely unrecognised, so a few weeks later I submitted a second report. This later report was also totally ignored, so I now began a one-man vendetta. I stopped and reported every speed restriction warning board that wasn't up to standard; I stopped with heavy Freightliners and passenger trains, in hope that the loss of time would bring a response from management. One week, I stopped every night with the newspaper train to report a warning board at Bescot which had no lights in it. There was an almost fanatical situation with the timing of this newspaper train and I felt sure someone from management would eventually send me a report for the lost time. I never heard a word.

After a long, frustrating campaign, I eventually wrote to the Staff Suggestions Team, suggesting that temporary warning magnets could be installed in rear of speed restriction warning boards to operate the AWS in the cab. This I felt would be an extra protection should the warning board lights go out. I did get a response, although I was told that this suggestion had already been submitted a number of times previously. Regretfully, management were not in favour of implementing the system. Whilst the placing of temporary magnets was quite feasible, the reasons given were that in closely signalled areas extra warnings could be confused with signals. There would also be some dispute over whose duty it would be to install the magnets, the signal technicians, or the platelayers. The railway inspectorate also felt that the placing of such magnets might discourage drivers from referring to their weekly temporary speed restriction notice.

Some time later the inevitable happened, albeit because of vandalism to a warning board, a driver on the West Coast Main Line failed to see a temporary speed restriction during darkness. The results were catastrophic, he passed over a 20 mph restriction at Nuneaton station at high speed and there was loss of life. I was deeply upset and I could only feel some sense of failure.

Criminal charges were filed against the driver of this train and I could only feel the injustice of it. As I felt it was a personal matter, I wrote to my trade union ASLEF Headquarters in defence of this unfortunate man. I wrote a long detailed letter explaining the lengths I had gone to, to get the matter of poor warning board lighting corrected. I hoped that what I had written might be used as evidence in this driver's defence. Regrettably, this letter too remained completely unacknowledged. Unfortunately, I was unaware that all union correspondence had to go via my local trade union secretary. Nevertheless, in this instance I felt that bureaucracy might have been swept aside, as my letter was in good faith and I felt it warranted the courtesy of a reply. My effort was all pretty futile and I really felt as though I was hitting my head against a brick wall.

Whilst this accident did bring some changes for the better, temporary speed restrictions always remained a problem. We had already got warning boards with intensified lighting in some instances. These were gas lit, although, if the restriction was on for any length of time, the gas bottles would run out leaving no warning lights at all. This situation was quite treacherous, at least with the three paraffin lamps in a warning board, if one went out, you still had two other lamps that could be seen.

With train speeds increasing, more time would be lost due to temporary speed restrictions. Management then had the idea that if a train was on a rising gradient, the warning board for a speed restriction need not be so far out. This would reduce the time the driver spent looking for the commencement of the restriction after seeing the advanced warning board. With the new proposals implemented, speed restriction advanced warning boards were thereafter placed at what was deemed a correctly calculated braking distance from the commencement of the restriction. With faster train speeds, an express train needed longer to slow down on a falling gradient, so these warning boards were sited farther away from the commencement. In theory this was the perfect solution, in practice it was a disaster. It seemed to be a licence for platelayers to site warning boards anywhere they chose, despite the braking distance supposedly being carefully calculated for them.

Within days of the new system being implemented, I worked an express towards Derby. At 90 mph I faced a temporary speed restriction at Elford, on seeing the advanced warning board I put the brakes on full. Emerging from an overbridge, there was the 20 mph and I was still going far too fast. I passed over the restriction at 40 mph scattering workmen from right and left. Again I had to stop and report that the warning board was not far enough out to give sufficient braking distance.

This speed restriction was on in both directions and I noticed that the warning board in the opposite direction was almost two miles out, and this was a rising gradient! The warning board for the up line falling gradient was just half a mile out. Nevertheless, on my return journey that day, both warning boards for this speed restriction had now been re-sited correctly, so I was happy with that.

Back at the depot, pen went to paper again; this situation was dangerous, I had nearly run men down. At this time I had been at Saltley for some years and we now had a new manager. John Ride was not only a fine railwayman, he was a nice approachable man and good at his job, he also saw to it that any reports from men always got a reply. This courtesy was certainly a step in the right direction.

John eventually invited me into his office to read out the response to my latest report from the area manager at Nottingham. When he finished he said, 'Dennis, I can only regard that as snotty'. Which indeed it was, in short the reply said that great trouble had been taken to calculate the correct distances and that the warning boards had been correctly sited. What the area manager at Nottingham didn't realise was that initially someone had got their up line crossed with their down line, a matter that was quickly rectified by the permanent way men after I had stopped to I reported it. Nevertheless this reply was demoralising and again I seemed to be flogging a dead horse.

For some years I repeatedly reported incorrectly sited warning boards; on one occasion one was found to be 2½ miles out on a level gradient. Yet it was an awfully long time until things were eventually put right. Magnets were eventually placed in rear of permanent and temporary speed restrictions so that the AWS would operate in the cab and apply the train brakes if the driver had not seen it. This again was certainly a move forward, there again successive governments starved the railways of investment and it was only after serious accidents that recommendations got some things put right.

One job that I now worked regularly I always enjoyed, perhaps it was because we signed on around 8.00 am and always got a decent finish, plus mileage bonus. On this turn we left New Street about 9.00 am and worked a Plymouth train to Gloucester, via Worcester. At Gloucester Central we detached, later attaching to the Plymouth-Newcastle service. This train we then worked through to Derby, where we were relieved. We again relieved a train from Leeds going south and worked this train back to New Street. The only drawback with the turn was that it was a favourite for Les Durnell and he would appear at any time to assess your driving capabilities. Initially, I was unaware of this and he caught me at Derby with young train spotters in the cab; we were always inundated by requests from lads to 'cab it'. He read the riot act to me and although I did try to point out to him that these lads were our best ambassadors, thinking it was better to encourage them than to have them throw stones from a bridge at you, needless to say Les would have none of it, rules were rules.

On another occasion on this turn the eminent railway enthusiast O.S. Nock rode with us to record the train performance. Visitors in the cab were always accompanied by a traction inspector, needless to say whose breath I could feel down the back of my neck for the whole trip! Les watched every deviation of the speedometer like a hawk. A log of the trip later appeared in the *Railway Magazine* and I couldn't help smiling at what was written. It said that the driver made a rather cautious approach to Birmingham New Street. With a permanent 30 mph speed restriction from Proof House Junction, reducing to 10 mph entering the station, what could any driver have done under these circumstances? I was hardly likely to 'stretch' the speed over these restrictions.

Much to my irritation, Les Durnell turned up on me a second time during the same week, I was beginning to think others would soon be talking about me! I immediately said to him that he had seen me drive on Monday, perhaps he might like to have a turn. His reply to this was that men thought that because he told others what to do, they had an idea that he couldn't do it himself.

Les happily took the controls and I have to say that he did the job as expertly as anybody. Ironically, when we arrived at New Street the platform inspector was waiting for me and asked me if I would ring the control, as they wanted a word with me. Les pricked up his ears and followed me into the inspector's office where I made contact.

'Ah driver, you were right time at Burton, two minutes late at Wichnor Junction, but right time at Tamworth, could you explain why?' the controller inquired. To which I replied, 'Perhaps you would like a word with Traction Inspector Durnell, he has accompanied us today'. Les frowned, as I passed him the phone. When the controller repeated his words, my inspector went absolutely ballistic. He when red in the face and was fuming, eventually he yelled down the mouthpiece. 'I won't have my drivers harassed in this way, this is ridiculous'. Obviously, Les did have his good points, but would he have behaved in the same way had I been driving?

The rule concerning the number of wheels allowed behind a passenger train brakevan had now been abandoned. The consequences were that trains were allowed to have just one guard's brakevan in the train. Station staff didn't bother to find out at which end of the train the brakevan was if they needed to load parcels, but waited until the train arrived at the platform. Half of the time the barrow was at the back of the train, only to find the brakevan was at the front end when the train arrived. When the train stopped, they then had to push the barrow the length of the train and still had to load up, which tended to delay departures. This had obviously taken place on this occasion as station staff were never fussy to a couple of minutes when the control asked what time a train had left a station. The station inspector had obviously said 'right time', to cover any overtime which was down to station duties. Derby power signal box had then notified the control of our time passing Wichnor Junction, telling him that we were two minutes late. The Tamworth porter had again reported us right time, as we were near enough for him. We eventually arrived in Birmingham on time, after recovering the few minutes lost. However, I was pleased that Les Durnell became aware of some of the hassle drivers were inclined to get.

Our weekly temporary speed restriction notice book was a rather complicated piece of literature, although I have to admit that it was difficult to see how this publication could have been simplified. Drivers had to sign every week to indicate that they had been given this notice. Any speed restrictions imposed after the book had been published were entered on a late notice board in the engineman's lobby. It was the duty of the shift foremen to update the late notices daily; therefore it was important that drivers examined this notice board when they signed on duty.

Routes over which a driver worked on a single day could involve several pages in the 'Speed Notice', as each route was split into sections. Although as a driver you read the notice initially before starting a journey, when you were actually driving, the dates at which restrictions started and ended tended to be not always easy to recall, nor were they always fully accurately publicised. A driver just had to be extremely vigilant the whole time; it wasn't practicable to keep ferreting in your bag to check the speed notice whilst running.

I stopped at Worcester on our Gloucester job on one Monday morning and unusually the signal on the end of the platform remained at danger. After a time, the station inspector informed me that there had been a derailment at Cheltenham and we were to be diverted via Honeybourne and Toddington. This was one of my old Western routes that I still signed for, but just as I was about to leave a Worcester driver appeared to conduct me. He need not have come with us, but he said it suited him to get out of the mess room and he would be glad to pass the time. I therefore vacated the driving seat and he was happy to drive. A temporary speed restriction of 40 mph had been imposed for perhaps a year or more at Pershore due to subsidence; nevertheless, although I had not been over the line for some time, much work had now been done to raise the overall line speed to 90 mph running. On a diversion like this, few drivers would have religiously referred to their speed notice after being told of a diversion. I certainly would not have done as it was daylight and the weather was fine, I would just have been extra vigilant. I was very lucky, as this would have been a grave mistake on my part. Although an advanced temporary speed restriction warning board for the long-standing 40 mph at Pershore had not appeared, the Worcester driver began to apply the brake. I was momentarily puzzled by this, but as we approached where the old subsidence speed restriction had been, it had that very day been made a *permanent* 40 mph. This was indeed entered into our speed notice, saying that the warning boards had be removed and the usual 'cut out' indicators for a permanent speed restriction were now provided. Doubtless, had I been driving, by the time I saw the 'cut out' numbers for the speed restriction I would have been unable to reduce the train speed sufficiently and would certainly have passed over the restriction far too fast. This incident shows the pitfalls that we could always face on a daily basis.

Whilst most days went routinely, later another pitfall occurred which eventually became a High Court case and I was called to the witness box to give evidence.

We worked a Corby to Bescot freight one night, which we took charge of at Leicester. Luck again was with me to some degree, we worked the last passenger to Leicester on this turn and I had a secondman accompanying me that I had quickly assessed previously as one of those that I would only let drive once! With a good experienced secondman I would have normally let him do the driving with the freight.

We set off from Leicester with a train of 48 standard wagon length units. On the rear of the train were some huge hexagon-shaped steel ingots from Corby foundry. My guard, Levi Lawrence, was of West Indian origin, a really nice man who was one of those that always had a great smile and possessed not an inkling of aggression. At Croft Sidings the signals were against us and the signalman eventually stopped us outside the signal box by exhibiting a red light. He said he had the Postal behind us and he therefore wanted us to shunt over into the up refuge siding, which held 60 wagons in length. The signalman made a point of asking us how many wagons we had got behind us, when told 48 in length, he commented that we would get inside easily. We then drew forward to clear the points and our guard eventually waved his lamp to call us back towards the siding. I had not done this move before, so I took things with caution. I was unsure whether the train would pull us into the sidings once I had given it a start, or whether I would have to push it back due to the gradient. Before we had got the train halfway inside there was an enormous bang, the locomotive stopped dead and our brew can, cups, bags and everything that was loose went flying across the cab. When I walked back to see what had happened, the train had gone down a short siding next to where we should have gone. The brakevan buffers were now sitting on top of the stop block, otherwise everything looked all right. Levi appeared unhurt, but he was extremely shocked.

My immediate thoughts were that things were not as bad as might have been. We could quickly detach the brakevan, go forward and then come into the siding that we should have come down, that would at least clear the line for the Postal. On the way back to the locomotive I made an examination of the rest of the train, unfortunately one box van standing right on the main line crossover had got its buffers interlocked with the wagons next to it. If I moved the train, it would almost certainly derail and make things far worse. I therefore had to make arrangements for the breakdown crew to come from Leicester. The Postal was now standing behind us at Narborough, so much manoeuvring had to be done for the breakdown train to access us.

It was dawn before the line was cleared and I eventually took the locomotive back to Leicester, where we caught the first passenger train home. Levi came home with us, he seemed quiet, but otherwise he appeared all right. He was obviously worried of the repercussions of this accident, as it was his duty to check the route points were set correctly before he had called the train back. Heaven only knows what a mess there would have been had I let the impulsive youth who was with me do the driving; I might well have had Levi's life on my conscience.

On return to Saltley, I made out the usual paperwork and went home. As I was in no way to blame I heard nothing more of the incident and some months went by. Working shifts it was not unusual to not see other men for weeks, I therefore had no idea that Levi had not returned to work after the accident. He had indeed been off work for some months.

The next thing I knew, the boss was interviewing me regarding this affair. I was then sent to Leicester to another inquiry with the area manager there. I was also grilled at some length by a trade union solicitor. After I had again given my account of the incident, the solicitor asked again how hard I thought I had collided with the stop block. I had just explained for the second time that the brakevan buffers were just resting on top of the stop block wooden beam, when he produced photographs of the same stop block completely demolished, saying, it didn't look like that to him. Although this stop block had probably been weakened by my collision with it, in fact another train from the quarry working in the siding had struck it a second time only a short time after. I had seen the gutted stop block myself, as I worked over the route with regularity. However, I got the impression that the union solicitor was not at all convinced that I hadn't completely destroyed the stop block.

The reason for the renewed interest in the accident was that National Union of Railwaymen had submitted a claim for compensation for my guard, but BR management had refused to pay, as they felt he had not adhered to the laid down instructions for these sidings. Lack of agreement between the two parties eventually brought the case to the high court. Here one has to bear in mind that most immigrant men working on the railway had come into a completely alien environment and they had taken on extremely responsible work. The guard's job did require a vast amount of knowledge; the railway system was very complex, yet their basic wage was incompatible.

Almost every small siding had unique special working; this was laid down in the General Appendix to the Rule Book. British Railways management were fully aware that these men could not possibly be fully conversant with the work expected of them. Nonetheless, there was an acute shortage of manpower in that grade, if these guards got into difficulty it was well known that they were advised to ask the driver.

At the court, many of the guard's colleagues sat in the public gallery; I was one of the first called to give evidence. The elderly judge overlooked us all; spread out in front of him were all the relevant rule books and appendices, plus a long diagram of the track layout at Croft Sidings. As I gave my account, the judge referred to the map intently as I spoke. Levi was then called, when he got to the point where we stopped clear of the points to go back towards the sidings, he said that the ground signal cleared and he signalled to call us back. At this point there were immediate gasps and much murmuring from the public gallery, as in fact there was no ground signal there at all for this movement. Everyone therefore obviously felt that he had immediately muffed his own chances of any compensation.

This particular set of points were what was known as 'undetected points', in which case the signalman had control of a single lever in the signalbox. When a signalman operated such points, it was the person's responsibility who was making the movement to pass over the undetected points to check that they were correctly set. After the signalman had operated undetected points, he would indicate this to the guard by waving a white light with a twisting movement of his wrist. Because the point lever had been operated it was by no means an indication that such points would be correctly set, they needed to be checked to see that they had come together properly. Regretfully, our guard took the signalman's indication that he had turned the points as a calling back signal. He therefore waved his lamp from side to side to call us back, which was a different interpretation entirely of signalling with a white light.

Once receiving the signal from the signalman that the points had been operated, the guard should have gone on to the ground and checked that the undetected points had gone over properly. After doing so, he should then have walked down the siding to examine all the other hand points, this to be sure that the route was correctly set for us.

Despite the uneasiness in the public gallery, no one involved in the court proceedings seemed to pick up on the error that the guard had mentioned that a signal had cleared that wasn't there at all! I felt, as his colleagues obviously did, that the British Railways solicitor would have jumped on this inaccuracy. It was in fact an indication that the guard had signed his name to a route that he did not have complete knowledge of.

A British Railways official now gave evidence of what the guard should have done, whilst the judge again referred closely to his map. At the point where we were initially called back into the siding, the train was occupying a slight right-hand curve. This meant that the guard's signal could only be seen from my secondman's side of the locomotive. My secondman therefore, had to relay our guard's signal to me. The man giving evidence then related that the guard should have checked all the points and then called the driver back whilst standing on the ground, instead of being in the brakevan. The management official then intimated that the guard should then have positioned himself in a place so that he would be clearly seen by the driver, as the train would ultimately be snaking into the siding over reverse curves. The judge then quickly asked at which point on the map should the guard have positioned himself, as to become in full view of the driver. The reply to this was that the guard should have gone over to the driver's side and stood in a position near the lineside where he would eventually come into my view.

To this the judge immediately retorted, 'Is that not a very dangerous practice?'

The official looked very puzzled; 'You have just said that this man should call his train back and then walk in front of it as it moves towards him, this he must do if he is to eventually be in full view of the driver'. A prolonged silence followed, and there was much deliberation; there really was no answer to this in court, although it was in reality regularly done as a matter of course. There was always a slight delay from the time a signal was given to the time a train moved, time enough for anyone to cross. Levi was finally awarded compensation, but the amount would hardly have been life changing.

I had an Irishman as a guard on another occasion; he was a lithe wiry character who had told me that his last job had been building the cooling towers at the new Didcot power station. I admired his nerve. Our train this night was a Tutbury to Westbury mineral train, although I still have no idea what the white mineral was under the sheeted wagons. All I know is that it was the heaviest mineral that I ever conveyed on any train. We often worked slack coal trains from South Wales; these were extremely heavy, particularly when wet. These trains soon became well known as 'Hot Box Specials'. The reason being, that we were rarely able to get from Gloucester to Landor Street Junction (Birmingham) without having to dispose of a cripple wagon somewhere, because the wagon had a hot axle, despite all the axleboxes on the wagons by this period being already converted to the oil filled type. In addition, we had to keep the train speed below 35 mph.

The Tutbury to Westbury for some time went via Banbury, but was later re-routed via Gloucester. Single manned and with a class '47', I set forth from Landor Street Junction on this night with the usual banker behind as far as Camp Hill. I had just the minimum brake force at my disposal; therefore this very heavy train had to be treated with every respect. At the top of the Lickey Bank I stopped at Blackwell for wagon brakes to be pinned down by the brakesman. The maximum tonnage of my train was contained in only about 30 wagons, only two of which were vacuum fitted wagons piped up to the locomotive. Because of the short train the brakesman and my inexperienced Irish guard apparently misjudged the train weight. There was a 'Right Away' indicator to the rear of the 'Stop and Apply Wagon Brakes' board, this board being situated at the top of the incline. I drew the train over on to the falling gradient and the 'R.A' eventually lit up to tell me that sufficient brakes had been applied and that the guard had rejoined his brakevan. Before I had reached this indicator, the brakes were full on and the train was gathering speed alarmingly. I sounded the rear horn to try to make my guard realise that I needed more assistance from the brakevan, that is, if his brake was not already applied. Our speed increased alarmingly and the fire from the locomotive brake blocks was now lighting up the fields. The train reached a very frightening 60 mph, all 12 of the locomotive wheels were now like 'katharine wheels'. Scared out of my wits, I sounded the horn at the bottom of the incline, near to the bank engine sidings as the locomotive lurched through the crossover on to the slow line. It was perhaps 1½ miles to Stoke Works Junction, at the speed the train was going I didn't feel I would have stopped there. There were 'catch points' ahead of Stoke Works loop exit signal and I therefore hoped that someone would telephone the signalman in Gloucester Panel signal box to tell him that the train was running away. I could see the locomotive and train going down the bank as it went off the end at Stoke Works Junction.

I breathed a sigh of relief as the train eventually ground to a stop only a matter of a few feet from this signal. Smoke was now pouring from the locomotive bogies, a blue haze of potentially explosive hot oil vapour filled the still air, I really felt the locomotive could burst into flames at any moment. The brake blocks were all glowing red and all were now worn down to just wafer thin.

Annoyed that I had been let down by the brakesman, I walked back to examine the train, only one of the vacuum fitted wagon brakes was working, the brake blocks on the second fitted wagon were cold and hanging away from the wheels. No brakes had been pinned down at all, they were just taken out of their racks and only light brake pressure was exerted from the weight of the brake handle. I was trembling and furious.

My guard eventually arrived at the engine, and to say he was terrified would be an understatement. He was shaking from head to foot and admitted that he had been kneeling on the brakevan floor saying 'Hail Mary's'. This could have cost both our lives, but there was little point in sounding off at him, he just lacked experience.

Now on level ground I eventually drew the few feet towards the signal at Stoke Works Junction and phoned the signalman. When he answered his first words were, 'You had a quick run down, didn't you?' He obviously knew that we were out of control; otherwise we would have normally stopped at Bromsgrove for the wagon brakes to be released. I took things very carefully from there on and warned the driver who relieved me to be extra vigilant because of the thin brake blocks on the locomotive. He looked at them at Gloucester and decided to carry on; I had already entered them for changing in the repair book. Back at Saltley, my guard made out his resignation there and then and I never saw him again!

Air brakes were being phased in gradually, although on passenger trains my personal preference was always for vacuum brakes. Whilst vacuum brakes needed more skill to control, when you applied the brake you always felt a slight tug from the train, this was reassuring and you always got a positive brake application. Air brakes did tend to be a bit unpredictable, as though some gremlin was always lurking there to try to catch you out. There wasn't a problem with the system; it was a phenomenon that found you occasionally having to make uncharacteristic applications of the brake to stop. Perhaps I was lucky, I never overran a station, but other men did, and it was so easy to do; yet there never seemed a conscious reason for it to happen.

Vacuum stock would also hold the brakes on for days after an engine had been detached; on the other hand, air brakes could leak off in minutes. In the early days, this caught shunters and guards unawares, even air trains of great length were known to move unexpectedly. A new concept had to be adopted quickly; hand brakes always had to be applied as soon as the locomotive was detached from any air braked train.

A brake continuity test now became vital too, the instructions of which were laid down specifically. However, some men interpreted these instructions in all sorts of ways and short cuts were taken, some of which had disastrous results. In the early days of air brake working, when a locomotive was attached to a train the guard had to do the brake test. He would go to the rear vehicle and open the train pipe air cock, the driver would then have to notice a considerable drop in brake pressure to be sure all the train was piped up and that all the intermediate air cocks were open between the wagons or coaches.

A guard told me that we were ready to leave a yard with a freight one night when I questioned him that he had not yet done the brake test, 'Yes I have, but nothing came out', he remarked. I immediately told him that he must have a cock shut between the wagons, which he refuted. As this was an unsatisfactory state of affairs, I walked back along the train checking all the connections. As he had said, all the cocks were open and all the pipes were connected correctly. I then opened the air cock on the rear wagon; instead of the usual considerable escape of air, there was just a Ha-a-a-a sound, as barely anything came out.

My guard, being yet another man from a distant country, was now completely baffled, and who could blame him? I then advised him there must be a blockage in the pipe of one of the wagons somewhere. I therefore got between every wagon, testing for air pressure. I got to the fourth wagon from the locomotive and no air passed that wagon at all. We were alone in Queens Head sidings, so I told him to take the wagon out of the train and leave it behind. I scribbled a note to give the reason why it had been left and we eventually got going.

I never had this happen again, but I was always conscious that it could. It was lunacy to leave anywhere without the correct brake test being carried out. Every time a train was re-marshalled in any way, the test had to be done, except when wagons were detached from the extreme rear and the rest of the train was left untouched.

Even before the new Didcot power station became on stream we took thousands of tons of pulverised coal there. This power station was to put an awful lot of work towards my depot.

Initially, there were three men on the engine; these coal trains were 'Block Trains' and fully air braked. The guard rode in the rear cab of the engine and a secondman was provided as the driver could not be diagrammed for a specific meal break. These 'Merry-go-Round' trains ran at 45 mph loaded and 55 mph when empty. The locomotives that worked these trains had slow speed devices fitted. When in operation a fine adjustment could control the train speed to just ½ mph for unloading. In the early days, we had class '47s', or two English Electric type '20s', or perhaps two class '37s' in multiple. Later times saw the new class '56s' on these jobs; whilst these were very strong locomotives, they were dreadfully unreliable initially. Our hearts went in our boots when we saw one, wondering if we would get through the day without our horse sitting down!

There were a few teething troubles with the later class '58s', but these were really nice engines. The cab was quiet, comfortable and warm and also tended to be a lot cleaner. Artisan staff didn't have to traipse in oil in the engine room and then pass through the cab as there was no access to the engine room from the cab. All maintenance work on these engines was done through side panels.

Towards my retirement we got the class '60s', which were exceptionally strong and eventually did away with the banking engine which usually pushed us from behind from Landor Street Junction as far as Bordesley Junction. The traction output on the Class '60s' was computer controlled, hence they stuck to the rail like glue, but by this time these clever electronics were getting over my head. Nevertheless, they were lovely to work on, albeit completely alone. Later years saw us single-manned on these trains, we had relief at Foxhall Junction (Didcot) for our break, a Didcot driver took the train through the plant for unloading and we returned with the same train.

On the railways, things, or people, did tend to get quickly labelled, like the tutor driver whose metal lamp melted when he touched a high amperage electrical contact.

The author's class '47'-hauled 'Merry-go-Round' train waits to leave Daw Mill Colliery bound for Didcot power station, 1978. *Author*

The author's MGR train with a class '56' at Buildwas in 1980. *Author*

He was never known by anything other than 'Torchy' afterwards. The unloading hoppers at Didcot power station were dreadfully unreliable initially; this caused coal trains to queue up in large numbers to unload. The power station therefore soon became known as 'Colditz', because once you went in, you never knew when you would get out! There were sometimes as many as five trains in front of you when you went in, with every train taking more than one hour to discharge their coal, if the plant didn't break down again, you were still in there an awfully long time. The plant operators were never very co-operative either; many times I have been the first train in on a Monday morning, only to see the hopper in front of you so full with coal that it was above rail level. It was then often 30 minutes before anyone was seen in the plant and the hopper again took at least another 40 minutes to empty before I was signalled in to unload. Delay to the first train compounded to subsequent trains for all the following week.

Having said that, delays were not always the fault of the Central Electricity Generating Board; I passed through the plant on one occasion and the snowplough on the rear class '20' locomotive had inadvertently screwed itself down, consequently it ripped off all the electrical trip switches on the plant weighbridge. On another occasion, the guard left the rear cab doors open of our two class '37s' in multiple. The 'magic eye' beam then passed through the cab, instead of the gap between the locomotive and the first wagon. The result was that the hopper operating arm swung out ripping off the second locomotive bogie brake cylinders.

The 'Merry-go Round' (MGR) trains were no doubt money-spinners on nights, but unfortunately on days you could forget any social life.

We also worked MGR trains from Daw Mill Colliery to Buildwas. The plant there was more reliable, but the morning syndrome was similar, the hopper would always be full as the first train went in. At Buildwas this policy was deliberate: the coal in the hopper beneath the rail was kept in reserve for the furnaces. Apparently it was easier to use this coal if necessary, rather than get coal back from the coal stack. Nevertheless, this again delayed all the following trains and the subsequent cost to the railways must have been colossal. The railways seemed fair game for the collieries too; they often piled the coal so high in the wagons that it was dangerously close to touching overhead wires.

Whilst the railway moved millions of tons of coal to power stations in these 'Merry-go-Round' trains, I often wondered how much profit was made. Countless hours of men's time were involved, all over the country, not to mention the hours the locomotives were in service, plus constant wear and tear.

Didcot power station plant always remained anything but reliable, but in later times, when we were single manned, once you had relief at Foxhall Junction if the train got stuck inside the plant during the day there was always a passenger train home.

The new concept of 'Block' trains ran faster, often up to 60 mph. Also, with the introduction of power signalling one would have expected communications to have been second to none. In reality, getting information as to where freight trains were became far worse than before the manual signal boxes were abolished. It was indeed as though the control and the regulator in the power signal boxes were not on speaking terms. The supervisor at Gloucester sent me to relieve a train in the Central station one night, it was an appalling night and I stood waiting at the signal for 40 minutes, no other train passed. My train was a 60 mph 'Block' train, when I asked the driver where he was at the time I was sent out, he said was still the west of Newport!

This same supervisor asked me again on another occasion if I would work a special train back to Landor Street Junction. As I was already a bit late, I said I would work the train it if it wasn't too far away. His words in reply were, 'I'll try to perform a miracle to find out where it is'. I listened intently to his conversation on the telephone; it went as follows, 'You say it passed Yatton at 20.10?; you had better look again hadn't you?, it is only 19.10 now!'

The supervisor shook his head in despair, saying, 'If I were you driver, I would catch the next train home'. I took his advice. These were not isolated cases, this happened country wide; with signalmen now knowing exactly where trains were almost to the yard, it was difficult for anyone to believe that communication with others was appalling.

Class '60' training at Derby. Left to right are, traction inspector Cyril Rist, tutor driver Harry Willetts, the author, driver Oscar Williams, traction inspector Gareth Jones, tutor driver Tony Shelley and driver Geoffrey Morris. *Dick Potts*

# Chapter Twelve

## Once in a Lifetime

After living together for only a short time my sister met one of my colleagues and later remarried. This left me a free agent again and I was to spend the next five years living alone. Whilst I had good times, I wasn't really cut out for bachelorhood. My military training had taught me to wash and iron; my barrack room duties had also opened my eyes to good standards of cleanliness. I always remembered the sergeant yelling, 'You don't need Jeyes Fluid, if it's clean, it won't smell'. Strangely, none of my mother's good examples had ever rubbed off on me, that was until the time came to do it myself! Also, my culinary skills would have done little to tempt any victim of famine.

Coming home to a cold house in the depths of winter was miserable. Fortunately, I was very rarely ill; I hadn't seen a doctor for 10 years following my accident caused by incessant shovelling. However, I did go down with a very virulent form of flu, for two days I was very poorly and could contact no one. On the third day of feeling wretched my father called at the house quite by chance. He immediately summoned a doctor, whose bedside manner proved pretty humiliating. He was a Scotsman and it was New Year's Eve, he made it quite obvious that home visits on this day were not on his agenda. I was always very particular regarding my personal hygiene, more so since my army days. As he left the bedroom, he remarked irately that I would feel much better if I got on my feet and had a shave! Thankfully, I never needed this man's 'services' again. Following this incident, my father urged me to have the telephone installed, which was a wise precaution.

I got involved with a number of women friends, but the dreadful shifts that I worked seemed to make relationships impossible. One young woman loved to dance and often dragged me almost screaming to the Tower Ballroom, Edgbaston. I always possessed about as much flexibility and rhythm in this field as a hippopotamus, my feet had similar dexterity. She would then stomp off the dance floor in absolute temper; needless to say that relationship was short-lived.

Another relationship almost broke the bank; each time we met she openly admitted to having had nothing to eat all day, so she was always ravenously hungry in the evening. She insisted that we dine out, plus she needed copious amounts to drink to follow, none of which ever appeared to touch the sides. There were no cheap places to eat then, and she was not content with the local café. Even so, the only thing the after dinner drinks did for her was to revitalise her appetite, so it was then beef sandwiches from the bar for supper, yet we had only stuffed ourselves to capacity 90 minutes earlier! I withdrew money from the bank on several occasions to cope. Finally, one weekend I was stony broke by Sunday night; there was little doubt, I was indeed the proverbial 'meal ticket'. Going 'Dutch' was unheard of at that time. Seeing this relationship was also going nowhere, I did find the courage to break it off. There were an awful lot of tears and consequently I ended up feeling terribly guilty.

There was no 'fanfare of trumpets' when my wife and I met, we immediately became inseparable friends. A country walk in the snow holding hands, or just an hour with the crossword brought us total contentment, it was so easy and so much happiness was to follow. Neither of us had much money; she had earlier walked out of an unhappy marriage with absolutely nothing, not so much as her treasured personal possessions, nor even a family photograph. She had never gone back, her memories were too painful.

The rostering of train crews was an unthankful job, yet at Tyseley the national agreements were always adhered to and the rostering was as fair as possible. Any 'spare' men could be moved two hours either way of their rostered 'spare' time. For example, if a man was '2 pm Spare', he could be diagrammed at any time from noon to 4.00 pm. Tyseley was limited to just one man for every job at the depot, plus the bare minimum of spare men to cover holidays and sickness.

All the Tyseley men that had transferred from Tyseley to Saltley found that the rostering at their new depot perplexing. So much so, that any sought after jobs sent from the diagramming office, turns that were a bit special, tended to be filled by familiar names with some regularity. Whilst Saltley had the same complement of men for each job as Tyseley did, plus an amount of spare men, I suspect to keep an extra float of men at the depot, what were termed 'ghost' diagrams were sent from the diagramming office. These were freight trains that never ran; nevertheless these jobs would be put into the links as normal train turns. With several of these 'ghost' diagrams in one link, drivers then had good cause to complain that they were always spare, consequently they didn't know whether they were coming or going. It was finally agreed that men on 'ghost' diagrams got the first priority for any train work which was on offer, in preference to any men who were actually booked 'spare'.

I was rostered on a 'ghost' diagram one week at 10.58 am. All the week the roster clerk crossed my name out on the roster and put me on another train turn, as was agreed. On the Saturday, I got wind that a steam special involving *Flying Scotsman* was diagrammed to Saltley and the booking on time was around 11.00 am. There was no doubt that, I stood first priority for this turn. This would perhaps be a once in a lifetime opportunity for me to drive this extraordinary locomotive. Regretfully, when Saturday's roster did appear, I was left on the 'ghost' diagram and one of a clique of familiar names had been moved over 3½ hours from his diagrammed turn. This was highly irregular and I obviously protested to the roster clerk. His reply was that he had not been advised that my 'ghost' train was in fact cancelled on the Saturday. He knew only too well that this 'ghost' turn never ran. I therefore missed out on this wonderful opportunity and I was obviously very disappointed.

I never lost my love for steam locomotives, although the chances now of getting on one were pretty remote. With very few steam specials and a host of drivers available to work them, who needed the deviousness of a roster clerk to hinder your chances?

Only a few weeks later, I checked the Sunday roster and couldn't believe what I was seeing. The Locomotive Club of Great Britain had organised two 'Farewell to the Gresleys' tours, my name was against one of them and another ex-Tyseley driver was working the other. It didn't take a genius to work out why we were rostered on these turns, the handwriting on the sheet was different, the normal roster clerk was on holiday! The man deputising on the rosters was branded by many as 'Wicked Wilf,' undoubtedly he was as straight as a die and would stand no nonsense from anyone. No doubt, it was the men who could not get their own way with him that gave him this unfair criticism. In later years, Wilf bent over backwards to help me when my wife was in hospital, so I have more than one reason to be eternally grateful to this very fair man. So eager were some drivers to work one of these turns, one actually wrote to the Divisional Manager's Office and volunteered to do the job without pay. That information came from a very reliable source. I worked with this man for many years afterwards and he never knew that I was aware of what he had done to try and deprive one of us Tyseley men from having one of these steam specials.

It wasn't until I was rostered to work this extraordinary job that the responsibility of what was involved dawned on me. It was getting on for eight years since I had set foot on a steam engine; the only former LNER locomotive that I had worked on was a solitary 'B1' class 4-6-0 as a fireman. That particular night always stuck in my mind. As Fred Gay and I approached a freight in the dead of night at Gloucester South Junction, the Bristol engine crew abandoned it to catch a quick ride home on another moving freight train brakevan. At a distance, the two plumes of steam going straight up in the air from the safety valves made us think at first that we were blessed with an ex-LMS class '8F'. The train had obviously stood there for some time; the only glimmer of light in the cab was from a flickering water gauge lamp and a dull fire. It was a still damp night and the yardsman at Gloucester immediately got line clear for us before we had got our bearings on this very unusual craft. Whilst I soon found out how to get the injectors working, the cylinder cocks were open and Fred moved everything within his reach to close them, he probably emptied all the sand boxes in the process. This LNER engine turned out to be a very good engine; the bucket seat was quite a novelty too. I was certainly soon doing well for steam, but at Cheltenham we still couldn't see were we were going as the cylinder cocks were still open! Fred had found it necessary to close the regulator each time we needed to catch sight of a 'distant' signal. With things going really well and some more light from the fire, I noticed a lever tucked away on my side of the footplate that we hadn't seen. I put my foot against it and the cylinder cocks closed. As Western men, it hadn't dawned on us to look anywhere else other than on the driver's side of the footplate. Ex-LNER locomotives were rare visitors over the North Warwick line, yet I had a super trip home. I showed off a little as we passed the 7.06 am departure from Henley-in-Arden which was standing in the bay. This train was utilised for training on the 'Western' hydraulics and there were several trainees and tutor drivers on it. We had a heavy train and were working hard up the bank, so I let our engine safety valves blow off steam just as we were passing ... big head!

My fireman on the Gresleys was to be Martyn Jones of whom I could not speak more highly of as a secondman. He was utterly trustworthy and a rather quiet studious young man who always seemed rather over qualified and a little out of place among many railwaymen. Nevertheless, with the best will in the world, I knew that Martyn could have had little experience on steam locomotives, particularly of this calibre. Our footplate inspector would again undoubtedly be Les Durnell, which was likely to have a tendency to take the shine off the day. Originating from Oswestry, his early experience would have extended to little more that the Great Western 'Manor' class.

So I signed on duty on Sunday 5th July, 1973 with mixed feelings of excitement and apprehension. The service minibus took us to Tyseley, where we first took charge of 'V2' class 2-6-2 No. 4771 *Green Arrow*. She was in faultless condition and had been carefully prepared for us, the oiling taken care of by the legendary Bill Harvey, an expert artisan who had given so much of his time and expertise into the preservation of this lovely locomotive. As expected Les Durnell also arrived, bringing with him no less than three hats for the occasion: his bowler hat, should there be any dignitaries around, his normal inspector's trilby, and a grease top driver's hat, if he needed to help out with the firing.

It was a beautiful summer's morning, yet the mood on the footplate was rather frosty. Bill Harvey was sombre, indeed a man of a very few words. I later learned that his opinion of Midland men had reached an all time low when this locomotive had worked a special to Stratford-upon-Avon the previous weekend. The driver's handling of 'his' locomotive had caused some sort of altercation between the two men, I think he was also now eyeing me up with doubtful prospects!

Another gentleman then joined us, as yet I had no idea of who he was, Les Durnell's watchful eye took care of any preliminaries. Had this man not have had the right credentials he would have been back down the steps in double quick time.

'V2' class 2-6-2 No. 4771 *Green Arrow* at Tyseley with Les Durnell, in the bowler hat, Martyn Jones my fireman and myself on 5th July, 1973. No. 4498 *Sir Nigel Gresley* is visible in the background. *John Sutton*

*Green Arrow* on the climb to Harbury tunnel on 5th July, 1973. *Vic Haddon*

Our guest on the footplate had a definite aura about him, in only seconds the mood on the footplate changed and pleasant conversation developed. With the exception of Bill Harvey, it took only seconds for me to realise that this man was the only one among us who was completely at home on the footplate of this strange locomotive. He was also about to take on the shovelling, a brave prospect, as I suspected that he was around 50 years of age.

Our train was very late arriving at Tyseley, there had been a fatality on the line *en route*, but we eventually backed on to 14 coaches. Single line working was in operation from Tyseley, as far as the ground frame at Solihull station, due to engineering work. The single line pilotman instructed me to proceed in the wrong direction over the down main line, whilst keeping a good look out for men working on the line. My immediate thoughts were that this cautious start would help my fireman to get things right on his side of the footplate before we really started to move.

We left Tyseley on the down main and I kept the speed at about 30 mph giving any workmen on the line good warning on the whistle. It wasn't unexpected, but Les Durnell just had to put his oar in from the very start. He had already been interfering with the men on the other side of the footplate. Approaching Olton he gave my sleeve a tug and with a very determined look and said, 'Isn't it about time you got this bloody machine moving?' He had in fact not noticed that we were running in the wrong direction over the down main. He must have immediately seen my anger, as I retorted, 'We are working over a single line in the wrong direction, the rule book says, run at reduced speed, giving a series of pop whistles!' This lapse on his part was obviously an awful embarrassment to him, although he was too dominant to admit it. He slunk to the other side of the footplate and on the up journey to Didcot I was left in silence.

South of Solihull we negotiated the 15 mph speed restriction through the ground frame points and were on our way. The signalman in Bentley Heath Crossing was no doubt reading the *News of the World*, as his distant failed to clear, although he was hardly likely to have been inundated with road traffic on a Sunday morning. The signal protecting the crossing was on a left-hand curve and hidden behind the embankment, so until this signal was seen at clear further caution was necessary.

Once clear of this obstacle, it was easy going to Leamington and our speed increased quickly. *Green Arrow* rode beautifully; her mechanical condition equalled her fine looks, there were no knocks or rattles whatsoever. Bill Harvey, her caretaker, had every right to be very proud. The 'V2' had no speedometer and with the line speed up to 90 mph standard, the locomotive proved extraordinarily stable. We were officially limited to 60 mph, but running down Hatton Bank we were going a lot faster than that, so good was the riding that even Les Durnell didn't appear to notice.

Humping 14 coaches up the gradient from Leamington was no mean task and the gentleman holding the shovel had already gained my respect. He was not just a good fireman, he was undoubtedly an artist. As we took the rising gradient, he planted his feet in one spot on the footplate and flicked the coal through the 'letterbox' firehole into the back corners of the wide firebox. He fired with a steady rhythm and barely broke into a sweat; he was indeed a joy to watch. The boiler pressure gauge needle never left the red line whilst the engine was under this continual thumping.

After Wormleighton Crossing, the valve travel was shortened and only seconds after both safety valves lifted, the boiler water level was still well up the gauge glass. At Banbury, we filled the tender tank and I hadn't realised that the saloon coach next to the engine had got a speedometer installed. How accurate this was I am unsure, but a voice whispered to me that we had reached 86 mph down Hatton; I was surprised, but nurtured some doubts. I have always been an avid Great Western fan, nevertheless this locomotive impressed me greatly and its performance was certainly to widen my outlook. Swindon did not totally have the monopoly of good design.

The going from Banbury to Didcot was effortless and our trip was completely trouble free, this was all thanks to my senior doing the 'spade work'.

At Didcot, we turned the engine on the triangle via Foxhall Junction and then changed footplates with 'A4' class 4-6-2 No. 4498 *Sir Nigel Gresley*. This was an unbelievably proud moment for me; to have a once in a lifetime opportunity to drive such a locomotive was beyond my dreams.

We left Didcot with 13 coaches and the footplate inspector was still causing some irritation to my colleague, he kept trying to fill the back end of the firebox as we always did in Western fashion. This obviously impedes the firing of the back corners of the fire with a wide firebox. On the slight rising gradient leaving Didcot we hadn't gone far before the inspector turned his attention to me. Although the valve cut off was already set at 25 per cent he accused me of working the engine too hard. I then rather abruptly asked him where he felt I should set the reverser, to which he ordered, 'Put it in the 15 per cent'. I complied with his wish, but passing Kennington Junction we were slowing down considerably. I deliberately avoided his gaze, but there was soon another tug at my sleeve, 'You will have to drop her down a bit', he sheepishly remarked. I had worked over this line for 15 years as a fireman; I could have told him that!

With the 'A4' gathering speed nicely I was looking forward to a spirited run. At Heyford the speedometer was showing 65 mph and I heard a voice call, 'Watch the speed'. I kept my head out and pretended not to hear, but seconds later Les was gripping my flesh with a very determined look, 'Watch the speed', he said again with gritted teeth. From there on I had to comply, but at 60 mph this thoroughbred was hardly taxed. All in all I had a wonderful day and for the whole journey had adequate steam; both engines were in absolutely faultless condition.

'A4' class 4-6-2 No. 4498 *Sir Nigel Gresley* arriving at Tyseley on 5th July, 1973. My grandparents lived in the row of houses on the left. *John Sutton*

When I signed on duty the following day there was a small parcel for me in the shed master's office. It was a copy of a now treasured book, *Steam in the Blood*, written by Richard Hardy and signed by him. He had indeed been our guest who had expertly handled the firing. Dick Hardy was at that time divisional manager at Liverpool, yet I had no idea who he was, or his status. Since reading his book we have always kept in touch, any railwaymen that knew him could only ever have had a total regard for this exceptional man.

I have to look back and smile at being told how to drive the engine by Les Durnell. I worked over the Didcot road day in and day out, I knew the gradients like the back of my hand. Not only did we work the 'Merry-go-Round' trains, we worked heavy Freightliners. The Freightliners left Didcot in the early hours and the controller would be put wide open, it would be wide open for at least the next hour, that is until the train got on the falling gradients towards Fenny Compton. What a thumping those class '47s' took; you could hardly imagine any large road vehicle taking such punishment.

So many good people sent me photographs taken on 5th July, 1973, which was no undoubtedly the most memorable day of my career. Unfortunately, I cannot now recall many of the photographers' names, but my sincere appreciation does go out to them all. These photographers I know include driver Vic Haddon and driver John Sutton, then there is the photographer of the fine monochrome picture of No. 4498 passing Radley, near Oxford. He sent the photograph to me and I apologise, occasionally names are lost with age.

Dick Hardy who did the firing for me on 5th July, 1973 seen here with driver Vic Waite of Leamington. At the age of 82 I asked Dick if he could still do it, he said he could, but he now has to move his right foot to swing round. *Peter Hardy*

*Sir Nigel Gresley* passing Radley on the return trip with myself as driver on 5th July, 1973. A treasured photograph sent to the depot for me by a complete stranger.

*Provenance Unknown*

# Chapter Thirteen

## The North Link

The High Speed Trains (HSTs) were introduced on the Intercity Cross-Country services and Saltley depot gained a good proportion of this work. I was soon trained on the class '254' HSTs and had a good grounding under the instruction of my fellow model engineer Harry Willetts. I was eventually deemed competent to drive this form of traction by traction inspector John Dorricote.

Around this period, a number of men that I had known all my working life were gaining positions in management; it was refreshing to see local men whom I had every respect for gain promotion. John Dorricote was a Wolverhampton man and at one time was regular fireman to my Uncle Bert, who was a driver at the GWR's Stafford Road shed. Uncle Bert was my father's brother and a bit of a controversial character; he followed my grandfather's principles by becoming secretary of the Wolverhampton Branch of the National Union of Railwaymen. Regretfully, as the biggest proportion of the footplate staff at Stafford Road Shed were ASLEF men, at times of dispute this tended to make my relative unpopular. However, he held on to good principles that he firmly believed in, he stuck by them and was therefore in turn respected by many men of other railway grades. Just like my father, he was afraid of no one and cared little for what others thought.

John Dorricote made an excellent inspector and was eventually to become chief traction inspector at Birmingham New Street. Few people worked harder than John in his early days as a fireman on the 'runners' at Stafford Road. He was always wise too, to the antics of some of the more devious members of the footplate grade. I think what made John a good inspector was his general approach to men; he was never seen to raise his voice. He also had the advantage of vast experience, which most enginemen tended to respect. I think it would be correct to say that our inspector at this time did get somewhat fraught with the lack of back-up from the management at Saltley regarding discipline. The trade unions were strong and there was still much emphasis by management on taking a more moderate approach to keep things running smoothly. This is was fine, but someone must carry the can, any position of trust brought with it some accountability when accidents occurred. There were no doubt a number of footplatemen at Saltley that took grave liberties and yet were to escape authority.

Reorganization of the links saw me in the new North link. Once again, along with my good friend Dick Potts, we went to learn the road north as far as York. This was a long process, taking some eight weeks. We had to learn the route several ways, via Pontefract and via Altofts Junction. Also via Sheffield and via Beighton Junction, this included the large freight yard at Tinsley.

When we were sent road learning it was winter and we were beset with the most awful cold weather. To get back home at a reasonable time we had to catch the 7.06 am departure from New Street every morning. This sticks in my mind as air braked passenger stock was now being used regularly on these trains. The early departure from New Street was timetabled first stop Burton-on-Trent. One week, because of the exceptionally cold weather, the train only managed to stop at Burton two out of the five mornings. The drivers were caught with their pants down as the air-brake system froze. It was then emphasised on all drivers that a running brake test should be carried out at intervals to avoid this happening in inclement weather. Again, this problem was never evident with vacuum-braked vehicles.

Driver Harry Willetts and myself during HST training. *Don Vincent*

Western Region Magazine cutting of my Uncle Bert with his fireman Reg Webb. The only picture I have of him, what the occasion was I am unaware. *Author's Collection*

Once more the Eastern Region had many different ways of working and much of the terminology used by railwaymen was again alien to us. This, just as we were coming to terms with the differing ways of working of the Midland Region. There were other problems too; some of the ways of working at this period of time seemed dreadfully slack on the Eastern Region. Alterations to track layout and speed restrictions, for some reason, sometimes failed to be published in the notices issued to us. A permanent speed restriction at Ferry Bridge, which had always been 60 mph, appeared on one Monday morning as 20 mph and no prior advice had been given. Another near disaster happened when the track layout was changed at Royston Junction one weekend; Midland Region men got no notification of this until the first express driver almost came to grief. These events tended to keep you on the edge of your seat when working over these lines; it was also something that we could have done without, as we had an awful lot to absorb as it was. York station had an absolute mass of ground signals and making moves around the station in foggy weather was a bit of a nightmare to us. We often worked trains that terminated at York and had to run round the stock for the return trip. This made me scratch my head a few times when working single manned.

Working the HSTs to York eventually became quite routine, in general things ran well and these trains were reliable. These were nice jobs for us too, as we usually had a couple of hours at York before returning. This gave me ample time to get well acquainted with this wonderful city.

The North link also had some freight work, which included Freightliners to Rotherham. We also had to learn Toton Yard and Crewe. Like York station, Crewe was also a bit daunting to anyone who had not spent their younger days in the area.

Many times I worked nuclear trains for Sellafield as far as Crewe. We relieved these trains at Landor Street Junction and worked via Castle Bromwich Junction, over the Sutton Park line through Walsall and Wolverhampton. I must have worked these trains for five years when the press got to know that nuclear fuel was passing through the City of Birmingham. There was quite a fuss for a time, but it all went quiet eventually, there didn't seem to be any great public outcry. I did work a train one day which was obviously of more significance than the normal 'nuclear flask'. This train carried an armed guard and technicians checked it with Geiger counters at intervals for any radiation leaks. Each time we stopped police appeared from nearby roads, so this was no run of the mill material, yet this train too passed through the sleeping city and many other towns.

The many clerical errors were not confined to the Eastern Region, I was talking to a young man in the mess room at Saltley one Friday afternoon and he advised me that a steam special was at Stratford-upon-Avon the following day. I asked him what time it would be leaving and was told 17.53 hrs, I was still always keen to see any steam locomotive. However, I eventually felt that he had obviously got the departure time wrong, as the special train that I was diagrammed to work from Stratford-upon-Avon was scheduled to depart at 17.53. Two trains could not leave Stratford at the same time, but at least I felt that I still might have a good chance of seeing this steam special.

When I signed on duty the following day, management had discovered that an error had been made in the diagrams; indeed both trains had initially been booked to leave at the same time. My train was therefore retimed to depart a few minutes after the steam special. The new departure time was 1800 and I was now re-routed via Henley-in-Arden. This, I discovered, was because the steam special was booked to wait at Bearley station for 20 minutes to pick up photographers who had filmed the train at Wilmcote, hence they would be rejoining the train by road.

My train was a six-car dmu, which I worked to Stratford empty from Tyseley Carriage Sidings. I was to work this special charter train to Crewe, via Sutton Park and Bushbury Junction, the train ultimately going forward to Morecambe.

I was pleased to be able to get a good view of No. 7018 *Drysllwyn Castle* and somewhat enviously watched her depart from Stratford in all her splendour. When I rejoined my train the chief traction inspector Harry Pratt was waiting for me. He had just left the steam special and was going home. Harry was my superior, but he had earlier come to Tyseley as a young driver for promotion and we had worked together many times. Little doubt, Harry was nothing short of a gentleman who often seemed a bit out of place amongst many of the coarser locomen. Harry had always been super keen and did most things strictly by the book; nevertheless he was great to work with. He too had earned his position and was no stranger to heavy work. He had spent his firing days at Bushbury shed (LMS), much of his work being done on the Eustons with 'Scots', 'Jubilees' and 'Black Fives'.

On this late Saturday evening, Harry had had a long day and needed to get back to Saltley where he had left his car. On the other hand, he seemed very apprehensive when I said I would stop at Landor Street Junction and drop him off, it was a only a 20 mph junction and no one would be aware that he would not be riding with me officially. He would be off in seconds, although he would be in full view of the signalmen in Saltley power signal box. He did agree to come with me, although I feel rather reluctantly.

I left Stratford at 1800 and the signals were against me at Bearley Junction, I could see the steam special waiting in the distance in Bearley station. Strangely, the signal cleared for me to go via Bearley, which I knew would cause us considerable delay whilst we waited for the steam special to clear the single line section to Hatton. The signalwoman, I thought, had obviously got it wrong, so I sounded the horn and waited for her to correct the mistake and re-route me via Henley-in-Arden. She made no effort to change the route, so I said to the inspector that I would walk to the signal box and inform her verbally. When I got several yards from the train, Harry shouted that she was now exhibiting a green handsignal from the box. Having given her every opportunity to reset the route, I rejoined the cab and drove to the box, as I was now thinking that there could be a problem on the line via Henley. At the signal box, I explained that I was re-diagrammed to go via Henley, this the signalwoman disputed as she assured me that she had checked with the control. Even after showing her the late notice that I had been given, nothing would change her stance. To add insult to injury, when I rejoined the cab, my guard, along with a courier for the party, had come to see what the delay was. With the vestibule door open I heard a passenger ask the courier what was the matter. His reply to this was that it appeared that the driver didn't know which way to go! Which you could say was a bit irritating.

However, as expected, the enthusiasts on the steam special were in no hurry to get moving until every possible photograph had been taken. I was eventually more than 30 minutes late leaving Bearley Junction and quickly dropped Harry off at Landor Street Junction as planned; I then did my level best to recover some of the lost time.

As this was just another time when communications had broken down, this incident would normally have been forgotten. Unfortunately, when I signed on duty on the following Tuesday there was a letter from the boss waiting. The report claimed that I had taken the incorrect route and not challenged the diversion. This meant that I had not given the signalwoman chance to correct her mistake and that

BRITISH RAIL : LONDON MIDLAND REGION

To: DRIVER HERBERT 494
SALTLEY

From: Area Manager
Saltley

o/r: OTC/690 D
ext: 050-2734
Date: 17.4.84

1C01 1800 STRATFORD - MORECAMBE
INCORRECTLY ROUTED VIA HATTON
& NOT CHALLENGED BY DRIVER
SATURDAY 14.4.84

Would you please submit your report on the above incident.

I attach a BR.2072/72 form for your reply.

[signature]

for Area Manager
Saltley

Copy of the report given to me for allegedly taking my train over the incorrect route.

they were in fact laying the blame for the lost time on me. I was absolutely seething at this, as I was in reality the only person to get things right. In my reply to this letter I felt it prudent to ask for an apology, particularly as I was put in a very embarrassing position in front of passengers. I knew that I was on to a winner, if need be I had the best witness I could possibly have had, the chief traction inspector. Although, I never mentioned this in any of my reports, Harry should not have been there officially and I would never have compromised him.

A new manager John Ride took over, who I knew well as he had been at one time diesel supervisor in Tyseley Carriage Sidings. John was a good man; he was an absolute 'toff' and in general kept things running smoothly as manager. I eventually received an acknowledgement from John Ride regarding this incident at Bearley, which stated that the matter had been referred back to the area manager at Coventry.

I therefore waited for more correspondence on the matter. After some weeks, the lack of any apology bugged me; I therefore submitted a second letter. In this letter, I stated that I was wrongly accused of taking my train over the incorrect route and was compromised in front of passengers. The fact that no apology was forthcoming, I could only treat as a discourtesy.

The following day I got an apology from John Ride in writing, unfortunately this gave me little satisfaction as John should not have been apologising for others in management who had got egg on their face. As the original report had come from the area manager at Coventry, I would have felt much happier if he had replied.

Initially, few drivers at Saltley were trained to drive the English Electric type 3s', or class '37s'. As these locomotives became more prominent in the Birmingham area, all drivers were eventually trained, including myself. I had my one week of training and on the following Monday night, with abundant knowledge fresh in my mind, I

## * DRIVER'S/† ~~GUARD'S~~ REPORT

* Station/Depot: Saltley  Date: 19th April 1984

Date of Incident: 14th April 1984  Place of Incident: Bearley Jct  Delay: 15 mins.

Train Reporting No.: 1K02  1800 hrs.  From: Stratford on Avon  To: Morecambe

Type of Traction: DMU  Loco/Unit No.: ___  Load of Train: ___ tons  No. of Vehicles: 6  No. fitted: ___  Brake force: ___

| | Name | Home Station |
|---|---|---|
| * Guard or Shunter in charge | | |
| Driver | D C Herbert | Saltley |
| Second Man | | |

Assisting Loco (if any) No. ___ Driver ___

Type of brake in use ___  Whether train loco E.Q. fitted ☐ YES ☐ NO

Position of passenger/goods switch ___

* Delete as applicable

† GUARDS: Defects in COACHING STOCK to be reported on form B.R. 29206

Dear Sir  Ref. OTC/690/D

REPORT (including weather conditions)
GIVE FULL PARTICULARS OF ANY DAMAGE TO TRAINS OR WORKS

Regarding incorrect routing of the above train.
The wrong routing of the 1800 hrs Stratford to Morecambe was brought about by a series of management errors.
ie. 1/ Diagramming two special trains to depart from Stratford on Avon at the same time.
2/ Failure to issue to the signalperson at Bearley Jct with Late Notice No 9489
3/ Incorrect advice from the control to the signalperson at Bearley Jct in the absence of Notice No 9489.
The wrong routing was challenged by myself and my duties carried out in a conscientious manner.
I therefore feel that a written apology from management would not be out of place due to unnecessary harrassment and the compromising position I was put into in full view of passengers.

(continue overleaf if necessary)

Signature: D C Herbert

Driver 474

My reply with a request for an apology.

John Ride, Saltley Manager and Mr H. Hook Area Manager Bescot on my 35 service year presentation.
*British Rail*

The final reply containing an apology from John Ride, on behalf of the Area Manager.

BRITISH RAIL : LONDON MIDLAND REGION

To: Mr D C Herbert
Driver 474
Saltley

From: Area Manager
Saltley

o/r: OTC/690/D/JM/GV
ext: 2734

Date: 18th June 1984

1L01 18.00 STRATFORD-MORECAMBE : 14.4.84

Thank you for your second report regarding the above train.

As previously stated, the matter was referred to the Area Manager, Coventry, on whose area the incident took place. I have now spoken to the Area Manager Coventry on your behalf and find that the cause of the matter lies with the notice distribution section at Crewe, who failed to send notices either to Control or Bearley Signalbox.

The person concerned at Crewe has now been suitably dealt with and under the circumstances, I offer my apologies for any inconvenience caused to yourself.

J Ride

for H Hook
Area Manager

took over this form of traction. I relieved a freight train outside the depot and when the signal cleared for my departure a blue fault light appeared on the panel and I was unable to gain power. I then became aware that the main air pressure had dropped and that the compressors were not running. It was standard procedure for us on any locomotive to toggle the switch on the compressor governor as a first instance. Knowing exactly where this governor was situated, I went into the nose end to trigger the switch. Low and behold it was nowhere to be found. Items of this nature were generally placed in an identical position on all locomotives of the same class. This obviously avoided drivers searching for components when problems occurred. With the seeds of doubt now sown in my mind I eventually had to alert the signalman to reverse the signals. This not only gave me time to think about the problem, but it allowed other trains to run by me, hence keeping traffic moving. There were a thousand places that this small switch could have been hidden on this engine and I had to ask the signalman to alert the maintenance staff. Being right outside the depot, it was only a few minutes before Mick Meryll the electrician appeared with his screwdriver long enough to clean the tubes of a 'Jinty'. In seconds he had the panels off the electrical control cubicles and I knew I was in very capable hands. Some 20 minutes went by when Mick emerged from the engine room looking puzzled.

'Where's the compressor governor on these he enquired?' I told him that I was freshly trained on these engines and to all intents and purposes it should have been in the nose end. Two pair of eyes were better than one and we both set about a further search.

With almost an hour gone by the compressors suddenly burst into life and Mick came out of the engineroom wearing a big smile. The compressors raced away until the maximum air pressure was attained when all went quiet. I made several applications of the brakes to reduce the air pressure again and the compressors burst into life again. This procedure was repeated several times and the problem had obviously cured itself. I eventually went on my way without further trouble, yet we never found the compressor governor. I can only assume that this locomotive had suffered modification by the research people who had failed to identify the alteration. It was usual practice to bring such modifications to the attention of drivers and maintenance staff by fitting a plaque on the side of the locomotive. There was no such notice and it was quite lucky that this problem occurred on a freight train within reach of the artisan staff. I could imagine such a problem occurring on a passenger train and being in a position to cause no end of delay to other traffic. It was therefore vital that certain components were placed in the same position.

This procedure should also have been extended to the positioning of the controls in the cab. I drove dmus for thousands of miles, but one day took to a set known to us as a 'Cravens'. These units were rare in our area and a short time after taking over I was driving at speed when platelayers appeared on the track in front of me unexpectedly as I approached a sharp curve in the track. In my haste to sound the horn my hands went everywhere before sounding the horn. In this instance the horn was a pair of buttons on the driving panel. The normal position for the horn was a lever down by your right knee and the operation of it had become automatic. Nevertheless, the vital split second that it took me to sound the horn could well have cost someone their life, indeed it did make the workmen jump clear and shake their fist at me as though I had been neglectful. We will not mention that they were working without a lookout!

Intercity Cross-Country eventually re-routed the trains to the North via Doncaster, which should not have been a problem, but the Eastern Region men's representatives would not allow Midland Region men over the East Coast Main Line from Doncaster to York. At that time too, 125 mph running required two drivers, which was an added problem. To avoid any dispute, our diagrams were changed and we then had relief at Doncaster and rode in the train to York. From York we worked a diesel unit stopping train back to Sheffield, via Pontefract. We then returned from Sheffield with the HST to Birmingham. On some turns we had relief at Sheffield going, worked a diesel unit stopping train to York, then travelled to Doncaster and worked the HST from there back home.

An amusing incident happened on this turn one Monday morning when I took to the diesel unit as usual at Sheffield. I got as far as Rotherham, where the station manager met me. I was instructed to stable the unit where it was and catch a bus service from the front of the station. Over the weekend, engineers had been replacing a bridge and things hadn't gone according to plan, consequently they were unable to reopen the line. My guard and I were the last to board the double-decker bus, which was very full as we had a school party from Sheffield on our train. These were young infants going to York for an educational visit. As we joined the bus the lady driver remarked that she hoped we knew the way to Moorthorpe, as she had no idea. Neither the guard, or myself, had ever been outside the station at Rotherham and felt that she must have been pulling our legs. When it took us an awful long time to get into open country we began to realise that she really had no idea of the route that she should be taking. We took several wrong turnings and at one point had to reverse up a farm track to turn. The ultimate was when she stopped to ask a motorist the way. The motorist looked at all the passengers and wasn't very complimentary as he felt he was being set up! No words would do justice to the look of amazement on his face.

Some of the young children then started to feel poorly and were sick, this in turn set others off and the poor teachers were in an awful mess. The teacher said to me that they had particularly gone by rail to York because they knew the children would be ill on a bus. They therefore hadn't made any provisions for the children feeling unwell, as they could have taken them into the toilets on the train.

We finally made it to Moorthorpe after almost 1½ hours on the bus and were all glad to get into the fresh air. Another diesel unit was waiting at Moorthorpe and I continued to York as scheduled, although very late.

I worked a special train to York on another Saturday and was diagrammed to return with the empty coaches to Landor Street Junction, as the stock would be going forward empty to Bristol. I had a Crompton Parkinson type '4' and stopped only at Derby and Sheffield *en route* to York. This was a nice turn; the Saltley guard who worked the train with me certainly had a soft number, the work he did amounted to giving me a green flag at Derby and Sheffield and doing a brake test for the return trip at York. The shunter did the necessary uncoupling when I ran round the train.

We had a good run home and I arrived back at Saltley in less than seven hours, well under my eight-hour day. On arrival at Landor Street I contacted the signalman, who then told me that an engine change was necessary, as the Bristol driver was not trained to drive Crompton Parkinson's. I found my guard asleep in the train and asked him if he would detach the engine, this was quite normal; freight guards were issued with protective clothing for the purpose. This guard was a contentious character and he immediately said that he was not going to detach, it wasn't his fault that the Bristol driver was not trained to drive these engines. He then picked up his equipment and walked off leaving me alone.

After 1½ hours the supervisor at Saltley sent a secondman, who was doing shed duties, to uncouple. I then eventually made overtime by the time I had disposed of the locomotive on the fuel line. There is little doubt that this guard should have been disciplined, as it certainly came into his remit to detach and secure the train whilst standing on an incline. Three weeks later I was surprised to see him at Tyseley wearing a new black serge suit … in a supervisory post!

I worked a summer special to York one day and again was very grateful that my charge was a stable type '4' Crompton Parkinson. I was diagrammed first stop Derby from New Street, but at Leicester Junction, just south of Burton-on-Trent station, whilst travelling at the correct speed of 50 mph the locomotive went into all sorts of unusual throes. The locomotive lifted several inches off the track and an awful lot of metallic noise went with it. I made an emergency brake application and immediately contacted the signalman at Derby power signal box and informed him that something pretty concerning had happened and it was now necessary for me to examine the train. Fortunately all the train wheels were on the track, but a few yards walk back to the junction points I found that a hefty steel wagon chain had been dragging the track and had caught in the junction points. The wheels of my train had severed it and hammered it had into the point diamond and there was no way I could get it out. I informed the signalman and continued my journey, but that day could well have been a very different story.

In steam days it was always the driver's prerogative that, if he felt his locomotive was not in good mechanical order, he would be provided with a replacement engine. This principle continued for a time after modernisation, but diesel traction was far more complicated than steam and eventually the onus was passed to the mechanical staff to have the final say if the locomotive was fit for service. There probably had been a dispute somewhere which had caused severe delay, because an entry in our weekly notices appeared emphasising that drivers could not refuse to take any form of traction from depots, any decision that the traction was fit for service would be made by the mechanical staff.

The very week that this instruction appeared in our notice, part of my diagram was to take a diesel multiple unit off Etches Park Sidings into Derby station and work forward to Nottingham, calling at all stations. With some two hours to spare, my guard and I walked from Derby station to Etches Park to prepare our unit. It was winter, but a lovely sunny afternoon. The old type dmus were now being phased out in favour of the new 'Sprinter' class '150s', which were being built at Derby works. Etches Park was obvious favourite to be the first place to be rid of all the old type units. As we walked to the sidings, I could see a row of the new class '150s' lined up with some precision, as if for an official photograph, all gleaming in the afternoon sun. On the left of this row was the most decrepit looking old type diesel unit as was ever seen, it comprised of a single unit, or 'Bubble Car', and a drive end trailer. A drive-end trailer was a coach with a driving cab, but having no engines. This meant that it was a two-coach unit with just two engines. When I asked the supervisor which train was ours, his immediate remark was, 'Just your luck mate, that's yours on fifteen'. It was all in a day's work, it really didn't matter in the least that we had this old unit; the new 'Sprinters' as yet were tied up with all sorts of new electronics that tended go wrong, familiarity with the old sets was to a degree comforting. However, as I got into the driving cab, I noticed that the windscreen wiper was broken, the arm had come adrift and the blade was hanging loosely vertically across the window. To add to this, the repair had been entered in the repair book by the previous driver, who had left the book open on the driving panel so that the repair would not go unnoticed by artisan staff. I immediately walked back to the supervisor's office and asked him to alert the fitting staff, at this time we still had 1½ hours before we were diagrammed to leave the sidings.

We prepared the unit for the road, but after the best part of an hour the artisan staff had still not appeared. A third visit to the supervisor and another call to the fitters brought the comment, 'What's the panic?' With less than 20 minutes before we were due to depart a fitter ambled down with a large screwdriver sticking out of one pocket. I was sat in the driving seat and I watched as he gazed up at the offending window wiper. As I dropped the side window, he said with a frown, 'It's broke'.

'I know it's broke mate, that's why I've asked you to mend it'. I replied.

'But we don't carry any spares for these old sets now', he answered.

'Ah, then I will need another unit, unless you care to take the blade off the rear cab of this power car', I said, knowing that the intermediate cab would not be in use whilst it was coupled to the drive end trailer. He agreed to do this and in a couple of minutes he had a replacement wiper blade. He climbed on to the front buffer and set to work. In a short while there was a string of curses. He then said that he had dropped the anchor spindle between the inner and outer panel work, now it would take well over an hour to get it out. I then reminded him that, had he come when I first requested, he would have had plenty of time, now I wanted another unit.

Back in the supervisor's office, I told the man in charge that the fitter could not effect a repair.

'What are you going to do then driver?', the boss questioned.

'Better still mate, what are you going to do?', I quipped.

'Are you refusing to take the unit then driver?'

'No, I understand that we now cannot refuse to take any traction unit, but there is snow forecast for tonight and just in case there is an accident, I want to make sure that you inform the control that I am leaving the sidings with restricted visibility, should the weather change'. At this he threw his pen down in anger and shouted, 'Take that bloody 'Sprinter' off ten!'

You only ever had to put the ball in someone else's court!

At home I realised a dream: with our finances stable my wife and I had a brick garage built, big enough to house a workshop. Having said that, the construction of this extension did become a problem in itself. After the plans were drawn up, we had three estimates from different builders. We chose the middle quote, as this builder was the only contractor to display the 'Master Builder's Federation' emblem.

I then cleared the site of the old wooden garage to be sure nothing delayed progress. On Monday morning two workmen appeared, a middle-aged man and a youth of school leaving age. They set to work digging the foundations, which owing to a number of previously dry summers, the regulations now deemed that they needed to now go down to a depth of one metre to avoid subsidence. With the older man doing much of the work, there was soon a 'mountain' of soil on the site. The house wall and my neighbour's garage wall meant that all the earth had to be thrown inwards. The building inspector arrived and ordered that the footings needed to be squared off at the bottom, as the hole got narrower the deeper it got. There was much muttering from the workmen, so I took a shovel into the footings and made sure they were right myself. It was no hardship; I was still adept with a shovel.

When I arrived home from work the following day, the builder's lorry had delivered the materials for the job, in doing so had wrecked my hedge getting on to the drive. The sand, cement and bricks had all been dropped amongst the great heap of soil surrounding the footings. With the site looking as if a bomb had exploded the two workmen were now mixing the cement for the bottom of the footings. To get the wet cement into the trench they had to wheel the barrow over the top of the heap of soil, knocking much of the loose earth back into the hole whilst doing so. Why this soil had not been taken away at first was mystifying, as it had to go eventually.

The bricklaying eventually started and the performance didn't end there, I began to feel sick inside. The younger man was arguing with his elder who should mix the mortar. I finally got to know that the young man was indeed the 'tradesman'; it was his first job following a short course at college. Whilst the older man was quite adept at bricklaying, I watched the younger man from our landing window, because his back was aching whilst he bent to work on the foundations, he had now chosen to press the bricks into the mortar with his feet!

There was a long saga of telephone calls and letters to the builder, followed by visits to the Citizen's Advice Bureau and the Master Builders Federation. All of which were pretty futile. It took six weeks to get the two garage walls built; arriving home from work, it was common to find both men in shorts sunning themselves on my lawn. It took several months to complete the work and we had to withhold the payment to get the work finished to a minimum standard. Even the builder took pity on us finally, by reducing the bill by £500!

Some time before the new garage-workshop was built, I had resurrected the drawings and some of the casting for the 3½ in. gauge 'County' class locomotive that I had started to build originally in my teens. With my first engine completed I needed another project for my relaxation. Also, economics had dictated the issue of starting any new project. With my new workshop fitted out and the installation of one of the first cheap foreign mill/drills, work on the second locomotive progressed well. Yet it still took a period of six years to complete. This was quickly followed by the construction of a Stuart No. 4 stationary steam plant.

The bodywork on my wife's car got beyond economical repair, so we invested in a new Mini Estate. This motor was perfectly turned out as Sir Michael Edwards had taken over the reins at British Leyland and was eagerly trying to enhance the company's reputation. So pleased we were with this vehicle that two years later we purchased another for myself. Regrettably this was a different story, the day I collected it, it had to go straight back in the workshop because the speedometer was not working. When I went for it the following day my stepson came with me and whilst on its first run, he pointed out that he could see through to the road from the air vent on the passenger side. When we looked, both air ducts had not been located at both ends and they were flapping around loose beneath the front wings. The following day I went to start it and there was a tinkling noise as parts of the carburettor fell on to the garage floor. I then decided that a thorough examination was necessary and I was aghast at the number of irritating faults that I found. Numerous grommets and insulators had not been fitted properly and the gaiter surrounding the radiator hung loosely in front of the grill, hanging on just one of the eight fixing points. Even after this examination, faults developed periodically, the engine stabilisers came loose, the locknut on the clutch had not been tightened and eventually I had difficulty selecting the gears. After a very small mileage, the front tyres wore out; the wheel alignment had not been set anywhere near correctly. Then the main battery lead burned through as it was in close proximity to the exhaust pipe. Little doubt, the workers who assembled this car did not deserve to be employed by anyone. From that time on, with the exception of having a new clutch fitted to my wife's car, no one else has ever put a spanner on either of the cars; all the work has been done by myself.

# Chapter Fourteen

## The Top Link

After several years in the North link I finally made No. 1 link, this again meaning a complete change of territory. The change of link started once more with many weeks of road learning. I now had to learn the routes to Bristol and Paddington, via Bicester and via Reading, also to Basingstoke and Kensington Olympia; the latter destination was where we had relief with the trains on the Brighton and Folkestone services. Going over these routes as a fireman, and as a 'Put Back Driver,' made learning much easier, but Paddington station had been completely remodelled, and modernisation in general had brought about a host of other changes. The 'New Line', as we always called the line to Paddington via Bicester, was now a single line over some distance from Princes Risborough to Ayhno Junction. All very different from when we used to attempt the 'ton' with the 'Kings'.

The principle of the top link had also changed since I was a fireman. Discontent amongst younger drivers, who felt that it was unfair for older men to have the best work, had brought about a partial compromise and some work sharing. No. 1 link was therefore now interspersed with some local work, passenger and freight; in addition the link carried a number of 'spare' turns. This meant a wide variety of work, apart from the normal express work, one day you could be on Royal Train working and the next on the shunting engine in Bromford Yard.

Initially, all mileage turns had always been double manned. Therefore the night car transporter trains that we now worked from Washwood Heath to Acton, not only carried a secondman, but also a guard, who rode in the rear cab of the locomotive. During my time in the top link, first the secondman, then the guard was abolished. We finally found ourselves working trains of a hundred standard wagon units in length completely alone. This was fine when things were going all right, but any trouble *en route* could become a nightmare with trains of this calibre. Plus the fact that these trains were often single-piped air-braked trains with continental type wagons, working the brake needed super skill, a fraction too much air released from the system and a train of this length would come to a stand, as the brakes were extremely slow releasing.

My friend Dick Potts had the unfortunate experience of coming to a stand across all the running lines at Southall, as the air train pipe hose on the last wagon of 100 wagons in standard length units chose to burst as the train was across the junction. It was therefore an awful long time before anything moved in any direction, as Dick was alone in the dead of night. It was finally sanctioned for him to run with the last wagon isolated and unbraked. He was advised to screw the wagon hand brake on which apparently did little for the wheel tyres of the wagon! This was totally against the rules, but there was no other way out at the time, as these lines were occupied almost as much at night as they were in daytime.

Each time drivers took on extra responsibility, we got productivity deals. These were never very substantial and, with the current rate of inflation, in a short time we found ourselves doing the extra tasks and being little better off.

With the introduction of electric train heating we had always to be particularly vigilant. Oscillation between coaches and poor jumper cable connections sometimes saw the system trip out. The only indication in the cab was a white indicator light which illuminated to show the heating was working. This was difficult to see in daylight, as it was not situated immediately in front of you. The buffet and restaurant cars also relied on the train heating system working, and the later air-conditioned coaches. If the system tripped out and went unnoticed, there was soon some irate person round your neck at the first port of call.

We worked the Bournemouth trains to Reading, initially with class '47s'. The locomotives for these turns usually went fresh off the depot at Saltley with full fuel tanks. In the earlier days, we came back with the same engine. With the steam heating boilers now gone, the water tanks for the boiler were converted to carry extra fuel, some 850 gallons in total. This obviously kept the locomotives in service for much longer periods.

When I took engines off the depot for the Bournemouth turns, I usually swept out both cabs and cleaned round with hot soapy water obtained from the depot toilets. The brown linoleum on the cab floors would look really good when cleaned. No one was ever designated to do the job of cleaning locomotive cabs and they could become pretty disgusting at times. Fitting staff trod oil about and previous drivers left litter, fag ends, apple cores and orange peel lying around. In many instances things were kept much tidier on steam engines.

Cleaning up one day I found a patch of cotton waste in the cab, this was very unusual, as this material was one of the first things to disappear with the advent of diesels. The loose fibres were detrimental to the finer working parts of diesels it was thought. When I went to ring off the depot on this day, the engine arranger had a little dig at me; he said that I looked like a typical old 'Western' man with a patch of cotton waste sticking out of my pocket. We laughed about it, but little did I know that this wad of cotton waste was to be my saviour later in the day.

I worked to Reading and on the return journey I noticed that a hydraulic buffer had fallen off a previous freight train, it was now lying on the edge of the track. I passed over it after leaving Banbury, in the vicinity of where Cropredy station was at one time. Some five miles on, at Fenny Compton, the train brakes started to apply, which I first thought was the communication cord being pulled. As I came to a stand, I looked back to see the guard down from the train and hurrying my way. He quickly told me that the locomotive was losing fuel rapidly and it was splashing on to the first coaches. When I looked out on the other side, a column of fuel was spurting from a three-inch diameter pipe with such force that it was clearing the up main line and going down the opposite bank. I quickly opened the engine room door to check the fuel gauge, which was already showing empty. Another look at the old boiler water tank gauge from the ground indicated about 100 gallons left in that tank. Off came my jacket, up with my sleeves and the only thing I had to stem the flow was the patch of cotton waste in my pocket! The fuel tank drain valve had sheared off as it had struck the buffer head on the track. I rammed the cotton waste home and found a stick from off the bank and forced the bung hard into the pipe. In just a few minutes we were on our way again, the trouble was now, that I could not be sure that the 'repair' would hold. Also, I would have no idea if the material did come out, that is until the engine stopped. On arrival at Leamington, I telephoned the signalman, telling him of the plight I was in, emphasising that there was just a piece of cotton waste stuffed in the pipe holding the remaining fuel in the tank. To avoid further delay, I advised him to tell the control that another locomotive would be necessary at Birmingham, as the train went forward to Newcastle and that was of course only if I was lucky enough to get that far.

Fortunately I made it to New Street, but alas, again the control had not heeded what I had said. I was surprised to see a fitter walking up the platform with two large containers of oil to fill the hydrostatic radiator fans! It was difficult to see how on earth the wires had got crossed again to such a degree. When I explained to the fitter what had happened, another locomotive was immediately summoned for the job, but some delay now occurred whilst the replacement engine came from Saltley, which I found extremely aggravating. In addition, no one ever thanked me for my quick thinking, which had also avoided a long delay at Fenny Compton. There were many drivers who would have rubbed their hands in such a situation and allowed the remaining fuel to drain away. Any delay would have been money in their pocket; they would happily have waited for an assistant locomotive to arrive. Having assistance in such circumstances rarely meant less than one hour delay.

The Bournemouth trains later ran with HSTs, although working them single manned we were officially not allowed to exceed 100 mph at that time, despite the line speed between Didcot and Reading being 125 mph. Most of us tended to stretch a point if we were running late and therefore got the thrill of 125 mph running. I did have the most eerie experience whilst doing this on one damp autumn night when running late. The signals were against me at Tilehurst; this just as I had attained 125 mph. As I made a full brake application, all eight wheels on the first power car started to slide. The speedometer went to zero and apart from the engine idling over, there was almost complete silence in the cab. We relied totally on the speedometer when braking from high speeds and this was a pretty alarming experience. There was certainly no room for 'fannying' around with the brake at this speed, yet if I allowed the wheels to slide it would do a lot of damage by grinding flats on the wheels. I quickly had to release the brake until the wheels began to revolve again, then make another full brake application. I was relieved to get things back in perspective, the train speed had if fact reduced considerably due to the braking effect of the other vehicles, but it was an unusual experience which did much to increase my heart rate.

Much of the work into Paddington we did with the English Electric class '50s', these locomotives were probably the best we had from this manufacturer. They were quiet, robust, reliable and comfortable; I enjoyed working on them. They had a top maximum speed of 95 mph at this period. Although, on favourable stretches of track they would comfortably reach 100 mph.

At a later time, I worked part of the 'Farewell to the Class 50s' tour with two locomotives in multiple, No. 50007 *Sir Edward Elgar* and restored No. D400, the leading engine painted in Great Western green and the second in BR blue. I worked the train from Reading to Birmingham, but unfortunately there was little chance of any brisk running, despite having the power of the two locomotives at my disposal. The locomotives by this time were reduced to 75 mph running and the mechanical inspectors present watched my speed closely. However, it was good to feel the surge of power when accelerating away from stations. My secondman on this turn was Neil Harris, who was one of the nicer young men that I had to work with at that time; he faithfully recorded the day on his camera.

These times brought an odd mix of youngsters who were 'apprenticed' to us. Young men were either attracted to the job by fervent enthusiasm, or fully aware that the work was less than energetic. Some were uncontrollably indolent; as long as they dragged themselves to work, they felt it was their right to finish their sleep out in the cab. Running into stations during daylight, nothing looked less professional than a secondman with his feet in the window reading *Tit-Bits* or *Reveille*. These young men would not have lasted a week with a firing shovel in their hands and this was to be a bone of contention with many conscientious drivers. Little wonder too, that management continually pressed the unions towards single manning.

Myself on class '50' No. 50007 *Sir Edward Elgar*. *Neil Harris*

'Farewell to the Class 50s' tour waiting line clear at Leamington. *Neil Harris*

In the cab during the 'Farewell to the Class 50s' tour. Note the locomotive was now limited to 75 mph stencilled on the panel. *Neil Harris*

An experience now springs to mind when I left Reading towards Paddington one evening with a class '50'. Approaching Twyford I had just reached maximum speed when I passed a High Speed Train doing 125 mph in the opposite direction. Nearing Maidenhead the signals in front of me reverted to danger and I had to make an emergency stop, coming to a stand in the station platform. I immediately contacted the signalman and he advised me that I had needed to examine my train. We had apparently left Reading with a door open on the first coach and the door had protruded well foul of the opposite running line. The passing HST had struck the door, which must have brought about a considerable impact with the combined approach speeds of both trains. The driver of the HST must have indeed suffered quite a traumatic shock.

I entered the first coach to find the coach door completely missing and shards of glass everywhere. Amazingly, although the train was full with passengers, they had all sat and said nothing, almost as though this was an everyday experience! Several other windows down the train were also smashed, one window seven coaches back from the engine. Yet no one had said anything, or even alerted the train guard.

When I reported the damage to the train back to the signalman, we were ordered to detrain everyone and go empty to the sidings at Paddington. Unfortunately, this experience was one of the drawbacks of single manned working. When the station 'right away' indicator illuminated, a driver was unable to watch the train leave the station if the platform was on the 'off' side.

The Bournemouth and Brighton services initially ran with eight to 12 coaches. Line speeds were eventually raised to compete with other forms of transport initially without problems. Later economies by InterCity management finally reduced trains to six vehicles and timings were further enhanced. When running at 90 mph with only six vehicles, I quickly became aware that certain signals were difficult to stop at. Indeed, once or twice, I sat with the brakes in the emergency position with my toes curled up, wondering if I would overrun the signal. When I realised this, I found it necessary to anticipate the offending signals by shutting the controller in advance of them until they came into view. At the most doubtful signals, I allowed the train speed to drop slightly until a clear signal was seen. However, there were soon a number of signals that were passed at danger by other drivers and management felt at first that men were exceeding the maximum line speed. Radar speed traps were set up regularly, but the overruns continued and drivers were disciplined. Three overruns and you were taken off main line working. Whilst it was a well-known fact to seasoned drivers that with only a short train the available brake power was less, the boffins would have none of this. Research had shown that the braking distance was the same however many vehicles were in a train formation. The theory was that the moving mass of weight was less with a small train; therefore the ratio of brake power should bring it to a stand in the same distance.

Despite the fact that the brake blocks on the class '47' locomotives now working the Folkestone and Brighton services were down to lasting only four days, the situation remained unaltered. Management were convinced that errors of judgement on the driver's part were always the reason for the signal overruns. The maintenance staff at Saltley literally changed brake blocks by the wagonload. Yet it still did not become evident to the management that something must be amiss. With the violent braking always necessary to stop these services, it was quite remarkable that there were not a proliferation of fires on locomotives, the undersides of which were invariably dripping with oil. When braking, the wheels would become a mass of fire, which was more noticeable at night; the fire from the wheels would light up the surrounding railway.

Things came to a head when I worked the 0900 from Poole to Glasgow on Easter Monday 1989. I took over the train at Reading with 12 coaches, 389 tons tare and this train was exceptionally well patronised. At Banbury people were having difficultly finding room to get on the train at all.

Fosse Road signal box had now been abolished and intermediate colour light signals had been installed at Fosse Road, these controlled from the new Leamington power signal box. This signal, Leamington DM33, was on a falling gradient and at 90 mph with 12 coaches on, I did not anticipate any problem at all stopping when this signal was against me. The train brakes had been working perfectly. Nevertheless, I was running on time and had shut off power prior to going on to the falling gradient at Harbury. On sighting the colour light distant signal at caution, my speed had already fallen to 85 mph. I made a full service brake application the very moment the signal came into view, which was some 400 yards before reaching the signal. As I passed the caution signal, the brakes had yet had no affect on the train speed whatsoever; I therefore pushed the brake valve into the emergency position. Again, with my toes curled up, I sat helplessly wondering if I would stop. I ground to a stand with a jerk, the engine right up to the stop signal with absolutely no leeway whatsoever. I knew that this particular signal had to be treated with respect with a train of six coaches, but stopping with 12 coaches at any time had never been a problem. I now realised that the trouble must have been the sheer weight of the number of people on the train, combined with the falling gradient.

Feeling that enough was enough, having to make emergency brake applications to stop trains in normal service should never have been an option. It was my opinion that all trains should come comfortably to a stand with average brake applications, leaving some yards to spare to accommodate any poor brake adjustment and wear on brake blocks.

Before signing off duty I made out a report, stating that there was some difficulty in stopping trains of certain formations at Leamington DM 33 signal. I explained that in this particular instance my train was abnormally overloaded. To accommodate all combinations of trains, I suggested that the line speed in rear of the distant signal should be reduced until such time as this repeating signal could be move farther out, therefore giving a greater stopping distance.

My letter brought the response from management that the matter would be investigated, but it also criticised me for not reporting the train brakes as faulty at the time of the incident. Regrettably, I was in a 'no win' situation; had I reported a brake problem, the train would have been severely delayed whilst carriage and wagon examiners were sent to meet the train. Doubtless, I would have been told that nothing was wrong; indeed I had stopped on every other occasion without any difficulty.

Initially, it appeared to me that the management had already made up their mind that this incident was due to a brake problem, not insufficient stopping distance. Nine months went by and I received no other communication whatsoever on the matter. Tests had however been going on behind the scenes. Nevertheless, although I thought that this was a safety issue, little progress seemed to have been made in a very long time.

In February 1990, a colleague had the misfortune to overrun the same signal and was immediately grounded pending the usual inquiry. I was then quick to write another letter stating that I had already indicated to management that there was some difficulty stopping trains of certain formations at this signal and that the repeating signal should be moved farther out, or the line speed reduced.

Unfortunately, the driver involved in the overrun had in fact had the same amount of experience as myself; therefore he should have shown more respect towards the inadequate stopping distance at this signal with only six coaches on. Nevertheless, there was a problem, which I felt may well catch drivers of lesser experience out; not every driver worked these trains on a day to day basis, in this instance it would be unfair to discipline these men. Not only did I point this out, but also I listed a number of other signals at which difficulty of stopping short trains had been experienced. I then threw the ball back into the management's court, by saying that a copy of my letter was being forwarded to my trade union representative, should any incident occur in the future at the offending signals.

The 'Corporate Image' had now begun to rear its ugly head. With strong murmurings of railway privatisation, management became more aggressive. A host of 'Team Leaders' were promoted to keep a closer watch on drivers. Now depots had not only a traction inspector, but also perhaps up to 10 others having a footplate supervisory authority. The amount of team leaders allocated obviously depended on the depot size. In the early days, just two locomotive inspectors had covered the whole Midland section of the Western Region.

Many younger men jumped at the opportunity to become a team leader which brought with it a considerably enhanced wage packet, and in addition less unsocial hours. Whilst a number of the newly promoted men were good conscientious railwaymen, there were also some who were little doubt downright rogues as drivers. Knowing these people's track record, it became pretty galling to have one of these men ride with you to assess your driving capabilities, as they were now required to do on a regular basis.

Higher management now began to dictate strict policies, which few in the inspectorate grade would dare challenge for fear that their position would be at risk. Many times I approached my latest traction inspector at Saltley, because changes were being made which I felt compromised safety. Particularly the fact that traction units were now beginning to re-enter service with faulty Automatic Warning Systems. Whilst my inspector would agree with me whole-heartedly in principle, he had become a puppet and therefore failed to challenge any unsatisfactory management policies. He told me that our sacred AWS was now only an aid to a driver and not to be relied upon.

John Dorricote, who I had known all my working life, had now attained the position of Regional traction inspector. John was one of the 'old school' and I had every respect for him. Even so, private conversations with him had shown some exasperation on his part with prevailing trends. With the present situation, I therefore expected little from my report regarding the limited stopping distances at some signals. I was pleasantly surprised when this turned out to be a wrong assumption.

After five weeks, I received a long handwritten letter from John Dorricote in reply to my letter, which turned out to be very much to my satisfaction. Following this letter, all six-coach trains were limited to 80 mph and the line speed approaching most of the suspect signals that I reported was also to be reduced. A personal whisper from John later, intimated that I was the only person he knew that had ever got the present management to change their minds.

I understand that the InterCity Director, Dr John Prideaux, was now a very unhappy man. He had to find an extra coach for many of his trains just to supplement the braking, and this was to upset his costings somewhat. To keep to the timetable, the locomotive-hauled Cross-Country services had to run at 90 mph. Furthermore, the new regulations regarding six-coach trains also applied to all Regions.

The amount of extra coaches now required were not easy to come by; old stock, which had stood in sidings for years was brought back into service. Most of which were so dilapidated that the coaches were just attached to the rear of the train for braking purposes and were locked out of service to the public. Having said that, it was still known for passengers to find a way into these vehicles.

Soon after the new regulations applied, I arrived at Reading after an uneventful trip, only to be met by a detective sergeant. I was hustled into a private room and quizzed at some length as to what had taken place at Leamington. My guard was interviewed separately and we had no idea what the police wanted to know. The wires had got crossed again and we were eventually released. It was only after the driver of the train behind us came into the mess room that the mystery was solved. Passengers for Leamington had somehow got into a locked up coach on the back of this train. Just as the train left the platform, the guard heard people shouting that they wanted get out. Some yards down the line, the guard had operated the emergency brake valve in the guard's compartment. He then released the people from the train and told them to walk back to the station, luggage and all along the ballast! This act was certainly not compatible with the rules and regulations; little wonder the Transport Police had taken a dim view.

Saltley depot was by this period under the administrative area of Bescot, nevertheless, we still had a depot manager who was the equivalent of the old shedmaster. Terry McKenna was our boss, who was probably the most enthusiastic manager that I ever worked under. He was a 'live wire' and liable to turn up at anytime, particularly if there had been a problem on the line. He was undoubtedly a dedicated railwayman who went through the footplate grades and diverted to management as a young driver. He had amassed great experience in management, by filling a number of positions outside the locomotive running side before becoming our depot manager. Terry's presence on engineering work at weekends, accidents, or just signal failures, had always been an asset. Stopped in a blizzard one night, at a remote junction, Terry was there, sweeping snow from points and hand cranking over electric points that had failed. He believed firmly in keeping the trains running, a trait that had rubbed off on many of us from the older men that we worked with. This incentive was probably a throw back from the war years when munitions, coal and foodstuffs had to be kept moving as lives depended on it. Whilst Terry eventually retired almost unrecognised, if there had been medals to be earned for devotion to duty and to the travelling public, Terry should have been bestowed with them all.

Most footplate men fiddled the system at some time; the loss of the eight-hour day by the implementation of flexible rostering had not gone down well with the men. The system of having been given a job, however short, and then disappearing had now long gone. Men therefore deviously devised a system where, after having a short job, they would put their driver's ticket in time order of booking off in the mess room under a newspaper on one of the tables. Drivers standing 'spare' then ferried the tickets into the time office at the appropriate time. This worked out well for a long time until Terry McKenna, who was always very sociable and kept in touch with all his men, saw something of interest in the newspaper covering the tickets of the men who had gone home early. There was quite a rumpus for a while after he had innocently thumbed through the newspaper and revealed the tickets. Hence the tickets then found there way into the kitchen drawer, then the cooker oven. Terry would have purges from time to time and sniff out the tickets, men would lose some pay, but there was never any bitterness, it was his job to manage and he was effectively a great man.

Royalty sometimes visited the Midlands and often passed through to other areas; being in the top link I was now regularly selected for Royal Train working. This did not mean that I drove the Royal Train regularly, as it more often than not meant that you were just standby. This, in fact, became a real irritation, as you could be taken off a straightforward passenger turn, only to find yourself sitting about doing nothing until the Royal Train had left the district. We were always required to come to work on these turns looking respectable, yet once the Royal Train had gone you could find yourself on any job. One night I was asked to help out with marshalling the depot, as one or two failures had occurred and the shedmen had got into a knot. As anyone can imagine, this did not go down well after I had donned a newly dry-cleaned uniform and had put an extra polish on my shoes.

Once again I received notification of Royal Train working, consequently on booking off duty the previous day I asked the train crew supervisor whether I was in fact working the job, or whether I was just standby again. I had known Terry Dugard an awfully-long time and hoped he would give me a clue, but he stuck to his orders and said he could not tell me for security reasons.

The following evening I booked on, only to be told that I was standby again. I asked who was working the Royal Train and was told Kenny McGlachan. Ken was reliable man, but he did have a habit of turning up at the very last moment on a regular basis. When he was a few minutes late, even for the Royal Train, the supervisor was not unduly worried.

Once more, looking smarter than usual, I retired to the mess room rather irritated. I sat there for a few minutes and a young driver passed the comment that I looked as though I had come for the Royal Train. When I told him that I had, but was now standby, he casually inquired as to who was working the job. When I told him Kenny McGlachan, he said that he would have a job to work it, he had signed on at lunch time. He had in reality worked a quick job to Gloucester, gone without his meal break and caught an earlier passenger train home. Two hours earlier he had indeed put his ticket under the newspaper and gone home!

To get our facts right, we sorted through the tickets, sure enough, there was Ken's ticket. Back at the supervisor's window, I said to the supervisor that I thought he had told me that Kenny McGlachan was working the Royal Train? Terry was already looking very anxious at Ken's late arrival when I dropped the bombshell that I was sure that he would find that Ken had booked on at lunchtime and had gone to Gloucester. In seconds Terry had got a telephone in each hand and there was a soon very urgent three-way conversation in progress. There had obviously been an error in the rostering and changing the driver on the Royal Train was not the easiest thing a supervisor could do without authority, again supposedly for security reasons.

Eventually, I was handed the working diagram, yet there was now another problem. George Stokes, the guard, and I were rostered to travel to Slough to pick up the Royal Train which was ultimately to take Her Majesty to Chester. It was already now too late for us to catch the local train from Duddeston station into New Street, which would in turn connect with the express to Reading. Frantic calls were quickly made for the minibus driver who was ordered to speed us into town. Unfortunately, this was the evening rush hour and we had to be on the 1808 departure from New Street station. Because of the sheer volume of traffic, we arrived on the platform just as the train was on the move, but fortunately we were able to scramble on board with some co-operation from the station staff.

George Stokes and I were able to get our breath back, but this was not to be our day, a points failure at Aynho Junction saw the train delayed for more than an hour.

BRITISH RAIL LONDON MIDLAND REGION

TO: DRIVER

474 HERBERT D.C.

FROM: CHIEF CLERK
B.O.P.
SALTLEY
EXT: 2867

DATE: 07/04/1992

ROYAL TRAIN WORKING

PLEASE NOTE THAT ON WEDNESDAY 15th APRIL 1992

YOU HAVE BEEN SELECTED TO WORK THE ROYAL TRAIN *******

WITH A BOOKING ON TIME OF 17 26 HRS

FULL REGULATION UNIFORM IS REQUIRED (WHICH INCLUDES HAT).ANY ITEMS OF EQUIPMENT OR UNIFORM YOU REQUIRE CAN YOU PLEASE ADVISE THE T.C.S. AS SOON AS POSSIBLE.

IT IS ESSENTIAL THAT YOU ALSO CARRY YOUR PHOTO IDENTITY CARD WITH YOU ON THIS DAY FOR SECURITY REASONS.

FOR CHIEF CLERK SALTLEY
FOR A.M. BESCOT

C.C.
T.C.M.
A.T.C.M.
T.C.S.
R/CLK.
A.T.I.

My advice for Royal Train working.

This meant that we would miss the local train from Reading to Slough that we were diagrammed to be on. At Reading we just missed another local train to Slough, which ran only at 30 minute intervals in the evenings. We worked out that the next train would get us to Slough with just eight minutes to spare before departure with the Royal Train, which indeed it did. We crossed by the footbridge where security men were searching the line for explosives etc. We put some boiling water on a tea bag and I walked up the platform with my cup in my hand as the Royal Train arrived.

Her Majesty arrived at the side of the station from Windsor and it was only seconds before we were on our way. So much for security, no one as much as asked me my name, not even the traction inspector who was in the cab! We ran exactly to time, as police helicopters kept watch from above; it was really like driving just another train.

I never received the usual letter of thanks from Buckingham Palace, neither did I get the usual £10 gratuity, I suspect Ken McGlachan got that!

On the retirement of Terry McKenna the depot manager, Colin Porter, succeeded him. Colin had also risen from the footplate grades and had worked his way to the top by first becoming outside foreman at Saltley, then train crew supervisor and ultimately depot manager. Colin had always been a committed railwayman and with his huge experience there were few who could tell him anything about railway work, or indeed the men that he had under his wing. Men respected his knowledge, yet he kept a low profile, whilst at the same time doing a good job. Things usually ran smoothly, yet I suspect that there was little that went on at the depot that escaped his awareness. Perhaps, like many of us older men, with the oncoming privatisation he knew that he too would be pushed out by the new organization. It was openly said that the older workers were too set in their ways for the future plans of the railways.

I worked to Paddington and back via Reading one Saturday afternoon. It had been a perfect trip over the 240 miles; I had the same locomotive all day and ran to time. As the class '47' had behaved impeccably, I had no reason at all to consult its repair book. Whilst I had passed countless signals during the run, regrettably, the last but one signal approaching New Street gave a 'wrong side' audible warning indication. Although the signal was showing a caution aspect, the AWS gave a clear indication by sounding the bell, instead of the warning horn. This was a serious failure and I immediately stopped at the next signal to inform the signalman. The signal technicians would then have to be sent to the offending signal and all subsequent trains passing this signal would have to be warned of the problem.

When I disposed of the traction unit on the fuel line at Saltley, I discovered from the repair book that the problem had occurred on the locomotive on other occasions, the equipment on the locomotive was therefore at fault. Earlier times would have seen the locomotive withdrawn from service at the first hint of a failure of this type.

We now had a new train crew supervisor and earlier encounters had already led me to realise that he was really was not up to the job. Anyone in this capacity required untold knowledge of railway work. With a 'wrong side' AWS failure it was now my duty to submit the appropriate form. When I asked this supervisor for the form, he gave me the form that I had often had to submit for 'right side' failures. I immediately told him that it was the incorrect form, where by he sorted through all the drawers of his desk. He then told me that it was indeed the right form; I protested that this simple form did not convey sufficient information for a 'wrong side' failure. He then insisted that he was right and that the requirements had since been amended. It then crossed my mind that if engines with faults of this nature had been re-entering service, perhaps he was right. Management was already allowing the equipment to be downgraded. Indeed, the Saltley traction inspector had earlier told me that the system was only a guide to drivers and never to be relied upon. Under the circumstances, I therefore filled in the form that he had given me and went home, although I was rather saddened of what the future held in due regard to safety.

My next turn of duty was 0200 on Monday morning for the Bournemouth 'sleeper'. When I did sign on, the supervisor was anxiously waiting for me.

'For God's sake, fill in this form will you, the wires have been red hot over this from Crewe, you should have done this before you went home on Saturday evening!', the boss remarked abruptly.

Getting home at midnight on Saturday and being back at work at 0200 hrs on Monday morning had done little for my frame of mind, the reply he got, regrettably, was colourful. When I eventually explained what had taken place on Saturday evening, although nothing was said, there were some raised eyebrows and rolling of eyes.

The night 'sleeper' came from the North and was divided at Birmingham. My train for the journey south then consisted of three sleeping cars plus several postal vans, and was booked to depart from New Street a few minutes after 0300.

We all hated this turn; we only had to run at about 50 mph to keep time. Any faster and you would be held at signals *en route*, hence you would be continually up and down from the cab contacting the signalman on the telephone. Running at 50 mph was pretty monotonous and it was a dickens of a job to stay awake at that hour!

This was not to be my night, the communication cord was pulled at Dorridge and I came to a stand on a high embankment on a devilishly wild night. There was some compensation, inasmuch as it was the sleeping car attendant on the nearest sleeping car to the engine who had stopped the train, he had smelled burning and had acted promptly. In earlier years there had been a serious fire on a sleeping car train at Taunton, which did involve loss of life; at the very least this man was vigilant. The brakes on the coach were not releasing properly and the wheels were already very hot.

Drivers were required to overcharge the air brake system when attaching to a train, or if fresh vehicles were added. This was to set up the system and overcome any minor maladjustments of the 'distributor valves' on the train. I had carried out this procedure several minutes before leaving New Street and the air trainpipe was given ample time to bleed down to the normal 70 psi, therefore on this occasion everything should have been alright. I finally found it necessary to isolate the brakes on this vehicle altogether, as each time I applied the brake the brakes would not release again. Isolating the vehicle brake was not a problem, I advised the signalman as to the cause of the delay and that the brakes on the first sleeping car on the train had been isolated. As the defective vehicle was running between postal vans and the other sleeping cars this was quite acceptable in an emergency.

When I arrived at Reading, the parcel vans next to the engine were removed from the train, the train also reversed to go out towards Basingstoke. This left the faulty coach on the back of the train, which was now an unacceptable problem. Unbraked passenger vehicles were definitely not allowed on the back of a train. I felt sure that the control would sanction the empty postal vehicles to be left on the back of the train, which would have allowed it to proceed to its destination. Unfortunately, with privatisation looming, the railway system was now being fragmented into separate sections, these parcel vans now belonged to a potentially different company.

It was unheard of, but the control cancelled the train, the sleeping passengers had to be detrained on to the platform at Reading and the coaches were then put into the sidings! To any conscientious railwayman this was unthinkable, people having paid an awful lot of money for a sleeping berth from Scotland to Bournemouth. Again this made me feel apprehension as to what the future held.

Back at my home depot, with the thoughts of this incident fresh in my mind, the supervisor who had failed to furnish me with the correct AWS fault form had now returned to duty. On seeing me, he called me into the office and I was stunned at what he inferred.

'Where did you get to on Saturday night?' He remarked. Baffled as to why he had said this, as I had spent some time making a special report out, plus time filling in the incorrect form that he had given me, I therefore asked him what he meant?

'You cleared off home before I had time to find the proper form for you', he replied. Incensed by this remark, without another word being spoken, I left the office and within 30 seconds I was knocking on the depot manager's door. Colin Porter was always approachable, I had known him since he was a young driver and I explained in detail what had taken place. I was reluctant to make an official issue over this, but I told the depot manager that I felt he should know that this man was certainly not to be trusted. He was indeed covering his own inability to do the job with downright lies. With drivers becoming ever more accountable for their actions, possibly to the point of being dragged to court, the last thing footplatemen wanted was for someone in management who was treacherous. Having said my piece, I went home and left Colin with his thoughts; I was very angry and it had not been a good day.

The fragmentation of the system, as the run up to privatisation took hold, became an exasperating time for anyone who had a love for railways. After running all the way from Kensington and making every effort to recover any lost time, you would be held outside New Street station because the InterCity platforms were occupied. The rest of the station could be empty and your train terminating, but the signalman could not put you into another platform. Drivers were often rostered to be picked up by the minibus service car to be taken to Saltley, this would go if the train was a few minutes late and leave you stranded and not knowing what time you would be collected.

I worked one of the Norwich trains from Leicester one morning, when the class '31' locomotive on the train had been reported as having a hot axlebox. A replacement class '31' was turned off Leicester depot and a change of locomotive was effected in the station. As the train was already considerably delayed, passengers for the North, who would normally have changed trains at Nuneaton, were advised to stay with my train to Birmingham, as their connecting train had now gone.

After leaving Nuneaton, I braked to reduce speed for the 30 mph permanent speed restriction through Arley tunnel, as I entered the tunnel the diesel engine shut down. This was a steep rising gradient and it was necessary to stop in total darkness to restart the engine. The reverser had to be put into neutral before the engine would start, if I did this on the move the train brakes would apply anyway. Fortunately, after a short time I was able to restart the engine, but once the locomotive put her head down on the pending falling gradient the engine shut down again. This was the classic symptoms of low radiator water, which indeed it did turn out to be. Knowing that at this time of day there was always at least one locomotive in Daw Mill Colliery Sidings that would be able to assist me quickly, I allowed the train to coast to the signal protecting the colliery sidings. My assumption was correct, when I stopped there were three locomotives in the sidings and without delay I asked the signalman to provide assistance. I expected to see one of these engines quickly come up to the ground frame and make movements to come on to the front of me. After some time, I asked the signalman what was going on, only to be told that a locomotive was being prepared at Saltley depot to render assistance for me. The locomotives in the sidings were now classed as freight engines and the signalman was not allowed to use them!

An assistant locomotive arrived over one hour later. The two men who were given the job to bring the engine were on overtime, both were notorious 'string pullers' and had obviously made little effort under these circumstances to get things moving as it was all money in their pocket. In the meantime, my guard had taken an awful lot of flak from a train full of irate passengers, who had now also missed their connection to the North from Birmingham.

This should have been just another day's work, but these events had a profound affect on me, my thoughts of what the future held were depressing. The majority of drivers of my calibre got a lot of job satisfaction out of running a train to time. People travelled for many reasons: perhaps to catch a holiday flight, see sick relatives, a job interview, or an important business appointment; it is imperative that these folk have reliable transport. The people on my train were inconvenienced for no other reason than bureaucracy; I found this very hard to accept. Perhaps the powers that be were right; we older men were too set in our ways?

A few days later, when working a local train on my old hunting ground around Tyseley, I noticed a train of petrol tanks on the up main line standing in the platform at Small Heath. The locomotive had failed and the train stood there for the whole of my shift, each time I passed the train was still there. Other trains were diverted on to the goods line to pass it. The new system of working now meant that the only replacement locomotive for this train was at Immingham on the East Coast; the long delay was waiting for this engine to arrive.

Both drivers and signalmen were susceptible to mistakes, both had demanding jobs and no one is infallible. I have said earlier that signalmen covered for drivers and this did go both ways. Even when the power signal boxes were commissioned, minor anomalies were covered over. I know men who overran signals by a short distance and when they contacted the signalman the reply they got was, 'I can't hear what you are saying driver?' This usually meant that the train had not got as far as the next track circuit and was therefore not showing on the panel diagram as an overrun. The signalman again was obviously keeping the incident between two people, probably not even the signal box supervisor would be aware.

A number of accidents and consequential court cases made management more accountable and loopholes had to be tightened. This in turn brought more bureaucracy and the whole railway system became awash with paperwork, there was soon a form for every minor occurrence.

On 22nd October, 1991, I worked the 1106 New Street to Paddington and *en route* I was routed into No. 9 platform at Reading. This was the up relief line platform and I approached at the maximum line speed of 60 mph. To my surprise, the signals reverted to red and I had to make an emergency brake application to stop. I didn't overrun any signals but the stop was very abrupt. Any signal irregularities were now followed by inquiries and accountability, this almost paranoia had given most drivers the jitters over any minor signal overruns. After all, a driver had no way to prove that a signalman had reversed his signals. This incident shook me, as I knew passengers were likely to be standing in readiness to alight at this point, I could imagine some elderly lady lying on the coach floor with a broken hip! So it was worrying.

However, when I contacted the signalman he immediately apologised, explaining that a points failure had occured at the east end of the station. Had he allowed me to run into No. 9 platform he would have been unable to get me out again towards Paddington. He then explained that when the Bournemouth had left No. 8 platform, he would put me in there. This I felt was a logical move on his part and that he was doing his utmost to avoid delay. Although I was shaken, there was nothing sinister about the incident and it therefore passed from my mind.

Two weeks later there was a familiar looking brown envelope in the lobby window sporting my name. This letter said that there had been a signal irregularity at Reading on the 22nd October and I was to give my reasons for not submitting Form 2351. It then criticised me and stressed the importance of submitting this form at the time of the incident and that I had failed in my duty.

Again I was rather angry, but I wrote back to say that the reversal of the signals was due to a deliberate act by the signalman to avoid delay to my train and not a technical problem.

A few days later another letter arrived for me on the same subject. What had taken place in the Panel box at Reading after the incident I have no idea, but there was a photocopy of the signal box log along with the letter. An entry in the log concerning the incident was that there had been a points failure at the east end of the station. The signal technicians had inadvertently interfered with the overlap track circuit on platform No. 9 whilst addressing the points problem, this automatically reversing the signals on the approach of my train.

This was a total fabrication so I found it necessary to write a second letter, saying that I wanted it on record that I was dissatisfied with the explanation given. The signalman had at the time accepted responsibility for reversing the signals. Nevertheless, this proves that collusion did occur in signal boxes, which could, in all seriousness, put a driver in the dock. A driver working alone had no other witness, a situation which many of us always found worrying.

Having completed two model locomotives and a stationary steam engine, I now looked for a complete change of workshop project. My thoughts were on making a traction engine, I loved to watch the gears on these machines revolving and I felt that gear cutting would stretch my engineering capabilities. A friend had suggested that I make a longcase, or grandfather, clock, but I dismissed this as totally out of my league. This was despite him telling me that the old clocks were never that accurate in their mechanism. In the old days the gears were hand filed and the clocks were made with basic tools, men often working by candlelight. He was quite right in this respect, with modern tools the job should be within the scope of anyone with a reasonable workshop, but I was still very sceptical.

I never jumped into any new project, purely for economic reasons, but my friend Dave Grainger had colluded with my wife prior to my birthday, consequently, inside some of the gift wrapping was a book, *How to Make a Longcase Clock*. The first paragraph of this book warned me that clock making was likely to be infectious. It then went on to explain the stages necessary for making the 'works' of the clock. The more I read, the greater my interest became. Some £30 worth of engraving quality brass would be most of what I would need to give me many hours of interest; this would be no great loss if the project failed.

The book preface was right, the work did get infectious and it became very difficult for me to find a compromise with what needed to be done around the house and also be fair to my wife. Many hours of work saw the making of the 'going train' of gears between the plate frames and the 3 ft-long pendulum hanging on the back. At this time the clock made its first erratic few ticks. This was just a start, for it was many weeks before it would keep running for any length of time. Few words in the dictionary would describe my exasperation during this period, but when I got up one morning to find it had been running all night the feeling of achievement was all worth while. What I needed to achieve could only be done by listening and it had taken a very long time for me to develop the 'ear' for this.

This success gave me the impetus to make the 'strike' chain of gears and also make the motion work to drive the hands round in relation to one another. I had never seen the inside of a grandfather clock before I started this work; therefore much credit went to the author of the book for getting me through to this stage. Again, it was wonderful to watch the striking sequence take place, each hour counted faithfully by the right number of chimes.

The Roman numerals on the brass chapter ring also took an awful long time to achieve. This was done by mounting it on the mill/drill on a rotary table and carefully etching the numerals out by hand, any errors here would of course be the first thing anyone would see.

With the movement working successfully, I felt that the purchase of English oak for the case would be justified. This cost around £200 at the time, a purchase that I have never regretted. The only sundries that I had to acquire were the clock bell, the gut lines for the weights and some decorative cast brass spandrels for the corners of the clock face. Every other thing was hand made, right down to the door hinges. From start to finish the project took just 12 months, at the time of writing it has been running for 16 years and this achievement the will always remain part of my life.

Someone got to know that I had made a grandfather clock; consequently I was asked if I would consider repairing their antique clock. This I felt was a bit daunting, I knew nothing of old clocks and felt that my inexperience could devalue their treasure. However, I agreed to take a look, low and behold the mechanism was exactly the same as the one I had just made. I was therefore able to make a new part and fit it successfully. These longcase clocks were the main timekeepers for almost three centuries, in all that time little inside them changed.

I fell in love with this antique timepiece; it had been fashioned in mahogany and had a painted enamel dial. This gave me the urge to start again; my next one would be in this medium and have a painted dial sporting a railway theme.

Dick Potts took up the challenge to do the oil painting on the dial, that is, after I had done the necessary preliminary work and marked the numerals. He had not painted on metal previously and what he was asked to do was also rather small, thus he had to do much exploratory work first. The final result has always pleased me and given me enormous pleasure over the years. The clock has stood in our living room for the past 15 years and has become part of our lives; it is amazingly accurate too, as the room temperature varies little it therefore does not alter the pendulum length to any degree. It will lose a few seconds during the winding process; otherwise it will strike the hour with regularity in unison with the Greenwich Time signal. It is little wonder that these clocks were the main timekeepers for three centuries.

The days of British Rail as we knew it were now numbered and it wasn't just the older men who became more disillusioned with each day. The paranoid approach to safety, and being continually spied on, was unsettling to anyone who had great experience and always had safety in mind.

Finally, in early 1993 I was offered a resettlement package for which I was ready to snatch anyone's hand off. Feeling this way was an awful pity, I loved railways and the camaraderie amongst the men that I worked with at Saltley. This, I feel sure, was unequalled in any other industry.

During my final week at work I got even more exasperated as to the changes being implemented. I signed on one morning at 0800 and was told that an electric multiple unit had failed in Redditch station earlier that morning. I was asked to take a class '47' locomotive, pick up some extension air brake pipes from New Street station and drag the failed unit to the maintenance depot at Soho. A few years earlier, when Terry McKenna was boss, someone would have already brought the pipes to Saltley by road. The locomotive would also have been ready to go to clear the line immediately I signed on. There had now been no passenger train service to Redditch, because of the failure, for almost two hours, yet no sense of urgency prevailed whatsoever. I prepared the engine, took it to New Street where the best part of another hour went by. Eventually, a traction inspector appeared carrying the necessary extension pipes and we departed from New Street somewhere around 1000. Finally, after first getting permission from the signalman to enter the single line from Barnt Green, we made our way towards the failed train.

*Above:* A group photograph prior to our retirement party. David Jones, Dick Potts, Bernard Rainbow and myself representing 177 years of railway service.

*Iris Herbert*

*Right:* The retirement cake made by Bernard Rainbow's sister, Margaret.

*Iris Herbert*

*Right:* An oil painting by Dick Potts that he gave to me on retirement. It depicts No. 6116 passing Handsworth Junction on the the 7.06 am Henley-in-Arden to Wolverhampton Low Level on the day that I was Dick's fireman when he had his practical driving examination with inspector Charlie Weston of Wolverhampton.

One of the first things hammered home to us early in our career were the rules regarding the protection of trains. This was done with explosive detonators placed on the line and it was absolutely vital that this procedure was understood from the onset. Originally, three detonators had to be placed 10 yards apart on the rail not less than ¾ mile from any obstruction. As train speeds increased, however, the detonators had to be set at 20 yards apart to give three precise explosions to warn on coming trains. In addition, the distance was extended to not less than 1¼ miles on high speed lines.

I ran through the section from Barnt Green at caution, eventually arriving at the point where the guard was protecting his train. The guard was a smart young man, obviously well 'aligned' during his training to the needs of looking professional for the future privatised companies. He stood bolt upright holding a pristine new red flag, its freshly dowelled wood contrasting to the vivid crimson colour of the material. When we came to a stand I noticed that the detonators, which should have been set at 20 yards apart, were strapped to the railhead all touching each other. It was obvious that this young man, in reality, had no conception of even the basic principles of what was required to stop a speeding train in an emergency. Under the circumstances this day, there was no danger, but the implications of this new imagery were not only worrying, they were frightening.

We cleared the line of the obstruction just after 1100; the line had been blocked for over four hours, the unit suffering just a simple pantograph problem. My thoughts flashed back to steam days when my locomotive had become completely derailed. Within 30 minutes, trains were running past me in both directions and the line opened again to normal traffic in four hours. Perhaps I was now getting out of touch with this 'progress'.

My last day came and I worked an express to Reading and back. The final locomotive that I drove was class '47' No. 47844, the train reporting number 1S76, a train bound for Scotland. I left the locomotive on the fuelling pit at Saltley, shut down the engine and screwed on the parking brake. The depot was silent; no other engine showed any sign of life. This was such a contrast to 25 years earlier; the depot was already less than a shadow of former times. I walked the 25 yards or so to the lobby, were I started to write my ultimate driver's ticket. A serious looking team leader sidled up to me saying, as if sharing a confidence, 'I noticed that you came over the crossing without wearing your high visibility jacket'. He was obviously unaware that it was my last day. I said nothing, yet this said it all for me.

Some 30 drivers took resettlement at the same time as myself. It had been leaked to us that older men did not fit the image of the new privatised companies. Ironically, the first time my wife and I went to catch a train from New Street with our concessionary passes, the train was cancelled. The announcement over the public address system apologised for any inconvenience caused - there was no driver!

Dick Potts, Bernard Rainbow, Dave Jones and myself pooled our resources and had a joint retirement party, which over 300 people attended. We specifically requested no presents, yet over £500 was raised for charity. Bernard Rainbow's sister made us a huge cake in Great Western style, and Dick presented each of his three retiring colleagues with one of his wonderful oil paintings. Each painting had some significance to the person receiving it. I had been a 'passed fireman' at the time that Dick had his practical driving test and I became fireman to him on that day. He therefore painted for me the very engine that we worked on. The prairie No. 6116 is seen passing Handsworth Junction on the 7.06 am ex-Henley-in-Arden to Wolverhampton Low Level. This is just one of a number of his oils that I still treasure.

Bob Court, President of the Elmdon Model Engineering Society, checks my work on the society's Hunslet after I had overhauled it. *Author*

# Chapter Fifteen

## Retirement

Whilst I had longed for retirement, finishing work just before I was 60 years of age gave me an underlying psychological feeling of guilt .This was despite completing 44 years of service and turning out to work during all weathers and at all times of day and night. I could not get to grips with collecting dole money for six months and the flurry of forms issued by the Department of Health and Social Security. I had been a wage earner since I was 13 years of age and my creator had blessed me with wonderful health, I really felt no older than I had 20 years earlier. Having said that, the railway management of the time clearly did not want the services of the older men and I told myself that a younger man now had job security because of my action. Nevertheless, I still thought inwardly that I should be doing something towards the economy, despite the fact that there was no work at all for anyone my age at that time.

I have always been a home loving person and being able to do things around the house initially for me was heaven, plus the fact that I now did not need an alarm clock! It was early summer; I loved my garden and had a particular passion for fuchsias. Unfortunately, my wife and I were now unable to up sticks and go out, or on holiday, at the drop of a hat. Since my father's death in 1976 we had become carers for my elderly mother who was suffering macular degeneration and the after affects of a stroke. This was a duty that lasted 14 years, a time during which my wife showed unrivalled patience towards her mother-in-law. This was a time also that put the strength of our marriage, and our love for each other, to the most stringent tests.

At this time I had no particular project to work on in my workshop; I enjoyed the out of doors and caught up with all the tasks around the house over the following summer. I had indeed been 'warned' about making yet another striking clock!

Of all people, it took the milkman to make me think that perhaps I had already become obsessive; I no doubt had begun to keep the shortest grass in Great Britain. As his mate walked up our drive to deliver milk to our home, he shouted over, 'Only one at 'Do-it-All' today!' I really don't know which of us was the most embarrassed when our eyes met and he realised that I had overheard.

My wife and I could rarely leave the house for long periods and therefore walked a great deal. One Sunday afternoon we found ourselves back at where it all began for me, at the old Tyseley shed, now the Railway Museum. The roundhouses were long gone, but part of the enginemen's lobby had been rebuilt and one of the turntables refitted. There was an awful lot of nostalgia there for me and I inwardly felt that I would like to see the site thrive as a museum. It had all started well, with some backing from the City Council and a host of dedicated professional railwaymen lavishing much of their time caring for the locomotives. Regretfully, inward political squabbling had by this time induced all the professional people to abandon the place, in fact the site was now looking rather like a scrap yard.

It was on this day that I came into contact with a rather forlorn band of men running the miniature railway. These were members of the 'Elmdon Model Engineering Society' who had recently moved to Tyseley hoping to be an added attraction for museum visitors. I learned that the society had found it necessary to abandon their previous site owing to constant vandalism and theft. Unfortunately, they now had just about 200 yards of straight track at the museum. I met the president of the society Bob Court; I had known his younger brother many years earlier as a fireman at Tyseley. Bob was kind enough to show us round and I felt some envy at the amount of workshop machinery available to the society. This had been donated to the museum from a number of sources, mainly the many technical colleges that the government of the time had seen fit to close. I was hooked, I joined the society there and then, it was only a few minutes' walk from my home and I knew I would be mixing with people of similar interests. This was also the first time in my adult life that I had the opportunity to make friends with people outside the railway industry. Unsocial working hours made liaisons with others difficult, only fellow railwaymen realised that once you turned out to work anything could happen; indeed you would never be sure of what time you would get home.

It is a small world and one of the first club members that I met was Barrie Chalmers. He had been a fireman at Tyseley in his younger days and his father Albert had also been a driver. Barrie was at the time the works engineer for Lucas Research. Stan Alderman's father was a driver at Tyseley too; I had worked with him any number of times, Stan ran his own engineering business in the Jewellery Quarter. I was privileged to meet Len Perks, an extremely skilled engineer, who rose to being the toolroom manager at Joseph Lucas. Then there was Ron Scott, with whom I was to become very close friends. Ron had finished his working days as managing director of a manufacturing company. This was a position he gained purely by his own endeavour, yet he had never lost sight of his grass roots. He had started work at the bottom, as an engineering apprentice for the BSA Company during the early days of the war. Like many young men of his era, he was soon in the army and serving in India on the North West Frontier. Ron had started life in the back streets of Aston, where he always insisted that the policemen were eight feet tall and always went around in twos!

He had a devilish sense of humour, often relating stories of his time in India. Usually at lunchtime, he would mention that the flies that got baked into army bread looked rather like currants! I learned such a lot about engineering from this gentleman, simply by talking to him; he was extremely adept in finding time for everyone. Ron was using his skills building a 5 inch gauge model locomotive for his grandsons; this was same design as my first attempt. Straight off the top of his head, Ron could recall the core diameters and pitch angles of any given screw thread, this again brought about by years of engineering experience. Similarly, I could recite the valve events of a steam locomotive in the same vein. With this interchange, I was able to offer a little in return and we learned much from each other.

Only one visit to Tyseley was sufficient to tell me that the society was already unhappy in its new surroundings. Any extension to the short length of miniature railway track had already been halted. This delay had hung on for some months, owing to lack of decision by the museum trustees regarding an access gate from the British Rail diesel maintenance depot. Hence the society membership became demoralised and attendances began to diminish.

The society members had also built a 7¼ inch gauge Hunslet saddle tank engine at Sandwell College during evening classes; necessity saw this valuable asset now standing outside in all weathers. There was little wonder that this small locomotive now wheezed up and down the track on open days with the frequent delays to recover boiler pressure.

The whole summer of 1994 the society spent painting picnic tables and buildings around the museum, yet any decision to extend the track remained in abeyance. An absolute wealth of engineering skills, enthusiasm and resourcefulness was wasted.

The late autumn brought an offer to move to another site. Whilst I had every interest in seeing my old work place survive as a museum the society's position was untenable. A meeting of members saw a unanimous decision to move.

An offer to relocate had come through the foresight of the then Chief Trustee of the Birmingham and Midland Transport Museum at Wythall. This was a dedicated gathering of men who leased the site to restore and operate classic buses for display to the public; there were no paid staff at the site whatsoever. Any museum funds relied on public attendances and Bob Lewis, the Chief Trustee, had realised that the gate money from omnibus enthusiasts alone would not keep the trust viable. He had therefore advocated a miniature railway as an extra attraction to families in general. Backed by his enthusiasm and given a pretty free hand the Elmdon Model Engineering Society burst back into life.

The ground leased by the Transport Museum was undulating; this meant that the siting of the railway track bed had to be correctly surveyed. It also meant a great deal of hard work, cuttings and embankments had to be made and the area landscaped. A viaduct had to be built to cross a redundant road entrance and the society wanted to incorporate a tunnel for general interest. To get the right effect, the tunnel had to be long enough and on a curve so that it could not be immediately seen through. The track, too, had to be at ground level, as there were road crossings within the museum which were constantly used by heavy buses. It was essential therefore that these crossings be properly engineered.

The invitation on to the Wythall site brought with it a firm commitment from the society to run trains on the museum open days, an obligation that after several years has always been fulfilled. In the early days this commitment did cause some nail biting, most members only had small locomotives that were not up to sustained public running. The society's 7¼ inch gauge Hunslet was the only suitable locomotive, but even this was 'poorly.' Working on an engine of this size was a new challenge for me, but it was eventually transported into my workshop and over the winter of 1995 I gave it a complete overhaul.

None of the new track was ready for the first Easter opening, so we laid the old track from Tyseley on to a steep grass embankment. This was an immediate success with the public, but it made the little locomotive work to its limit. The descent was a bit uncertain too, and was to cause some anxious moments with drivers. I have to admit that I had to keep my fingers crossed during this early period; the Hunslet had to be 100 per cent reliable. Fortunately, she never let the society down.

During the summer of 1995 some of the track became serviceable in sections at a time, although the completed circuit was to take another two years. This first summer brought the society more luck; an elderly gentleman came to the museum on one of the open days and quietly asked us if we would like another engine. When he said it was an 8 ft-long 7¼ in. gauge 'Black Five', we all looked at one another in silence with our mouths open! He was a local man and he went on to explain that he had built the locomotive some years earlier, but poor health and age now prevented him from doing essential repairs. A public 'Right of Way' had also been recently re-opened at the rear of his home and he now felt doubtful for the locomotive's security.

The following Wednesday four of us went to the gentleman's home and loaded this wonderful gift on to a trailer. This engine too then ended up in my workshop for an overhaul, we had to be sure that the boiler was in good repair and safe to use amongst the general public.

Several months later saw the engine back at Wythall and our commitment to run trains became somewhat more assured. Several times we invited the gentleman back to the museum to see, and perhaps drive, his locomotive. Sadly, it was an offer that, for reasons only known to himself, he never accepted before he passed away.

My 3½ in. gauge model of No. 1011 *County of Chester* that I made ready for the Model Engineering Exhibition at Stoneleigh in 1996. *Author*

My 7¼ in. gauge 'King' class locomotive after three years' work. *Author*

The track circuit was completed in 1998 and with a piper heralding the first train the First Citizen of Bromsgrove did us the honour of cutting the ribbon.

Today, the Elmdon Model Engineering Society still holds very good relations with the present Transport Museum trustees. Attendances have greatly improved and much enthusiasm by the dedicated volunteers annually sees other classic buses restored for the enjoyment of the public.

At the Wythall museum I have been involved with an awful lot of very nice people ... and have since never found the need to attend any gym to pump iron in order to keep fit!

Having some space in a marriage, keeps it healthy; whilst I spent time with my hobby, my wife did voluntary work for the Citizen's Advice Bureau. For many years she found this work very rewarding and also met any number of lovely people. Social evenings widened our outlook and brought us into contact with many new friends. When the Citizen's Advice Bureau Office closed through financial restraints, my wife went on to the schools Volunteer Reading Scheme. We have never got bogged down into any rut. I have never gone into my workshop during the evenings, or after Sunday lunch, these times together have always been special for us both.

In 1997 I started another project, the building of a 7¼ in. gauge 0-4-0 tank engine. Working on other locomotives of this size and their working capability had won me over. I purchased a partly-built engine, which had been up for sale for some time and I had heard it said by others that they would not touch it with a barge pole. When I viewed it, I was attracted to the new, very well manufactured, commercially made copper boiler. The partially constructed chassis was pretty awful; it was not difficult to see that perhaps several people had had a 'knock' at it over time. There were varying standards in the workmanship and at some time the chassis had been dropped. The wheels were locked and in an effort to get them to revolve there were deep gouge marks in the axles through the use of mole grips.

The chassis was eventually dismantled and many of the parts discarded. I rebuilt the whole thing from scratch, finally steaming it 18 months later. By this time any number of different locomotives were appearing on the Wythall track.

We had begun to get many regular visitors with children, a number of whom were grandparents with grandchildren. To add some variety, I painted my locomotive blue and called it 'Thomas'. This sounds a bit 'twee', but the children adore it and we always have to be very vigilant when it is stationary, as they are inclined to want to stroke it, and it does get very hot! Much of the time I hand the driving of it over to other club members, my main satisfaction was in the engineering and seeing it run well.

I also get enormous satisfaction in seeing children getting pleasure from the railway. In my early days, coal was the life blood of this country, yet I heard it said by one child, 'Why is he putting those black stones in there?' It is difficult for us to conceive that some children these days have never seen coal. My ultimate pleasure came one day when I sat a child on the driving seat of *Thomas*, he looked at me with a smile as wide as anyone has ever seen, saying, 'These are better than computers, aren't they?', a moment that I will always treasure.

The year 1999 brought an extraordinary challenge, I was asked to make a replica 1724 James Harrison wooden regulator clock, a devilish project that is still on going today, seven years later. James Harrison was the brother of John Harrison, famous for solving the maritime problem of longitude, and whose sea clocks are today on display in the Maritime Museum in Greenwich. Historians tell us that John Harrison was the brainchild behind these 1724 wooden regulator clocks, which apparently had extraordinary timekeeping qualities for those times. They were reputed to be accurate to one second a month.

Having already made two clocks, when I was asked to take on this venture my immediate thoughts were that it could hardly be rocket science. After all, the old craftsmen had worked with primitive tools, often in poor light. This was to be incredibly naïve thinking and this venture has since taken me to the outer bounds of total frustration. My wife has never passed comment on any of the things that I do, but with this undertaking she became aware of my exasperation, on several occasions she has suggested that I take a break from it. Much of this difficulty occurred because the drawings that I had were very basic, giving only the wheel pitch circles. There were no profiles shown for the gear teeth and this seems to be where the secret lay. Consequently, I have had to work from photographs. There were no drawings at all for what is known as the motion work, this is the set of gears that make both of the clock hands revolve at the correct ratio.

The main frame of the clock is made of oak, as are the main driving wheels. The only exception being the 'scape' wheel, which is made of brass. The 'scape' wheel is the cog that makes the clock tick and regulates its timekeeping. All the wooden driving wheels have their teeth inserted separately, so that the grain of the wood runs along the length of each tooth. This gives the teeth strength; cross grain would cause them to break off. In itself, this has been an infernal task, as I never realised how accurate the gear teeth profiles had to be despite being made of wood.

The 'scape' wheel revolves purely under its own weight by lying on small wooden rollers; any variation in the torque from the gear train causes the 'scape' wheel to hesitate. The pallets, which engage the brass 'scape' wheel are made of lignum vitae, a very hard tropical wood. These wooden pallets never wear, as they hop in and out of the 'scape' wheel without causing any friction. This gives rise to the name 'grasshopper' that Harrison gave to his escapement. If the 'scape' wheel does hesitate, the pallets miss engaging the ratchet teeth; the wheel lifts off its rollers and starts to spin rapidly. The pendulum brings the opposite pallet into contact with the 'scape' wheel, which has now become a very effective circular saw. In turn both pallets are then destroyed and hours of work ruined. On many occasions I have watched the clock work for a considerable time, turned my back for only minutes, only to find bits of wood from pallets and gear teeth strewn about the floor. There is little wonder that this escapement was not used to any degree by other clock makers. It does tend to need the patience of a saint to get it to work reliably.

My latest project will little doubt be my 'swan song'. I was recently offered the chance to purchase every casting for a 7¼ inch gauge Great Western 'King' class locomotive. The deal came with the drawings, the frame steel for both engine and tender, and other sundries. Whether it was a rational decision to take on such at task at my time of life only time will tell. However, I decided to think positively and have already enjoyed the many hours of work put into this huge challenge. At 73 years of age, every day is a bonus, I would have changed nothing, and I count my blessings each day.

My old depot still survives today as an EWS freight depot. The few staff there still run the Welfare Fund and retired people are annually invited to a reunion dinner and occasional trips during the summer. With limited numbers now at the depot, I find their generosity towards elderly staff staggering. The Welfare Fund Committee too, must give much of their free time in the interest of others. There again, railway workers are unique.